Privacy and Security Policies in Big Data

Sharvari Tamane
MGM's Jawaharlal Nehru Engineering College, India

Vijender Kumar Solanki
Institute of Technology and Science Ghaziabad, India

Nilanjan Dey
Techno India College of Technology, India

A volume in the Advances in Information Security,
Privacy, and Ethics (AISPE) Book Series

www.igi-global.com

Published in the United States of America by
   IGI Global
   Information Science Reference (an imprint of IGI Global)
   701 E. Chocolate Avenue
   Hershey PA, USA 17033
   Tel: 717-533-8845
   Fax: 717-533-8661
   E-mail: cust@igi-global.com
   Web site: http://www.igi-global.com

Library of Congress Cataloging-in-Publication Data

Names: Tamane, Sharvari, 1973- editor. | Solanki, Vijender Kumar 1980- editor. |
   Dey, Nilanjan, 1984- editor.
Title: Privacy and security policies in big data / Sharvari Tamane, Vijender Kumar Solanki, and Nilanjan
   Dey, editors.
Description: Hershey, PA : Information Science Reference, [2017] | Includes
   bibliographical references and index.
Identifiers: LCCN 2017003838| ISBN 9781522524861 (hardcover) | ISBN
   9781522524878 (ebook)
Subjects: LCSH: Big data--Security measures. | Data protection. | Privacy,
   Right of. | Telecommunication policy.
Classification: LCC QA76.9.B45 P75 2017 | DDC 005.8--dc23 LC record available at https://lccn.loc.gov/2017003838

This book is published in the IGI Global book series Advances in Information Security, Privacy, and Ethics (AISPE) (ISSN: 1948-9730; eISSN: 1948-9749)

British Cataloguing in Publication Data
A Cataloguing in Publication record for this book is available from the British Library.

For electronic access to this publication, please contact: eresources@igi-global.com.

Advances in Information Security, Privacy, and Ethics (AISPE) Book Series

Manish Gupta
State University of New York, USA

ISSN:1948-9730
EISSN:1948-9749

MISSION

As digital technologies become more pervasive in everyday life and the Internet is utilized in ever in-creasing ways by both private and public entities, concern over digital threats becomes more prevalent.

The **Advances in Information Security, Privacy, & Ethics (AISPE) Book Series** provides cutting-edge research on the protection and misuse of information and technology across various industries and settings. Comprised of scholarly research on topics such as identity management, cryptography, system security, authentication, and data protection, this book series is ideal for reference by IT professionals, academicians, and upper-level students.

COVERAGE

- Privacy-Enhancing Technologies
- Data Storage of Minors
- IT Risk
- Risk Management
- Network Security Services
- Global Privacy Concerns
- Computer ethics
- Device Fingerprinting
- CIA Triad of Information Security
- Privacy Issues of Social Networking

IGI Global is currently accepting manuscripts for publication within this series. To submit a proposal for a volume in this series, please contact our Acquisition Editors at Acquisitions@igi-global.com or visit: http://www.igi-global.com/publish/.

Titles in this Series

For a list of additional titles in this series, please visit: www.igi-global.com/book-series

Security Breaches and Threat Prevention in the Internet of Things
N. Jeyanthi (VIT University, India) and R. Thandeeswaran (VIT University, India)
Information Science Reference • copyright 2017 • 276pp • H/C (ISBN: 9781522522966) • US $180.00 (our price)

Decentralized Computing Using Blockchain Technologies and Smart Contracts Emerging Research and Opportunities
S. Asharaf (Indian Institute of Information Technology and Management, Kerala, India) and S. Adarsh (Indian Institute of Information Technology and Management, Kerala, India)
Information Science Reference • copyright 2017 • 128pp • H/C (ISBN: 9781522521938) • US $120.00 (our price)

Cybersecurity Breaches and Issues Surrounding Online Threat Protection
Michelle Moore (George Mason University, USA)
Information Science Reference • copyright 2017 • 408pp • H/C (ISBN: 9781522519416) • US $195.00 (our price)

Security Solutions and Applied Cryptography in Smart Grid Communications
Mohamed Amine Ferrag (Guelma University, Algeria) and Ahmed Ahmim (University of Larbi Tebessi, Algeria)
Information Science Reference • copyright 2017 • 464pp • H/C (ISBN: 9781522518297) • US $215.00 (our price)

Threat Mitigation and Detection of Cyber Warfare and Terrorism Activities
Maximiliano E. Korstanje (University of Palermo, Argentina)
Information Science Reference • copyright 2017 • 315pp • H/C (ISBN: 9781522519386) • US $190.00 (our price)

Online Banking Security Measures and Data Protection
Shadi A. Aljawarneh (Jordan University of Science and Technology, Jordan)
Information Science Reference • copyright 2017 • 312pp • H/C (ISBN: 9781522508649) • US $215.00 (our price)

Developing Next-Generation Countermeasures for Homeland Security Threat Prevention
Maurice Dawson (University of Missouri-St. Louis, USA) Dakshina Ranjan Kisku (National Institute of Technology, India) Phalguni Gupta (National Institute of Technical Teachers' Training & Research, India) Jamuna Kanta Sing (Jadavpur University, India) and Weifeng Li (Tsinghua University, China)
Information Science Reference • copyright 2017 • 428pp • H/C (ISBN: 9781522507031) • US $210.00 (our price)

Security Solutions for Hyperconnectivity and the Internet of Things
Maurice Dawson (University of Missouri-St. Louis, USA) Mohamed Eltayeb (Colorado Technical University, USA) and Marwan Omar (Saint Leo University, USA)
Information Science Reference • copyright 2017 • 347pp • H/C (ISBN: 9781522507413) • US $215.00 (our price)

www.igi-global.com

701 East Chocolate Avenue, Hershey, PA 17033, USA
Tel: 717-533-8845 x100 • Fax: 717-533-8661
E-Mail: cust@igi-global.com • www.igi-global.com

Table of Contents

Section 4
Data Mining

Section 5
Big Data Privacy and Security

Section 6
Is IoT Driving a Big Data?

Section 7
Big Data Analytics

Detailed Table of Contents

Section 1
Fundamentals of Big Data

Chapter 1

    Sharvari C. Tamane, MGM's Jawaharlal Nehru Engineering College, India
    Vijender K. Solanki, Institute of Technology and Science Ghaziabad, India
    Madhuri S. Joshi, MGM's Jawaharlal Nehru Engineering College, India

The chapter is written on two important buildings, the basics of Big data and their security concern. The chapter is classifying in different sections. The chapter starts with the basic of big data and is concluded with security concern. The chapter is enriched with different category examples to make texts easy for author understanding. The chapter begins with the introduction of big data, their memory size followed by the examples. The chapter explains the category of big data in type of structured, semi-structured and unstructured data. The discussion on operational data service and big data application is also included to ensure the basic understanding to readers. The second portion of chapter which is based on security in big data. It's explaining the issues and challenges in big data. The section also focusing on the shift paradigm from cloud environment to big data environment changes and the problems encounter by organizations. The section discusses the framework issue and concluded with the necessity of understanding security in the big data, keeping in view of expansion of information technology infrastructure in the 21st century.

Section 2
Big Data Tools and Technologies With Case Studies

Chapter 2

    Krishnan Umachandran, Nelcast Ltd., India
    Debra Sharon Ferdinand-James, The University of the West Indies, Trinidad and Tobago

Continued technological advancements of the 21st Century afford massive data generation in sectors of our economy to include the domains of agriculture, manufacturing, and education. However, harnessing such large-scale data, using modern technologies for effective decision-making appears to be an evolving science that requires knowledge of Big Data management and analytics. Big data in agriculture, manufacturing, and education are varied such as voluminous text, images, and graphs. Applying Big data science techniques (e.g., functional algorithms) for extracting intelligence data affords decision markers quick response to productivity, market resilience, and student enrollment challenges in today's unpredictable markets. This chapter serves to employ data science for potential solutions to Big Data applications in the sectors of agriculture, manufacturing and education to a lesser extent, using modern technological tools such as Hadoop, Hive, Sqoop, and MongoDB.

Chapter 3

    Meenu Gupta, Ansal University, India
    Neha Singla, Punjabi University, India

Data can be anything but from a large data base extraction of useful information is known as data mining. Cloud computing is a term which represent a collection of huge amount of data. Cloud computing can be correlated with data mining and Big Data Hadoop. Big data is high volume, high velocity, and/or high variety information asset that require new form of processing to enable enhanced decision making, insight discovery and process optimization. Data growth, speed and complexity are being accompanied by deployment of smart sensors and devices that transmit data commonly called the Internet of Things, multimedia and by other sources of semi-structured and structured data. Big Data is defined as the core element of nearly every digital transformation today.

Section 3
Non-Relational Databases

Chapter 4

    Sonali Tidke, SPPU, India

MongoDB is a NoSQL type of database management system which does not adhere to the commonly used relational database management model. MongoDB is used for horizontal scaling across a large number of servers which may have tens, hundreds or even thousands of servers. This horizontal scaling is performed using sharding. Sharding is a database partitioning technique which partitions large database into smaller parts which are easy to manage and faster to access. There are hundreds of NoSQL databases available in the market. But each NoSQL product is different in terms of features, implementations and behavior. NoSQL and RDBMS solve different set of problems and have different requirements. MongoDB has a powerful query language which extends SQL to JSON enabling developers to take benefit of power of SQL and flexibility of JSON. Along with support for select/from/where type of queries, MongoDB supports aggregation, sorting, joins as well as nested array and collections. To improve query performance, indexes and many more features are also available.

Chapter 5

Jens Kohler, University of Applied Sciences Mannheim, Germany
Christian Richard Lorenz, University of Applied Sciences Mannheim, Germany
Markus Gumbel, University of Applied Sciences Mannheim, Germany
Thomas Specht, University of Applied Sciences Mannheim, Germany
Kiril Simov, Bulgarian Academy of Sciences, Bulgaria

In recent years, Cloud Computing has drastically changed IT-Architectures in enterprises throughout various branches and countries. Dynamically scalable capabilities like CPUs, storage space, virtual networks, etc. promise cost savings, as huge initial infrastructure investments are not required anymore. This development shows that Cloud Computing is also a promising technology driver for Big Data, as the storage of unstructured data when no concrete and defined data schemes (variety) can be managed with upcoming NoSQL architectures. However, in order to fully exploit these advantages, the integration of a trustworthy 3rd party public cloud provider is necessary. Thus, challenging questions concerning security, compliance, anonymization, and privacy emerge and are still unsolved. To address these challenges, this work presents, implements and evaluates a security-by-distribution approach for NoSQL document stores that distributes data across various cloud providers such that every provider only gets a small data chunk which is worthless without the others.

Chapter 6

Shraddha Pankaj Phansalkar, Symbiosis International University, India
Ajay Dani, G. H. Raisoni Institute of Technology, India

Contemporary web-applications are deployed on the cloud data-stores for realizing requirements like low latency and high scalability. Although cloud-based database applications exhibit high performance with these features, they compromise on the weaker consistency levels. Rationing the consistency guarantees of an application is a necessity to achieve the augmented metrics of application performance. The proposed work is a paradigm shift from monotonic transaction consistency to selective data consistency in web database applications. The selective data consistency model leverages consistency of critical data-objects and leaves consistency of non-critical data-objects to underlying cloud data-store; it is called selective consistency and it results in better performance of the cloud-based applications. The consistency of the underlying data-object is defined from user-perspective with a user-friendly consistency metric called Consistency Index (CI). The selective data consistency model is implemented on a cloud data-store with OLTP workload and the performance is gauged.

Section 4
Data Mining

Chapter 7

Rashmi Agrawal, Manav Rachna International University, India
Neha Gupta, Manav Rachna International University, India

In today's era, educational data mining is a discipline of high importance for teaching enhancement. EDM techniques can reveal useful information to educators to help them design or modify the structure of courses. EDM techniques majorly include machine learning and data mining techniques. In this chapter of the book, we will deliberate upon various data mining techniques that will help in identifying at-risk students, identifying priority learning needs for different groups of students, increasing graduation rates, effectively assessing institutional performance, maximizing campus resources, optimizing subject curriculum renewal. Various applications of data mining are also discussed by quoting example of various case studies. Analysis of social networks in educational field to understand student network formation in classrooms and the types of impact these networks have on student is also discussed.

Section 5
Big Data Privacy and Security

As Big Data is group of structured, unstructured and semi-structure data collected from various sources, it is important to mine and provide privacy to individual data. Differential Privacy is one the best measure which provides strong privacy guarantee. The chapter proposed differentially private frequent item set mining using map reduce requires less time for privately mining large dataset. The chapter discussed problem of preserving data privacy, different challenges to preserving data privacy in big data environment, Data privacy techniques and their applications to unstructured data. The analyses of experimental results on structured and unstructured data set are also presented.

This chapter presents a survey of the most important security and privacy issues related to large-scale data sharing and mining in big data with focus on differential privacy as a promising approach for achieving privacy especially in statistical databases often used in healthcare. A case study is presented utilizing differential privacy in healthcare domain, the chapter analyzes and compares the major differentially private data release strategies and noise mechanisms such as the Laplace and the exponential mechanisms. The background section discusses several security and privacy approaches in big data including authentication and encryption protocols, and privacy preserving techniques such as k-anonymity. Next, the chapter introduces the differential privacy concepts used in the interactive and non-interactive data sharing models and the various noise mechanisms used. An instrumental case study is then presented to examine the effect of applying differential privacy in analytics. The chapter then explores the future trends and finally, provides a conclusion.

Section 6
Is IoT Driving a Big Data?

Chapter 10

Abhijeet Chandrakant Dabre, Smt. Kashibai Navale College of Engineering, India
Sandesh Shivaji Mahamure, Smt. Kashibai Navale College of Engineering, India
Snehal Pandurang Wadibhasme, Smt. Kashibai Navale College of Engineering, India

This chapter specifically with Internet of Things (IoT), initially presents what exactly it is? It's just a smart route to improving daily life activities by connecting devices to widely used Internet. Then gradually put a view on history, which closely talked about traditional ways of communication mechanisms, moving forward it touches the current ideology of IoT. Further in this chapter authors discussed different aspects of IoT which was explained by different philosophers and it clears the idea of how to introduce, how to learn and how to launch IoT in different sectors (such as education, power generation, water management, road safety, automobiles etc). The practicality of the knowledge explains the usefulness of IoT and also explains how it impacts on the overall growth of the country and why every individual attracted towards this smart network of things. At the end, this chapter accomplished with the need of IoT in developing countries, how IoT provides efficient solutions to overcome upcoming challenges and finally briefs about why it is recommended.

Section 7
Big Data Analytics

Chapter 11

Lokukaluge P. Perera, Norwegian Marine Technology Research Institute (MARINTEK),
   Norway
Brage Mo, Norwegian Marine Technology Research Institute (MARINTEK), Norway

Modern vessels are monitored by Onboard Internet of Things (IoT), sensors and data acquisition (DAQ), to observe ship performance and navigation conditions. Such IoT may create various shipping industrial challenges under large-scale data handling situations. These large-scale data handling issues are often categorized as "Big Data" challenges and this chapter discusses various solutions to overcome such challenges. That consists of a data-handling framework with various data analytics under onboard IoT. The basis for such data analytics is under data driven models presented and developed with engine-propeller combinator diagrams of vessels. The respective results on data analytics of data classification, sensor faults detection, data compression and expansion, integrity verification and regression, and visualization and decision support, are presented along the proposed data handling framework of a selected vessel. Finally, the results are useful for energy efficiency and system reliability applications of shipping discussed.

Chapter 12
Big Data Predictive Analysis for Detection of Prostate Cancer on Cloud-Based Platform:
Microsoft Azure 259

Ritesh Anilkumar Gangwal, Dr. Babasaheb Ambedkar Marathwada University, India
Ratnadeep R. Deshmukh, Dr. Babasaheb Ambedkar Marathwada University, India
M. Emmanuel, Pune Institute of Computer Technology, India

Big data as the name would refer to a subsequently large quantity of data which is being processed. With the advent of social media the data presently available is text, images, audio video. In order to process this data belonging to variety of format led to the concept of Big Data processing. To overcome these challenges of data, big data techniques evolved. Various tools are available for the big data naming MAP Reduce, etc. But to get the taste of Cloud based tool we would be working with the Microsoft Azure. Microsoft Azure is an integrated environment for the Big data analytics along with the SaaS Cloud platform. For the purpose of experiment, the Prostate cancer data is used to perform the predictive analysis for the Cancer growth in the gland. An experiment depending on the segmentation results of Prostate MRI scans is used for the predictive analytics using the SVM. Performance analysis with the ROC, Accuracy and Confusion matrix gives the resultant analysis with the visual artifacts. With the trained model, the proposed experiment can statistically predict the cancer growth.

Preface

Big data is becoming a very essential component for the industries where large volume of data with large variety and at very high speed is used to solve particular data problems. This large volume and variety of data is sometimes structured, sometimes unstructured (means the data which does not have proper predefined format) and sometimes semi-structured. The volume and variety of this data are increasing in size day by day which makes it difficult to understand through general computer programs and to analyze it later. Big data is first captured, stored, processed, analyzed and then used with other available data in the company to make it more effective. Therefore, big data is never operated in isolation and can't be handled by traditional database management systems. Big data is generated by various sources and therefore new tools, technologies and methodologies are required to manage, organize, secure and analyze it.

Cloud computing provides various services and resources from remote data centers to organizations or individuals. It is a technology used to reduce complexities of computing needs and getting results quickly and cost effectively. The services provided are either public or private or hybrid. It can be delivered wherever and whenever one may need in a pay-as-you-go fashion. Cloud based platforms with these advantages are utilized as prospective mass for big data. Most important challenge in cloud computing and big data is the privacy and security policies of the data. Big data security may involve protection of big data and big data analytic techniques as important issues. Recent work on big data mainly focuses on management and analysis. However, there is less focus on privacy and security policies.

OBJECTIVE OF THE BOOK

The main objective of this book publication is to cover the fundamental concepts of big data management, analytics and recent research development in security and private policies of big data. It also includes various real time/ offline applications and case studies in the field of engineering, computer science, information security, cloud computing with modern tools & technologies used.

The impact of this edited book is focused on in depth information about big data, big data analytic methods, recent tools and technologies used, along with, technical approach in solving real time/offline applications and practical solutions through case studies in big data analytics. Companies may get different ways to monitor data coming from various sources and modify their processes accordingly to prevent it from catastrophic events through case studies. Retailers may provide different offers to customers to manage data in real time to market their products and increase sell. This book also provides guidelines on various applications and use of tools and technologies for the same. The applications discussed in this book are related to the following areas:

- Development of data analytics in shipping.
- Internet of things in real life applications.
- Big data predictive analysis for detection of prostate cancer on cloud-based platform Microsoft Azure.

The target audience and potential uses include:

1. The researchers, academician and engineers who gets more insights on big data and analytics.
2. Readers who may discover new things for marketing and at the same time they learn how to protect big data from risk and fraud.
3. Audience who can use various technologies provided in this book to develop their applications.
4. The students of various universities studying computer science and engineering and information technology, master of computer applications and management.
5. This book will provide correct information to business.
6. Audience can contribute in businesses by providing IT services.

ORGANIZATION OF THE BOOK

The book consists of an introductory chapter followed by 12 chapters that are organized in seven sections as shown in Table 1. The first chapter focuses on big data fundamentals and data types with its applications. The second section, consists of Chapters 2 and 3 which relate to Big data tools and technologies with case studies. The third section of the book encloses three chapters that introduced the non-relational databases with examples. The fourth section contains a chapter concerning data mining details. Chapter 8 and Chapter 9, the fifth section, introduce big data privacy and security concepts with issues and future research directions. The sixth section included relationship between IoT and big data with IoT applications. The last section, seventh, having Chapters 11 and 12, focuses on big data analytics technologies with different case studies.

Section 1: Fundamentals of Big Data

This section elaborates the fundamental concepts of the Big data with characteristics and applications. The intention is to clear the basic concepts of big data.

Chapter 1 introduces fundamentals concepts of big data, its characteristics, data types, operational data services for big data, applications of big data and big data and security concern. It also focuses on induction of big data in security and big data security challenges. The chapter discusses various approaches with use cases to big data operation management.

Section 2: Big Data Tools and Technologies With Case Studies

Chapter 2 covers the continued technological advancements of the 21st Century afford massive data generation in sectors of our economy to include the domains of agriculture, manufacturing, and education. However, harnessing such large-scale data, using modern technologies for effective decision-making appears to be an evolving science that requires knowledge of Big Data management and analytics. This

Table 1. Organization of the book

Section 1: Fundamentals of Big Data		
Chapter 1 The Basics of Big Data and Security Concerns		
Section 2: Big Data Tools and Technologies With Case Studies		
Chapter 2 Affordances of Data Science in Agriculture, Manufacturing, and Education		**Chapter 3** Evolution of Cloud in Big Data With Hadoop on Docker Platform
Section 3: Non-Relational Databases		
Chapter 4 Data Management in NoSQL	**Chapter 5** A Security-by-Distribution Approach to Manage Big Data in a Federation of Untrustworthy Clouds	**Chapter 6** Selective Data Consistency Model in No-SQL Data Store
Section 4: Data Mining		
Chapter 7 Educational Data Mining Review: Teaching Enhancement		
Section 5: Big Data Privacy and Security		
Chapter 8 Privacy Preserving Data Mining on Unstructured Data		**Chapter 9** Differential Privacy Approach for Big Data Privacy in Healthcare
Section 6: Is IoT Driving Big Data?		
Chapter 10 Internet of Things in Real Life: Applications		
Section 7: Big Data Analytics		
Chapter 11 Development of Data Analytics in Shipping		**Chapter 12** Big Data Predictive Analysis for Detection of Prostate Cancer on Cloud-Based Platform: Microsoft Azure

chapter also focuses on issues, controversies and problems related to various applications. It served to employ data science for potential solutions to Big Data applications using modern technological tools such as Hadoop, Hive, Sqoop and MongoDB to extract important data and to take important decisions.

Chapter 3 discusses big data concepts in detail with recent tools and technologies like Hadoop, NoSQL data stores, big data mining process, Hadoop using Docker containers, its working and benefits. These tools and techniques are used to enhance decision making, insight discovery and optimization process. This chapter also covers how data growth, speed and complexity have been accompanied by deployment of smart sensors and devices using Internet of Things, multimedia and by other sources of semi-structured and structured data. It also focusses on differences between online and offline Big Data forms.

Section 3: Non-Relational Databases

Chapter 4 discusses concepts of MongoDB, a NoSQL database management system in detail. It also explains its uses for horizontal scaling across a large number of servers. Author proposes a database partitioning technique for horizontal scaling to manage and access a database in a faster and easier way. Chapter also explains features of MongoDB along with support to queries and functions that includes select/from/where, aggregation, sorting, joins as well as nested array and collections. Chapter also focuses on how to improve query performance by giving various examples.

Chapter 5 introduces challenging questions concerning security, compliance, anonymization, and privacy emerge in cloud computing and provided solutions for the same. It also demonstrated that the approach is viable with NoSQL document stores. Moreover, the implemented prototype showed the feasibility of the approach in practice. The chapter not only built the foundation to transfer the SeDiCo concept to NoSQL architectures, but also revealed further open research questions in Big Data scenarios.

Chapter 6 presents a paradigm shift from monotonic transaction consistency to selective data consistency in web database applications. It also explains how the selective data consistency model leverages consistency of critical data-objects and leaves consistency of non-critical data-objects to underlying cloud data-store? The chapter further focuses on the architecture of the application implementing selective data consistency model. The chapter may help users of transaction-based databases to realize their consistency requirements with CI and relates CI to the conventional SQL isolation levels.

Section 4: Data Mining

Chapter 7 deliberates various data mining techniques that will help in identifying at-risk students, identifying priority learning needs for different groups of students, increasing graduation rates, effectively assessing institutional performance, maximizing campus resources and optimizing subject curriculum renewal. Various applications of data mining are also discussed by quoting example of various case studies. Analysis of social networks in educational field to understand student network formation in classrooms and the types of impact these networks have on student is also discussed.

Section 5: Big Data Privacy and Security

Chapter 8 mainly focuses on how to mine and provide privacy to individual data. It also proposes private frequent item set mining techniques using map reduce for privately mining large datasets. The chapter discussed different challenges to preserve data privacy in big data environment and techniques to preserve data privacy and their applications for unstructured data. The analyses of experimental results on structured and unstructured data sets are also presented.

Chapter 9 presents a survey of the most important security and privacy issues related to large-scale data sharing and mining in big data with focus on differential privacy as a promising approach for achieving privacy especially in statistical databases often used in healthcare. A case study is presented utilizing differential privacy in healthcare domain, the chapter analyzes and compares the major differentially private data release strategies and noise mechanisms such as the Laplace and the exponential mechanisms. The background section discusses several security and privacy approaches in big data including authentication and encryption protocols, and privacy preserving techniques such as k-anonymity. Further, the chapter introduces the differential privacy concepts used in the interactive and non-interactive data sharing models and the various noise mechanisms used. An instrumental case study is then presented to examine the effect of applying differential privacy in analytics.

Section 6: Is IoT Driving a Big Data?

Chapter 10 presents basics of Internet of Things (IoT). IoT is a smart route widely used to improve daily life activities. Chapter focuses on history of IoT with traditional ways of communication mechanisms. Further it discussed different aspects of IoT which was explained by different philosophers to clear the idea of how to introduce, how to learn and how to launch IoT in different sectors such as education, power generation, water management, road safety, automobiles etc. Chapter also provides practical knowledge to explain the use of IoT and impact of IoT on overall growth of the country. Further author provided in detail need of IoT in developing countries with solutions to overcome upcoming challenges.

Section 7: Big Data Analytics

Chapter 11 presents data handling issues of shipping industries such as monitoring modern vessels, ship performance and navigation conditions which are also categorized as big data challenges. How to overcome these challenges and various issues related to these are discussed in this chapter. The basis for data analytics under data driven models is presented and developed with engine-propeller combinator diagrams of vessels. The respective results on data analytics of data classification, sensor fault detection, data compression and expansion, integrity verification and regression and visualization and decision support, are presented along with the proposed data of handling framework of a selected vessel. Finally, the results of energy efficiency and system reliability applications of shipping are also discussed.

Chapter 12 presents Microsoft Azure tool to overcome big data challenges. Microsoft Azure is an integrated environment for the Big data analytics along with the SaaS Cloud platform. Chapter presented a case study for the Prostate cancer data to perform the predictive analysis for the Cancer growth in the gland. An experiment depending on the segmentation results of Prostate MRI scans is used for the predictive analytics using the SVM. Performance analysis with the ROC, Accuracy and Confusion matrix gave the resultant analysis with the visual artifacts.

This book is expected to assist researchers, academicians, and science and engineering students in contributing in businesses by providing IT services. It addresses innovative conceptual framework for various applications and insights on big data and analytics. The book is expected to serve as a reference for the post-graduated students as it offers the requisite knowledge for understanding in depth information about big data and recent tools and technologies used. It also discovers new things for marketing and at the same time they learn how to protect big data from risk and fraud. This book is based on research studies carried out by experienced academicians and is expected to shed new insights for researchers, academicians, and students, and improves understanding of big data concepts by technologies provided in this book to develop their applications.

Sharvari Chandrashekhar Tamane
MGM's Jawaharlal Nehru Engineering College, India

Vijender K. Solanki
Institute of Technology and Science Ghaziabad, India

Nilanjan Dey
Techno India College of Technology, India

Acknowledgment

"There's a difference between interest and commitment. When you're interested in doing something, you do it only when it's convenient. When you're committed to something, you accept no excuses - only results." —— Kenneth H. Blanchard

We would like to say 'THANK YOU' to Almighty, our parents for endless support, guidance and love through all our life stages. We are heartiest thankful to our beloved family members for standing beside us throughout our career, move our career forward through editing this book. Our great thanks to our students, who have put in their time and effort to support and contribute in some manner. We dedicate this book to all of them.

We would like to express our gratitude to the all people support, share, talked things over, read, wrote, offered comments, allowed us to quote their remarks and assisted in editing, proofreading and design; through the book journey.

We believe that the team of authors provides the perfect blend of knowledge and skills that went into authoring this book. We thank each of the authors for devoting their time, patience, perseverance and effort towards this book; we think that it will be a great asset to the all researchers in this field!

We are grateful to the IGI-publisher team, who showed us the ropes to start and continue. Without that knowledge we wouldn't have ventured into starting this book, which ultimately led to this! Their trusting for us, their guide and providing the necessary time and resource, gave us the freedom to manage this book.

Last, but definitely not least, we'd like to thank our readers, who gave us their trust and hope our work inspired and guide them.

"Take a minute: look at your goals, look at your performance, see if your behavior matches your goals." —— Kenneth H. Blanchard

Sharvari Chandrashekhar Tamane
MGM's Jawaharlal Nehru Engineering College, India

Vijender K. Solanki
Institute of Technology and Science Ghaziabad, India

Nilanjan Dey
Techno India College of Technology, India

Section 1
Fundamentals of Big Data

Chapter 1
The Basics of Big Data and Security Concerns

Sharvari C. Tamane
MGM's Jawaharlal Nehru Engineering College, India

Vijender K. Solanki
Institute of Technology and Science Ghaziabad, India

Madhuri S. Joshi
MGM's Jawaharlal Nehru Engineering College, India

ABSTRACT

The chapter is written on two important buildings, the basics of Big data and their security concern. The chapter is classifying in different sections. The chapter starts with the basic of big data and is concluded with security concern. The chapter is enriched with different category examples to make texts easy for author understanding. The chapter begins with the introduction of big data, their memory size followed by the examples. The chapter explains the category of big data in type of structured, semi-structured and unstructured data. The discussion on operational data service and big data application is also included to ensure the basic understanding to readers. The second portion of chapter which is based on security in big data. It's explaining the issues and challenges in big data. The section also focusing on the shift paradigm from cloud environment to big data environment changes and the problems encounter by organizations. The section discusses the framework issue and concluded with the necessity of understanding security in the big data, keeping in view of expansion of information technology infrastructure in the 21st century.

INTRODUCTION

Big data is a buzzword used to describe and transfer a massive volume of structured and/or unstructured data into knowledge. It is so huge that it is very difficult to process it using traditional database and software techniques. Big data helps companies to improve the performances of their applications and make faster intelligent decisions. Big data refers to Petabytes or Exabytes of data consisting of more than

DOI: 10.4018/978-1-5225-2486-1.ch001

Gigabytes to Terabytes of records of more than lac users, all from different sources. These sources may include: web, sales, customer contact center, social media, mobile data etc. One must be familiar with the other terms of data as shown in Table 1. Big data is always not referring to big volume of data but also refers to the technology that deals with the large amount of data and the infrastructure needed to store that data. When dealing with larger data sets organizations face difficulties in being able to capture, organize, manage and integrate big data as standard tools and procedures are not designed to search and analyze massive data sets. It may take so many minutes/days/years to transfer the data from one location to other. Businesses or enterprises expects more fast processing and transfer of data to perform different operations on it. Ninety percent of data currently available in the world is generated in last few years.

Characteristics of Big Data

Big data (Sharvari, 2015) is typically broken down by three main characteristics: Volume (i.e. quantity of big data), Velocity (i.e. processing speed of big data) and Variety (i.e. various categories of big data: structured or unstructured?). Even two more important characteristics are available, Veracity: (i.e. how accurate is that data in predicting business value?) and Value (conversion of data into actual business value). In a simple language, big data is defined as it is so large and comes in various categories that it becomes very difficult to process it using relational database management systems. It is the requirement of the industry that it should be provided with useful insight and gain correct content. Data should be processed with recent tools and produce important & meaningful information.

According to the study of IBM CMO (IBM, 2014), 2.5 exabytes of data is generated every day. Google generates approximately one Gigabytes of data, Twitter may generate greater than 500 Megabytes of users and 400 Megabytes of tweets and Facebook may generate more than 25 Terabytes of data daily. This leads to huge processing of data every day with new technologies like MapReduce.

Table 1. Bytes and bigger bytes

Data	Unit Size	Binary Size
1 bit	A binary digit	-
8 bits	1 byte or 10^0	2^3
1024 bytes	1 kilo bytes (1 KB) or 10^3	2^{10}
1024 KB	1 Mega Bytes (1MB) or 10^6	2^{20}
1024 MB	1 Giga Bytes (1 GB) or 10^9	2^{30}
1024 GB	1 Tera Bytes (1 TB) or 10^{12}	2^{40}
1024 TB	1 Peta Bytes (1 PB) or 10^{15}	2^{50}
1024 PB	1 Exa Bytes (1 EB) or 10^{18}	2^{60}
1024 EB	1 Zetta Bytes (1 ZB) or 10^{21}	2^{70}
1024 ZB	1 Yotta Bytes (1 YB) or 10^{24}	2^{80}
1024 YB	1 Bronto Bytes (1 BB) or 10^{27}	2^{90}
1024 BB	1 Geo Bytes or 10^{30}	2^{100}
…	…	…

A company may wish to analyze large volumes of data in real time by quickly assessing the value of their customers and may have potential to provide additional offers to those customers to buy new things. This can be done by finding the exact amount and type of data to be analyzed to improve the business value. As big data includes structured or unstructured data generated from various sources like e-mail, social media sites, text streams etc. companies needs to organize, manage and perform different operations on it by using different software tools and technologies.

Managing and analyzing data have always offered the greatest benefits and challenges for organizations of all sizes and across all industries. Managing data includes, ensuring high quality of data, easy access to data, performing analysis on data, providing data as an input to various applications and locating valuable information out of large amount of structured or unstructured data. Analyzing data has different types: Basic Analytics for insight, advanced analytics for insight, operationalized analytics and monetized analytics.

Basic Analytics for insight type is used to understand data more clearly. Analysis in this method is done by slicing and dicing of data, reporting, simple visualizations and basic monitoring methods. Advanced analytics for insight type is more complex analysis method than previous type. This type includes predictive modeling, pattern matching techniques, text analytics and data mining techniques. Operationalized analytics type becomes a part of the business process operations, for example weather forecasting, mobile phones, insurance company etc. Monetized analytics are utilized to drive revenue, the income returned by an investment.

To access structured or unstructured data we may need to deal with lots of complexity. For example, businesses need to struggle to capture information about their customers, products and services. If number of customers buying the same product in a same way is small, things are quite straightforward and simple but over the period as number of customers grow, number of companies increase and market also grows things are somewhat complicated. Therefore, to survive, companies need to add more product options with new features and distribute it to customers through various geographical areas. This struggle is not only related to businesses but also to research and development organizations. Organizations require more computing power to run software's, more computing power to process images and also to get more sources of scientific data. Complexity in data is present because data comes from different sources and in different formats.

Types of Big Data

Big data comes from different sources like weather stations, sensors, social media, smart phones, healthcare, insurance companies, stock exchange, tablets etc. All these data sources are managed and searched independently. But the challenge here is, how to intersect all this structured/unstructured data as data management methods are different for different types of data. Organizations are finding ways to make use of this information. Following section provides insight on types of big data.

Structured Data

Structured data is a data which has some fixed format. Generally structured data is arranged in rows or columns of tables, called as relational database or relational data. Other examples may include data mart, data warehouse, graphical information etc. This type of data is organized and searchable by data type within the actual content. This data is easy to manage and process by traditional data management tools. Most of the organizations are using traditional methods for managing and processing their data effectively. Data can be generated either by machine or by humans. Data which is created (Judith et al., 2013) by a machine without human intervention is called as machine generated data. Data created by humans in interaction with computers is called human generated data. Examples of machine generated data are as follows: medical devices, sensors (Radio Frequency ID (RFID) tags, smart meters), web logs, global positioning system (GPS) data, point of sale data (purchase transaction data), financial data, stock trading data etc. Human generated data may include: click streams data (data generated after you click a link), gaming data and Company data: name of employees, age, income, address, phone numbers, etc. Some of this data may not be considered as large volume of data but if collected for millions of users then the size of data is astronomical. This large volume of data can be made useful after analysis to take important business decisions.

Unstructured Data

Unstructured data neither has predefined format nor organized in a predefined manner. This type of data is irregular and ambiguous which makes it difficult to understand using traditional computer programs/ database management systems. These days it is said that 80% of data in the world is in unstructured format, primarily in text and it is growing significantly every day.

This data needs to be processed to extract useful information from it. This processed data should be converted into structured data and then can be analyzed and used to take important business decisions. As this process is very difficult, expensive and time consuming, every time it is not possible to convert unstructured data into structured format. This may lead to various issues related to relational database management system.

Email data can be considered as unstructured data. Even if it has some implied structure, it cannot be considered as structured type data as it doesn't fit into relational databases and cannot be parsed by traditional data management tools. Other examples of unstructured data include: document, text files or pdf files, books, articles, spreadsheets, web pages, image files, presentation files, video files, audio files, social media data, customer reviews, call center conversations etc. All these files don't have predefined format to store a data. Similar to structured data, unstructured data is also generated by either machine or human. Data which is captured through satellites about weather, scientific data for seismic imagery/atmospheric/high energy physics data, surveillance data and radar or sonar data comes under the category of machine generated data. Company data, email data, social media data (blogs, tweets, Facebook data, LinkedIn data, news feeds, discussion boards, video sites), mobile data (text, image, etc), website data comes under the category of human generated data. Unstructured text data are analyzed by using text analytics methods to extract significant data. This data is later transformed into structured data to utilize it in various ways.

Sometimes data comes continuously, may or may not be from various sources, may or may not be with different varieties to your systems in real time which may lead to a problem of managing and processing data using traditional methods. This may also overwhelm your systems. Therefore, we need newer information management tools and technologies to deal with real time large volume and large variety of data. To consume, process and analyze data in real time we have to consider following things: low latency, scalability, versatility and native format. If the amount of time required to respond to a particular query in real time applications is low, then it is suitable for real time data. If the system is capable of sustaining in high volume of streaming data, then that system is capable for real time data. Versatility means the system must support all types of data streams: structured, unstructured or semi-structured. Data should be used in its original format otherwise it will be quite expensive and time consuming to convert it into some other format and then use it. There are chances of changing the meaning of data after conversion.

Semi-Structured Data

In addition to previous data types there is one more data type available called as semi-structured data type. This data type is a combination of structured and unstructured data. This type of data doesn't store data in rows and columns but it has some properties through which it can be analyzed easily. XML files, NoSQL databases, SWIFT, EDI and Java Script Object Notation (JSON) are the examples of this datatype.

Operational Data Services for Big Data

Companies need analysis of big data to solve a particular problem. They use big data analysis results with existing business data to make their decision more effective. There are varieties of operational data services available which are used in combination with big data analysis results. One of the most useful services of operational database is the data persistency service. This service prevents databases to change the data without permission and data will be available whenever required. Data persistency can be maintained by storing data using relational database management system. Data may include information about customer transactions or operational details of the business. Data may be available in more than one database. Relational databases play an important role in big data management but other methods are also available to manage big data. Non-relational databases are one of the important databases playing a major role to manage big data. It doesn't rely on table of rows and columns. There are number of non-relational databases available each with different capabilities. NoSQL or Not an SQL or Not Only SQL is one of the important kind of non-relational databases available. NoSQL databases (Sharvari, 2016) provide a mean for storing, managing and organizing huge volumes of unstructured data other than tabular form. NoSQL databases are having more simple and flexible modeling constraints than relational databases which are beneficial for developers, analysts and the other users for performing interactive queries. Different types of problems may have different types of analyses methods. NoSQL allows different structure for different types of analyses. For example, some are implemented as key-value stores, which aligns data as a collection of key value pairs, while another developing model is a graph database, in which graph structures are used for semantic type queries with different nodes, edges and its associated properties for retrieval and storage purpose. It also provides pointers to know elements which are adjacent to it and avoids use of index lookups. Riak an Berkeley databases and Neo4J & Graph databases are the examples of key-value stores and graph databases respectively. Some databases stores data column wise instead of row wise, these are called as column stores. In document stores stored values are called documents and they are provided with some structures and encoding to manage the data. This encoding can be done in XML, JSON or BSON. Difference between key value pair and document store is that key value store uses unique key to extract the data while document store provides resources for querying. Another NoSQL data store is tabular store which stores data in three-dimension table. The values stored in the table are indexed by row key, column key and a timestamp key. The third dimension is used to store timestamp value. The timestamp value is generally used to preserve history of data entered into the table. NoSQL databases also has object data stores and object databases which works similar to objects maintained in object oriented programming languages.

Benefits of NoSQL databases over relational databases:

- NoSQL databases are more scalable and provide better performance than relational databases for structured or unstructured and large volume of data.
- Data structures used in NoSQL for each database is different than relational databases and therefore performs few operations fasters than relational databases.
- NoSQL databases are suitable for applications with huge volumes and variety of data.
- NoSQL databases are also suitable for applications that are provided as services which are accessible from any location with different devices.
- It also allows object oriented programming.

BIG DATA APPLICATIONS

In 2012, a few data scientists have thought of a few applications as "Future of Big Data" and now in 2017, it is found to be the applications found in our day to day life. Now it is our turn to envision new application today which can be the new future of Big Data.

Big Data based products have penetrated in every field to such an extent that a due care is cautioning about the usage of how the data is to be used. This takes us to look into the dark side of Big Data. The power of Big Data is there in developing many applications- mainly in extracting a reduced, small inferential information out of a huge data (Roy, 2014).

Since year 2011 two terms were coined – Big Data and Cloud computing. Though they have many aspects in common, their origins are different.

The notion of word 'Big' is also changing day by day. A few applications are discussed below to give an idea about the type of systems which can be developed using Mining on the Big Data.

Usage Example of Big Data: USA 2012 Election

US 2012 Election was an example of hi-tech election making use of Computers, Social Networking, Big Data frameworks and predictions. The election campaign was carried out using the technology by both parties. Even the Data Analysis prediction was also done using Big data. Summary of techniques, technology, websites used by both the contestants is given below which tells us the information as a case study.

Barack Obama

- Model used is predictive modeling.
- **Portal:** mybarackobama.com.
- Information Pushing technique used was to drive traffic to other campaign sites.
- YouTube channel also had found more than 230,000 subscribers and 245 million page views.
- As a part of Publicity, a contest was kept to dine with Sarah Jessica Parker.
- It was claimed that the Facebook page recorded more than 32 million "likes".
- A team of Computer programmers was running 66000 computer simulations on every single night. The service was taken from Amazon web services.
- Every single night, the team ran 66,000 computer simulations, (www.Reddit.com).

Another Contestant was Mitt Romney.

Mitt Romney

- Here the model Used was data mining for individualized advertisement targeting.
- YouTube channel showed up more than 23,700 subscribers and 27 million page views which was huge.
- Application Used by Mitt Romney's campaigners was - Orca big-data app.
- The stunt used for Publicity was a program of Ace of Spades HQ (It is a humor-driven U.S.A. based Political Blog covering current events, news, legal issues).

The environment of USA elections is very different than our Indian Elections. But here we are quoting this example with this data because the Mining techniques were used extensively on Big Data as a real-time application in this 2012 USA election.

The Story of Spreadsheets

All of us know the use of spreadsheets. But as the Big Data aspects started penetrating in different areas it affected various fields. People started imaging various possible instrumentation for using the available data. One of such word got coined is Narrative-driven Data analysis. A company was formed called as Narrative Science.

Chief Technology Officer (CTO), Kris Hammond of Narrative Science was a very dynamic person. He explored the other applications of narrative-driven data analysis. Many Companies had a lot of data in the form of spreadsheets (rows and columns). They started collecting / compiling that data. The data suddenly grew up and they ended up with very large data repositories which was very difficult to be managed. The problem was: What is to be done with that data?

Kris Hammond thought that there is an opportunity to extract and communicate the insight concept which is locked within the company data. He said "We will bridge the gap between the data you have, the insights that are in the data. We can compile, and communicate that information to your customers and to your management, and to various teams. We will convert it into something that's intelligent instead of just a list, or rows and columns, or a graph. You will be getting a real narrated story out of the data" as shown in Figure 1.

The point to ponder here is: The journalism applications of this type began which are more empowering than the earlier ones.

Spreadsheets pushed us into a cognitive corner. Then we have to work hard to infer meaning out of the data.

With that in mind, we might think that spreadsheet's days are counting down?

No. There will be always be some people who will require a spreadsheet. He will look at the data from that angle of data. Some people will go ahead like in the case of above example of narrative-driven data analysis.

Thus, the older spreadsheets can be converted into more meaningful data as per the users' requirement.

Figure 1. Conversion of spreadsheet to story

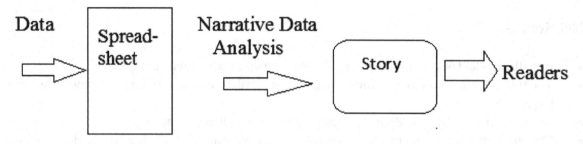

Mining NASA's Astronomical Literature

The field of literature also is an example of huge data and has potential of mining the data and finding the inferences. One such example is given here which is tried on the NASA's Astrophysics Data System.

NASA's Astrophysics Data System (ADS) has been working since 1980s. ADS provides access to abstract of all the articles, research papers of more five lakhs of papers. A team of three data scientists namely- Robert Simpson, Karen Masters and Sarah Kendrew thought of developing an Information System using Data Mining over the three databases i) Abstracts and Titles of all the papers from Astrophysical Journal (ApJ), ii) Astronomics & Astrophysics (A&A), and iii) Minutes & Notices of Royal Astronomical Society (MNRAS). They got some very interesting results after this data mining which are given in short in the following Figure 2.

Figure 2. Percentage of astronomical papers published with one, two, three, four or more authors
(Credit: Robert Simpson; Mac et al., 2012)

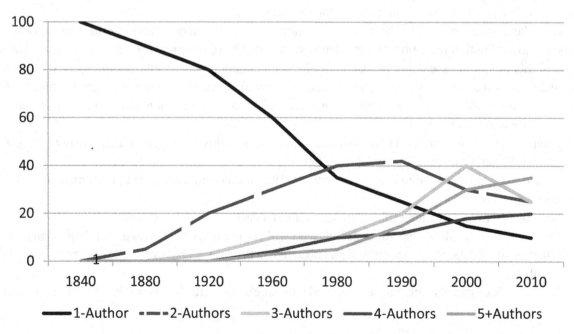

Observations

Single author papers were very prominent for most of the 20th century. Around 1960, two or three author papers started showing up which was the era of communication and hence the joint research work showed the results. There is big trend towards collaborative work. Such type of information is not possible without mining the Big Data.

Software Technologies which are used to develop this type of application were Ruby and Perl languages to grab the data, MySQL database to store and query it and JavaScript (scripting) to display the data in the front end (Mac et al., 2012).

BIG DATA AND SECURITY CONCERN

Many organizations are declaring themselves as big data compliant organizations. They are making advertisement and working on further research for using big data, but security point of view it's very important to know the pros and cons of any new technologies. The big data is new technology for the organization that is relying on updated IT infrastructure. if we do not get the issues and benefits of Big data then it may prove beneficial as well as it could make vulnerability for the organization data as well.

The salient feature which is need to understand that big data is basically works with open source code and we can say platform independent language like JAVA, which means it's important to safeguard against the backdoors intruders. It requires the authentications from users and multiple location data access, which may not be easy to bridge towards securing infrastructure. Further in security (Tim et al., 2009), log files and audits are an important bench mark which is again a challenge in front of organization that is deploying big data in their organization. Also, it should be kept in mind that when the security is benchmark the malicious data and inadequate data validation solution is challenges for us.

The study of big data means to make setup of information technology in the term of infrastructure as well in term of tuning software. The big data also support to save each and every small piece of code, web logs, click stream data and social media content to gain better insights about their customers and their business. But without knowing the repercussions, it may prove fatal also to organization if its insecure and it is taken out by somebody else illegally, which create a good picture of security incident in big data, however it is not a common practice but its need to align the keep in view of security concerns. If we look up the difference between cloud and big data, the responsibility in big data infrastructure is always more than cloud. Because in cloud the security is concern for the third-party alliance where we are using the cloud while in big data the infrastructure is organization based and it give support to save the minute's details of data which itself give a challenge to big data experts to ensure the security of the data to organization.

Induction of Big Data in Security

The big data and security induction is important with the change age of information technology. Prior to that security incident and event management (SIEM) is widely use towards securing by logging system and it's widely reliable for the IT organization, but with the emergence of Big data technologies, used as potential savior for the security and providing better than the SIEM and many other tools which are responsible to give security to the IT infrastructure.

Making one step next, the challenges of detecting and preventing advance threats could be solved by Big data security analysis, even big data help in identifying detection and suggesting prevention to make security fold infrastructures. In big data, we have also opportunity to analyze the log in systematic ways which helps a lot to save loss of data by stopping security incidents in the organization, there are many more suggestions e.g., Intrusion detection and prevention system, help in security using big data. At the morale, big data results more practical and better approach than previous held technique towards securing the infrastructure organization.

Security and Big Data Framework

If we are working with big data, we have to work with Hadoop, which is a traditional data warehouse and connect with relational database which is having vast amount of data. Hadoop is design in such a way that it can easily process large amount of data, irrespective its structure. In the heart of Hadoop, a Map Reduce framework, which is work to creating web search indexes? The Hadoop Distribution File System, allows every server in a cluster to fail without cancelling the different process and in parallel ensuring the security with the existing framework, the framework is good security complaint and provide a wonderful security to the data.

Big Data Security Challenges

The big data ensure the wonderful future for technologist and confirm the jubilant opportunity for variety of users irrespective they are scientist, industry experts or the marketers. It is giving a varied new opportunity to variety of users to ensure secure and perfect system. However, it's also keep in mind that without planned security and other solutions, big data could be proved a big challenge also to the inducer who are planning to deploy big data in their organization.

Scope of Big Data Security

The scope of big data security is certainly high in coming trends; the important fact could be seen with the three different areas like the data sources, big data framework and analytics. The data sources are more important and concern to security because big data provide the variety of information through different forms, and as its changes as the requirement emerges so it's certainly tough to secure the data in the different format. The table and form changing dynamically as the need arise give a challenges to security concerned to ensure that the data is safe and all the things are at par secure, The big data framework weather as discussed above is Hadoop or different like MongoDB or other is certainly secure but the open source code and ignorance of small-small incidents in log and audits leads to the big vulnerability and give a big planning to ensure that big data framework ensure security to the organization, the important view from which the big data is center of attraction is big data analytics. Which is now a day a powerful tool for organization. The management require the different type of results in terms of graphs and trending feature, whose outcome is purely conditional basis, so it's very important to conform the big data analytics. The organization who are shifting from cloud to big data is also wide in market give a good massage that there is nice opportunity for security experts to work with big data. In the cloud the security concern remains for the external agencies while in the big data its completely taken care by the big data infrastructure designer and developers so it's quite visible that vast scope of big data security is for sure in coming time.

The limitation of traditional encryption approaches is big challenges for big data due to availability of plenty of encryption schemes. It is also need to ensured that the data which is get exported from simple database to big data environment then how to ensure the schema of security with simple to complex database design. In fact, with the changes, the different approaches tuning itself leads to a big concern for big data security, and it require a massive plan to confirm the security in big data.

The Vormetric Data Security architecture gives strong feature in the big data framework provides encryption, key management and access control in systematic procedure. It also offers granular control, robust encryption and analytics support. It also enables security to leverage centralized control from the distributed sources and optimize with compliances. It's easy to use and provide a support with securing big data framework with data. Organization has opportunity to get data from variety of sources, which can be of structured as well as unstructured. The sources of data could be from data warehouses, system logs and different applications like spreadsheets etc., required to submit in big data framework. In order to ensure security, we can use vormetric transparent encryption as well as vormetric application encryptions, which ensure the suitable platform for the security in the big data environment.

In the big data framework, the data use regularly transfer from multiple nodes from one node to another node in the network infrastructure. During that the sensitive information, could be stored in log files, and during audits its noticed that it is vulnerability prone which is immediately noticed to avoid any security accident in the data warehouse. In addition, Vormetric protection for huge database, its noticeable to organization benefits and enable maximize the business befits of big data schema and its investment to the organization.

In the big data, many forms include, on-demand graphs, automated report and adjunct query these outputs contain the very important and sensitive information which is very important for the organization. And its very potential target for the intruders to get it done for business. To make available big data annalistic security, the use or vormetric transparent and application encryption is absolutely ease of use and perfect to use to ensure secure platform for organizations.

Lack of Designed Security

The big data platform is used to get different type of formats and data, which signify that its required to give attention to designed a secure mechanics, else it will be tough to ensure the security with multiple formats and data through various nodes in the channel. Few more issue in context of security could be the Anonymity Concern, Big Data Diversity in Complex, Data Breaches are now common, Security Spending is still low, Big Data Skill Gap, Data brokers.

In short, we would like to brief that the security is the important concern in the big data technologies due to the merging demand in the corporate and deploying information technology require a lot of schema planning to confirm that big data technologies is secure and will be effective for the organization. A small mistake may lead to big security accident which may cost a huge to organization so due care shall be taken to ensure secure schema.

REFERENCES

Hurwitz, Nugent, Halper, & Kaufman. (2013). *Big Data for Dummies*. Wiley.

IBM. (2014). *International Technical Support Organization, Information Governance Principles and Practices for a Big Data Landscape*. University of Illinois.

Mac Slocum, A. A. (2012). Big Data Now: Current Perspectives. O'Reilly Media.

Mather, T., Kumaraswamy, S., & Latif, S. (2009). *Cloud Security and Privacy, An Enterprise Perspective on Risks and Compliance*. O'Reilly.

Tamane. (2015). Text Analytics for Big Data. *International Journal of Modern Trends in Engineering and Research, 2*(3).

Tamane. (2016). *Non-relational databases in big data*. 2nd International Conference on ICT for Competitive Strategies, Udaipur, India.

Section 2
Big Data Tools and Technologies With Case Studies

Chapter 2
Affordances of Data Science in Agriculture, Manufacturing, and Education

Krishnan Umachandran
Nelcast Ltd., India

Debra Sharon Ferdinand-James
The University of the West Indies, Trinidad and Tobago

ABSTRACT

Continued technological advancements of the 21st Century afford massive data generation in sectors of our economy to include the domains of agriculture, manufacturing, and education. However, harnessing such large-scale data, using modern technologies for effective decision-making appears to be an evolving science that requires knowledge of Big Data management and analytics. Big data in agriculture, manufacturing, and education are varied such as voluminous text, images, and graphs. Applying Big data science techniques (e.g., functional algorithms) for extracting intelligence data affords decision markers quick response to productivity, market resilience, and student enrollment challenges in today's unpredictable markets. This chapter serves to employ data science for potential solutions to Big Data applications in the sectors of agriculture, manufacturing and education to a lesser extent, using modern technological tools such as Hadoop, Hive, Sqoop, and MongoDB.

INTRODUCTION

Data science as a new field of endeavor is increasingly in top demand (American Statistical Association, 2016) as technological advancements afford the availability of an abundance of real-time information (e.g., via social media or global positioning system) to users. Organisations and institutions face operational challenges such as fierce price wars, stronger competition, overhead controls, waste reduction, operational excellence, stressed customer demands, and reduced buying power. Such challenges may prompt "panic" decision-making in the absence of data science wherewithal by institutions/organisations in key sectors like manufacturing, agriculture, and education. Moreover, the education sector, unlike

DOI: 10.4018/978-1-5225-2486-1.ch002

other service sectors, is not always prompt in responding to changing needs of the education market. Responsively, businesses and institutions can now tap into data they never knew earlier existed, making customized dynamic decisions with intelligence of no perceived boundaries. Data science as an information work space for data analytics affords in-depth processes such as scoring, predicting cross- field inputs, and functional algorithms, resulting in data warehousing and intelligence tools used appropriately for decision-making. Artificial intelligence plays a critical role in data analytics for decision making as it allows the computer system to almost think and find, while correlating varied pieces of information, producing meaningful results for analysts such as those in the agricultural sector (Roy, 2013, May 22; Tapia & Corchado, 2010). The challenge in this process is the evolution of data cognitively engaged and skimmed for decisions. The dawning of the field of data science enables market testing for possible products and services that are the real frameworks for revenue. Employing data science techniques in creating and analysing Big Data for supporting critical decision-making can enhance an institution/ organisation's ability to satisfy customers' changing needs and build market resilience in key sectors such as agriculture, manufacturing, and education. To this end, this chapter specifically aims to achieve the following objectives:

- Explain the need for data science wherewithal.
- Analyze the use of data science in agriculture.
- Describe the use of analytical tools in data science.
- Analyze the use of data science in manufacturing.
- Describe uses of data science in education.

BACKGROUND

Survival in today's competitive global economy requires institutions and organisations to continually strategize for accessing and allocating their budgets, conducting customer research, and revisiting set targets in keeping with current market trends in sectors like agriculture, manufacturing, and education sectors. The success of such strategic decision-making is largely dependent on ready access to high quality operational and market intelligence data. One mechanism that can contribute to this success is the use of data science. As a new burgeoning field with attractive and stable employment potential, data science is described as "… an interdisciplinary field about processes and systems to extract knowledge or insights from data in various forms, either structured or unstructured,…" (Stansbury, 2016, 1. Data Science/Data Administration section). Big Data is also defined as a collaborative phenomenon for guiding real-time insights into organisational and institutional operations through mathematical, statistical, computational, and data management skills (Magoulas & Lorica, February, 2009; National Science Foundation, 2012). Institutions and organisations can extract new sources of information that were previously unexplored through the application of data science. For example, the use of an evolving algorithm from voluminous data for such tasks as deciding priorities or choices, deep-cutting conventional approaches and the supplemental combination of observations, patterns, trends, sequences, similarities and data behavior are now possible for arriving at a superior solution. Data science is a composite clustering of machine learning, Big Data processing, and statistical routing along with expert convolutions for arriving at a best optimal range of solutions that can be customized by the user for effective results. Scenarios, situations, circumstances and other fluctuations can also be merged into the algorithm for an objective analysis for a more precise synthesized solution (Jimenez, 2013; Zenodo, 2016). Therefore, the result is a combination of both quantitative and qualitative reasoning so that the numerical decisions are forged with conceptual reinforcements.

REACHING BIG DATA

Issues, Controversies, Problems

The use of Big Data has been gaining more attention by decision-makers over the past decade. Casey (2012), a researcher of Google trend, found that the higher their GDP, countries were inclined to support economic success by focusing on the future. Such futuristic projections require high-powered analytics for overall data management with volume, velocity and variety of information assets that demand cost-effective and innovative forms of processing for enhancing decision making. The value captured from these data depict large economies of scale that reflect innovativeness in data system integration, particularly among business systems, manufacturing performance and shop-floor process systems. The shop-floor process is a crucial concern in facilitating the deployment of plant-wide Big Data systems from job-related to manufacturing-led matters such as indicators for productivity and safety as indicated in Table 1. Implicit in manufacturing operations are internal rejections that do not meet set standards of quality. The desired state for achieving operational excellence in reducing these internal rejections and optimizing safety would translate into higher productivity, survival, and longevity for the manufacturing enterprise. A similar scenario would exist for satisfying customers in reducing customer-end rejections for growth and survival of the business. Big Data in manufacturing is based on centralized architecture to evolve the data intelligence in manufacturing that is addressed through data science initiatives.

CORDIS (2012, September 1) emphasized the benefit of using modern technology to address apparent challenges in managing voluminous data. Similarly, Jain and Bhatnagar (2016a) purported that modern technology provides innovative ways for reusing and extracting valuable information from such data. Likewise, an information perspective is a robust process which brings valuable message development through the manufacturing organisation, comprising the gamut of surprise, regularization, and uniqueness. In agriculture, the emphasis is on enhancing water use effectively to increase accessibility, convenience and affordability of water. Such valuable information is knowledge and hence, it is an intellectual property and needs to be duly protected that include the following reasons:

Table 1. Integration of operational and customer satisfaction indicators

Sl. #	Implicit	Explicit	Desired State	
			Indicator	**Framework**
1	Internal Rejections	Operations Excellence	Productivity	Survive
2			Safety	Longevity
3	Customer End Rejections	Customer Satisfaction	Development Lead Time	Growth
4			Weekly Refill	Survive

Source: (Umachandran, 2016)

- For rightful ownership.
- For use, nurture and propagation.
- From wrongful acts and omissions.
- From inappropriate claims and ownership.

Ongoing research to safeguard against these threats to intellectual property include user authentication, computer attack signature identity, and traitor identification. Fouad et al. (2016) used a biometric approach to user authentication that employs user keystroke recognition. They found the biometric approach to be more secure than the traditional passwords that often fall prey to theft. The "fingerprint" left by computer users (sincere or illicit) in log files have also been used by researchers in developing a dataset generator tool that easily reproduces the patterns of attack signatures found in these log files (O'Shaughnessy & Gray, 2013). Mohanpurkar and Madhuri (2016) have proposed a traitor identification system that protects numeric relational databases by embedding secured fingerprinting in them. Further, the machine learning of data processing should also ensure the data quality in a closed loop, whether such data are unsupervised (exploration), supervised (learning and testing), or reinforced (optimizing and reporting) for impacting the solution process. Creation and management of agricultural information on climate forecast is a demanding data task, possible requiring a re-thinking, reducing, re-using and recycling of information for crystalizing knowledge. This revitalizing of information ultimately depends on the management of resources and on individuals for effective utilization as shown in Figure 1.

Knowledge and information sources are tools that can be used to provide answers to specific questions relating to brief facts, statistics, technical instructions, background information, or needed sources located at other information sites. Knowledge and information sources include the following types:

Figure 1. Considerations for effective utilization of information resources
Source: (Umachandran, 2016)

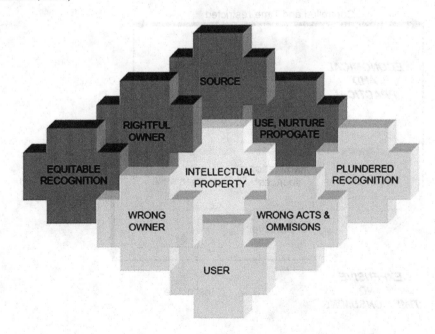

- Instinctive.
- Explorative.
- Experimentative.
- Archival (Latent).
- Transactional (Practicals).

Nazim and Bhaskar (2011) claimed that explicit knowledge is prescribed and methodical, targeting a specific scientific plan or program and then stored. Tacit knowledge is personalized and enriched with individual experience, including intangible factors such as personal beliefs, perspectives, instincts, and values. The effectiveness of the knowledge process is its capture, share and transfer of both tacit and explicit. An effective transformation of knowledge in an organisation reduces duplication, improves productivity, and reduces costs. Figure 2 represents considerations for the control and timeliness of knowledge sources.

The competitive advantage of leveraging knowledge and information sources is derived from creating actionable intelligence from these data. The leap in technological support such as cloud implementations, advanced business analytics, cyber security, communication tools, information security, protection, and business acumen help to create such actionable intelligence. Moreover, there are various options for information sources every day that can possibly lead to a decision fatigue and overload of information. It is exhausting to deliberate on the different options or be told by others what to do. Hence, there is a need for technology to intervene and facilitate an objective solution. Data science can satisfy this need in affording an understanding of the overall scenario and recognize trends and patterns occurring by employing algorithms in taking in data and either accepting or converting data by pattern and behavior

Figure 2. Considerations for the control and timeliness of knowledge sources
Source: (Umachandran, 2016)

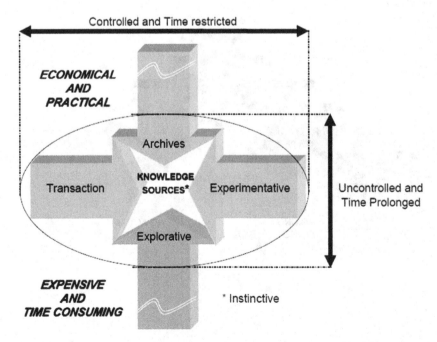

analysis. But, over-reliance on the converted data can cause an oversight of the context, which very often is acquired through instinctive understanding and the value of human conversations. Ultimately, the Big Data created provides the user with the following options:

- USE.
- Mis-USE.
- Manipulate.
- Hush / Archive / Remnant.

Data science takes advantage of Big Data because of its exceptional scale and heterogeneous characteristic (e.g., texts, images, graphs, or sequences) that allow for deeper insights into the data for improving the quality of products and services offered through its multi-disciplinary functionality. To this end, several techniques are employed for reaching Big Data across domains (e.g., agriculture, manufacturing, and education) that include the following: Stochastic Methods; Graph and Text Mining; Monte-Caro model; Signal and Image processing as well as Predictive Machine Learning (Jimenez, 2013; Roy, 2013, May 22). Harnessing this collective knowledge, thinking, creativity, and problem-solving address a series of demands and encounters by traversing around the possible options. Many decisions and choices are sometimes determined by emotions, instincts, and reactions to situations that can be too subjective for the common good. Alternatively, an unbiased operating system should be used for generating, processing, and sustaining an objective evaluation, which is capable of enduring large volumes of data from various sources and matching these with the right expectations of the business or organisation. Thus, data science is the underlining leverage for providing actionable intelligence data for improving business performance. This leveraging is only possible through the data warehousing (DW), computations (DC), engineering (DE) and mining of data, while being mindful of the options for use or misuse of these data as shown in Figure 3. Sifting through various and voluminous data requires an automated effort in data science.

Insights gained from leveraging data for improving strategic planning, resource allocation, and client reach, have a positive impact on economies. Specifically, this impact provides information solutions that demonstrate the importance of synergizing information and technology systems for producing data with actionable insights in critically responding to issues that impact the major applications of both public and private section organisations. Inferences are made from the factual information provided to develop a logical step-by-step analysis for arriving at solutions to problems. The ability to reason abstractly is important and logical thinking help in arriving at valid conclusions by recognizing faulty arguments,

Figure 3. Considering relationship options for leveraging data
Source: (Umachandran, 2016)

RELATIONSHIP OPTIONS

Data Warehousing	USE - misUSE
Data Computing	misUSE - Manipulation
Data Engineering	Manipulate - Hush
Data Mining	Hush state to Use state

while gaining confidence over decisions taken. The right data, as depicted in Figure 4, when mined for arriving at logical conclusions are very useful warehouse data. Data mining (DM) is an analytic process that allows for locating and interpreting information for more informed decisions. It is a fusion of applied statistics, intelligence, machine learning and data management systems for extracting the best possible solution from large amounts of data valuable (especially for the treatment of diseases) (Kausar et al., 2015). In addition, data warehousing (DW) has observations and examples as attributes. It is a central repository of all organisational data arranged so as to be accessed by Data Object Abbreviation Standards (DOAS). DOAS is a list of abbreviations used for data object naming by developers and information deliverers. The data are updated in real time from source systems (e.g. email) or populated from data feeds from source systems or legacy systems. Data warehousing (DW) becomes necessary when data integration, information delivery mechanism, and complex data transformations exist.

Data obtained by computation are based on patterns and not totally correct data due to invalidation. Through user authentication, the protocol authorizes the user to make changes according to the conferred access rights (read only/edit). The manipulated data are engineered after data computation (DC). Data engineering (DE) helps to build systems, infrastructure, and massive reservoirs for Big Data. Data stacks use a Hush function to map data of arbitrary size to data of fixed size by looking up and detecting duplicated records in a large file. Data hush /archive /remnant are mined from the healthy hack engineered contents. The value or data science captured from these data can inform large economies of scale. This large scaling requires, among other considerations, designing and building Big Data systems for gaining

Figure 4. Reaching right data
Source: (Umachandran, 2016)

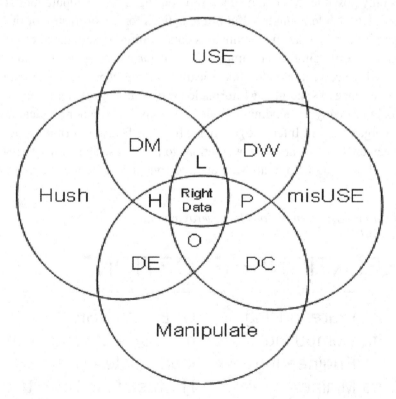

knowledge through data-mining and machine-learning to achieve the following: successful information research, predictive analysis, customization, technological solutions, and informed business decisions as shown in Figure 5.

Data, in different file formats as listed in Figure 6, should be monitored during the data acquisition stage by handling data with standard exchange classification code to include the following:

- Technology assisted creation,
- Standard file format,
- Geographical information,
- Conversions,
- Surveying compatibility.

The Oregon Health and Science University has released a list of recommended file formats for long-term data preservation file storage and access. The file formats used will affect the accessibility of files at a later date, so those listed in Figure 6 are recommended for storage purposes (OHSU Library, 2012).

Figure 5. Data processing for informed decision making
Source: (Umachandran, 2016)

Figure 6. Data files formats
Source: (Umachandran, 2016)

DATA FILES FORMATS

Raw data	.doc / .xls / .gif
Data Set	.pdf
Posters	.jpeg
Images	.bmp and fash automations
Charts	.dib
Models	.ppt / .tiff etc.,

Further, terminal, text, pipe and sockets can read a binary data file written by another statistical system, (cannot be avoided) even though the originating system is not available. Data files from specific versions of the one system may not have been updated to the most recent versions of the other system. Image format files may require use of external conversion software to first convert the image into one of the formats required when data import/export happens. There are also problems with flow in data science. Decision making is done with error deduction, dependent associations, cluster formations, classification, regression, and summarization of the mined data when subjected to an algorithm that facilitates the evolution of a series of optimal solutions in decision making. Inroads into these problems include "handling a set of base predictors for a given classification task and then integrate the output information using an integration technique" (Ripon et al., 2016, Introduction section).

FUTURE DIRECTIONS FOR REACHING BIG DATA

In moving forward, the business or institution should spare no effort in acquiring the wherewithal for employing high-powered analytics for the overall management of Big Data with volume, velocity and variety of information assets in order to enjoy the affordances of reaching Big Data. Research should also be ongoing regarding the impact of these high-powered analytics to justify the investment made for having such wherewithal. Additionally, applicable safeguards should be taken to protect the intellectual property arising from Big Data "reach" to include user authentication, computer attack signature identity, and traitor identification. But, solely relying on the converted data can result in overlooking context, so decision makers are strongly advised to engage in human conversations for a full instinctive understanding of the Big Data.

DATA SCIENCE IN AGRICULTURE

Modern Industrial farming is mono-cultured on a large-scale with enough support for sustainable organic agriculture. Industrial management principles are becoming applicable to Agriculture as Farming is an industry today. Shekar and Otto (2012) believed that a Government's role was crucial in proactively facilitating policy development on business models in ICT, skill application for ICT, and supporting infrastructure for gadgets and free download applications. These developments will benefit the farming industry in taking advantage of the ongoing technological wave in gaining accessing to a growing body of organic knowledge in the Agricultural sector.

This organic knowledge is factually altering the approach in cultivation, breeding, and harvesting in plantations and animal rearing. In addition, the rainfall for agricultural vegetation and diseases in animals are rampant and drastically affecting agriculture as a sustainable and prospective business. Understanding microbes, gene pairing, cropping history-patterns, agronomic practices, weather, climate, and environment is a very huge chunk of data incomprehensive to normal human beings. It is necessary to include technology to support data science in agriculture for suitable decision making. Considerations for Big Data in agriculture are listed in Figure 7 and include core technologies, improvised technologies, schemes and services, events, Agri IT, market orientations and other general considerations.

Figure 7. Considerations for agricultural big data
Source: (Umachandran, 2016)

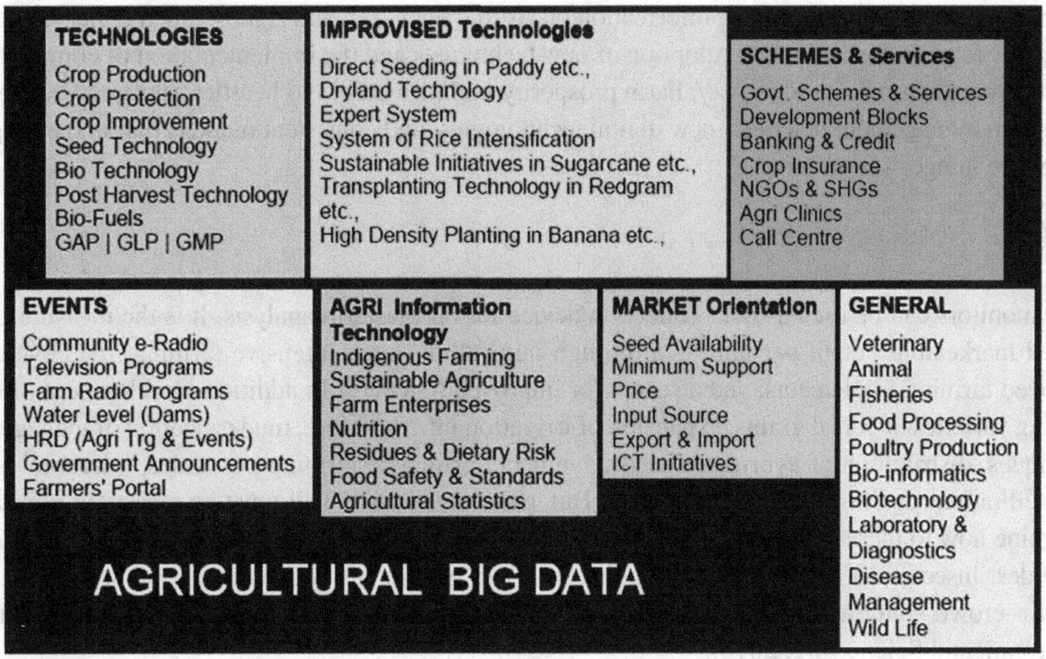

Farming Parameters in Agriculture

Amedie (2013) highlighted the bio-variability in the complex interactions between the physiological process affecting crop growth and weather conditions. Responsively, all involved should work collaboratively to achieve a full understanding of the complexities involved in crop growth affected by weather conditions to include the impact of technology on society. Pezeshkirad et al. (2014) studied the use of computers and the Internet in the Agricultural Extension context and found that these are perceived as having high value by Agriculturalists. The collaborative approach among Agriculturalists coupled with technology use can result in clearly understood outcomes, content development, and additional advice for special agricultural needs. Agriculture as an industry is becoming more competitive and now demands a business approach that includes the use of business principles, techniques, structures, practices (e.g., business analysis, accounting, insurance, financing, capital resources, contract planning, and marketing), and the application of computer technology in order to succeed (Hashimoto & Day, 1991). Animal and plant science principles cover genetics, health and well-being, diseases and pests, and management practices along with technology related applications in natural resources, the environment, and sustainability. The parameters for Farm Management are as follows.

Productivity

It is possible to reduce hunger and poverty through farming by sustainably increasing agricultural productivity. This productivity is measured by the ratio of outputs to inputs in agriculture; output is usually measured as the market value of final output, which excludes intermediate products. Agricultural productivity is calculated by comparing an index of agricultural inputs to an index of outputs. After machinery mechanizations in farming practices, information and computer technologies (ICTs) can now be used to inform productivity such as having information on fishing densities, and rightly timed climatic changes in weather (e.g., in fog and rain). Adoption of new techniques and the implementation of competitively new measures can raise productivity. Farm prosperity includes access to heartier seeds, more effective tools, farm management practices, new digital technologies, and consistent markets that in the long run can reduce hunger and poverty.

Yield

Yield monitors can be used as data-collection device for on-the-farm analysis. It is the measure of the desired marketable output per unit area through innovation, more intensive farming, the creation of improved farming implements, and a search for improved practices. In addition, development of high-yielding varieties of cereal grains, expansion of irrigation infrastructure, modernization of management techniques, distribution of hybridized seeds, synthetic fertilizers, farming pesticides, microbiological, and facilitations can also be good indicators. But, concentrations in soil must be measured in order to determine how to increase organic yields without the environmental degradation, additional fertilizers, pesticides, insecticides in land cultivation. Moreover, a geographic information system (GIS) can be used for crowd sourcing to manage food security and reorganize crops to ensure that maximum use (Environmental Science.org, 2016).

Income

Calculating income from farming requires knowledge of the amount of money earned from farming operations and the returns from secondary derivatives of the original produce, then deducting land value, cost on efforts that induced sprout, rent for any appliances and services, which can then give an idea of net farming income (Sharma, 2013). In addition, farmers also earn money from other sources such as farm wastes or renewable energy. Wind, solar, and biomass energy can be harvested forever, providing farmers with a long-term source of income (Union of Concerned Scientists, n.d.). Renewable energy can be used on the farm to replace other fuels or sold as a "cash crop".

Livelihood Impact and Rural Prosperity

Agricultural growth options and linkages with agricultural investments are key components of an agricultural development strategy. Importantly, a real demand for the goods produced in the local market must exist for sustainability of the farming activity. Simultaneously, favorable Export sector policies should exist to support the balances of linkages between demand and supply through changes in income and productivity. All permutations and combinations of livelihood strategies can contribute to the following:

- Farm and off-farm.
- Livestock-oriented, diversified-oriented, and off-farm-oriented.
- Dependent on - only farm, farm and non-farm, only non-farm, and non-labour.
- Consider the share of forestry and animal husbandry in household income.

- Household dependence - less dependence, moderate dependence, high dependence, and very high dependence on forest/livestock income.

Farming Technologies

Technological advancement aims at making the agricultural industry more productive beyond plant yields by employing a range of farming technologies as depicted in Figure 8. The food production process starting from soil preparation to planting, harvesting, storing, and transporting has new technologies which dramatically improves efficiency.

Farming Resources

Farm production operation include crops, livestock, wild crop harvesting, or handling. Resources needed to support farming management include but not limited to the following: Water, Land, Agriculture Practice, Livestock, Weather, Integrated farming, Forestry, Herbs and Spices, Integrated livestock, People capacity, Money flow and Insurance as shown in Figure 9. These resources are commonly shared through networking with stake holders by serving farming and related information on variables to farmers, consumers, community, media, policy makers, government departments.

Mobile Network, Innovative Partnerships, and Impact

The agricultural marketing sector has access and profitability advantages. Greater access to information and buyers, especially via mobile networks with high connectivity bandwidths, steadily adds to farm

Figure 8. Farming technologies
Source: (Umachandran, 2016)

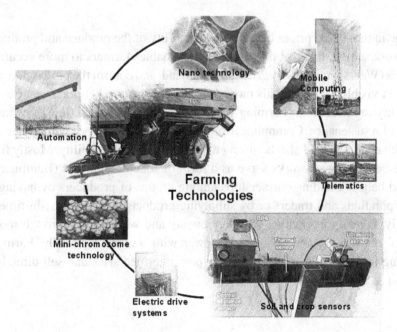

Figure 9. Supporting resources for farm management
Source: (Umachandran, 2016)

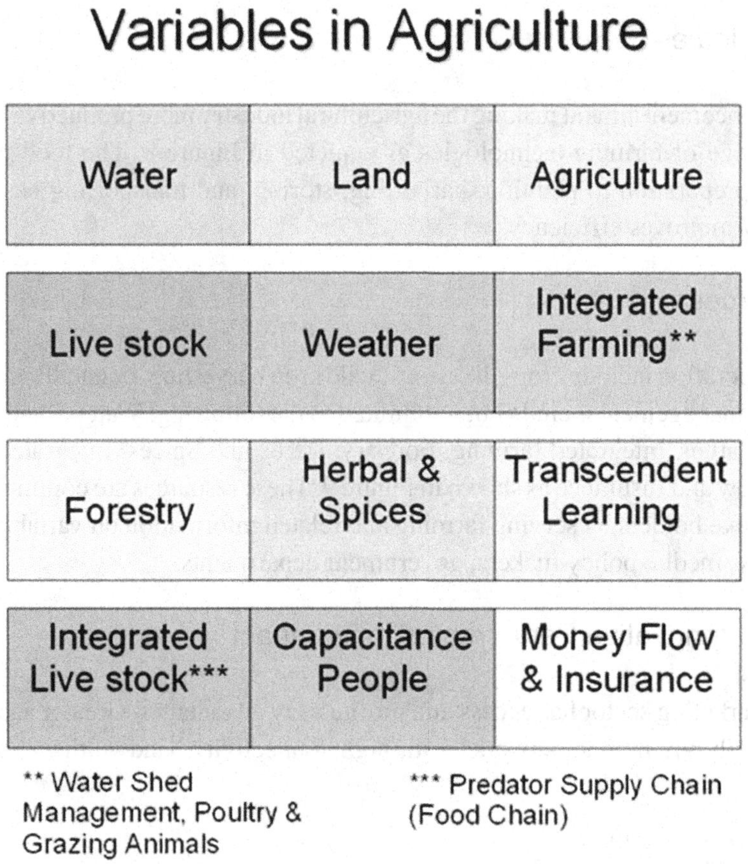

Variables in Agriculture

Water	Land	Agriculture
Live stock	Weather	Integrated Farming**
Forestry	Herbal & Spices	Transcendent Learning
Integrated Live stock***	Capacitance People	Money Flow & Insurance

** Water Shed Management, Poultry & Grazing Animals

*** Predator Supply Chain (Food Chain)

market knowledge in timing the prices based on perishability of the produce and products. Augmenting the agricultural work setting, this real time information enables farmers to more accurately understand weather conditions (Wehrspann, 2016) agricultural demand, and control the production and management of supply chains. A visible Market avoids monopoly or spurious market practices. Businesses aspiring towards profitability in the chain of Farming within the shortest possible time of economics and commerce is necessary for sustenance. Communication channels with producers, wholesalers, intermediaries, dealers, and small vendors should also be strong to realize such sustainability. Mostly fuelled by mobile technology, these developing networks serve as a form of social commerce (Baumgarten et al., 2016; Odella, 2017) and help in building partnerships among groups of producers by having direct communication with corporations and traders or by supplying products based on just-in-time and /or quality needs, accordingly. Directly interacting with key buyers and wholesalers through mobile technology enhances farmers' networking and negotiation power with traders, especially. Farmers have greater insight into pricing in multiple markets, how to bypass intermediaries and sell directly to larger-scale buyers (Halewood & Surya, 2012).

FUTURE RESEARCH FOR DATA SCIENCE IN AGRICULTURE

Following-up with research to understand the impact of an investment into technology adoption for deriving the maximum benefits of data science in Agriculture can assess the following outcomes:

- Reduced Logistics and Transportation costs.
- Enhanced marketing plans informed by multiple market pricing.
- Broader and deeper networks.
- Innovative partnerships.
- Informed use of inputs.
- Improved farm Business Management.

DATA SCIENCE ANALYTICAL TOOLS

Analytical tools should be used to support a variety of processes in data science. For example, in the manufacturing work setting, these analytical tools can augment data workflow, beginning with capturing data, engineering and processing data, and ending with visualizing and communicating the result. Different applied modes of reasoning are used as shown in Table 2. The commonly used programming language for such analysis is Python, and it is an open source suited for scientific computing because of its extensive ecosystem of scientific libraries and environments. Data science analytical tools for Big Data technology follow the process of predictive modeling, machine learning, data visualization, and data pipeline technology (speed analytics) tools for generating, capturing, analyzing, and feeding processed data back into the system. Four modern applications operationalized in this regard are Hadoop, Hive, Sqoop, and MongoDB.

Hadoop

A modern technological tool used in data science is Hadoop, a high-level software framework with user interfaces like SQL for storage and large-scale processing of datasets on clusters of hardware. Such high density data processing was previously challenging to handle with the large volumes of data produced, but is now achievable as well as the consumption of these data in decision making (Jain & Bhatnagar, 2016b). Hadoop helps in data transfer to and from data storage locations as shown in Figure 10.

Table 2. Applied modes of reasoning

Logical	Data Mining and Data Warehousing
Pattern	Data Warehousing and Data Computing
Opportunity	Data Computing and Data Engineering
Hack	Data Engineering and Data Mining

Source: (Umachandran, 2016)

Figure 10. Hadoop data transfer and storage
Source: (Umachandran, 2016)

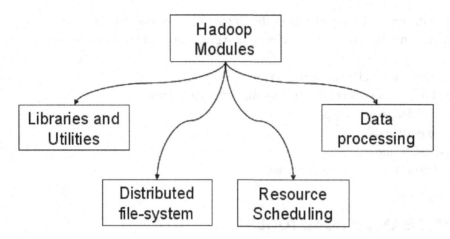

LIBRARIES, UTILITIES, AND DISTRIBUTION

Big Data classification changes over time with technological enhancements across sectors due to the variation in dataset size, software, and tools that are specific to each. Hence, data science tools should not identify a minimum volume requirement for Big Data classification but also ensure a load balance among request servers (Panda et al., 2017) in order to potentially enhance decision-making. Further, a distributed file-system provides high aggregate bandwidth across clusters such as in the following:

- It is a Client-server link through TCP / IP.
- File system indexing through snapshots in node's memory (single point for storage and management of metadata) structures.
- Assured file-system against corruption and loss of data.
- RAID storage on Hosts is optional.
- Mounted on an OS using file:// URL, stores data on a FTP file server.

Scheduling of resources include but are not limited to the following:

- File access through Thrift web app (HTTP) command line interface on network libraries.
- Inventory Management of the Queuing queries through First-In-First-Out.
- Prioritization and rescheduling of tasks through java virtual machine to facilitate data to work and reside on the same node.

Hive

Similar to a SQL database, Hive is a data warehouse on Hadoop used for segregating, summarizing, and analysing Big Data as depicted in Figure 11. In accelerating the query and indexing of these data, Hive also compiles, transacts, and stores Metadata. The compressed data from algorithms are mined with the help of UDF.

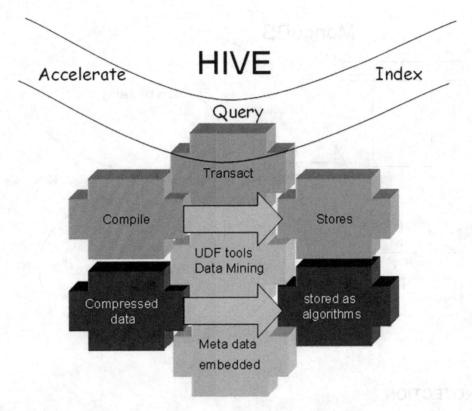

Sqoop

Functioning as a plug connector, Sqoop operates on a command-line interface application and is likened to a SQL query. Sqoop is used for importing and populating HIVE in transferring Big Data between relational databases and exporting to an external Data Warehouse, providing the wherewithal to achieve the following data functions:

- Import data,
- Transfer and copy to external systems,
- Analysis.

MongoDB

MongoDB is a horizontal platform in a database that is placed on different hardware and multiple machines for improving performance through Data Modeling as represented in Figure 12. This modelling is done in different ways to include the following: embedding, growth and relationship modeling, tree structures, memory storage through pipeline and operators, replication of concepts, concerns and failovers, using JavaScript Object Notation, schema design, indexing and working with language drivers.

Figure 12. MongoDB: Data modeling for performance improvement
Source: (Umachandran, 2016)

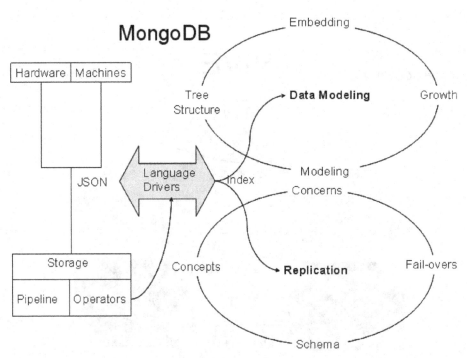

DATA PROTECTION

Today, data science has covered all verticals such as biological sciences, medical informatics, health care, social sciences, and humanities. Knowledge and information sources are usually protected by registrations such as patents, copyrights, and trademarks from transmission pilfers that include plagiarizing, hacking, and phishing. Knowledge propagation is required in industries to create institutionalism of the process as latent, expressed, documented and practiced. More importantly, organisational learning demands that the expected knowledge content is readily available beyond the threshold of performance and incentivized for cutting edge delivery. Therefore, industries create knowledge-level matrix than silos of excellence. Potential knowledge becomes depleted and obsolete over time depending on the needs, demands, and importance the society attaches to changing scenarios. Hence, a Kinetic form of Knowledge is required. To expect everyone to be instinctive or explorative in this fast world is not worth the wait and not economical for Manufacturing activity. Progressive researchers are the ones who propagate kinetic knowledge through ATE (Archives, Transactions, and Experimentations).

DATA SCIENCE IN MANUFACTURING

Excellence in the manufacturing industry has a push and pull to its dimensional structure:

1. **PUSH:** Operational excellence.
2. **PULL:** Customer Delight.

The rapid growth of social media, mobility and radio frequency identification (RFID) can allow manufacturers to reach un-tapped data that were not readily accessible before (Roy, 2013, May 22). Today, the manufacturing sector is taking the lead in job creations, technological innovation, and GDP growth by adopting technologies. This adoption adds value to the manufacturing sector in enabling departments to quickly respond, becoming agile to market trends, optimizing resource utilization, controlling environmental impact, managing revenue fluctuations, and sustaining profits through new markets (Morel et al., 2007). Still, enhancing efficiency in business operations relies on pushing operational excellence in managing the process flow and sustained with a focus on best practices and employee engagement. Customer satisfaction in manufacturing is more concentrated towards conformance to a standard or specification in quality, delivery and time that would "pull" customers, making it necessary to continuously monitor the quality of service – expected vs received.

Quality control (QC) involves constant inspection throughout the manufacturing process of products for adherence to set standards. This process is carried out by trained inspectors that include capturing data on internal rejects. Quality assurance (QA) represents responsibility of everybody involved in the creation of a product or service in building reliability into every stage of product development and manufacturing processes. Figure 13 gives further details on the key variables for consideration in deriving quality output. The data documented in this process includes customer end rejects. Progressing towards Total Quality Management (TQM) is a culture development for continuous improvement with a focus on customer empathy.

Further, manufacturers can collaborate with retailers in discussing ways to maximize the use of Big Data from smartphone and other BYOD technology for customer-oriented product designs. To illustrate, in a retail setup that facilitates one-to-one interaction with a potential customer, a specially developed app can monitor the customer's movements one entering the store. Through Wi-Fi detection and connectiv-

Figure 13. Achieving quality output
Source: (Umachandran, 2016)

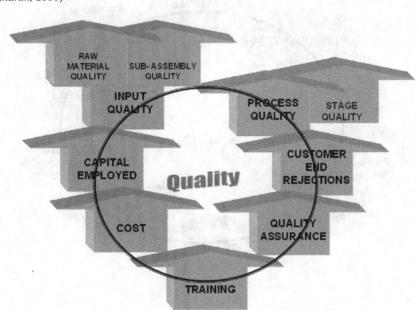

ity, an in-store mode would be activated sending a message to the Stores' personnel and simultaneously directing the customer to the relevant Customer Service Representative desk in that store. These messages would be facilitated through transmitters at specific distances to the stock room area, switching and adjusting to correspond Stores' personnel regarding the customer's specific needs (from the phone data browsed earlier by the customer). Customer proximity to the Stores entry can be achieved through the installation of Bluetooth transmitters, while signals generated within the stores would be guided by gadgets installed inside the store. Easy scale back using network elements and communications solutions would reduce the complexity of multiple vendors working together, integrating services of the store's direct dial extensions, voicemail, call trees for the toll-free number, and the ability to make calls from laptops.

In this illustration, innovative data applications and tools such as utility of Smartphones would work in tandem with downloaded applications in the phone and permitted to track and offer an augmented experience tailored to one's needs. Not only is a customer delight possible but it can invoke new inputs for new designs. Big Data is used in designing new products for flexible, secure, cost-effective innovations with new standards of performance supported by reliable maintenance of these products.

An important aspect of sustaining product quality is reliability-centered maintenance that is based on resource and process reliability as shown in Figure 14. Data on maintenance hovers over the following elements: diagnosis, analysis, adaptive process, sensitivity, priority-feasibility- effectiveness, sudden rupture/breakdown, bench-strength of manpower resources, spares, and inventory.

Figure 14. Reliability-centered maintenance
Source: (Umachandran, 2016)

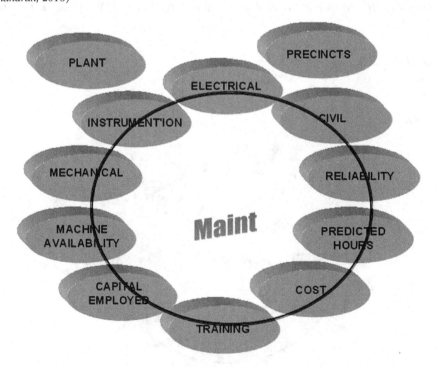

The manufacturing process is completed only when a range of post-production services, as elaborated in Figure 15, add value to the product or service. This output exposes the failures of the production activities, requiring a quick turnaround to fulfill customer expectations. Such responsive action can ensure the timely dispatch of the suitable output by coordinating logistics support, which is usually a contracted activity.

Added to the success factors for quality output is the process of purchasing materials. This purchasing process is based on the scheduling and execution done mostly on a two-bin pull system that requires the following elements: a physical material flow, lead time of delivery, and quality acceptance. The breakdown of maintenance, spares, and other immediately required materials would be purchased on an individual case, allowing adjustments of the purchase documents manually in every step of the purchasing process. Another critical success factor is the lowering of levels of inventories for cost effectiveness. Simultaneously, much caution should be taken to ensure zero time is lost in supplying requested materials to the shop floor, and the stores activities for receipts-storage-protection-indenting-delivery should be a dependable chain. These cautions help to ensure that holding cost is also controlled.

Data Science applications require a new work culture as data transparency is highly vulnerable for exploitation at the hands of unscrupulous persons. The simple terms sincerity, honesty, trust and loyalty mean a lot in all the people resources involved with such data. How to build these intricate characteristics into an organisational dimension is a great challenge. Humanistic studies would be more required to handle complex technological issues. Organisations would evolve to become lean (work) as automatic data capture and linkages gain momentum with sufficient care to audit and edit the inputs. Therefore, Data Science will become inevitable as an Enterprise's ultimate macro decision-making tool with micro insights and within tolerable errors.

Figure 15. Post-production services
Source: (Umachandran, 2016)

FUTURE DIRECTIONS FOR BIG DATA IN MANUFACTURING

Embracing data science in the manufacturing sector through the use of Big Data technology has many affordances. The more the data, the greater the possibility to connect the links for effective decision-making that can result in significant gains in flexibility and agility to the local and global manufacturing markets. Providing products and services to these markets that meet specifications for quality, delivery, and time would "pull" customers, but such quality must be continuously monitored for sustaining market share. In addition, protecting the information sources (e.g., patents, copyright, and trademarks) behind the development and production processes of manufacturers is a strategic imperative for survival. As such, it is highly recommended that manufacturers explore ways and means to protect their information sources from transmission pilfers that include plagiarizing, hacking, and phishing.

DATA SCIENCE IN EDUCATION

The Education sector continues to generate massive amounts of data as learning becomes more flexible and digital for the digital natives in the 21st Century classroom (Ferdinand, 2016). However, recent research reveals that this sector has not taken full advantage of using data science for offering programmes that readily respond to the changing education and training needs of the labour market (Jacks, 2014; Shacklock, 2016). The need exists to provide a sustainable framework for filling the education market shortfall in providing technical knowledge and skills sets for building technical capacity in the business sector. Institutions need to provide technologically savvy or "smart" campuses (Bures et al., 2016) and different education and training products for unique subject matter consolidation, customization, and delivery. Education and training institutions should include a coherent approach to knowledge and skills development maintained across all sectors in the economy (UK Government, Department for Business, Innovation & Skills, 2015). Education and training should be conducted in line with the following principles:

- **Proportionate:** Reduced bureaucracy; appropriate for the size and nature of the organization.
- **Timely:** Complete quickly with reduced disruption and uncertainty.
- **Challenging:** Continuous rigor, examining and evaluating multiple options in delivery.
- **Inclusive:** Open to Individual organisations and key users having the opportunity to commence, contribute, and conclude.
- **Transparent:** All reviews and reports should be published.
- **Value for Money:** Costs commensurate with quality of services.

Using Big Data for Student Recruitment and Retention

The success of training and education institutions partly relies on vibrantly recruiting and retaining students. To this end, Big Data can help to identify critical student patterns such as attendance and interactions through the use of sensors (Grunerbl et al., 2013; Zappi et al., 2012). Such Big Data can help educators and trainers to personalize learning for students in potentially improving their learning performance (Jacks, 2014; Shacklock, 2016). Additionally, Big Data can give insight into how institutions can design learning to help students reach their highest level of achievement in the shortest possible time, affording high turnaround time from student enrollment to graduation. Higher student retention will increase tuition revenue and the competitiveness of an institution for attracting new students. Similarly, training institutions can use available Big Data to design and offer programmes along with an establish mechanism for coordinating and utilizing industry resources for closing identified skills gaps. Such coordination would provide trainees with marketable and meaningful learning experiences that would enhance both recruitment and retention.

Learning Analytics for Improving Learning Performance

Learning Analytics is intended to provide an analysis of data on students' performance for determining meaningful improvements. Without harnessing and visualizing the massive education data collected by institutions and organisations in an understandable way (less statistical), the data will be of little use for most decision makers. In addition, this data representation must allow the individual learner as well as educators to make use of it (Khalil & Ebner, 2015). Currently, learning analytics research indicate an understanding of its scope and uses for improving student performance (U.S. Department of Education, 2012). As a result, developing data-driven analytics based on learning and performance activities can now be easily quantified and counted such as the distribution of scores for individual online assessments. The challenge is to develop analytics for solving particular problems. One mounting problem experienced in digital spaces used by students is cyberbullying and very prevalent in social media that they frequently use (Sarna & Bhatia, 2016). They reported that cyberbullying is known to have devastating effects (e.g., depression and attempted suicide) on student users. In an attempt to address cyberbullying, typically experienced by students in a regular school day, Sarna and Bhatia (2016) surveyed algorithms for cyberbullying detection, which revealed the extent of cyberbullying in social media messages. Consequently, the offenders were identified for the attention of the designated authorities. Successful gains that learners and educators can achieve and the positive change that would emerge from Big Data learning analytics can also be afforded. For example, data analytics on online assessment can help to address issues of delayed feedback some instructors experience due to busy work schedules and subjective nature of human marking (Ferdinand & Umachandran, 2016). Automated assessment can provide immediate feedback to students with a high level of accuracy and objectivity that can help students identify gaps in learning and correct these promptly. As a result, students would be in a better position to progress at a faster rate that can potentially improve their learning performance (NORWIG, 2015).

FUTURE DIRECTIONS FOR BIG DATA IN EDUCATION

The harnessing of Big Data in the educator sector can provide real-time information for augmenting the recruitment and retention of students such as student interaction and attendance patterns using sensor technology. These inputs to data warehousing for applications like Hadoop and HIVE allow for the segregating, analyzing, and summarizing of data. Learning Analytics is emerging as a robust technological field that can empower instructors and learners with information for making decisions on improving student learning performance. Knowledge and practice on these applications are recommended as part of the education and training curriculum that give students a competitive edge in entering the employment arena.

CONCLUSION

Embracing data science in the Agriculture, Manufacturing, and Education sectors affords many benefits. Reaching Big Data through data science is critical to the business or institution's decision making process as it provides actionable insights for improving internal operations such as strategic planning, resource allocation, and client reach. Agriculturalists can benefit greatly from the enhanced networking through technology in understanding and meeting their stakeholders' needs. Manufacturers can also use the real-time information from harnessing Big Data to response quickly and responsibly to changing market trends. Educational and training institutions can reap the benefits of using Big Data technology applications such as Hadoop and Hive for learning analytics on students' performance for determining meaningful improvement. However, enjoying the affordances of data science in these sectors requires a technology adoption investment in order to reach Big Data for achieving effective decision-making.

REFERENCES

Amedie, A. F. (2013). *Impacts of climate change on plant growth, ecosystem services, biodiversity, and potential adaptation measure* (Master's thesis). Retrieved from http://bioenv.gu.se/digitalAssets/1432/1432197_fantahun.pdf

American Statistical Association. (2016). *Data Science Tops List of Fields with Massive Potential.* Retrieved May 27, 2016, from http://www.amstat.org/

Baumgarten, M., Mulvenna, M. D., Rooney, N., & Reid, J. (2016). Keyboard-based sentiment mining using twitter. *International Journal of Ambient Computing and Intelligence*, 56–69.

Bures, V., Tucnik, P., Mikulecky, P., Mls, K., & Blecha, P. (2016). Application of ambient intelligence in educational institutions: Visions and architectures. *International Journal of Ambient of Ambient Computing and Intelligence*, 7(1), 94–120. doi:10.4018/IJACI.2016010105

Casey, J. (2012, April 5). Google Trends reveals clues about the mentality of richer nations. *Ars Technica*. Retrieved from *http://arstechnica.com/gadgets/2012/04/google-trends-reveals-clues-about-the-mentality-of-richer-nations/*

CORDIS. (2012, September 1). *Big data public private forum* [Online forum comment]. Retrieved from http://cordis.europa.eu/project/rcn/105709_en.html

Environmentalscience.org. (2016). *Agricultural science and GIS.* Retrieved from http://www.environmentalscience.org/agriculture-science-gis

Ferdinand, D. (2016). *Flexible Learning Environments: Theories.* Trends, and Issues. doi:10.13140/RG.2.1.3958.2488

Ferdinand, D., & Umachandran, K. (2016). Online assessment: Product development in academic writing. *Maha Journal of Education*, 2(1), 73–78.

Fouad, K. M., Hassan, B. M., & Hassan, M. F. (2016). User authentication based on dynamic keystroke recognition. In Information Resources Management Association (Ed.), Identity Theft: Breakthroughs in research and practice (pp. 403-437). Information Resources Management Association. doi:10.4018/IJACI.2016070101

Grunerbl, A., Bahle, G., Hanser, F., & Lukowicz, P. (2013). UWB indoor location for monitoring dementia patients: The challenges and perception of a real-life deployment. *International Journal of Ambient Computing and Intelligence, 5*(4), 45–59. doi:10.4018/ijaci.2013100104

Halewood, N. J., & Surya, P. (2012). Mobilizing the agricultural value chain. In World Bank (Ed.), *2012 information and communication development* (pp. 21-43). Retrieved from http://siteresources.worldbank.org/EXTINFORMATIONANDCOMMUNICATIONANDTECH NOLOGIES/Resources/IC4D-2012-Chapter-2.pdf

Hashimoto, Y., & Day, W. (Eds.). (1991). *Mathematical and Control Applications in Agriculture and Horticulture:Conference Proceedings*. Amsterdam, Netherlands: Elsevier Science & Technology.

Jacks, D. (2014). *The learning analytics workgroup: A report on building the field of learning analytics for personalized learning at scale*. Retrieved from https://ed.stanford.edu/sites/default/files/law_report_executivesummary_24-pager_09-02- 2014.pdf

Jain, A., & Bhatnagar, V. (2016a). Olympics Big Data prognostications. *International Journal of Rough Sets and Data Analysis, 3*(4), 32–45. doi:10.4018/IJRSDA.2016100103

Jain, A., & Bhatnagar, V. (2016b). Movie analytics for effective recommendation system using Pig and Hadoop. *International Journal of Rough Sets and Data Analysis, 3*(2), 82–100. doi:10.4018/IJRSDA.2016040106

Jimenez, A. (2013). *Seven big data lessons for farming*. Retrieved from http://www.e-agriculture.org/news/seven-big-data-lessons-farming

Kausar, N., Palaniappan, S., Belhaouari, S., Abdullah, A., & Dey, N. (2015). Systematic analysis of applied data mining based optimization algorithms in clinical attribute extraction and classification for diagnosis for cardiac patients. In A. Hassanien, C. Grosan, & M. F. Tolba (Eds.), *Applications of intelligent optimization in biology and medicine* (Vol. 96, pp. 217–231). doi:10.1007/978-3-319-21212-8_9

Khalil, M., & Ebner, M. (2015). *Learning analytics: Principles and constraints*. Academia. Retrieved from https://www.academia.edu/13200536/Learning_Analytics_Principles_and_Constraints

Magoulas, R., & Lorica, B. (2009). *Big data: Technologies and techniques for large-scale data*. Retrieved from http://assets.en.oreilly.com/1/event/54/mdw_online_bigdata_radar_pdf.pdf

Mohanpurkar, A. A., & Madhuri, S. J. (2016). A traitor identification technique for numeric relational databases with distortion minimization and collusion avoidance. *International Journal of Ambient Computing and Intelligence, 7*(2), 114–137. doi:10.4018/IJACI.2016070106

Morel, G., Valckenaers, P., Faure, J., Pereira, C., & Diedrich, C. (2007). *Manufacturing plant control challenges and issues*. Retrieved from https://hal.archives-ouvertes.fr/hal-00147431/document

National Science Foundation. (2012). *NSF leads federal efforts in big data*. Retrieved from http://www.nsf.gov/news/news_summ.jsp?cntn_id=123607

Nazim, M., & Mukherjee, B. (2011). Implementing knowledge management in Indian academic libraries. *Journal of Knowledge Management Practice, 12*(3). Retrieved from http://www.tlainc.com/articl269.htm

Norwig, C. (2015). *Learning Analytics can shape the future of adult learning*. Retrieved from https://ec.europa.eu/epale/en/blog/learning-analytics-can-shape-future-adult-learning

O'Shaughnessy, S., & Gray, G. (2013). Development and evaluation of a dataset generator tool for generating synthetic log files containing computer attack signatures. In I. G. L. Global (Ed.), *Pervasive and ubiquitous technology innovations for ambient intelligence environments* (pp. 116–127). IGI Global. doi:10.4018/978-1-4666-2041-4.ch011

Odella, F. (2017). Technology studies and the sociological debate on monitoring or social interactions. In I. G. L. Global (Ed.), *Biometrics: Concepts, methodologies, and applications* (pp. 529–558). IGI Global. doi:10.4018/978-1-5225-0983-7.ch022

OHSU Library. (2012). *Recommended file formats for long term data preservation*. Retrieved from http://www.ohsu.edu/xd/education/library/data/plan-and-organize/file-formats.cfm

Panda, S. P., Mishra, S., & Das, S. (2017). An efficient intra-server and inter-server load balancing algorithm for internet distributed systems. *International Journal of Rough Sets and Data Analysis, 4*(1), 1–18. doi:10.4018/IJRSDA.2017010101

Pezeshkirad, G., Hajihashemi, Z., & Chizari, M. (2014). Use of Computer and Internet in Agricultural Extension as perceived by Extension Workers. *International Journal of Agricultural Management and Development, 4*(4), 277–285. Retrieved from http://www.scopemed.org/?mno=177470

Ripon, S. H., Kamal, S., Hossain, S., & Dey, N. (2016). Theoretical analysis of different classifiers under reduction rough data set: A brief proposal. *International Journal of Rough Sets and Data Analysis, 3*(3), 1–20. doi:10.4018/IJRSDA.2016070101

Roy, D. (2013, May 22). The unvarnished truth about big data. *Computerworld*. Retrieved from http://www.computerworld.in/feature/unvarnished-truth-about-big-data-103412013

Sarna, G., & Bhatia, M. P. S. (2016). An approach to distinguish between the severity of bullying in messages in social media. *International Journal of Rough Sets and Data Analysis, 3*(4), 1–20. doi:10.4018/IJRSDA.2016100101

Shacklock, X. (2016). *From bricks to clicks: The potential of data and analytics in higher education*. Retrieved from http://www.policyconnect.org.uk/hec/sites/site_hec/files/report/419/fieldreportdownload/frombric kstoclicks-hecreportforweb.pdf

Sharma, U. C. A. (2013, October 22). *Karniti Part 7: Agricultural income and some misbeliefs under I.T*. Retrieved from http://www.caclubindia.com/articles/karniti-part-7-agricultural-income-some-misbeliefs-under-i-t-18678.asp

Shekar, M., & Otto, K. (2012). ICTs for health in Africa. In E. Yonazi, T. Kelly, N. Halewood, & C. Blackman (Eds.), *eTransform Africa: The transformational use of ICTs in Africa*. Retrieved from http://www.cmamforum.org/Pool/Resources/ICTs-health-Africa-2014.pdf

Stansbury, M. (2016, May 9). *e-Campus News: 3 blossoming fields of study with massive potential*. Retrieved from http://www.ecampusnews.com/technologies/fields-of-study/

Tapia, D. I., & Corchado, J. M. (2010). *An ambient intelligence based multi-agent system for Alzheimer health care*. Retrieved from https://pdfs.semanticscholar.org/169e/2cc3edcdabe237c4b7b7bedb766734 020c40.pdf

UK Government, Department for Business, Innovation & Skills. (2015). *Combined triennial review of the industry training boards (Construction, Engineering Construction and Film) Final Report, December 2015*. Retrieved from https://www.gov.uk/government/uploads/system/uploads/attachment_data/file/485876/BIS-15-686-combined-triennial-review-of-the-industry-training-boards-December-2015.pdf

Union of Concerned Scientists. (n.d.). *Renewable Energy and Agriculture: A Natural Fit*. Retrieved from http://www.ucsusa.org/clean_energy/smart-energy-solutions/increase-renewables/renewable-energy-and.html#.V7_kQDUXVf4

U.S. Department of Education. (2012). *Enhancing teaching and learning through educational data mining and learning analytics: An issue brief*. Retrieved October 13, 2016, from https://tech.ed.gov/wp-content/uploads/2014/03/edm-la-brief.pdf

Wehrspann, W. (2016, April 12). Industry Insider: Robb Fraley. *Farm Industry News*. Retrieved from http://farmindustrynews.com/crop-protection/industry-insider-robb-fraley

Yonazi, E., Kelly, T., Halewood, N., & Blackman, C. (Eds.). (2012). *eTransform Africa: The Transformational Use of Information and Communication Technologies in Africa*. Retrieved from http://www.gsdrc.org/document-library/etransform-africa-the-transformational-use-of-information-and-communication-technologies-in-africa/

Zappi, P., Benini, L., & Troster, G. (2012). Collecting datasets from ambient intelligence environments. In I. G. L. Global (Ed.), *Innovative applications of ambient intelligence: Advances in smart systems* (pp. 113–127). IGI Global. doi:10.4018/978-1-4666-0038-6.ch009

Zenodo. (2016, October 20). *Legal interoperability of research data: Principles and implementation guidelines*. Retrieved from https://zenodo.org/record/162241#.WHPHE_2FOic

KEY TERMS AND DEFINITIONS

Big Data: A collaborative phenomenon for guiding real-time insights into organisations and institutional operations through mathematical, statistical, computational, and data management skills.

Data Mining: An analytic process that allows for locating and interpreting information for more informed decisions.

Data Object Abbreviation Standards: A list of abbreviations used for data object naming by developers and information deliverers.

Data Science: A composite clustering of machine learning, Big Data processing, and statistical routing along with expertise convolutions in arriving at the best optimal range of solutions that can be customized by the user for effective results.

Data Warehousing: A central repository of all organisational data arranged so as to be accessed by Data Object Abbreviation Standards (DOAS).

High-Powered Analytics: The overall management of data with volume, velocity, and variety of information assets.

Yield: The measure of the desired marketable output per unit area.

Chapter 3
Evolution of Cloud in Big Data With Hadoop on Docker Platform

Meenu Gupta
Ansal University, India

Neha Singla
Punjabi University, India

ABSTRACT

Data can be anything but from a large data base extraction of useful information is known as data mining. Cloud computing is a term which represent a collection of huge amount of data. Cloud computing can be correlated with data mining and Big Data Hadoop. Big data is high volume, high velocity, and/or high variety information asset that require new form of processing to enable enhanced decision making, insight discovery and process optimization. Data growth, speed and complexity are being accompanied by deployment of smart sensors and devices that transmit data commonly called the Internet of Things, multimedia and by other sources of semi-structured and structured data. Big Data is defined as the core element of nearly every digital transformation today.

INTRODUCTION

Big data is a term that indicates a very large amount of data which floods and controls a business on a daily basis. Moreover, what really matters are the manipulations of data in industry specific environment. Big data can be analyzed for insights that lead to better decisions and strategic business moves. The data has to be surveyed regularly, analyzed before it undergoes any business action. The general advantages of big data are uncovered truths, predict product and consumer trends, reveal product reliability, brand loyalty, manage personalized value chains and discover real accountability. IT industry is arranging big data processing on regular basis with the good relation to Cloud Based IT solutions (Bollier, 2010). Cloud-based Big Data solutions are hosted on Infrastructure as a Service (IaaS), delivered as Platform as a Service (PaaS), or as Big Data applications (and data services) via Software as a Service (SaaS)

DOI: 10.4018/978-1-5225-2486-1.ch003

manifestations. Each must follow some of the Service Level Agreements (SLAs) for the business development. Cost effectiveness is a must to provide a better service to the industry. *For* example, applications and better customer experiences are often powered by smart devices and enable the ability to respond the moment customer act. Smart products being sold can capture an entire environmental context. New analytical techniques and models are being developed by business analysts and data scientists to uncover the value provided by this data (Bhosale & Gadekar, 2014).

Goals of Big Data

- The enterprises should invest in acquiring both tools and skills as Big Data analytics strictly depend on analytical skills and analytics tools.
- The Big Data strategy must involve an evaluation of the decision-making processes of the organization as well as an evaluation on the groups and types of decision makers.
- To discover new metrics, operational indicators and new analytic techniques, to look at new and existing data in a different way. This, generally, requires setting up a separate Big Data team with research purpose.
- The Big Data is required to support concrete business needs and provides new reliable information to decision makers.
- The most suitable technology can, only, meet all the Big Data requirements due to presence of different workloads, data types, and user types. For example, Hadoop could be the best choice for a large-scale Web log analysis but is not suitable for a real-time streaming at all. Multiple Big Data technologies must coexist and address use cases for which they are optimized.

In this, we are mainly focusing on Hadoop, working of Big Data on Docker platform and its relation with Cloud Computing.

MAIN FOCUS OF THE CHAPTER

While the term "big data" is quite new in the IT field, the act of storing large amounts of information for eventual analysis is old aged.

Big data represents a prototype shift in the technologies and techniques for storing, analysing and leveraging information assets. That can be characterized by 7 V's (Khan M. Ali-ud-din et al., 2014) (Figure 1):

- Volume
- Velocity
- Variability
- Variety
- Value
- Veracity
- Visualization

Figure 1. 7Vs of big data

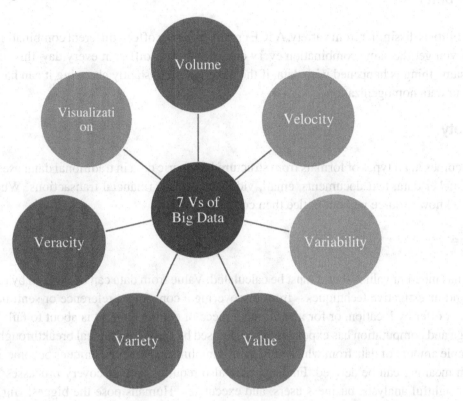

Volume

Volume reflects the amount of unique data which converts low-density data into high-density data that has value and processes high volumes of low-density data, such as clicks on a web page, network traffic, sensor-enabled equipment capturing data at the speed of light, twitter data feeds and many more. The amount of data varies from company to company ranging from terabytes to petabytes. Data collection by organizations takes place from a variety of sources, including social media and information from a sensor or machine-to-machine data, business transactions.

Velocity

Velocity is a fast rate for receiving data and mayhap acted as upon. The highest velocity data normally streams directly into memory against being written to disk. Some of the Internet applications (IoT) have health and safety branches that require real-time evaluation and action. As an example, consumer e-Commerce applications assay to combine mobile device location and personal predilections to make time sensitive offers that's why data streams is at unprecedented speed and must be dealt with in a timely manner. RFID tags, sensors and smart metering are driving the need to deal with torrents of data in near-real time.

Variability

Variability is dissimilar from variety. A ICE cream shop may offer 4 different combinations of ICE cream, but if you get the same combination every day and it tastes different every day, this reflect variability. The same thing is happened with data, if the meaning is constantly changing it can have a huge impact on your data homogenization.

Variety

Data comes in all types of formats from structured, numeric data in traditional databases in unstructured stock ticker data, text documents, email, video, audio and financial transactions. When data changes from a known source without notice then complexity arises.

Value

Data has inherent value—but it must be calculated. Value from data can be derived by range of quantitative and investigative techniques – from discovering a consumer preference or sentiment, to making a relevant offer by location, or for identifying a piece of equipment that is about to fail. The cost of data storage and computation has exponentially decreased by the technological breakthrough, thus providing an ample amount of data from which numerical sampling and other techniques become appropriate from which meaning can be derived. Finding value also requires new discovery processes involving clever and insightful analysts, business users, and executives. Humans pose the biggest Big Data challenge, which is learning to ask the right questions, recognizing patterns, making informed assumptions, and predicting behavior.

Veracity

Veracity speaks to the exactness and precision of data and chaos or dependability of the information. With many types of enormous information, quality and exactness are less controllable however with the assistance of huge information investigation innovation, it permits us to work with these kinds of information. The volumes compensate for the absence of value or precision.

Visualization

Visualization is critical in today's world. Using charts and graphs to visualize large amounts of complex data is much more effective in conveying meaning than spreadsheets and reports chock-full of numbers and formulas.

The term "Big Data" is used only when we are discussing about petabytes and Exabyte`s of data which cannot be integrated very easily. Big data is the term used to refer to the incrementing of data which is otherwise hard to store and procedure through the traditional database technologies. In other words, big data is defined as a set of technologies and techniques that involve new methods of integration to uncover big unseen values from big data sets that are assorted, complex, and of a huge scale.

BIG DATA TECHNOLOGIES

Big data includes the following technologies. Here, we mainly focus on Hadoop which is explained below.

- Collecting
- Storage
- Computation
- Stream Processing
- Data Mining

Collecting

It includes following factors (Jlassi & Martineau, 2016):

- **Scribe:** Scribe is a server for accumulating log data that's streamed in real time for clients. It is designed and developed by Facebook which is no longer in use.
- **Apache Kafka:** Kafka is partitioned, replicated, distributed commit log service which provides the functionality of a messaging scheme that allows producers send messages over the network to the Kafka group which in turn helps them to consumer (Kreps et al., 2011).

Storage

It includes following terms

- Hadoop
- NoSQL Data Stores
- HBASE

Hadoop

Hadoop is an Apache open source software framework for storage of data and running applications on groups of product whose hardware is written in Java that allows distributed dispensation of large data sets across groups of computers using simple programming models which distributes storage and computation across clusters of computers (see figure 2). It has been designed to move away from single server to thousands of machines, each offering local computation and storage. It also enables massive storage, enormous processing power and the ability to handle simultaneous tasks or jobs. The Following terms are used in Hadoop (Blazhievsky, 2013):

- **Open-Source Software:** It is a free of cost software that is developed and maintained by developers and is available with multiple versions.
- **Framework:** It is an area which enables complete software applications from developing to running phases.
- **Massive Storage:** Hadoop, primarily, breaks the large amount of data into small units which are stored on hardware.

- **Processing Power:** Hadoop simultaneously procedures for large amounts of data using several low-cost computers for fast results.

The following are the main objectives of using Hadoop in Big data.

- Hadoop stands out because of its capability to store and process large amount of data quickly. The main considerations are volumes and variety of data consistently increasing from Social Media and IoT (Internet of Things).
- Its distributed computing model quickly processes Big Data. It is done by adding nodes to the computer which helps in faster processing.
  - Pre-processing of data is not required here before storing it. It is so flexible that it can be used in any way and for all types of data.
- Data and application processing are protected against hardware failure is another unique advantage of Hadoop. The jobs are automatically redirected to other nodes when a node goes down in order to make sure that the distributed computing does not fail and it automatically stores multiple copies of all data.

1. Hadoop Distributed File System

The file system of Hadoop was designed and developed using a distributed file system service that runs on hardware. HDFS can tolerate high levels of faults by even using low cost hardware and it holds a very large amount of data, providing easier access. For storing of large data, the files are stored across

Figure 2. Framework for basic component of Hadoop

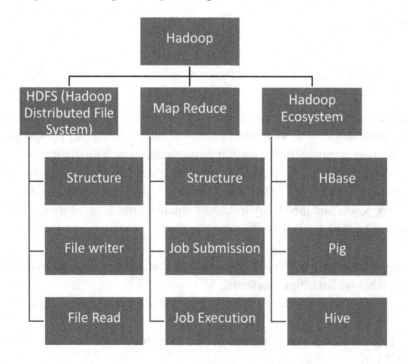

multiple machines by splitting them into various parts. These files are stored in such a way that they can be easily retrieved in future (Meo, 2014).

Although Hadoop Distributed File System, it can work directly with any mountable distributed file system such as Local FS, HFTP FS, S3 FS, and others. The Hadoop Distributed File System (HDFS) completely works on the Google File System (GFS), thereby, providing a distributed file system which is reliable as well as fault tolerant.

Following are the features of HDFS:

- It is primarily meant for large storage and data processing.
- It provides a command interface to interact with HDFS.
- To easily check the status of the cluster, the built-in servers of namenode and datanode help users.
- HDFS provides file permissions and authentication.

2. HDFS Structure

In HDFS, the architecture with master/slave concept is used where master consists of a single NameNode that manages the file system metadata and one or more slave DataNodes that store the actual data. The NameNode determines the mapping of blocks to the DataNodes that takes care of read and write operations with the file system. They also handle block creation, deletion and replication based on instructions given by NameNode. A file in an HDFS namespace is split into several blocks and those blocks are stored in a set of DataNodes (see Figure 3).

- **Namenode:** The namenode is the service hardware that contains the GNU/Linux operating system and the namenode software. It can be run on commodity hardware. The system has the namenode which acts as the master server and does the following tasks:

Figure 3. HDFC structure

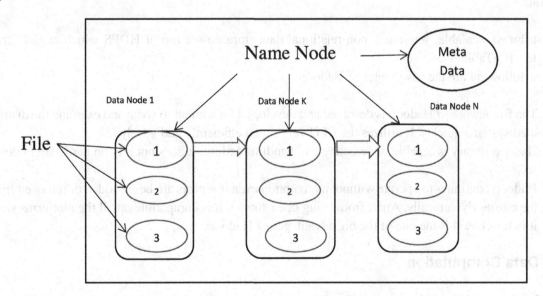

- It handles the file system namespace.
- It controls client's access to files.
- It also executes file system operations like opening, renaming and closing of files and directories.
- **Datanode:** The Datanode basically refers to commodity hardware with the GNU/Linux operating system and Datanode software. Every node, in a cluster, is accompanied by a separate Datanode which manage the data storage of their system. Datanodes perform various operations such as read-write on the file systems block creation, deletion, and replication according to the instructions of the Namenode, as per client request.
- **Block:** In general, the user data is stored in the files of HDFS. Blocks are the file segments which store data as elementary components of the file system. In other words, the minimum amount of data that HDFS can read or write is called a Block. The default block size is 64MB, but it can be varied as per the need to change in HDFS configuration.

NoSQL Data Stores

A NoSQL database gives a mechanism for storage and retrieving of data like Apache HBase is an open-source, distributed, versioned, non-relational next generation of data storage and retrieval applications who has their separate data base whereas other NoSQL databases like UnQLite does not have a separate server process. It has following types:

- Key Value Store
- Document Store
- Column Store
- Graph Database
- Content Delivery Network

Hbase

A distributed, scalable, versioned, non-relational data store on the top of HDFS which models after Google's BigTable.

The following are the advantages of Hadoop

- The framework of Hadoop is designed and developed for a client to write and examine the distributed systems quickly. It utilizes the CPU very much efficiently and wisely.
- Hadoop library is capable of detecting and handling failure; it does not rely on hardware in doing so.
- Hadoop continues to operate without interruption even if servers are being added or removed from the cluster dynamically. Apart from being open source, it is compatible on all the platforms since it is Java based is the one of the big advantages of Hadoop.

Big Data Computation

The data can be computed by using following methodologies.

- MapReduce
- Apache Spark

Map Reduce

MapReduce is a type of framework where an application can be written for processing a large amount of data in reliable manner. A MapReduce algorithm specified in two ways are Map and Reduce where Map converts a set of data into another set where individual elements are broken down into tuples (key/value pairs). Secondly, the output from a map acts as input to the Reduce task which combines these data into a smaller set of tuples. It can also be defined as:

Hadoop = HDFS + MapReduce

The MapReduce becomes advantages in the fact that it scales data processing over multiple computing nodes. Sometimes it is not an easy task to fragment a data processing application into mappers and reducers. But scaling the application to run over hundreds, thousands, or even tens of thousands of machines in a cluster are just a configuration change, once we write an application in the MapReduce form. This scalability feature has eventually involved many programmers to custom the MapReduce model.

MAP Reduce Algorithm

MapReduce program is executed in three stages, namely map stage, shuffle stage, and reduce stage (Blazhievsky, 2013; Dean. & Ghemawat, 2008)(Figure 4).

Figure 4. Map reduce structure

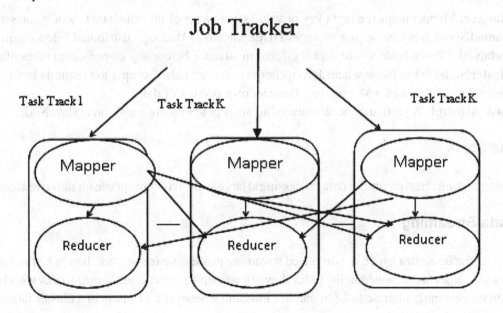

- **Map Stage:** The map stage carries out the primary function of breaking large amount of data which is input to the map into several small bundles of data. This process is completed by moving the total data line by line from HDFS to the mapper.
- **Reduce Stage:** This stage is the combination of the Shuffle stage and the Reduce stage. It basically processes the data from the mapper and after processing, it produces a new set of output, which will be stored in the HDFS.
- During a MapReduce job, Hadoop sends the Map and Reduce errands to the suitable servers in the cluster.
- The agenda has the task to manage all the details of data passing, such as authenticating task completion, distributing tasks, and replicating data around the cluster between the nodes.
- Most of the calculation takes place on nodes with data on local disks that decreases the network traffic.
- The cluster collects and reduces the data to form an appropriate result after the completion of given tasks, and sends it back to the Hadoop server.
- Job tracker controls almost everything about computing.
- Key concepts of Map-Reduce.
  - The computation goes with data.

Terminology Used in Map Reduce:

- **SlaveNode:** It is a Node where Map and Reduce program executes.
- **JobTracker:** It is used for scheduling of jobs and also tracks the allocated jobs to Task tracker.
- **Task Tracker:** It tracks the task and reports status to JobTracker.
- **Job:** It is a program in execution of a Mapper and Reducer across a dataset.
- **PayLoad:** Applications form the core of the job by implementing the Map and the Reduce functions.
- **Mapper:** Mapper maps the input key or value sets to a set of intermediate key or value set.
- **NamedNode:** It is a Node that manages HDFS known as Hadoop Distributed File System.
- **DataNode:** It is a Node where data is offered in advance before any dispensation takes place.
- **MasterNode:** It is a Node where JobTracker executes and also accepts job requests from clients.
- **Task:** An execution of a Mapper or a Reducer on a portion of data.
- **Task Attempt:** A particular occurrence of an attempt to execute a task on a SlaveNode.

Apache Spark

It is quicker and universal engine for data processing at large scale. It is appropriate for iterative algorithms.

Big Data Streaming

It includes Apache Samza which is a dispersed streaming processing framework. It uses Kafka for assurance that messages are managed in the order they are written to a partition. Samza works with Hadoop YARN to transparently migrate tasks to another machine whenever a machine in a cluster fails.

Big Data Mining

It includes Apache Mahout that delivers open source implementations of dispersed and scalable machine learning algorithms mainly focused in the areas (Miller, 2013):

- Collaborative Cleaning
- Classification
- Clustering
- Dimension Reduction

There are certain considerations before using Big Data Technologies:

- Processing a large quantity of data not only organised, but also semi organised and unstructured from a inclusive variety of resources.
- The analysis of data that is collected must be done against a reference sample or in another case. Sampling of data is not as operative as the analysis made upon a large amount of data.
- when business measures of the data are not a priority, it must do Iterative and explorative analysis.
- Cracking about the business challenges which are not properly addressed by a relational database approach.

HADOOP USING DOCKER CONTAINERS

Docker provides easy to use interface to Linux containers and also easy-to-construct image files for those containers. In other way, we can say that Docker is based on light weight virtual machines. Users can specify the Docker images as they want for their containers. User's code run in a software environment which is provided by these containers. It simulates from the software environment of the Node Manager (Yeh, 2016).

Docker containers can include special libraries that is necessary for an application, and they can have different versions of Python, Perl and also Java. Indeed, these containers can run a different flavour of Linux than what is running on the Node Manager.

Docker containers allow each software to have independent environments during installation. This enables all the groups to use the same cluster for their jobs. This prohibits the need for a separate cluster for each of use case which further becomes a resource-management unpleasant experience.

Docker architecture is based on (The Digital Enterprise A Framework for Transformation, vol. 5, pp. 1-124) open source container platform that allows developers to manage and run distributed applications (Figure 5). Docker consists of Docker engine which can also be known as a daemon, Docker Hub that consists of online registry for sharing Docker Containers. Applications run on multiple platforms such as windows computers and Linux servers that are built with Docker.

Docker image consists of a base operating system such as Ubuntu along with a custom software stack which is further used to create containers. By installing libraries, users can build custom containers on top of a base operating system. The resulting container can be shared on Docker Hub.

Figure 5. Docker architecture

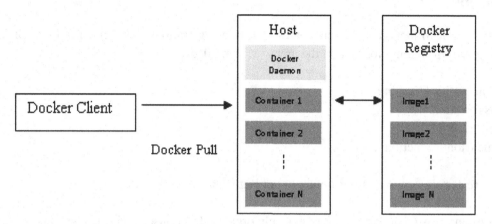

Why Do We Use Docker?

According to a workload perspective, platform-as-a-service (PaaS) offering the Data Cloud provides which can also be called by company "Hadoop dial tone." It enables the users to load data into Hadoop Distributed File System (HDFS) through a variety of large and event-oriented mechanisms and APIs, and deploy Pig, Hive, MapReduce and other applications in order to operate directly on that data, irrespective of deploying or configure Hadoop.

As the company allows the users to observe job performance on the basis of some infrastructure metrics, such as CPU consumption and memory, otherwise, it abstracts away the concept of clusters, nodes, and other level concerns of infrastructure metrics. This provides the company with the ability to partition and allocate resources at its wariness. For cloud providers, Virtualization (Berreis, 2016) is best possible way to solve this partitioning/allocation problem.

Here we are introducing two terms (Figure 6 and Figure 7):

- Heavy Duty Virtualization
- Light Duty Virtualization

Heavy Duty Virtualization

The heavy-duty virtualization has long been available for a number of virtualization platforms: VMware, Virtual Box, and as a disk image usable by KVM and others. Because of partition issues in heavy duty virtualization, working of Hadoop is not possible on this platform.

Light Duty Virtualization

Docker technology is based on the concept of light duty virtualization which is used as to host multiple machines on single platform. Docker is different from other platforms we may have used: it works with Linux containers. While "virtual machine" software typically isolates access to hardware so that a guest operating system can run. A "container" is nothing but really just a partition of the host operating system.

Figure 6. Heavy duty virtualization

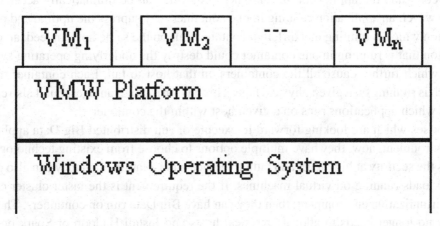

Figure 7. Light duty virtualization

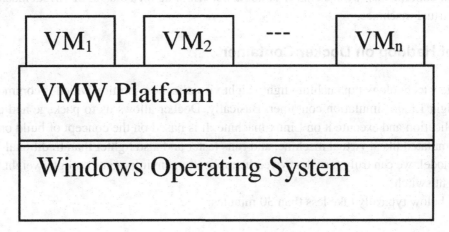

Each container runs on the same Linux Kernel as the rest of the system and has its own view of the file system and its own set of resources.

The virtualization technologies used by containers and virtual machines are not same as they are different with each has its own strengths and weaknesses. The heavy weight virtualization or hypervisor used by virtual machines (VMs) provides strong fault tolerance, its isolation and security. An application running on VM will not negatively impact the performance or stability of an application that is running on other different VM but on the same host. The application can go so far as it can crash the operating system running in the VM, but there is no impact on other VMs running on same host and also each VM can run a different operating system. When selecting an application to perform a specific task, this gives maximum flexibility to the users. However, this flexibility and security comes at the expense of using a lot of extra CPU and memory resources – and ultimately this overhead can lead to higher costs.

The container technology that is based on operating system virtualization uses significantly less extra CPU and memory than hypervisor which is based on heavy weight virtualization. There is no overhead which is further having each container that is run on a completely installed operating system (OS). This lightweight approach or light weight virtualization can improve I/O performance that further lead to reduce the costs and the application development lifecycle can be dramatically accelerated by the containers. However, an application running in one container may supress the uptime and performance of an application which is running in a different container but on the same host. Indeed, an error occurs in an application that is running in one container could destroy the underlying operating system on the physical host which further cause all the containers on that host to fail. Each container must use the same OS which is running on a given physical host. This has various advantages, but it also creates some limitations on which applications runs on a given host within the container.

The enterprises which are looking forward to execute or run distributed Big Data applications in a virtualized environment, now, they have multiple options to choose from existing technologies. If main requirement is the security at high level and fault tolerance and isolation, then they can also choose their Big Data workloads running on virtual machines. If the requirement is the faster cluster creation in a light weight virtualization environment, then they can have Big Data run on containers. The Enterprise in IT industry no longer needs to allocate physical hosts and install Hadoop or Spark on bare metal servers while standing up new Big Data applications in their data centers. Hadoop and Spark can now run on Docker containers or even a cluster of containers running on a cluster of virtual machine, within a cluster of virtual machines.

Working of Hadoop on Docker Container

Docker is a new technology but enabling lightweight virtualization solution which is commonly known as a lightweight Linux simulation container. Basically, Docker allows us to package and configure a run time application and execute it on Linux machine. It is based on the concept of build once and run anywhere, simulated like a virtual machine, and runs faster and also lighter than traditional VMs. With the Docker model, we can truly turn heavyweight application environments on light weight just like on and off of light switch!

The steps below typically take less than 30 minutes:

- Download and Import the Docker Images,
- Run the Docker Containers,
- SSH and Start the Pivotal Hadoop on Docker Cluster,
- Test HDFS and MapReduce for Hadoop on Docker,
- SQL on Hadoop, and
- Test.

The following are the key concept of Docker images (Subramanya, 2016):

- Containers share host kernel,
- Image and Image Registry,
- Build Images,
- Images are layered and hence extensible.

The following is the Procedure of creating Docker environment:
Each cluster node is virtual node powered by Docker. Each node of the cluster is a Docker Container. Docker Containers run on a Docker Hosts. Each Hadoop cluster will have multiple nodes. In the context

of this work, the Docker container guarantees the same function as the virtual machine and it has the same architecture. It is based on a management engine; it has the same role of the hypervisor in the traditional virtualization. However, the resources policy used for the containers management is more flexible than the one issued from the policy used in the full virtualization approach. we can do the following things (Shyni et al., 2016).

- Fix the number of the CPU cores to allocate to each container, or
- Define a relative share of the CPU resources between all containers on the physical host. In the second policy.
- The containers benefit from free CPU resources disposed on the physical host and releases them when they will be used by another process.

Concerning the memory resources, a container requires consumed memory not provisioned memory, thus the containers offer better management of idle resources than VM. The Docker technology introduces policies to manage four resources: memory, CPU, network IO and disk space management. Containers are able to share the same application libraries and the kernel of the host. The intermediate level that transforms instructions from guest to host OS is limited, therefore the container technology presents a lower overhead, it is considered as light virtualization. In big companies like Facebook and Yahoo, a cluster of Hadoop contains a large number of machines. The optimization of the resource exploitation offers the opportunity to reduce costs and increase benefits. The company's profit from the virtualization in the cloud to improve resource exploitation. As the energy management presents an important field, much research over the Cloud aim minimize the electric consumption of the data centre. In this, we analyse the effect of the use of virtualization tools over the energetic consumption. It is important to mention that the energetic gain over a cluster of four machines will be weak. The idea is to detect the variation of the consumption as small as it is. In a large cluster scale, the variation in energy consumption is not negligible and has an important impact on the overall cost.

Benefits of Running Hadoop on Docker (Jlassi & Martineau, 2016)

- Light weight container virtualization platform.
- Run without the extra load of a hypervisor.
- Separate our applications from infrastructure.
- **Portable:** Run on developer host
- Since Docker is based on Linux Virtual Environment, so, it has fast container set up, uses less resources, easy commands and easy networks and volume set up.
- Quick installation.
- Same process/images for development/QA/production.
- Same process for single/multi-node.

Big data app developers are increasingly leaning toward containerization of their apps using Docker. In addition, there is quite a bit of interest to run Docker on top of bare metal, rather than VMs, to provide a cost-performance ratio for Hadoop-like applications.

COMBINING TECHNOLOGIES: CLOUD COMPUTING USING HADOOP

Big Data and cloud computing are linked together (Changqing et. al., 2012). It enables companies of dynamic sizes to get more value from their data than by blaming fast analytics with a small amount of previous costs. This will further manage companies to earn and store even more data by creating more need for processing power and driving a clean circle. The services of cloud computing can be private, public or hybrid.

Cloud computing allows companies to utilize resources as a utility. It ensures more attractive benefits for both businesses as well as end users. Out of which, three of the main benefits of cloud computing includes:

- **Self-Service Provisioning:** It allows clients to easily use the resources for any type of work at any time whenever they want.
- **Elasticity:** Companies can go up as computing needs increase and then go down again as demands decrease.
- **Pay Per Use:** At a granular level, Computing resources are measured by allowing users to pay only for the resources and workloads as per the usage.

In today's complex environments, data enters from various sources. In the company, we have known orderly, analytical and operational sources with further addition of sources that we may have never thought to use before, such as log files beyond the technology stack. Outside the company, we own data beyond our enterprise SaaS and PaaS applications. In addition, we are entering, and licensing data from both free and subscription public sources, all of which differ in structure, quality and volume.

Without a doubt, cloud computing plays an important role for many use cases such as a data source, analytical services, providing real-time streams as well as a device transaction hub. But logically, the best strategy is to develop the analytics to the data then in the end there are various decisions to make. The physical severance of data centres, discrete security policies, ownership of data, and data quality processes, in addition to the impact of each of the five V's requires architecture decisions. So, this entreats an important distributed processing architecture. Assuming multiple physical locations of large amount of data, what is the design pattern for a secure, low-latency, possibly real-time, operational and analytic solution?

Big data analytics are often linked with cloud computing because the analysis of large data sets in real time requires a platform like Hadoop to store large quantity of datasets across a distributed cluster and MapReduce to coordinate, join and process data from various sources.

Because of big data requires too much time and costs too much money for loading into a traditional relational database for the analysis part, new approaches for storage and analysing data have emerged that depends less on data schema and data quality. Instead, raw data with extension of metadata is massed up with in a data lake and machine learning and artificial intelligence (AI) programs which further use complex algorithms to look for repeatable patterns.

Cloud computing and big data are related to each other. Big data deliver users the ability to use object computing to process distributed queries over multiple datasets and return resultant sets with in a timely constraint. Cloud computing supply the underlying engine with usage of Hadoop which is a class of distributed data-processing platforms. The use of cloud computing in big data is shown in Figure 8. A large set of data source from the cloud and Web are stored in a distributed with fault tolerance database

Figure 8. Cloud computing usage in big data

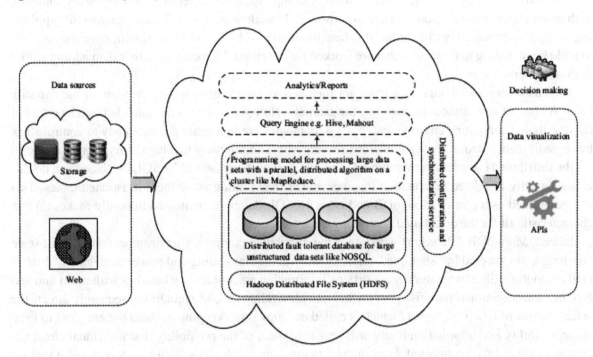

which further processed through a programming model for large datasets by using a parallel distributed algorithm in a cluster. The main aim of data visualization, as shown in Figure 8, is to analyse analytical results that are presented visually through different graphs for decision making.

Big data deploy distributed storage technology that is based on cloud computing instead of local storage attached to a computer or electronic device. The evaluation of Big Data is driven by cloud based applications, a fast-growing technology, developed using virtualization platform (Table 1). Therefore, cloud computing not only distribute facilities for the computation and evaluation of big data, but it also serves as a service model.

To address the data storage required, cloud computing infrastructure can serve as an effective platform to perform analysis of big data and its correlation with a new pattern for the provision of computing infrastructure and processing method of big data for all types of resources that are available in the cloud through data analysis. There is various cloud based technologies that have to survive with this new environment as we are dealing with big data for which concurrent processing has become increasingly complex.

Table 1. Relationship between cloud computing and big data

	Google	**Microsoft**
MapReduce	AppEngine	Azure using Hadoop
Big data analytics	BigQuery	Azure using Hadoop
Relational database	Cloud SQL	SQL Azure
NoSQL database	AppEngine Datastore	Table Storage

Generally speaking, we can state that distributed computing gives better force and versatility, mutually with lesser expenses and expedient time to showcase. Nonetheless, it additionally requires that applications ought to be sorted out to exploit this new foundation. The applications should have the capacity to scale by including more servers that are worked for the cloud, for example, rather than adding ability to existing servers.

The customary social databases were not intended to exploit even scaling in view of the capacity layer. A class of new database structures, for example, NoSQL databases are intended to take effect of the distributed computing environment. NoSQL databases are in a general sense ready to control stack by spreading information among numerous servers which additionally making them a characteristic fit for the distributed computing environment. The min part of the reason of NoSQL databases can do this is the capacity of related information together, rather than putting away them in isolated tables. This can be utilized as a part of MongoDB and other NoSQL databases which additionally makes them a characteristic fit for the distributed computing environment.

Indeed, MongoDB database is worked for the distributed computing environment. Its crucial scale out design, empowered by "sharding," relates well with the flat scaling and power managed by distributed computing. Sharding naturally apportions information equally among bunches with multi hub and equalizations questions crosswise over them. Notwithstanding this, MongoDB consequently directs the arrangements of repetitive servers which is called as 'copy sets,' keeping in mind the end goal to keep up accessibility and information trustworthiness regardless of the possibility that individual cloud occurrences are taken disconnected. For example, to guarantee high accessibility, clients can turn various individuals from a copy set as individual cloud occurrences over various accessibility zones and additionally on server farms. MongoDB has likewise connected with various driving distributed computing suppliers, for example, Amazon Web Services, Microsoft and SoftLayer.

NoSQL, MPP databases, and Hadoop are new innovations that have created to address chal-lenges of Big Data that further empower new sorts of items and administrations to be dispersed by the business. Out of which organizations are utilizing the capacities of both frameworks, a standout amongst the most widely recognized routes, by coordinating a NoSQL database, for example, MongoDB with Hadoop.

The association is effectively made by winning APIs that licenses examiners and in addition information researchers to perform muddled, review questions for examination of Big Data and dreams while keeping up the proficiency and straightforwardness to utilization of a NoSQL database. NoSQL, MPP databases and Hadoop are blending to each different as NoSQL frameworks ought to be utilized to seizure Big Data and give operational astuteness to clients. This further empowers MPP databases and Hadoop to be utilized to give systematic vision to examiners and information researchers. Together with this we can state that NoSQL, MPP databases and Hadoop permit organizations to abuse on Big Data.

Considerations for Decision Makers in Big Data

There are numerous Big Data innovations that are created enough to be utilized for mission that is basic and generation utilize cases, it is as yet encouraging in a few respects. As needs, be to this, the path forward is not generally clear. As associations advance Big Data methodologies, there are various measurements that are to be considered while selecting innovation accomplices which incorporates the accompanying:

- Online in opposition to Offline Big Data.
- Software Certifying Models.

- Community.
- Developer Demand.
- Agility.
- General Purpose vs. Niche Solutions.

Online in Opposition to Offline Big Data

Huge Data can take both online and in addition disconnected structures. Online Big Data states to information that is made, devoured, changed, achieved furthermore broke down continuously keeping in mind the end goal to bolster dynamic applications and clients. Enormous Data is begin on the web. The stopping of administrations for these applications must be low. The accessibility must be high with a specific end goal to meet SLAs. This involves a huge cluster of utilizations that are accessible on long range interpersonal communication news nourishes with a specific end goal to examine continuously servers to complex CRM applications. For Examples: MongoDB database and other NoSQL databases.

Disconnected Big Data fuses applications that pant, change, achieve furthermore examine Big Data as far as a bunch setting. They normally don't make new information. The reaction time can be moderate (up to hours or days) for these applications, which is regularly middle of the road for this kind of utilization case. Since they every now and again deliver a static (versus operational) yield, for example, a report or dashboard, additionally they can even go disconnected temporarily without affecting the entire objective or finished result. The cases of disconnected Big Data applications may incorporate Hadoop-based workloads, present day information stockrooms, separate, change, stack applications which is known as ETL, and business knowledge devices.

The associations which are assessing Big Data advancements to embrace, utilization of their information. The operational utilize cases for those hoping to fabricate applications that bolster continuous, they will need an operational information store like MongoDB database. Maybe to illuminate basic leadership forms for those that need a place to comportment long running examination disconnected, the disconnected arrangements like Hadoop can be a successful device. Associations taking after both utilize cases can do as such pair, and they will once in a while discover increments between online and in addition disconnected Big Data advancements. For example, MongoDB offers mix with Hadoop.

Software Certifying Model

There are three general sorts of ensuring for Big Data programming advances:

- **Patented:** The product item is held and controlled by a product organization. Assist, source code is not accessible to proprietors. Clients normally guarantee the item through an everlasting permit that empowers them to inconclusive use, with yearly conservation charges for support and programming updates. A portion of the illustrations incorporate databases from Oracle, IBM and Teradata.
- **Open-Source:** The product item and in addition source code both are openly accessible to utilize. Organizations give the product item by offering commitments and nearby items with esteem included constituents, for example, administration devices and bolster administrations. The illustrations may incorporate MongoDB by MongoDB, Inc. furthermore, Hadoop by Cloudera and others.

- **Cloud Service:** The administration is facilitated in a cloud-based environment outside of clients' server farms and conveyed over general society Internet. The plan of action is metered (i.e., pay-per-utilize) or membership based. Cases incorporate Google App Engine and Amazon Elastic MapReduce.

For some Fortune 1000 organizations, rules and inner systems around information protection constrain their capacity to influence cloud-based arrangements which brings about most Big Data activities that are driven with advancements orchestrated on start. The greater part of the Big Data engineers are web organizations that built up capable programming and equipment, which they publicly released to the bigger group. Therefore, the vast majority of the product utilized for Big Data activities is open-source.

Community

There is a chance to learn from others in these early days of Big Data. Organizations should contemplate how many other enterprises are being followed by using the same technologies and also with similar objectives. The organizations should consider the following in order to understand a given technology's adoption:

- The number of users.
- The ubiquity of organized events that are local as well as community.
- The health and activity of online opportunities such as Google Groups and StackOverflow.
- The accessibility of conferences, regularity of occurrence and well attentive or not.

Developer Demand

The chance to take a shot at extreme issues by offering to the designers, furthermore by utilizing an innovation that has solid engineer consideration, a lively group, and a promising long haul future, associations can pull in the hopeful personalities. They can likewise surge the pool of competitors that are anything but difficult to learn and use by picking innovations which are regularly the ones that request most to engineers. Moreover, we can state that, advancements that have solid designer plea tend to make for more profitable groups who feel they are allowed by their instruments as opposed to loaded by ineffectively planned, legacy innovation. The groups having profitable designer will lessen time to advertise for new activities and diminish advancement costs.

Agility

So as to be coordinated, Organizations ought to utilize Big Data items that empower them. This will profit by advances that escape the way and allow groups to accentuation on what they can do with their information as opposed to masterminding both new applications and in addition foundation. This will make it simple to investigate a difference of ways and premises for separating esteem from the information and to emphasize quickly because of changing business needs.

In this unique circumstance, spryness incorporates three essential segments:

- **Affluence of Use:** An innovation that is simple for designers to secure and fathom either in view of its engineering, the accessibility or plausibility of devices and data, or both will empower groups to get Big Data ventures progressing and to comprehend esteem rapidly. Innovations with startling expectations to absorb information and lesser assets to bolster instruction will make for a more drawn out street to venture execution.

- **Technological Powerfulness:** The item ought to roll out it modestly simple to improvement requirements, for example, displaying of information, its utilization, where information is dragged from and its preparing as groups advance new discoveries and acquaint to inner and outer requirements. Dynamic information models which is otherwise called blueprints and adaptability are abilities to search out.

- **Licensing Autonomy:** Open source items are commonly simpler to support due to groups can begin expediently with free group plans of the product. They are additionally much of the time simpler to scale from a confirming viewpoint, as necessities increment groups can purchase more licenses. By differentiation we can state that by and large licensed programming merchants require a major sum, forthright patent acquirements that would make it firmer for groups to move rapidly and to scale later on.

MongoDB's riches of utilization, dynamic information model and open source protecting model make it the most light-footed online Big Data arrangement accessible.

REFERENCES

Berreis, T. (2016, March 15). *Virtualisierung und Containerisierung*. Retrieved from https://wr.informatik.uni-hamburg.de/_media/teaching/wintersemester_2015_2016 /nthr-1516-berreis-virtualization_and_containerization-ausarbeitung.pdf

Bhosale, H. S., & Gadekar, D. P. (2014). A Review Paper on Big Data and Hadoop. *International Journal of Scientific and Research Publications*, *4*(10), 1–7.

Blazhievsky, S. (2013). *Introduction to Hadoop and MapReduce and HDFC for Big Data Application*. SNIA Education.

Bollier, D. (2010). *The Promise and Peril of Big Data: Aspen Institute*. Washington, DC: Communications and Society Program.

Changqing, J. (2012). Big data processing in cloud computing environments. *IEEE International Symposium on Pervasive Systems, Algorithms and Networks (ISPAN)*, 17–23. doi:10.1109/I-SPAN.2012.9

Dean, J., & Ghemawat, S. (2008). MapReduce: Simplified data processing on large clusters. *Communications of the ACM*, *51*(1), 107–113. doi:10.1145/1327452.1327492

Hashem, I. A. T., Yaqoob, I., Anuar, N. B., Mokhtar, S., Gani, A., & Ullah Khan, S. (2015). The rise of big data on cloud computing: Review and open research issues. *Journal of Information Systems*, *47*, 98–115. doi:10.1016/j.is.2014.07.006

Jlassi, A., & Martineau, P. (2016). Benchmarking Hadoop Performance in the Cloud - An in Depth Study of Resource Management and Energy Consumption. *Proceedings of the 6th International Conference on Cloud Computing and Services Science*, 1-12. doi:10.5220/0005861701920201

Khan, M. (2014). Seven V's of Big Data understanding Big Data to extract value. *American Society for Engineering Education (ASEE Zone 1), 2014 Zone 1 Conference of the IEEE*. DOI: 10.1109/ASEEZone1.2014.6820689

Kreps, J., Narkhede, N. & Rao, J. (2011). *Kafka: A Distributed Messaging System for Log Processing*. Available at http://research.microsoft.com/en-us/um/people/srikanth/netdb11/netdb11papers/netdb11-final12.pdf

Marr, B. (2014, March 2). *Big Data: The 5 Vs Everyone Must Know*. Retrieved from http://www.epm-channel.com/2015/02/02/big-data-the-5-vs-everyone-must-know/

Meo, P. D. O. (2014, December 15). *Hadoop Lab*. SuperComputing Applications and Innovation Department. Retrieved from https://hpcforge.cineca.it/files/CoursesDev /public/2014/Tools_Techniques_Data_Analysis/presentations/Docker_NGS_lab_v1.1.pdf

Miller, H.E. (2013). Big-data in cloud computing: a taxonomy of risks. *Information Research, 18*(1), paper 571. Available at http://InformationR.net/ir/18-1/paper571.html

Shyni, S., Joshitta, R. S. M., & Arockiam, L. (2016). Applications of Big Data Analytics for Diagnosing Diabetic Mellitus: Issues and Challenges. *International Journal of Recent Trends in Engineering & Research, 02*(06), 454–461.

Subramanya, S. (2016). Evaluating and Deploying Sql-On-Hadoop Tool. *Bay Area Big Data Meetup*.

Talia, D. (2013). Clouds for scalable big data analytics. *Journal IEEE Computer Society, 46*(5), 98–101. doi:10.1109/MC.2013.162

The Digital Enterprise A Framework for Transformation. (n.d.). Available at http://www.tcs.com/SiteCollectionDocuments/Perspectives/The-Digital-Enterprise-Vol-5-1013-1.pdf

Yeh, Y. H. (2016). Dockerized Hadoop Platform and Recent Updates in Apache Bigtop: Apache Big Data. Vancouver: Academic Press.

Section 3
Non-Relational Databases

Chapter 4

MonogDB:
Data Management in NoSQL

Sonali Tidke
SPPU, India

ABSTRACT

MongoDB is a NoSQL type of database management system which does not adhere to the commonly used relational database management model. MongoDB is used for horizontal scaling across a large number of servers which may have tens, hundreds or even thousands of servers. This horizontal scaling is performed using sharding. Sharding is a database partitioning technique which partitions large database into smaller parts which are easy to manage and faster to access. There are hundreds of NoSQL databases available in the market. But each NoSQL product is different in terms of features, implementations and behavior. NoSQL and RDBMS solve different set of problems and have different requirements. MongoDB has a powerful query language which extends SQL to JSON enabling developers to take benefit of power of SQL and flexibility of JSON. Along with support for select/from/where type of queries, MongoDB supports aggregation, sorting, joins as well as nested array and collections. To improve query performance, indexes and many more features are also available.

INTRODUCTION

Today is era of computing system which are generating enormous data every day through various web and business applications. This data need to be stored in easy to access and retrieve format. A huge amount of such data is processed by RDBMS (Relational database management system). Relational model was proposed by E.F. Codd in 1970. This model is well suited for storing data in structured format for client-server programming. But with increase in generation and complexity of data, relational model is being inefficient to fulfill today's need.

NoSQL provides support for such large applications. NoSQL is schema less database management model which does not restrict user to store data in fixed type. MongoDB is one such DBMS developed using NoSQL concepts. MongoDB is a document based database management system.

Few reasons why NoSQL is better for data management than SQL are:

DOI: 10.4018/978-1-5225-2486-1.ch004

1. SQL cannot scale up to the current requirements of big data storage. RDBMS stores data using relations. Data is correlated with some common characteristics between stored data which results in the schema of RDBMS. This schema does not allow SQL to store unpredictable and unstructured information. Big data applications require to store data without fixed structure which NoSQL supports. NoSQL avoids major join queries making access to data faster and easy to store.

2. RDBMS requires data to be normalized into logical tables to avoid data redundancy and duplication. Though it helps in managing data efficiently, increase in data complexity hampers performance of SQL. In contrast, NoSQL stores data in the form of collections which makes data access faster. NoSQL processes complex data in real time.

3. SQL works on ACID (Atomicity, Consistency, Isolation, Durability) properties while NoSQL supports CAP (Consistency- Availability – Partition tolerance) theorem and works on BASE (Basically Available, Soft State, Eventually Consistent) properties.

Considering all this points, objective of this chapter is to focus on why and how MongoDB is useful for various business requirements. This chapter also gives various details about managing data using MongoDB.

BACKGROUND

NoSQL

NoSQL (Moniruzzaman & Hossain, 2013) is a non- relational database management system which does not restrict data storage in predefined schema. Websites like Google or Facebook collects terabytes of data from various sources for their users (Ricardo & Susan, 2016). It is not feasible to store such data in fixed schema and typically requires horizontal scaling. In such situation, NoSQL databases has become alternative for relational databases by providing flexible, horizontally scalable, schema-less data model.

Use of NoSQL

Now a days, many third parties are capturing user data easily for their use and analysis. Data like user personal information, social graph, location details, log file are few examples where data has been increasing tremendously. SQL databases are designed for fixed schema data with limited size. NoSql databases are evolved and becoming popular where such type of data is required to handle properly.

NoSQL is in used from more than a decade, it is facing various challenges. Following are few challenges which can be considered before choosing NoSQL for enterprise applications:

1. **Maturity:** RDBMS is in use from a long time and it is very stable and having rich in functions provided for handling data. In contrast to this, most of the NoSQL variations are still in development phase where many key features not yet implemented.

2. **Support:** RDBMS vendors provide assurance and support of data recovery for any kind of failure. Since most of the NoSQL systems are open source projects, guaranteed support cannot be assured for these systems.

3. **Administration:** Though NoSQL aims at providing a solution without administration, today NoSQL requires lot of skill to install and maintain later at all stages.
4. **Expertise:** As of today, in every industry, lots of SQL developers are available while most of NoSQL developers are still in learning mode.

Comparison of SQL and NoSQL

Comparing features of SQL with NoSQL (Chodorow, 2013), following are the basic points of difference.

CAP Theorem (Tauro, Patil & Prashanth, 2013) (Brewer's Theorem)

NoSQL follows CAP theorem, also called as Brewer Theorem. Three basic requirements stated by CAP theorem should be considered while designing a database for distributed architecture.

1. **Consistency:** Data in the database should remain consistent after any kind of transaction on database.
2. **Availability:** System is always available without any downtime.
3. **Partition Tolerance:** System must function reliably after partitioning of server though they may not communicate with each other.

Though it is not possible to fulfill all 3 requirements, CAP suggests to fulfill at least 2 requirement from above. Hence available NoSQL database follow different combinations of the C, A, P from the CAP theorem.

1. CA i.e. Consistency and Availability where all nodes are always in contact and are available. But the system fails, if partition occurs.
2. CP i.e Consistency Availability where after partitioning, consistent data will be available, may be not accessible all the time.
3. AP i.e. Availability with Partitioning where system is still available under partitioning, but some of the data may be incorrect.

Table 1. Comparison: SQL vs. NoSQL

SQL	NoSQL
SQL is structured query language where data is stored in predefined format	NoSQL means Not Only SQL where data is not required to be stored in predefined schema.
It uses structured query language to manipulate database	There is not declarative query language for manipulating data
Separate tables are used to store data and relationships.	It has Key-value pair, column oriented, document oriented and graph based databases for data storeage.
DML, DDL, DCL are used for data manipulation.	It supports eventual consistency rather than ACID properties.
It is used for storing data which is predictable and it's structure is already known	It stores unstructured, unpredictable data
Uses ACID properties	Based on CAP Theorem.

Figure 1. CAP theorem diagram for distribution
(Sources: Brown, 1970)

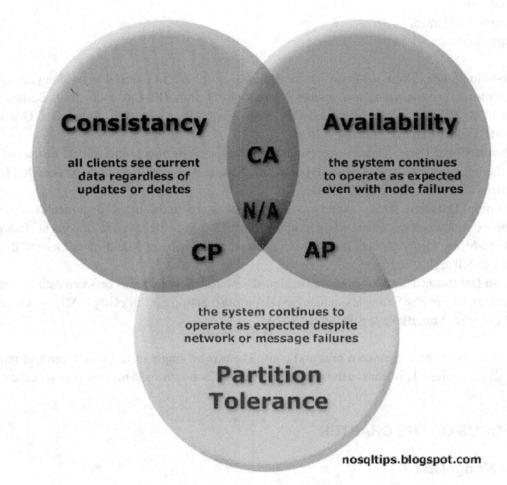

BASE Theorem

Eric Brewer has formulated BASE theorem and is also known for CAP theorem.
    A BASE system is focused on consistency.

1. Basically Available (BA) states that system guarantees availability (A from CAP theorem).
2. Soft (S) state indicates that the state of the system may change over time though input is not send. This can happen because of the eventual consistency model.
3. Eventual (E) consistency means the system will become consistent over time. During that period, system doesn't receive any input that.

NoSQL Database Models

NoSQL has four different models (Kumar, Charu, & Bansal, 2015) each with its own attributes:

- Key-value store.
- Column store.
- Document Oriented.
- Graph databases.

1. **Key-Value Store:** These databases are designed to store data in indexed key-value pair format. Examples of this type of database includes Azure Table, DyanmoDB, Cassandra, Riak, BerkeleyDB, CouchDB, FoundationDB, MemcacheDB, Redis,Fair Com c-treeACE, Aerospike, OrientDB, MUMPS (Luk, Blake & Silberglitt, 2016)
2. **Column Store:** These databases stores data tables as sections of columns of data instead of storing them in rows. Examples include HyperTable, HBase, BigTable, Accumulo, Cassandra, Druid, Vertica (Luk, Blake & Silberglitt, 2016).
3. **Document Database:** This is expansion of key-value stores. In this model documents stores more complex data. Each document has a unique ObjectID used to retrieve the document. Examples include MongoDB, Apache CouchDB, Clusterepoint,Couchbase, MarkLogic, OrientDB (Luk, Blake & Silberglitt, 2016).
4. **Graph Database:** These databases are designed for data where relations between data can be represented using graphs. Examples include Neo4J,Virtuoso,Stardog,InfiniteGraph,Allegro, OeirenDB and Polyglot (Luk, Blake & Silberglitt, 2016).

All above models have their own pros and cons. There is no single model which can suit requirements of all enterprises. This leads to the motto of NoSQL "Choose the best tool for your specific case".

MAIN FOCUS OF THE CHAPTER

What Is MongoDB?

MongoDB is flexible and scalable document – oriented database stores (Tauro, Patil & Prashanth, 2013). The reason to consider MongoDB for a business is its feature like creating geospatial indexes, easy

Figure 2. Key value store in NoSQL database
(Sources: Vorhies, 2014)

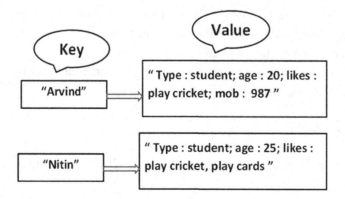

Figure 3. Column store in NoSQL database
(Source: Ranjan, 2015)

Row ID	Columns...		
1	**Name**	**Website**	
	Preston	www.example.com	
2	**Name**	**Website**	
	Julia	www.example.com	
3	**Name**	**Email**	**Website**
	Alice	example@example.com	www.example.com

Figure 4. Document oriented NoSQL database representation
(Sources: Subramanian, 2016)

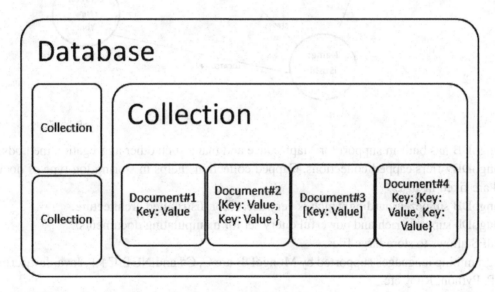

scaling out and default support for aggregation in MapReduce format (Tauro, Patil & Prashanth, 2013). MongoDB is schema-free database system where structure and keys of a document are not predefined. Besides this, MongoDB also supports arrays and embedded documents.

Key Features

Here are some features of MongoDB that all not available in similar options of database stores.

1. **Indexing:** Supports of creating generic secondary indexes makes MongoDB useful for faster execution of variety of queries. MongoDB also provides support for creation of various indexes like geospatial, unique and compound.
2. It is a document oriented database store, simple to create and easy to program.
3. MongoDB supports JavaScript (Tauro, Patil & Prashanth, 2013). This helps in creating and using JavaScript documents Instead of using stored procedures.

Figure 5. Graph store in NoSQL
(Sources: Eifrem & Rathle, 2013; as cited in Vorhies, 2014)

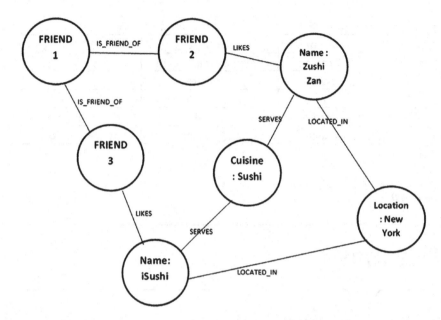

4. MongoDB has built-in support for MapReduce and many such other aggregation methods.
5. MongoDB offers capped collections. Capped collections helps in storing log type of documents and are fixed in size.
6. MongoDB supports sharding which is very useful for distributed architecture.
7. MongoDb supports rich and powerful query set for manipulating documents.
8. GridFS allows to store large files.
9. Programming languages supported by MongoDB are C, C# and.NET, C++, Java, Javascript, Perl, PHP, Python, Ruby etc.
10. It supports Server-side JavaScript execution.

Following are some tools which are available for monitoring MongoDB and few are GUI based tools.

Monitoring (Luk, Blake & Silberglitt, 2016)

1. Munin provides MongoDB plugin for Network and System monitoring.
2. Gangila is a Distributed high-performance system monitoring tool which provides MongoDB plugin.
3. Similarly Cacti, Open source web based graphic provides plugin for MongoDB.

GUI (Truica, Radulescu & Boicea, 2015)

1. **Fang:** A web-based UI developed using Django and jQuery.
2. **Futon4Mongo:** A web UI which is clone of CouchDB Futon.
3. **Mongo3(Truica, Radulescu & Boicea, 2015):** Ruby based interface.

4. **MongoHub(Truica, Radulescu & Boicea, 2015):** A native OS X application.
5. **Opricot:** PHP based MongoDB browser.
6. **phpMoAdmin:** PHP based MongoDB management tool.
7. **MongoVUE(Truica, Radulescu & Boicea, 2015):** Windows based GUI for MongoDB.
8. **RockMongo(Truica, Radulescu & Boicea, 2015):** PHP based GUI for administration of MongoDB.

Basics of MongoDB (Tauro, Patil & Prashanth, 2013)

- A document is the basic unit of data in MongoDB. It's similar to a row in RDBMS.
- A collection is similar to RDBMS table.
- A single instance of MongoDB can host multiple independent databases.
- Each MongoDB instance can have set of its collections and have a set of permissions to access and control them.
- MongoDB has a simple but powerful JavaScript shell.
- Every document has a key, "_id". It has a unique value which can be used to access documents in a collection.

Installing MongoDB on Linux/Windows Operating System

Installation of MongoDB is a simple process. For most of the platforms precompiled binaries are available and archive can be downloaded from http://www.MongoDB.org, extract and execute binary. The MongoDB server needs a data directory to write files and a port to listen for client connections.

Installing MongoDB on Windows

1. Download zip file for MongoDB site www.mongodb.org. There are 32 bit and 64 bit releases for Windows. Choose appropriate version and download zip file. Extract archive using available extractor.
2. Create a directory where MongoDB can store database files. By default, it tries to use C:\data\db as default data directory.
3. User can select any other path in the file system for directory creation.
4. If directory is created on any other path, it is required to specify the path when MongoDB is started.
5. After creating data directory, open command prompt and go to path where MongoDB is installed (where MongoDB binary is extracted).

```
C:> bin\mongod.exe
```

6. If installation path is other than default path, argument –dbpath is required to specify path of directory of installation

```
C:> bin\mongod.exe –dbpath d:\mydb\db
```

To see more options, use command mongo.exe – help

MongoDB as a Service (Tauro, Patil & Prashanth, 2013)

MongoDB also works as a service on Windows. To install, use –install option with full path and execute as given below

```
C:> c:\mongodb\bin\mongodb.exe - dbpath d:\mydb\db -install
```

To start or stop service, control panel access is required.

Installing MongoDB on Linux OS

As mentioned in previous section, choose correct version of MongoDB installation.

1. Download zip file from MongoDB site www.mongodb.org.
2. Create a directory to store database files. By default, the data directory will be /data/db path (Note: use chown command to give write permission if not available by default).

```
$ mkdir -p /data/db
```

Here, -p attribute is used to create *db* and its parent directory *data* if not created already

3. Uncompress the.tar.gz file using tar –xzf <name-of-tar- file> command. Eg.

```
$ tar -xzf mongodb-linux-i386-1.6.2.tar.gz
```

4. Change to uncompressed directory

```
$ cd <name-of-uncompressed-directory>
```

Eg.

```
$ cd mongodb-linux-i386-1.6.2
```

5. To start database, use command

```
$ bin/mongod
```

6. If extracted tar directory is in different path, give –dbpath while starting server

```
$ bin/mongod  -dbpath /home/mongoserver/db
```

This will start your MongoDB server. In above installation, it is assumed that user will run client and server on same machine with default port. If mongod server and mongo client/shell are running on different machines using other than default port above commands need to be modified.

- To start MongoDB server with port other than default port, user –port attribute as below.

```
$ bin/mongod -dbpath /home/mongoserver/db -port 20000
```

- To start client mongo shell, use command

```
$ bin/mongo igi-global.example.com:20000
```

This connects to server running on igi-global.example.com on port number 20000.
Here, shell is logged in and connected to default database "test".

- To connect to database other than default database, specify database name separated by / after port number.

```
$ bin/mongo igi-global.example.com:20000/userdb
```

connects mongo shell to database userdb on port 20000.

- ○ To start mongo shell without logged in to any database, user –nodb option. It is useful if user want to run some JavaScript and connect to database at later point.

```
$ bin/mongo -nodb
```

MongoDB Shell

MongoDB has JavaScript shell which allows user to interact with a MongoDB instance from the command line. Shell is used for performing administrative tasks, monitoring current tasks or just trying various commands. To start mongo shell,

```
$./mongo
```

The shell is JavaScript interpreter and hence can run JavaScript program.

```
> x = 10
    10
> y = 20
20
> x + y
    30
```

User can also use standard JavaScript libraries

```
> Math.sin (Math.PI/2);
    1
```

```
> "Welcome to JavaScript ".replace ("JavaScript", "mongo shell");
        Welcome to mongoshell
```

It is possible to define and call JavaScript functions on shell

```
> function add (a, b)
    {
        return a+b;
    }
> add (3, 4)
    7
```

While writing multiline commands, shell detects if command is complete. And will allow user to continue writing on the next line.

Mongo shell allows connecting to as many databases as required which is useful in multi server environments. connect () method is used for connecting to different databases and assign the resulting connection to variable of choice. For example, with sharding, use may require to connect to each shard,

```
$ shard1=connect ("local host: 20000");
$ shard2=connect ("localhost: 30000");
$ shard3=connect ("localhost: 40000");
```

Now, user can use shard1, shard2, shard3 variables like db variable is used in previous commands or later in other sections.

MongoDB Client

Mongo shell works as MongoDB client which is much more powerful tool than executing only arbitrary JavaScript. By default MongoDB get connected to "test" database available on server and assigns this database connection to the global variable db. This variable is used for executing commands on server through the shell. After connecting to server thru shell, client can choose database to work with using "use" command.

```
> use mydb
    Switched to db mydb
> db
    mydb
```

Creating a Database

Database is used to store a group of collections. A single instance of MongoDB can host several databases, each of which works independently. Every database has its own set of permissions. MongoDB stores each database in separate files on disk. Like other identifiers, database is having its naming convention as (Tauro, Patil & Prashanth, 2013)

- Empty string " " is an invalid database name.
- Characters like space, $,., /, \, or null characters (\0) are not allowed.
- Name of Database must have all lowercase characters.
- Name of Database is limited to maximum 64 bytes.

Following few databases are reserved and can be accessed directly

- **Admin:** This database is root of all database in terms of permissions. If a user is added in "admin" database, it gets permissions of all databases. "admin" also stores some commands which can be executed on server.
- **Local:** This database stores collections that are accessible by a single server locally.
- **Config:** It is used to internally store information about each shard in sharded setup.

Syntax to Create Database

```
> use databasename
```

If database does not exist, "use" command creates a new database or returns an existing one.
    Example: To create a database mydb

```
> use mydb
        Switched to db mydb
```

To check current database, use command db.

```
> db
mydb
```

To check list of available databases, use command

```
> show dbs
local         0.78432 GB
test          0.25132 GB
```

Here, currently created is not listed. A database will be listed only when it has at least one document. User can insert a document and then use above command to enlist new database.

```
> db.company.insert({ " Name": " Ishaan", "Department": "Manufacturing", "Date
": new Date()});
> show dbs
local         0.78432 GB
mydb          0.25132 GB
test          0.25132 GB
```

Dropping a Database

If a database is not required anymore, dropDatabase () (Truică, Boicea & Trifan, 2013) command is used to drop database.

This deletes current database and all its contents.

Syntax is: db.dropDatabase();

Example:

```
> show dbs
local        0.78432 GB
mydb         0.25132 GB
test         0.25132 GB
>use mydb
> db.dropDatabase();
{ "dropped":  "mydb", "ok": 1 }
> show dbs
local        0.78432 GB
test         0.25132 GB
```

Creating Collection

A collection holds a number of documents. A document is similar to a row in a relational database while collection is similar to a table in relational database. Collection don't have schema. It means that documents in a single collection can have any number of different forms. For example, a single collection can have documents of type:

{ "Name": "Sonali", "Department": "IT"}

{ "Name": "Ishaan", "Department": "R&D", "Project": "Robotics" }

Naming Conventions of Collection

While naming a collection user should consider following:

- Empty string " " is an invalid collection name.
- Null character (\0) is not allowed in collection name.
- As "system" keyword is reserved, collection name can not be prefixed with keyword "system".
- User created collection can not contain reserved character "$" in its name.

Sub Collections

Collections can be organized by sub collections separated by the dot (.) character. For example, user can create a "Movie" collection with sub collections "Bollywood" and "Hollywood". These sub collections can be accesses as

```
>db.Movie.Bollywood.insert({ "Title": "DDLJ", "Year": "1995"})
>db.Movie.Hollywood.insert({ "Title": "MIB", "Year": "2001"})
```

createCollection()

This command is used to create a new collection. Note that it is not required to create collection before using it. Storing a document in a collection will automatically create a collection if it does not exist.

```
Syntax: db.createCollection(name,options)
```

Here name is the name of collection to be created, options is an optional document about specifying default parameters. Following are few options available to use. All below options are optional (Table 2).

Example:

```
> use mydb
switched to db mydb
> db.createCollection("mycoll");
{ " ok": 1 }
> db.createCollection("capcoll",{ capped: true, size: 70000, max: 1000 });
{ " ok": 1 }
To list available collections:
> show collections
capcoll
mycoll
```

Dropping a Collection

Db.collection.drop() is used in MongoDB to drop a collection from database.

Example:

```
> use mydb
switched to db mydb
> show collections
capcoll
```

Table 2. Common options available with createCollection()

Option	Description
capped	If true, creates capped collection. Since capped collections are fixed size, it overwrites its oldest entries when reaches maximum size. With capped as true, it is necessary to use size parameter.
size	Specifies size in bytes for a capped collection.
max	Specifies maximum number of documents allowed for a capped collection.
autoIndexID	Creates index on _id field.

```
mycoll
> db.mycoll.drop()
true
> show collections
capcoll
drop() returns true on successful completion and false if fails.
```

Basic Shell Operations

Basic four operations of shell are create, read, update and delete (CRUD) (Arora & Aggarawal, 2013). This operation allows manipulating and viewing data in the shell.

Create

MongoDB provides function insert to create and add a new document in the collection.

Example, to store details of employee in collection company, user can use following command

```
> emp={ " Name": " Sonali", "Department": "IT", "Date ": new Date()};
        {
" Name": " Sonali",
 "Department": "IT",
 "Date ": " Sat Jul 16 2016 11:20:21 GMT - 0500 (EST)"
        }
```

Since the object is a valid document, it can be added using "insert" method in a company collection as

```
> db.company.insert(emp);
```

To insert one more document,

```
> db.company.insert({ " Name": " Ishaan", "Department": "Manufacturing", "Date
": new Date()});
```

The details of document added can be viewed using find command as

```
> db.company.find().pretty();
{
        "_id": ObjectID("4b23c3ca9538f49b20a2d"),
" Name": " Sonali",
 "Department": "IT",
 "Date ": " Sat Jul 16 2016 11:20:21 GMT - 0500 (EST)"
        }
{
        "_id": ObjectID("4a45f3rr9538f49b20a2d"),
```

```
" Name": " Ishaan ",
 "Department": "Manufacturing",
 "Date ": " Sat Jul 16 2016 12:30:43 GMT - 0500 (EST)"
        }
```

As shown, _id key is added automatically and other key/value pairs are stored as it is. pretty () after find() is used to display formatted output which can be omitted.

Read

find()(Arora & Aggarawal, 2013) demonstrated above shows all documents available in the collection. To display only one document in the collection, user can use findOne() instead of find().
> db.company.findOne();

```
{
        "_id": ObjectID("4b23c3ca9538f49b20a2d"),
" Name": " Sonali",
 "Department": "IT",
 "Date ": " Sat Jul 16 2016 11:20:21 GMT - 0500 (EST)"
        }
```

Update

After storing a document, user may require to modify the document. Update operation is used to modify the document. Update takes two parameters: first is condition to search document in collection and second is modified document. Following example demonstrates this:

To add key "location" in document emp,

```
> emp.location = "Pune"
```

To perform update, search document emp using available key like name and replace with modified new document as

```
> db.company.update("Name":"Sonali"},emp);
> db.company.findOne();
{
        "_id": ObjectID("4b23c3ca9538f49b20a2d"),
" Name": " Sonali",
 "Department": "IT",
 "Date ": " Sat Jul 16 2016 11:20:21 GMT - 0500 (EST)",
"location": "Pune"
        }
```

Another example of document update is complete replacement. For example, User want to change following document

```
{
        "_id": ObjectID("4b23c3ca9538f49b20a2d"),
"Name": " Sonali",
 "Department": "IT",
 "Date ": " Sat Jul 16 2016 11:20:21 GMT - 0500 (EST)",
"Location": "Pune"
        }
```

as new document given below

```
{
 "EName": " Sonali",
"Details":
{
 "Department": "IT",
 "Location": "Pune",
 "Designation": " TeamLeader"
                },
                "MgrID": "123"
        }
```

In new document, Name key is modified EName, MgrID key is added newly and Department, Location keys with new key Designation is updated under embedded document Details. To replace existing document with above new document, following method can be followed.

```
> var temp= db.company.findOne({ "Name": "Sonali " });
> temp.Details = {  "Department": temp.Department,  "Location": temp.Loca-
tion, "Designation": "TeamLeader" };
> temp.EName= temp.Name;
> temp.MgrID = " 123";
> delete temp.Date;
> delete temp.Name;
> db.company.update({ "Name": "Sonali", temp });
To check updated document,
> db.company.findOne({ "Name": "Sonali " });
```

Note: If collection has more than one document matching same condition given in findOne(), duplicate key on update error may generate.

Delete

To delete any not in use document, remove command is used. remove () (Truică, Boicea & Trifan, 2013) without any argument permanently deletes document from collection.

```
> db.company.remove ();
```

This command removes all documents from the collection but not collection and indexes on it. To delete document/s matching particular criteria, remove () is used with some condition.

```
> db.compnay.remove({ "Name": "Ishaan" });
```

removes matching document/s having value "Ishaan" for key "Name".

Deleting all documents from collection using remove() method without specifying condition to is time consuming. If collection is not required anymore, good to remove collection also instead of only documents. This can be achieved using drop_collection command.

```
> db.drop_collection ("company");
```

It takes very less time to drop collection with all documents and available indexes on document.

Note: To know details of any built-in function, type function name without parenthesis. This will show JavaScript code of the function.

```
> db.foo.update
```

This shows details of update function.

Querying

find() is used to query MongoDB documents. find() can be used with arguments or without arguments. First argument in find specifies the criteria for the output documents.

eg: db.company.find() returns all documents in a collection. To return restricted documents from collection, it is required to specify key-value pair as search criteria. This is same as where clause in RDBMS queries.

Example:

```
> db.company.find ({ "Name": "Sonali" })
```

This query will return all documents where value for key Name is Sonali.

Note that string value in search criteria must be enclosed in double quotes (" ")

Sometimes it is required to specify multiple conditions for searching required document. This can be done by separating search conditions using comma (,) and will be treated as conditional AND during execution.

Example:

To find documents where department is "IT" and location as "Pune" in company collection,

```
> db.company.find({ "Department": "IT", "Location": "Pune" })
```

Above query performs horizontal filtering of document ie output documents will contain all key-value pairs available. Vertical filtering is provided by specifying keys to return from documents. Sometimes it is required to return only few keys from documents. In such case, second argument to find() is list of keys to be returned. For example, if it is required to return only name and location in output documents, query will be

```
> db.company.find({ }, { "Name": 1, " Location": 1 })
```

Here first argument { } will return all documents and second argument allows to output only Name and Location keys for all documents. In above query, "1" is used to include key in output while "0" omits key in output. Note that output documents will have _id key by default.

To return documents with all keys other than _id, query will be

```
> db.company.find({ }, { _id: 0 })
```

In all above queries, comparison criteria is for equality. Now let's see some examples where find() uses other criteria than equality.

Like comparison operators in other languages, MongoDB provides "$lt", "$gt", "$lte", "$gte", "$ne" as comparison operators for <, >, <=, >=, != respectively(Tauro, Patil & Prashanth, 2013).

Consider a collection "users" with "age" as as one of the keys. To find documents with age greater than 20, query will be

```
> db.users.find({  " age ": { "$lt": 20 } })
```

To find users with age between 20 to 30 inclusive of both, query will be

```
> db.users.find({ "age": { "$lt": 20, "$gt": 30 } })
```

These types of queries are very useful for data comparison queries. For example, to find all users having data of joining between Jan and Dec 2014, query can be,

```
> start = new Date("01/01/2014")
> end = new Date("31/12/2014")
> db.users.find({ "joining": { "$lt": start, "$gt": end } })
```

To find documents matching exact dates may not be very useful as dates are stored with time in milliseconds. To query a document having key value not equal to specified value, $ne (not equal) operator is used.

For example, to find all users who do not have Country as India, query can be

```
> db.users.find({ " Country": { "$ne": "India" } })
```

Conditional AND is performed by separating multiple search criteria with comma (,). Similarly OR-ing can be performed either using $or or $in.

$or

When user needs to match documents using conditional OR, $or is used. For example, if user want all documents where age is above 18 or Country is India, query can be

```
> db.users.find({ "$or": [ { age: 12}, { Country: "India"} ] })
```

Note that $or accepts search conditions in array format.

$in

$in is used when user has to match more than one possible values to match for a single key. For example, to find all documents where age of user is either 18 or 25 or 36, query will be

```
> db.users.find({ "age": { $in: [18,25,36] } })
```

$in allows to specify criteria of different types as well. For example if user_id key is combination of few numeric and few text values, query will be

```
> db.users.find({ "user_id": { "$in": [1234, "Sonali" ] } })
```

This query will return all documents where user_id is either 1234 or "Sonali"
$nin works opposite as that of $in. $nin will return documents not matching with given values.

```
> db.users.find({ age: { $nin: [18,25,23] } })
```

This will return all documents where age is not from 18,25,23.
Note than in "$" prefixed keys, conditionals are used as inner document key while modifiers are used as an outer document key.
It is possible to nest multiple search criteria together. For example, to find all documents where Country is India or age is 18,25 or 36.

```
> db.users.find({ $or: [ { age: { $in: [18,25,36 ] } }, { Country: "India" } ]
});
```

Table 3. Summary of CRUD operations (Arora & Aggarawal, 2013)

Operation	MySQL	MongoDB
Schema creation	CREATE SCHEMA `BlogDB`	mongo BlogDB
Table creation	CREATE TABLE IF NOT EXISTS `BlogDB`.`users` (`id` INT NOT NULL, `first_name` VARCHAR(64) NULL, `last_name` VARCHAR(45) NULL, PRIMARY KEY (`id`));	Creation at first insert:db.articles.insert ({ user_id: "1", first_name: "Ciprian", last_name: "Truica" }) Explicit: db.createCollection("articles")
Create an index	CREATE INDEX IDX1 ON USERS(first_name)	db.articles.ensureIndex({dirst_name: 1})
Drop a table	DROP TABLE USERS	db.articles.drop()
Insert	INSERT INTO USERS(id, first_name, last_name) VALUES (1, "Ciprian", "Truica")	db.articles.insert({ _id: "1", age: 45, status: "A" })
Select	SELECT * FROM USERS	db.articles.find()
Select fields	SELECT frist_name, last_name STATUS FROM USERS	db.articles.find({ }, { first_name: 1, last_name: 1 })
Select with where	SELECT u.first_nameFROM `BlogDB`.`users` AS uWHERE u.id = 1;	db.articles.find({user_id:"1"}, { "first_name": 1});
Update	UPDATE `BlogDB`.`articles` SET title="MongoDB" WHERE id = 1;	db.articles.update({_id: "1"}, $set: { "article.title": "MongoDB" }}, {upsert: true});
Delete	DELETE FROM USERS	db.articles.remove()
Delete using where	DELETE FROM USERS WHERE id="1"	db.articles.remove({ _id: "1" })
Delete a table from dictionary	DROP TABLE `BlogDB`.`articles`	db.articles.drop()

Querying Using Regular Expressions

While performing search operation on strings, exact match for the string is required. Regular expressions are useful when string matching with flexibility in search string is required. For example, to find documents where username is Sonali or sonali, query will be

```
> db.users.find({ "username": /Sonali/i})
```

Here / and i flag combination is used to perform case insensitive matching. As MongoDB user PCRE (Perl Compatible Regular Expression) library to match regular expressions; any format allowed in PCRE is accepted in MongoDB.

Querying Arrays

To query an array is similar to that of other queries of find type. Consider a collection vehicles where user has documents with key car as an array type.

```
> db.vehicles.insert({ car: [ "Maruti","Renault","Benz","Hyundai" ] })
```

To query this document,

```
> db.vehicles.find({ car: "Renault" })
```

Insert few more documents in vehicles collection as

```
> db.vehicles.insert({ car: [ "Maruti", "Benz", "Renault" ] })
> db.vehicles.insert({ car: [ "BMW", "Benz", "Hyundai" ] })
> db.vehicles.insert({ car: [ "Maruti", "Renault", "Benz", "Hyundai", "BMW" ]
})
```

To match more than one element in an arry, $all is used. To find all documents where array contains both "Maruti" and "Benz" as value, query is

Query will be,

```
> db.vehicles.find({ car: { $all:  [ " Maruti", " Benz" ] } })
```

$size

To query documents of array type based on size, $size operator is used. For example, to find documents where car array is having 3 elements, query will be

```
> db.vehicles.find({ car: { $size: 3 } })
```

Note that $size cannot be combined with other conditionals.

Querying Embedded Documents

Like normal documents, find query also works on embedded documents. For embedded documents, query can be for whole document or for an individual key-value pair.

Consider following document with embedded document

```
{
"Name":
        {
        " First": "Sonali",
        "Last": " K"
        },
"Address":
        {
        "City": "Pune",
        "State": "Maharashtra",
        "Country": "India"
        },
"Contact": [ 1234567890, 0987654321]
}
```

To find document with name as "Sonali K", query will be

```
> db.people.find({ "Name": { First: "Sonali", Last: "K" } })
```

Restriction in the above query is that if "Name" is updated with any new key or if order of search criteria between Last and First is reversed, above query will not work. This problem can be solved using query

```
> db.people.find({ "Name.First": "Sonali", "Name.Last": "K" })
```

Use of Modifiers in Update Command:

Modifiers in update allow operations such as alter, add, remove key, manipulate arrays and embedded documents.

Increment and Decrement Modifiers

$inc modifier is used for changing value for an existing key or to create a new key if it doesn't exist. It is commonly used to update a key with changeable, numeric value.

For example, if user want to maintain hit counter for a URL, "url" collection with a document is

```
> db.url.insert({ " address": www.example.com", "type": "informative website"
});
```

After creating a document, when a visitor visits the page, it is required to increment hit counter by 1. This can be performed using,

```
> db.url.update({ "address": "www.example.com" }, { "$inc": { "counter": 1 }
});
> db.url.findOne() ;
{
        "_id": ObjectID("4b23c3ca9543f49a21a2d"),
        "address": www.example.com,
        "type": "informative website",
        "counter": 1
}
```

As counter key was not available in existing document, it is newly added and initialized at 1. To increment counter by 5, modify above query as

```
> db.url.update({ "address": "www.example.com" }, { "$inc": { "counter": 5 }
});
> db.url.findOne() ;
{
        "_id": ObjectID("4b23c3ca9543f49a21a2d"),
```

```
        "address": www.example.com,
        "type": "informative website",
        "counter": 6
}
```

Note that $inc is used for incrementing or decrementing (with negative value) integer, long or double type values only.

$set Modifier

$set modifier is used to set value of a key. If key does not exist, new key will be created. For an existing document of following type in collection "company"

```
{
        "Name": "Sonali",
        "Designation": "TeamLeader"
}
```

new key Department is added using $set as

```
> db.company.update({ "Name": "Sonali" }, { "$set": { "Department": "IT" } });
```

$set modifier is used for changing the type of an existing key. To change Department key in to an array type key,

```
> db.company.update({ "Name": "Sonali" }, { "$set": { "Department": ["IT",
"Production", "R&D" ] } });
```

$set allows to make modifications in embedded document too. For example, following is a document with embedded document.

```
{
 "EName": " Sonali",
"Details":
{
 "Department": "IT",
 "Location": "Pune",
 "Designation": " TeamLeader"
                },
                "MgrID": "123"
        }
```

In embedded document, to modify "Location" from "Pune" to "Mumbai"

```
> db.company.update({ "Name": "Sonali}, {"$set": {"Details.Location": "Mumbai"
} })
```

$unset Modifier

It may be possible that user want to remove any exiting key from a document. $unset modifier is used for that.

```
> db.company.update({ "Name": "Sonali" }, { "$unset": "Designation": 1 });
```

Here, key designation is removed from document where value of key "Name" is "Sonali".

Array Modifiers

To modify key of type array, array modifiers are available. $push adds an element at the end of an array for existing key. If key does not exist, new key will be added. For example, in company collection, if findOne() returns

```
{
        "Name": "Sonali",
        "Designation": "TeamLeader"
}
```

To add an array named "Skills", command can be

```
> db.company.update({ "Name": "Sonali"}, { "$push": { "Skills": [
"C","C++","JAVA", "NoSQL" ] });
```

To add more elements in array,

```
> db.company.update({ "Name": "Sonali"}, { "$push": { "Skills": [ "Adv. JAVA",
"PL-SQL" ] });
```

To add embedded document as an array element

```
> db.company.update({ "Name": "Sonali"}, { "$push": { "Projects": {"ID1: "Mo-
bile Botnet", "ID2": "Desktop Botnet" } } });
```

To add more elements in array,

```
> db.company.update({ "Name": "Sonali"}, { "$push": { "Projects": {"ID3: "Cloud
Computing", "ID4": "Cloud Botnet" } } });
```

$addToSet

While adding elements in a document, user may require to avoid duplicate key-value pair. $addToSet is useful for such condition. Suppose collection "company" consists of document of following type:

```
{
        "_id": ObjectID("4b23c3ca9538f49b20a2d"),
        "Name": "Sonali",
        "Email": [ sonali@abc.com", sonali123@xyz.com, sonali@pqr.com ]
}
```

While pushing new element in key "Email", $addToSet is used to avoid duplicates as:

```
> db.company.update({ "Name": "Sonali" }, { "$addToSet": { "Email": { "$each":
[ sonali@abc.com", sonali123@example.com ] } } });
```

Here, sonali@abc.com will not be added as it is already available in the array. $each is used with $addToSet to add multiple unique values.

$pop

$pop is used to remove elements from any end of an array. { $pop: { key: 1 } } removes last element of the array while { $pop: { key: -1 } } removes first element of the array. **$pull** removes an array element based on specific condition instead of its position. Following example removes completed tasks from todo list:

```
> db.todo.insert({ "list": [ "jumping", "walking", "running", "swimming",
"skipping", "pushup" ] });
> db.todo.update({ }, { "$pull": { "list": "running" } });
> db.todo.update({ }, { "$pop": { "list": 1 } });
> db.todo.update({ }, { "$pop": { "list": -1 } });
```

Limiting, Skipping, and Sorting Output

Many times it is required to limit output to some number of documents or skip some documents in result. Also, sorting result based on key is a common requirement – MongoDB gives following functions to perform this. To limit the result to some number, limit() is used after find().

```
> db.users.find().limit(10)
```

This will return only top 10 documents from the output returned by find query.

To skip few documents from the resultant documents, query will be

```
> db.users.find().skip(2)
```

This will skip() first two documents and will output other documents.

To sort output, sort() is used with required criteria. Sort takes a set of key-value pairs where key specifies the name of the key for sorting and value specifies direction of sorting. For ascending order "1" is used while "-1" returns descending order sorting. For multiple keys, output will be sorted in given sequence.

For example

```
> db.users.find().sort({ "Name": 1 })
```

Will return output sorted in ascending order based on value of Name key

```
> db.users.find().sort({ "Name": 1, age: -1 })
```

Returns output sorted in ascending order using "Name" key and descending order on "age" key. skip(),sot() and limit() can be combined to get required result.

CONCLUSION

In this chapter, author has covered all basics related with MongoDB. MongoDB has a very rich set of queries. This allows to perform all basics operations on MongoDB documents.

REFERENCES

Arora, R., & Aggarawal, R. (2013). Modeling and Querying Data in MongoDB. *International Journal of Scientific & Engineering Research*, 4(7), 141–144.

Brown, C. (1970, January 01). *NoSql Tips and Tricks*. Retrieved from http://blog.nosqltips.com/search?q=cap%2Btheorem

Chodorow. (2013). *MongoDB: The Definitive Guide*. New York, NY: O'Reilly Media.

Kumar, R., Charu, S., & Bansal, S. (2015). Effective way to handling big data problems using NoSQL Database (MongoDB). *Journal of Advanced Database Management & Systems*, 2(2), 42–48.

Luk, T., Blake, M., & Silberglitt, B. (2016). *Comparing MongoDB GU*. Retrieved September 19, 2016, from https://scalegrid.io/blog/which-is-the-best-mongodb-gui/

Moniruzzaman, A. B. M., & Hossain, S. A. (2013). NoSQL Database: New Era of Databases for Big data Analytics Classification, Characteristics and Comparison. *International Journal of Database Theory and Application*, 6(4), 1–13.

Oussous, A., Benjelloun, F. Z., Lahcen, A., & Belfkih, S. (2015). *Comparison and Classification of NoSQL Databases for Big Data*. Paper presented at International conference on Big Data, Cloud and Applications, Tetuan, Morocco.

Ranjan, N. (2015, January 03). *NoSQL database - Different types of NoSQL database*. Retrieved from http://www.devinline.com/2015/01/nosql-intorduction.html

Ricardo, C. M., & Susan, D. (2016). *Databases Illuminated* (3rd ed.). San Diego, CA: Jones & Bartlett Learning.

Subramanian, S. (2016, May 19). *A Primer on Open-Source NoSQL Databases - DZone Database*. Retrieved from https://dzone.com/articles/a-primer-on-open-source-nosql-databases

Tauro, C. J. M., Patil, B. R., & Prashanth, K. R. (2013). *A Comparative Analysis of Different NoSQL Databases on Data Model, Query Model and Replication Model*. Paper presented at International Conference on Emerging Research in Computing, Information, Communication and Applications, ERCICA 2013, Bangalore, India.

Truică, C. O., Boicea, A., & Trifan, I. (2013). *CRUD Operations in MongoDB*. Paper presented at International Conference on Advanced Computer Science and Electronics Information (ICACSEI 2013). doi:10.2991/icacsei.2013.88

Truica, C. O., Radulescu, F., & Boicea, A. (2015). *Performance Evaluation for CRUD Operations in Asynchronously Replicated Document Oriented Database*. Paper presented at International Conference on Controlled Systems and Computer Science(CSCS). doi:10.1109/CSCS.2015.32

Vorhies, B. (2014, July 23). *Lesson 5: Key value stores (aka 'tuple' stores)*. Retrieved from http://data-magnum.com/lesson-5-key-value-stores-aka-tuple-stores/

KEY TERMS AND DEFINITIONS

BASE: Basically Available Soft state Eventually.

CAP: Consistent Available Partition tolerance.

Capped Collection: Fixed size collections.

Collections: Equivalent structure for RDBMS tables.

CRUD: Create, Read, Update, and Delete.

Documents: Row equivalent of RDBMS. MongoDB stores data in documents instead of row.

Embedded Documents: Storing documents with in documents.

Modifiers: Symbols or keywords used to perform some special operations on queries.

Chapter 5
A Security–By–Distribution Approach to Manage Big Data in a Federation of Untrustworthy Clouds

Jens Kohler
University of Applied Sciences Mannheim, Germany

Markus Gumbel
University of Applied Sciences Mannheim, Germany

Christian Richard Lorenz
University of Applied Sciences Mannheim, Germany

Thomas Specht
University of Applied Sciences Mannheim, Germany

Kiril Simov
Bulgarian Academy of Sciences, Bulgaria

ABSTRACT

In recent years, Cloud Computing has drastically changed IT-Architectures in enterprises throughout various branches and countries. Dynamically scalable capabilities like CPUs, storage space, virtual networks, etc. promise cost savings, as huge initial infrastructure investments are not required anymore. This development shows that Cloud Computing is also a promising technology driver for Big Data, as the storage of unstructured data when no concrete and defined data schemes (variety) can be managed with upcoming NoSQL architectures. However, in order to fully exploit these advantages, the integration of a trustworthy 3rd party public cloud provider is necessary. Thus, challenging questions concerning security, compliance, anonymization, and privacy emerge and are still unsolved. To address these challenges, this work presents, implements and evaluates a security-by-distribution approach for NoSQL document stores that distributes data across various cloud providers such that every provider only gets a small data chunk which is worthless without the others.

DOI: 10.4018/978-1-5225-2486-1.ch005

INTRODUCTION

No other trend has changed the entire Information Technology during the last decade as Cloud Computing actually has done. Slowly, the hype about this buzzword abates and enterprises recognize the true added value of renting computing resources from the cloud. Cloud Computing in the context of this work is defined by the five essential characteristics listed in Mell and Grance (2011), with the on-demand self-service where customers are able to rent computing capabilities by themselves whenever they need them, followed by the requirement of a broad network bandwidth access. Furthermore, resources from the cloud are pooled together with the usage of virtualization from a provider perspective, which enables a rapid elasticity to provide requested resources. Finally, all provided resources are monitored (i.e. measured) by both, the providers and the consumers to have a provable accounting model. For most enterprises, the essential benefit is the dynamic scalability of computing resources along with cost advantages from the pay-as-you-go billing models (Furht et al., 2010). But also other benefits like working independently from any location, the fast deployment of resources and the development of new business models and markets with high-dynamic (i.e. elastic) IT infrastructures were key drivers for the development of Cloud Computing (Gens & Shirer, 2013).

Moreover, a new business case regarding Cloud Computing is now emerging: Big Data. Here, huge amounts of unstructured data at a great velocity must be managed, i.e. stored, analyzed, interpreted, corrected, etc. The notion of Big Data was firstly introduced by Pettey and Goasduff (2011) in 2011 where the three above-mentioned properties volume, variety and velocity are explained in greater detail. With respect to this, Cloud Computing is able to offer dynamically scalable resources to address these three challenges: instead of huge initial or new investments in better hardware, the required capabilities can be rented on-demand. Then, they can be used for a certain time, be dynamically scaled according to the data volume and velocity, and finally just turned off when they are not required anymore. Thus, two of the three Big Data properties are addressed, but variety is still a challenging issue. Here, NoSQL (not only SQL) databases offer promising features to efficiently store unstructured data. These new kinds of databases are considered in more detail in this chapter and are therefore defined in the following section.

Additionally, it is a fact that the more data are collected, the more important becomes privacy and security for enterprises as well as for end-customers. This becomes even more challenging, if data are managed in the cloud at an external provider. Therefore, the increasing usage of cloud services is accompanied by concerns regarding security, compliance, and privacy and customers depend on the security measures of the service providers. Moreover, for customers it is not transparent, which security measures are implemented by the provider Neves, Correia, Bruno, Fernando,and Paulo (2013), Sood (2012), and Cloud Security Alliance (2013). Hence, challenges of data privacy and compliance still are the most significant obstacles for an increased usage of Cloud Computing (Gens & Shirer, 2013).

To address these challenging security concerns and to ensure data privacy, several different approaches exist, e.g. encryption with digital signatures. A different approach is developed with SeDiCo at the University of Applied Sciences in Mannheim. SeDiCo (A Secure and Distributed Cloud Data Store) is a framework for distributed and secure data storage. With this framework, sensitive data can be segregated from non-sensitive data and stored at physically different places such as different cloud providers. Thus, the actual place of the data is disguised, as every chunk of data is worthless without the others. For example, bank accounts can be stored separately from the owners' names and thus, even if an attacker gets access to one of the partitions, the compromised data does not contain useful information. A simplified example that illustrates this basic principle is shown in Figure 1.

Figure 1. Security-by-distribution example

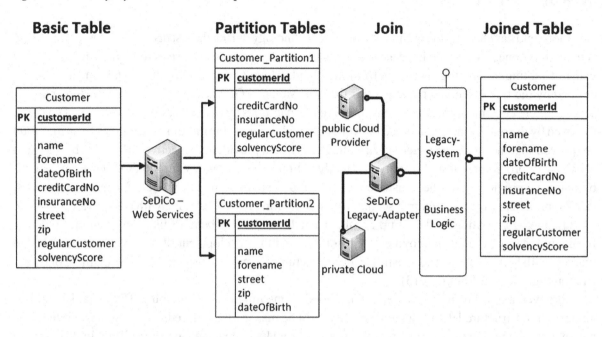

The example illustrates that when data from Customer_Partition1 is stolen or accidentally made publically available, the data (e.g. the credit card number or the insurance number) cannot be misused, as the data from the corresponding Customer_Partition2 (e.g. the corresponding name or address, etc.) is still secure and unknown to the thief or the public.

Currently, the SeDiCo framework supports relational database architectures. In widely distributed systems – particularly with respect to Big Data – those database architectures reach their limits. Here scalable databases which can be distributed to many computing nodes are considered adequate. This requirement entailed a new generation of database architectures, which can be summarized under the NoSQL umbrella. These databases were designed for a wide horizontal distribution and allow the processing of large amounts of data. In combination with that, Cloud Computing is considered suitable for those heavily distributed systems due to its cost advantages (pay as you go), but also with respect to the above-mentioned security risks. Considering this demand of data privacy with Big Data applications, this work enhances the current relational SeDiCo framework with NoSQL document stores. As this term covers much (also very different) database architectures, the focus of this work is limited to document stores. According to NoSQL Archive (2016), these architectures are mostly applied in today's practical use cases. As the existing relational SeDiCo prototype is implemented in Java and uses Hibernate as persistence framework (Kohler & Specht, 2012); Kohler, Simov, & Specht, 2015a), this work transfers the approach with the usage of Hibernate OGM (Object Grid Mapper) (RedHat, 2015) and MongoDB (2016) as the underlying document store. Finally, the prototype is evaluated with respect to its data access performance.

The contribution of this chapter to the current state-of-the-art is stated as follows:

- The conceptualization and definition of a security-by-distribution approach for NoSQL document stores.

- The creation of a framework that enables the processing of Big Data with dynamically scalable cloud capabilities, while security and privacy is maintained according to the security-by-distribution approach.
- A prototypical implementation of the framework that uses NoSQL document stores to manage unstructured data in different document stores and clouds.
- An evaluation of the implementation that compares the performance of the security-by-distribution approach to a non-distributed implementation.
- A detailed discussion and interpretation of the achieved performance measurements and their impact on other NoSQL databases.

TYPES AND EXAMPLES OF NOSQL DATABASES

First and foremost, some foundations have to be outlined to reach a common understanding about the used notions. Hence, this section provides a brief overview of NoSQL architectures and Hibernate OGM. Furthermore, this chapter introduces the concept of vertical partitioning within the SeDiCo framework.

NoSQL

The term NoSQL initially interpreted as no SQL but later interpreted as not only SQL and finally accepted by the NoSQL community was firstly proposed by Emil Eifrem of Neo4J (Neo Technology Incorporation, 2016). Hence, the term NoSQL refers to a whole generation of new database architectures and emerged as a countermovement to relational databases. Moreover, it covers a lot of database architectures and it appears to be difficult to find common features, which apply to all NoSQL architectures. Edlich, Friedland, Hampe, Brauer, and Brückner (2011) take the plethora of definitions and conclude that NoSQL databases show the following common characteristics:

- The underlying data model is not relational.
- They focus on horizontal scalability.
- Simple data replication mechanisms are used.
- They are Open Source.
- They are schema-free or have only weak schema restrictions.
- They provide a simple API but less powerful query possibilities (compared to SQL).
- They use a different model of consistency: BASE (Basically Available, Soft State, Eventual Consistency) vs. ACID (Atomicity, Consistency, Isolation, and Durability) (Edlich et al., 2011).

Especially the latter property requires a more detailed consideration. The hypothesis of BASE is based on the CAP-Theorem (Consistency, Availability, Partition Tolerance), which proves that in distributed systems always only two out of the three properties can be fulfilled simultaneously (Gilbert & Lynch, 2002; Brewer, 2000). Figure 2 illustrates this correlation.

While the ACID properties focus on consistency and availability, NoSQL databases have in common that they break up with the solid consistency property and accept a weaker one. Thus, these databases achieve a much better availability and partition tolerance at cost of consistency for certain periods of

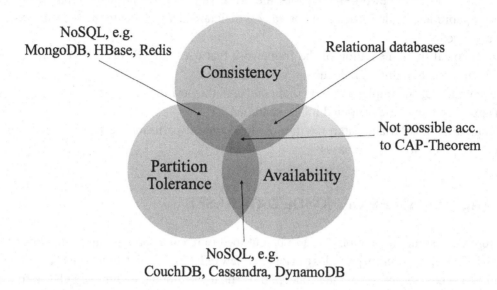

time. With respect to Big Data scenarios, this higher availability and the partition tolerance offer appealing benefits in terms of velocity and veracity.

Generally, NoSQL databases can be divided into four basic architectures: key-value, document stores, column stores, and graph databases (NoSQL Archive, 2016). Key-value stores store values with specific identifying keys, document stores store data in JSON (JavaScript Object Notation) (Crockford, 2006). The primer use case of these two architectures is a fast read and write access due to simple data schemes. Column stores are similar to relational databases; however, they persist data In-Memory and moreover, in columns instead of rows. This results in a good data analytical performance (i.e. read operations), as they are executed column wise and not row by row or tuple by tuple. Therefore, this architecture is used mainly in data warehouses with only few data manipulations but complex and long-lasting queries. Finally, graph databases use graphs as the underlying data model. Hence, benefits arise in special use cases where data are described as graphs with relationships. Figure 3 illustrates the data structure of the 4 NoSQL architectures schematically in which objects of a type customer are persisted. The attributes are displayed shortened due to better readability.

A good starting point for a general overview and detailed statistics about the current usage of NoSQL architectures is provided by (NoSQL Archive, 2016). According to these statistics, document stores are the most popular NoSQL architectures at the moment. These statistics also show that MongoDB as a concrete document store implementation currently plays a major part in the NoSQL area. In document stores, data are stored in different so-called documents and one or more documents are stored in files. The most common used notation for these files is JSON at the moment. A typical use case for document stores are highly unstructured data where a tremendous performance loss is experienced when these data are stored in a relational database in 3rd normal form. Above that, the other 3 architectures are also represented within the top 20 and these include Cassandra (Lakshman & Malik, 2010) and HBase (Apache Software Foundation, 2016a) as examples for column stores, which store data similar to relational data, but column-wise, i.e. columns are placed directly after each other in the storage engine. This improves the query performance when data is analyzed with complex queries (that include e.g. aggregate or sum

Figure 3. Structure of customer data in different NoSQL architectures: 1) key-value store, 2) column store, 3) document store, and 4) graph database

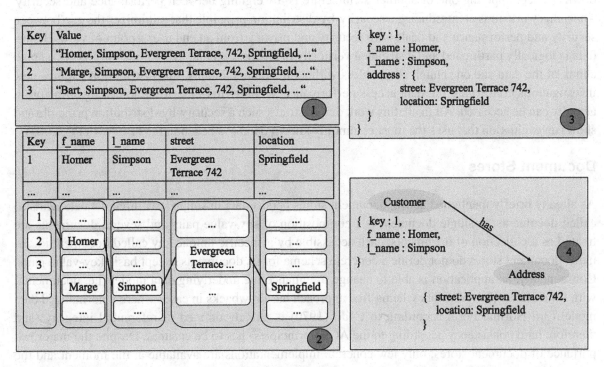

functions, etc.) because data is not iterated (slowly) row by row but columns are analyzed as a whole. Hence, a typical use case for such column-based data stores is a data warehouse with a lot of analytical queries but only few write operations. Furthermore, Redis (Redislab, 2016) as a key-value store, that store data in key-value pairs, which improves read and write performance in simple data structures, as the entire data set can be regarded as a hash set has to be mentioned. A common use case for such kinds of architectures are data caches. Last but not least, Neo4J (Neo Technology Incorporation, 2016) as an example for a graph database that stores data in a set of nodes with connecting edges that represent relations between the nodes can be mentioned as one of the 4 basic NoSQL architectures. Here, traditional and well-investigated graph algorithms can be used to analyze the data. This architecture is mostly used in highly related data, such as social networks or recommendation systems (e.g. customers that bought this article also bought this one). However, it has to be mentioned that compared to relational ones, these NoSQL databases are still comparatively rarely used. Based on these figures, this work focuses on document stores and therefore a more detailed overview of the general architecture is outlined in the following section.

Above all, it has to be noted that all 4 basic architectures and their respective database implementations and systems, are intended to improve the overall read and write performance and are focused on highly distributed system architectures where data is shared, distributed or replicated among many different heterogeneous nodes. Therefore, a lot of different use cases are thinkable for each architecture. A few examples are mentioned above, besides e.g. high-availability clusters, dynamically scalable distributed cloud architectures, etc. However, data security and privacy are not in the main focus of current implementations. A survey of different documentations (Mongo DB, 2016 ;Apache, 2016a;2016b; Neo4j,

2016) show that security is mainly dealt with in the sense of losing data if one or another node breaks down. Hence, applying one or another architecture is a weighing between performance and security. Thus, this work aims at introducing a security-by-distribution principle that minimizes the gap between security and performance and deals with security and privacy from an end user's point of view. Hence, data is logically partitioned and distributed vertically in a way, such that every node only stores a small chunk of the data and one chunk is worthless without the others. Finally, this distribution requires new investigations concerning the data access performance, as data first have to be joined again before it actually can be accessed. All in all, this work demonstrates such a security-by-distribution principle and shows an evaluation that uses the most commonly known database benchmark: TPC-W (TPC, 2003).

Document Stores

As already briefly mentioned above, document stores persist data in single structured data elements so called documents. A single document is a composition of key-value pairs and several documents are treated as a collection of documents, each accessible by a specific unique key called document id. Finally, document stores do not define a concrete schema for its documents except basic key-value pairs. Consequently, an application is able to change or enhance the underlying data model (i.e. documents) with little effort. However, this schema-free approach has drawbacks in cases where a normalized data model (3rd Normal Form according to Codd (1970) is already defined or referential integrity (and therefore hard consistency according to the ACID principles) has to be ensured. Despite the major importance of document stores, only few concrete implementations are available at the moment and the most popular among these are MongoDB and CouchDB (NoSQL Archive, 2016). These two are similar in their basic architecture. In both, a database instance contains one or more databases, each database contains collections of documents, and every document is assigned to a specified document collection, as sketched in Figure 4.

Figure 4. Structure of a document store instance

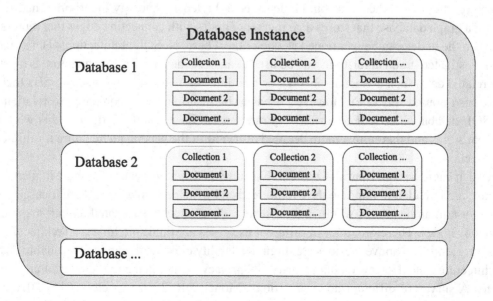

Compared to relational database architectures the collection corresponds to a table and the concrete document to a tuple (or a row) respectively. Table 1 illustrates this comparison in a broader overview.

Moreover, MongoDB and CouchDB have in common, that both use JSON as the basic data structure. A JSON object consists of key-value pairs, where the keys uniquely identify their corresponding value. A value can be one of the following datatypes: a (generic) object, an array, a character string, a boolean value or null. Figure 5 shows an example of such a JSON object, illustrated by an exemplified customer object in order to stick with the motivating example in Figure 1.

Here, JSON and its key-value pairs are illustrated with the attribute name followed by a colon and the actual value of the attribute (e.g. C_LNAME: Simpson). Above that, Figure 5 shows a nested structure with the attribute (C_BANKACCOUNT) which stores an array of (IBAN, BIC, and CREDITCARD attributes). Furthermore, it has to be noted that the types of the data (string, integer, etc.) are implicitly specified by the respective attribute values. Besides that, both MongoDB and CouchDB are schema-free databases. This basically means, that the schema – the concrete structure of persisted data – is created at runtime by the database and has not to be defined at the design time of the data model. This concept implies that documents within a collection not necessarily have the same structure. This is a major difference to relational models, as in relational tables the schema is predefined by the columns of the tables.

Table 1. Comparison of relational and document oriented database architectures

Relational Architecture	Document-Oriented Architecture
Database Instance	Database Instance
Database	Database
Table	Collection
Row (Tuple)	Document

Figure 5. A customer JSON object stored as a document

```
1 ▾  {
2         $id :           "Customer:04b24313-f210-4f0-989c",
3         $type :         "entity",
4         $table :        "Customer",
5         C_ID :          "04b24313-f210-4f0-989c",
6         C_FNAME :       "Homer",
7         C_LNAME :       "Simpson",
8 ▾      C_BANKACCOUNT : {
9             IBAN :          "987654321000123456",
10            BIC :           "BICXXX",
11            CREDITCARD:     "123456"
12 ▴     }
13 ▴  }
```

Lastly, both databases support the basic CRUD (create, read, update, delete) operations. Yet, also queries with higher complexity, such as complex joins over various document collections are possible with MapReduce functions (Moniruzzaman & Hossain, 2013). However, in order to not lose the focus of this work, the interested reader is referred to Apache Software Foundation (2016b) for concrete examples and further information about MapReduce.

Vertical Partitioning

This concept is not primarily focused on performance improvements but aims at creating a secure data store by using several database instances. Vertical partitioning in the context of this work is the logical separation of a tuple. As a result, 2 or more partitions logically contain the same tuple, but every partition contains only a part of it.

The basic concept of this approach is to identify relationships between data attributes, which bear a high potential risk when they are stored together. To ensure proper and consistent queries, the primary key is replicated in every partition and the tuple is joined during a query via its reference to the primary key. Finally, the vertical partitioning and distribution approach is considered as an appropriate solution to meet the above-mentioned Cloud Computing challenges: data compliance, privacy, security, and anonymization.

CRUD Operations for Vertically Partitioned Data

Generally, the idea of persisting objects from an application logic in a database is based on the underlying data model. Object-oriented programming languages operate with objects of specific types, created from classes. These objects contain attributes as well as methods which are in essence executable program code. On the contrary, relational databases use predefined data models with tables, columns, and rows. This shows that the mapping of tables to object-oriented classes turns out to be a non-trivial problem and this challenge is known as the Object Relational Impedance Mismatch (Ireland et al. 2009). Table 2 illustrates this mismatch in more detail and considers relational as well as NoSQL architectures.

Object Grid Mapping Frameworks

To overcome these challenges, so called Object Relational Mappers (ORM) have been and currently are developed. Figure 6 shows a typical architecture from an application to its database that uses such an ORM. The most popular example for such a framework in Java is Hibernate ORM.

Finally, ORMs implement logic that abstracts from a concrete database system and thus, they provide a unique interface that encapsulates all CRUD methods. Using this interface then allows exchanging databases without modifying the actual program logic. With respect to Figure 6, similar architectures for the other NoSQL architectures (key-value, column stores, and graph databases) apply.

Above that, it can be stated that documents in a document store do not differ so drastically from the object-oriented concepts with methods and attributes as the relational model does. Yet, a key difference is e.g. relationships between different objects. They have to be embodied as nested objects in the documents. This shows that specific aspects of the Impedance Mismatch like inheritance or encapsulation are still challenging aspects. Furthermore, the document stores discussed above use JSON to store Java objects and as a consequence, a mapping between Java and JSON is necessary. Above that, it has to be

Table 2. Impedance mismatch of relational and NoSQL architectures

Impedance Mismatch Challenge	Object-Oriented Class	Relational Database Table	Key-Value Store	Document Store	Column Store	Graph Database
Structure	Attributes and methods explicitly describe semantic of a class	Only implicit semantics with table attributes (i.e. columns)	Only implicit semantics with values that are stored with corresponding key	Only implicit semantics with documents that are stored with a corresponding document id	Only implicit semantics with table attributes (i.e. columns)	Only implicit semantics with values and their relationships that are stored in a graph
Inheritance	A class/object is part of an inheritance hierarchy	Not available	Not available	Not available	Not available	Implicit with an is-a relationship
Instance	Object represents behavior	Tuple represents a statement of truth (Codd, 1970)	Key-value pair represents a statement of truth	Document represents a statement of truth	Column represents a statement of truth	Nodes and their relationships represent statements of truth
Encapsulation	Attributes are encapsulated by methods (Information Hiding)	Table attributes are directly accessed	Values are accessed by their key	Documents are accessed by their document id	Columns are directly accessed	Graph with nodes and their relationships are directly traversed
Identity	Every object is uniquely identified by its object id	Every tuple is uniquely identified by its primary key	Every value is uniquely identified by its key	Every document is uniquely identified by its document id	Every tuple is uniquely identified by its primary key	Every node is uniquely identified by its node id
Data access	Discrete	Set-oriented	Discrete	Discrete	Set-oriented	Discrete
Maintenance	Developer	Database administrator	Database administrator	Database administrator	Database administrator	Database administrator

mentioned that for NoSQL architectures other mapping frameworks are available: e.g. Hibernate OGM (RedHat, 2015), Kundera (Impetus, 2016), DataNucleus (DataNucleus, 2016) and each of these mapping frameworks provides support for the mapping of several different NoSQL architectures.

Finally, another challenge is the still emerging market of NoSQL database implementations. In contrast to generic relational database drivers, e.g. JDBC (Java Database Connectivity) (Oracle, 2014) which are able to communicate with various different relational databases, in NoSQL, drivers are database-specific and cannot be used for different NoSQL databases generically. This means that persisting objects in different document stores, requires the encapsulation of different document store drivers into a single interface that acts as a generic database driver similar to JDBC.

As an exemplary mapping framework for document stores, Hibernate OGM (Object Grid Mapper) (RedHat, 2015), is outlined in more detail now. The framework aims at being compliant to the Java persistence interface JPA and Hibernate ORM (Object Relational Mapper). Hence, it uses well-known interfaces which facilitates and enables a simple change from relational to NoSQL architectures. Hibernate OGM reuses the Hibernate ORM engine to persist objects in NoSQL databases. To be precise, Hibernate OGM reuses the entire Object-Lifecycle-Management from the relational ORM implementation (RedHat, 2016b). Thus, the inbound requests of the application are processed by the Hibernate ORM core first and are then forwarded to the Hibernate OGM core. The abstraction from a single database is

Figure 6. ORM general, relational, and non-relational high-level architecture

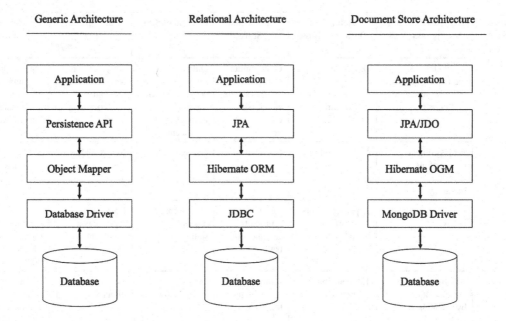

realized by DatastoreProvider and GridDialect. The DatastoreProvider abstracts the connection to the database including transactions and sessions. The GridDialect abstracts from the actual architecture of the database (i.e. key-value, document, column store, or graph database). Moreover, accessing data with CRUD operations is realized with a Query Parser which abstracts from SQL as the standard relational query language. So, every query is translated to a query suitable for the respective database architecture. Finally, this abstraction fosters the above-mentioned database abstraction and enables the exchange of the underlying database architecture without modifying the application logic.

PERFORMANCE HANDLING

On the one hand, data storage in public cloud scenarios offer enormous cost advantages for enterprises, due to the dynamic scalability, pay as you go models, etc. On the other hand, public clouds cannot guarantee data security and privacy. Hence, SeDiCo offers an approach for an enhanced level of security and privacy by vertically distributing database data (Kohler & Specht, 2012; Kohler, Simov, & Specht, 2015b).

The entire SeDiCo framework is based on a security-by-distribution principle. This notion is inspired by traditional principles like security-by-compromise which is known to delay the authentication process by an incrementing timer if an authentication attempt was proven false, e.g. in the case of a misspelled password. Other principles with respect to this are e.g. security-by-analysis, where an application or an entire environment is tested against certain attacks by penetration testers, or security-by-design, where already at the design time of an application or environment security measures are taken into consideration. According to these principles, security-by-distribution aims at establishing a certain level of security and privacy with the separation of logically coherent data and their storage at different locations (in the context of this work in different clouds).

Persisting objects in relational databases requires a mapping of a table to a class containing the table's attributes (i.e. columns) as object variables. Thus, each object (or so-called entity) represents a row of in the corresponding database table. In contrast to that, document stores persist objects in documents in JSON format and each document contains all attributes of the entity (or object) as key-value pairs. Figure 7 illustrates this, again with a customer example.

At this point two major differences of document stores to relational databases can be clearly recognized:

Firstly, document stores do not define a concrete schema despite the key-value pairs. This leads to the fact that a collection of documents may also contain documents with different structures (see Figure 7). This schema-freedom implies two questions regarding the vertical partitioning and distribution approach of SeDiCo:

- How can data of a child-object be vertically partitioned?
- How can an array of data in a document be vertical partitioned?

With respect to these challenges, it has to be noted that the properties in JSON may also contain other JSON objects or even arrays. These key differences have to be considered in the vertical partitioning and distribution approach presented in this work and are therefore elaborated in more detail now.

To transfer the basic security-by-distribution approach from the relational model to a document store, the following 5 scenarios have to be considered.

Scenario 1

In order to outline the first scenario in more detail, Figure 8 illustrates a simple use case.

Figure 7. Persisting a Java object in a document store

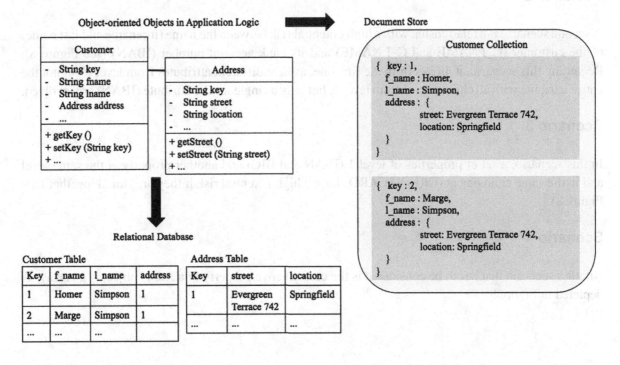

Figure 8. Scenario 1 and 2: basic security-by-distribution approach, based on a NoSQL document store

```
 1 ▼ {
 2       $id :           "Customer:04b24313-f210-4f0-989c",
 3       $type :         "entity",
 4       $table :        "Customer",
 5       C_ID :          "04b24313-f210-4f0-989c",
 6       C_FNAME :  "Homer",
 7       C_LNAME :  "Simpson",
 8 ▼     C_BANKACCOUNT : {
 9         IBAN :            "9876543210000123456",
10         BIC :             "BICXXX",
11         CREDITCARD:   "123456"
12 ⌐     }
13 ⌐ }
```

In the first level, there are simple properties ($id, $type, $table, C_ID, etc.), whereas the property C_BANKACCOUNT contains an entire object, called child-object. This C_BANKACCOUNT forms the second level of properties containing IBAN, BIC, and CREDITCARD. In the following, the first level will be referred to as level 0 and the second, nested level will be referred to as level 1.

Considering this basic example, it might be the case that the relationship of a property of level 0 (e.g. C_LNAME) contains a high security and privacy risk if it is stored together with another level 0 property (e.g. CREDITCARD).

Scenario 2

A second scenario is a relationship with a high potential risk between the name (forename and last name) of the customer (C_FNAME and C_LNAME) and its bank account number (IBAN) (see Figure 8). Regarding this scenario, it differs from the first one, as here different attributes from level 0 but not the entire attribute with all child objects from level 1, but only a single level 1 attribute (IBAN) are involved.

Scenario 3

In this scenario, a set of properties of level 1 (IBAN and BIC) and another property at the same level and in the same child object (CREDITCARD) have a high potential risk if they are stored together (see Figure 8).

Scenario 4

Another scenario that has to be considered is the case where a property of a JSON object is an array, as depicted in Figure 9.

Figure 9. Scenario 4: advanced security-by-distribution approach of a NoSQL document store

```
1  ▾  {
2         $id :            "Customer:04b24313-f210-4f0-989c",
3         $type :          "entity",
4         $table :         "Customer",
5         C_ID :           "04b24313-f210-4f0-989c",
6         C_FNAME :  "Homer",
7         C_LNAME :  "Simpson",
8  ▾      C_BANKACCOUNT : {
9  ▾          {
10                IBAN :          "987654321000123456",
11                BIC :           "BICXXX",
12                CREDITCARD:     "123456"
13 ˪          },
14 ▾          {
15                IBAN :          "123456789",
16                BIC :           "BICYYY",
17                CREDITCARD:     "9999999"
18 ˪          }
19 ˪      }
20 ˪  }
```

Figure 9 shows a customer, who owns 2 bank accounts (line 8, Figure 8) and each bank account has the same data schema (IBAN, BIC, and CREDITCARD). In contrast to the relational model, where such a one-to-many relationship has to be resolved with at least two tables, in document stores, the array elements are persisted in the same document as the parent-object. This case bears a high potential risk if all properties of all bank accounts (IBAN, BIC, and CREDITCARD) are stored together in just one single document.

Scenario 5

Additionally, it has to be noted that JSON permits that two objects in the same array have a different schema (i.e. different properties). Here, the schema-free approach of document stores becomes perceivable and this should not be restricted by the vertical partitioning and distribution approach of SeDiCo. An example for this is illustrated in Figure 10.

This time, the different bank accounts are stored in the C_BANKACCOUNT array in single elements but with different data schemes, e.g. one bank account has only an IBAN and a BIC and the other one has just a CREDITCARD number.

Finally, these challenges show that persisting objects according to the security-by-distribution approach of SeDiCo is more complex compared to relational databases. Therefore, the following sections address these challenges and outline possible approaches to solving them.

Figure 10. Scenario 5: advanced security-by-distribution approach of a NoSQL document store

```
1 ▾  {
2        $id :          "Customer:04b24313-f210-4f0-989c",
3        $type :         "entity",
4        $table :        "Customer",
5        C_ID :          "04b24313-f210-4f0-989c",
6        C_FNAME :  "Homer",
7        C_LNAME :  "Simpson",
8 ▾      C_BANKACCOUNT : {
9 ▾         {
10            IBAN :            "9876543210000123456",
11            BIC :             "BICXXX",
12           },
13 ▾        {
14            CREDITCARD:    "9999999"
15           }
16        }
17 ▾ }
```

APPROACH

The previous section showed that it is necessary to specify which attributes of an object have to be persisted in which partition. This information is defined in an XML file (an exemplified excerpt can be found in Figure 11) and this so-called specification file builds the foundation for the vertical data partitioning and distribution approach.

Scenario 1

With respect to the first scenario depicted above, the user has to specify the distribution accordingly. Compared to the relational approach, the partitioning of the child-objects (and all grandchild objects, and so forth) have also to be specified. Transferred to a document store, this is done by extending the XML schema as illustrated in Figure 11

Although objects in documents do not have columns but properties, here the tag column was retained to be compatible to the previously used nomenclature from the relational approach. Moreover, in this case, the separation of both properties is relatively simple. The property of level 0 (e.g. C_LNAME, line 8 in Figure 11) is stored in one partition and the property containing the entire child-object (all properties of C_BANKACCOUNT from the JSON in Figure 8 in scenario 1) is stored in the other partition (lines 15-18 in Figure 11).

Scenario 2

To vertically partition and distribute the data from scenario 2, the properties C_FNAME and C_LNAME (lines 7 and 8 in Figure 8) have to be persisted in one partition and the IBAN (line 16) has to be stored

Figure 11. XML configuration file for scenario 1

```
1   ...
2   <targets>
3     <target isPrimary="true">
4       ...
5       <dbType>MongoDB</dbType>
6         <partition>
7           <column name="C_FNAME"></column>
8           <column name="C_LNAME"></column>
9         </partition>
10    </target>
11    <target>
12      ...
13      <dbType>MongoDB</dbType>
14      <partition>
15        <column name="C_BANKACCOUNT">
16          <column name="IBAN"></column>
17          <column name="BIC"></column>
18          <column name="CREDITCARD"></column>
19        </column>
20      </partition>
21    </target>
22  </targets>
23 </config>
```

in another partition. In this scenario, all documents have the same schema. Thus, the partitioning and distribution schema from scenario 1 with the nested structure can be reused partly (Figure 12).

Scenario 3

To distribute data in this scenario, a separation on level 0 is not sufficient because the data has to be separated on the level of the child-object (here level 1). Again, the approach used in scenario 1 and 2 can be applied, but with a different nested structure and this is depicted in Figure 13.

Scenario 4

Just like in the previous case the relationship between IBAN, BIC and CREDITCARD is identified as a high potential risk relationship. Therefore, each of the array objects has to be vertically partitioned and distributed. As the schema of the array is homogeneous in this case, the partitioning and distribution from the previous scenarios can also be reused here, again with a different nested structure which is illustrated in Figure 14.

Figure 12. XML configuration file for scenario 2

```
1    ...
2    <targets>
3      <target isPrimary="true">
4        ...
5        <dbType>MongoDB</dbType>
6          <partition>
7            <column name="C_FNAME"></column>
8            <column name="C_LNAME"></column>
9          </partition>
10       </target>
11       <target>
12         ...
13         <dbType>MongoDB</dbType>
14         <partition>
15           <column name="C_BANKACCOUNT">
16             <column name="IBAN"></column>
17           </column>
18         </partition>
19       </target>
20     </targets>
21   </config>
```

Figure 13. XML configuration file for scenario 3

```
1    ...
2    <targets>
3      <target isPrimary="true">
4        ...
5        <dbType>MongoDB</dbType>
6          <partition>
7            <column name="C_BANKACCOUNT">
8              <column name="IBAN"></column>
9              <column name="BIC"></column>
10           </column>
11         </partition>
12       </target>
13       <target>
14         ...
15         <dbType>MongoDB</dbType>
16         <partition>
17           <column name="C_BANKACCOUNT">
18             <column name="CREDITCARD"></column>
19           </column>
20         </partition>
21       </target>
22     </targets>
23   </config>
```

Figure 14. XML configuration file for scenario 4

```
1   ...
2   <targets>
3     <target isPrimary="true">
4       ...
5       <dbType>MongoDB</dbType>
6       <partition>
7         <column name="C_LNAME"></column>
8         <column name="C_BANKACCOUNT">
9           <column name="IBAN"></column>
10          <column name="BIC"></column>
11        </column>
12      </partition>
13    </target>
14    <target>
15      ...
16      <dbType>MongoDB</dbType>
17      <partition>
18        <column name="C_FNAME"></column>
19        <column name="C_BANKACCOUNT">
20          <column name="CREDITCARD"></column>
21        </column>
22      </partition>
23    </target>
24  </targets>
25 </config>
```

Scenario 5

To partition and distribute these data vertically, the property IBAN is stored in one partition and the properties BIC and CREDITCARD are stored in another partition. However, in this case, the array has a heterogeneous schema and the array elements are different. Hence, in the specification file, the partitioning and distribution for each array element has to be done separately. This is addressed by extending the schema of the specification file and here, two approaches are viable:

- Identification via attribute is Array.

An option for specifying all necessary information for the distribution of each array element is to explicitly specify the distribution of every single element in the specification file. In this case, the individual array elements are referenced by their index position. To distinguish arrays from simple properties, the keyword isArray is used. This strategy is considered feasible if the exact size of the array and the positions of the array elements can be determined in advance. Figure 15 illustrates the specification of an array with the isArray keyword in line 8 and in line 23 respectively.

Figure 15. Specification of a vertical distribution of a homogeneous array in a document store

```
1   ...
2   <targets>
3     <target isPrimary="true">
4       ...
5       <dbType>MongoDB</dbType>
6         <partition>
7           <column name="C_LNAME"></column>
8           <column name="C_BANKACCOUNT" isArray="true">
9             <column name="0">
10              <column name="IBAN"></column>
11            </column>
12            <column name="1">
13              <column name="BIC"></column>
14            </column>
15          </column>
16        </partition>
17    </target>
18    <target>
19      ...
20      <dbType>MongoDB</dbType>
21        <partition>
22          <column name="C_FNAME"></column>
23          <column name="C_BANKACCOUNT" isArray="true">
24            <column name="2">
25              <column name="CREDITCARD"></column>
26            </column>
27          </column>
28        </partition>
29    </target>
30  </targets>
31  </config>
```

In this example, the property C_BANKACCOUNT holds an array containing different elements. The element at index 0 holds the IBAN, the element at index 1 contains the BIC, and the array element at index 2 the CREDITCARD (lines 8, 12 and 24 in Figure 15, respectively). Note that if a property exists in several arrays, the property is replicated, which possibly might contradict the entire security-by-distribution approach.

- The storage of associations as typed descriptions.

A second option is to assign object types to the array elements and to specify the distribution of these properties. To facilitate this, the XML schema of the specification file has to be extended, too. Here, an additional node type is used which holds 0, 1 or n nodes as its children. Thus, all necessary information can be provided for the partitioning and distribution of the objects to multiple different partitions. Figure 16 (lines 7, 10, 19, 22) shows an excerpt of such a specification file which uses this typed description. Thus, every array element belongs to such a typed description, and here again, if an array element is defined for several types, it is also replicated. Finally, this approach is recommended if the schema of the array is not predefined and is likely to be changed, i.e. in scenarios where the array elements are not known in advance.

Figure 16. Specification of a vertical distribution of a heterogeneous array in a document store

```
1    ...
2    <targets>
3      <target isPrimary="true">
4        ...
5        <dbType>MongoDB</dbType>
6          <partition>
7            <type name="Customer">
8              <column name="C_LNAME"></column>
9            </type>
10           <type name="C_BANKACCOUNT">
11             <column name="BIC"></column>
12           </type>
13         </partition>
14       </target>
15       <target>
16         ...
17         <dbType>MongoDB</dbType>
18           <partition>
19             <type name="Customer">
20               <column name="C_FNAME"></column>
21             </type>
22             <type name="C_BANKACCOUNT">
23               <column name="CREDITCARD"></column>
24               <column name="IBAN"></column>
25             </type>
26           </partition>
27       </target>
28     </targets>
29   </config>
```

IMPLEMENTATION

The relational SeDiCo implementation uses the Object Relational Mapper Hibernate. Therefore, the usage of Hibernate OGM as the mapping layer is considered adequate for the NoSQL document store approach. Above that, compared to the other mapping frameworks (sec. related work), Hibernate OGM supports all popular NoSQL architectures and a plethora of concrete implementations of them. Above that, the framework is currently developed by RedHat has an active user community which facilitates and supports the development process. These reasons substantiate the wide distribution of Hibernate OGM and explain (to a certain extent) its current state as the mostly applied mapping framework in the Java community nowadays.

In the relational version of SeDiCo, the framework interrupts the execution of the CRUD methods with the so-called Hibernate Lifecycle Events. The respective CRUD operation is canceled and instead, the tuples are processed in a virtual table which either realizes the join (in the case of a query) or the partitioning and distribution (in the case of a manipulation).

Unfortunately, it is not possible to use this relational approach for the vertical partitioning and distribution of documents in document stores for the following reasons:

- The usage of a virtual table is not suitable in the context of document stores. In fact, technologically this would be possible, but then the schema-freedom of document stores would also be restricted to a virtual table schema.
- Another drawback is the heterogeneity of NoSQL architectures (key-value, document, column stores and graph databases) in general. Distributing data vertically on the basis of the respective NoSQL architecture would result in the development of single implementations for every respective architecture. Furthermore, this would entail the translation of every query language of each database architecture. With respect to this, it must be noted that even MongoDB and CouchDB (as 2 document stores) already implement different query languages and above that, the integration of only one database driver would not be sufficient for a generic NoSQL solution.

Finally, it can be concluded that although the usage of a virtual table is technologically possible, it is not recommended.

Taking a closer look at this problem it is obvious, that the challenges for a vertical partitioning and distribution approach for NoSQL databases are caused by the heterogeneity of those data stores. Yet, these issues are already partly solved by Object Grid Mapper frameworks (OGMs), as they abstract from those different architectures. In general, these frameworks map the structure of objects to the data schema of the respective NoSQL architecture and integrate the necessary database drivers for the connection to the respective database system.

A further advantage of OGMs is the independency from the underlying database system. With these frameworks, the vertical distribution can be performed on the data model defined by the application logic and the OGM is used to translate the partitioning and distribution to the concrete underlying database system. This abstraction also enables to simply exchange the underlying NoSQL database, or expressed the other way around: All databases supported by Hibernate OGM can be used with the vertical partitioning and distribution approach of this work.

Finally, the challenge of joining data from the cloud partitions arises. Joining the partitioned and distributed data is done on the OGM layer via the document returned from the document store. In general, the partitioned objects are joined based on their document id, similar to the join via primary keys in the relational implementation. For the implementation of this work, this approach was chosen to achieve an independency from the underlying NoSQL database architecture. However, a drawback of this design is that data which are joined on the basis of the documents are stored as character strings because of the JSON format. Yet, this means that the join of the partitioned objects is not type-safe, as type-safety cannot be ensured during the runtime of the application. Yet, the actual object (in the context of this work it is a Java object) is already instantiated before the actual join has taken place. Thus, it must be concluded that as soon as child-objects with different attributes are vertically partitioned and distributed (see scenario 5), the join of these child-objects cannot be guaranteed to be type-safe anymore. The use cases depicted in the other scenarios are not affected by this, as there, the data schemes are homogenous.

EVALUATION

For the evaluation, MongoDB (MongoDB, 2016) as the most prominent and most widespread document store was used (NoSQL Archive, 2016). The performance analysis was done with an adapted version of the database benchmark TPC-W (TPC, 2003), to establish comparability between this work and results of previous works within the SeDiCo framework, e.g. (Kohler & Specht, 2012; Kohler, Simov, & Specht, 2015b). Thus, in this work also the customer table from the TPC-W benchmark was used. However, compared to the previous SeDiCo works, the evaluation scenario was slightly changed, such that the influence of cascading an object graph could be evaluated too. Therefore, the TPC-W address table that references the customer table (1 customer can only have 1 address) was introduced.

All following measurements were performed with the SeDiCo document store implementation (SeDiCo Document Store) and the following statistics show the comparison to a non-distributed and non-partitioned NoSQL document store (NoSQL Document Store). For the latter case, a typical Hibernate OGM implementation was used as described in RedHat (2016a).

To eliminate side-effects like network bandwidth, unpredictable workloads of the cloud servers, all measurements were conducted exclusively with locally installed MongoDB instances (version 3.0). All measurements were performed 3 times and the average of these measurements is presented in the following figures (Figure 17-20). Finally, the used hardware environment was a standard PC with an Intel Core i5-4200 CPU with 2,3 GHz, 8GB DDR3 RAM with 1600 MHz and Microsoft Windows 8.1 Pro 64bit.

Figure 17. Create performance comparison

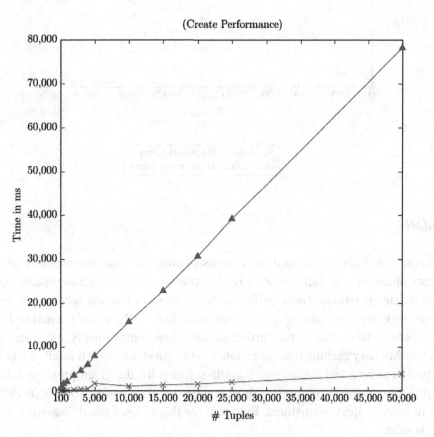

Figure 18. Read performance comparison

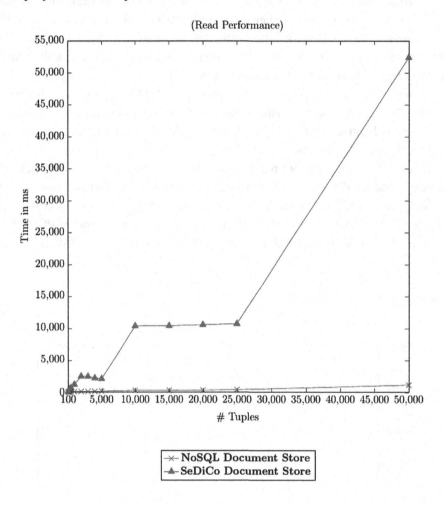

CONCLUSION

Compared to a traditional non-partitioned and non-distributed setup, the performance degrades by factor ~11 for create operations, by factor ~20 for read operations, by factor ~3 for update operations, and by factor ~2 for delete operations. These performance losses show that the security-by-distribution approach is an outweigh between security and performance. Especially, in the context of Big Data when the velocity attribute is the crucial factor, further performance improvements, e.g. query rewriting and optimization or In-Memory caching have to be taken into consideration. All in all, it can be stated that the approach proves to be a technologically feasible solution for the given problem definition. It can also be stated that the developed approach is able to realize security-by-distribution (to different clouds) in the context of NoSQL document stores. Evidence for this technological feasibility is given by the prototype of this work.

Figure 19. Update performance comparison

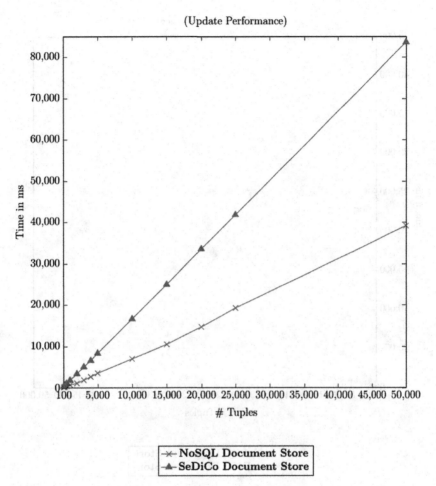

However, during the implementation and evaluation, the following restrictions have to be considered. Currently, it was not possible to show the feasibility of vertically distributing the attributes of different child-objects within an array for document stores (scenario 5). This was mainly caused by the choice of Hibernate OGM as the mapping framework. In Java, the concept of having objects of different types in an array is realized by inheritance. Assuming for example three classes A, B, and C, with the inheritance hierarchy, in which B contains other attributes as C. In Java (as a statically typed language) an array of type A might reference different objects of classes B and C.

Unfortunately, Hibernate OGM does not support different inheritance relationships. Only the strategy table per concrete class (RedHat, 2016a), which creates individual documents for each class instead of storing all array objects in one single document is supported. Thus, creating classes with defined object data types at runtime is not possible. In order to overcome this challenge, a non-type-safe, i.e. a script-based programming language (e.g. Groovy, which is similar to Java and is able to execute Java code) that is able to instantiate variable types of classes and objects at runtime could be used.

Finally, the benefits and drawbacks of the implementation can be summarized as follows in Table 3.

Figure 20. Delete performance comparison

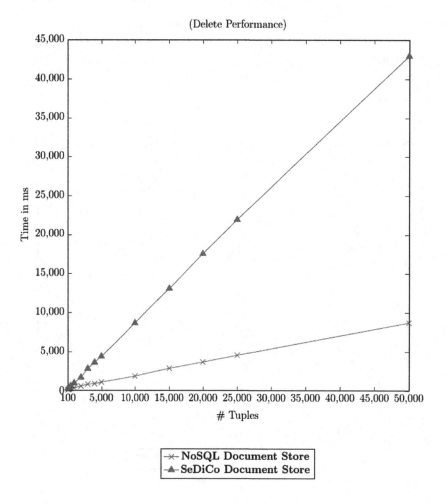

Table 3. Benefits and drawbacks of the proposed implementation

Benefits	Drawbacks
Feasible implementation of the security-by-distribution approach	In case of heterogeneous data schemes, type-safety of the objects cannot be guaranteed
Independence from the underlying NoSQL or relational data store	Performance losses because of the vertical partitioning and distribution approach

RELATED WORK

The problem definitions regarding IT security in Cloud Computing are manifold. Accordingly, (Yildiz, Abawajy, Ercan, & Bernoth, 2009) developed an approach to increase the security of a cloud infrastructure based on defined guidelines for participating parties referring to network, process, and system access. Other works like C. Wang, Chow, Wang, Ren, and Lou (2013); Juels and Oprea (2013), and B. Wang, Chow, Li, & Li, 2013 aim at increasing trust in public cloud services by assessing the integrity of the service via automated frameworks. For example, C. Wang et al. (2013) proposes a framework where the assessment of a cloud service is possible without gaining knowledge of the concrete data stored in the cloud. In B. Wang et al. (2013), this concept is enhanced by a security mediator, which minimizes the computing complexity and network overhead of the framework. Other works mentioned below study the use of encryption of data, stored in the cloud. Those technologies are applied to protect data from unauthorized access. Such an unintentional access by third parties might happen not only by external but also internal parties – for example, the cloud provider itself (so-called Insider Jobs). Further research like Sood (2012) and Saleh and Meinel (2013) show that encryption is actually a very effective protection for data in public clouds. Finally, other works e.g. (Banerjee et al., 2013; Sang, 2013) demonstrate attempts to detect attackers, to block them or allow better forensic investigations. Above these works, Tchepnda, Moustafa, Labiod, and Bourdon (2009) provide a broad overview about current security threads and challenges in today's heterogeneous networks. Further interesting security and privacy-related topics with a special focus on Cloud Computing and Big Data (e.g. the introduction of watermarks in multimedia data) are discussed in Dey and Santhi (2017).

The presented related work so far illustrates the wide range of this research field. According to Juels & Oprea, 2013) and Sood (2012), cloud providers offer a high level of security even if different well-known technologies (e.g. databases, network topologies, applications, etc.) are used in Cloud Computing. Accordingly, the authors suggest to distributing data according to their sensitivity. (Sood, 2012) also propose an algorithm for evaluating the sensitivity of information and the classification of information security in confidentiality, integrity and availability, also known as the CIA principle. A similar distribution of data is also proposed by the framework HPISecure (Saleh & Meinel, 2013). There, data is separated in encrypted data blocks and is stored distributed and thus, HPISecure offers an approach to the distributed storage of data in a Software as a Service model in an encrypted way. Comparatively, this work presents an approach which is focused on database data and thus, applicable in all service (IaaS, PaaS, and SaaS) and deployment (public, private, hybrid, and community) models according to the NIST (National Institute for Standardization and Technology) definition in Mell and Grance (2011).

Furthermore, regarding the approach proposed in this work Sood (2012) and Saleh and Meinel (2013) have to be emphasized, as those approaches also foster a vertical distribution of data in different cloud services. But in contrast to the approach of SeDiCo, those studies do not cover concrete database data but file systems.

Yet, in the context of Big Data and with respect to the conceptual database view of this work, there are numerous applications, use cases, and analytical scenarios thinkable. Current research work shows examples of not only analyzing huge amounts of data to receive a detailed overview about the past, but also to predict the future with artificial intelligence approaches. Interesting works in the field of professional sports was conducted by Jain et al. (2016). In the academic environment an approach with ambient intelligence is presented by Mikulecký, Olševicová, Bures, and Mls (2011) for the management of academic institutions (e.g. student data, research capabilities, etc.). Another application domain are recommendation systems, in which recommendations for a customer are presented based on other customers' orders. Here an interesting example can be found in Jain et al., 2016). Interestingly, such analyses require logic that is able to deal with fuzzy, incomplete and uncertain data sets. Here, Ripon et al. (2016) provide an overview about different classification methods (i.e. K-nearest neighbor, Naive Bayes and an Apriori algorithm) for such data sets, which they call rough sets. Classic examples of

Big Data come from social networks like Facebook, Twitter, or the like. Analyzing these kinds of data also requires new methods and algorithms and a good example for such algorithms (based on Twitter data) is presented in Baumgarten et al. (2013). Above these new challenges, which also provide a lot of opportunities, security and privacy are issues that have been hardly dealt with so far. Nevertheless, there are further research works that take these also challenging concerns into account. Mohanpurkar et al. (2016) for example present an approach which integrates fingerprints into the underlying data set. Thus, data integrity, i.e. the fact that data is not altered by unauthorized entities can be preserved and so data manipulations can be eliminated. Besides these works, collecting such huge amounts of data is another interesting topic. As already mentioned above, nowadays social networks provide a good foundation, if there is a critical mass of users achieved. With respect to this, Zappi et al. (2010) outlined a framework that shows a sensor-based data collection approach from the cradle to the grave. Another issue with respect to Big Data is the collection of huge data amounts. Here, especially user-specific data which are used to predict future behaviors and enables enterprises to draw conclusions on specific users are challenging. Here, a good overview about the current discussion and methodologies how such data are collected and what further implications come with such collections can be found in Odella et al. (2016), Bhatt, Dey, and Ashour, 2017), and Saleh et al. (2016). Moreover, Big Data not only focuses on user data, but also provides a huge data store for machine intelligence. As an example for building an intelligent agent, Mason et al. (2015) provides a framework for building a robot that is able to mimic emotions based on collected data.

Finally, other OGM frameworks besides Hibernate OGM have to be mentioned. Here, Kundera developed by Impetus Labs (Impetus, 2016) which is also able to persist objects in many different NoSQL architectures via JPA is an example of another OGM. Furthermore, DataNucleus (2016), a framework that supports a plethora of relational as well as NoSQL architectures via JPA and JDO can be mentioned as a viable alternative to Hibernate OGM.

SUMMARY, OUTLOOK, AND FUTURE PERSPECTIVES

According to Kohler, Simov, and Specht (2015a), and Kohler and Specht (2012, 2015b), the presented security-by-distribution approach is a suitable solution to address concerns regarding security, compliance and data privacy in Cloud Computing. This work showed that the approach is also viable with NoSQL document stores. Moreover, the implemented prototype showed the feasibility of the approach in practice. Yet, the evaluation of this work revealed an inferior performance compared to a traditional non-partitioned and non-distributed Hibernate OGM implementation. In particular, create and read operations suffer from severe performance losses (factor ~11 and factor ~20 respectively), but also update and delete operations are affected (factor ~3 and factor ~2 respectively). This shows that further research work is necessary. Here already applied strategies from the relational approach like caching or query rewriting as outlined in Kohler and Specht (2015a)and Kohler, Simov, Fiech, & Specht (2015) seem to be promising.

Furthermore, it has to be stated that this work also showed the necessity of further research work to adapt the security-by-distribution approach to NoSQL architectures. First and foremost, this work was restricted to document stores and the transfer to key-value, column stores, and graph databases are still open challenges. Addressing these challenges might reveal further challenging aspects which are not obvious at first sight. This was the case in scenario 5 of this work, where the vertical partitioning and distribution approach yield to problems with the schema-freedom concerning type-safe datatypes in the application logic. Hence, as a final conclusion it can be noted that this work built the foundation to transfer the SeDiCo concept to NoSQL architectures, but also revealed further open research questions which have to be addressed in the near future to fully exploit the advantages of these architectures, especially in nowadays Big Data scenarios.

REFERENCES

Apache. (2016a). *Apache HBase Reference Guide*. Retrieved January 3, 2017, from https://hbase.apache.org/book.html

Apache. (2016b). *Cassandra Documentation*. Retrieved January 3, 2017, from http://cassandra.apache.org/doc/latest/

Apache Software Foundation. (2016a). *Apache HBase Website*. Retrieved October 1, 2016, from http://hbase.apache.org/

Apache Software Foundation. (2016b). *Hadoop MapReduce Tutorial*. Retrieved October 1, 2016, from https://hadoop.apache.org/docs/r1.2.1/mapred_tutorial.html

Banerjee, C., Kundu, A., Basu, M., Deb, P., Nag, D., & Dattagupta, R. (2013). A service based trust management classifier approach for cloud security. *2013 15th International Conference on Advanced Computing Technologies (ICACT)*, 1–5. http://doi.org/ doi:10.1109/ICACT.2013.6710519

Baumgarten, M., Mulvenna, M. D., Rooney, N., Reid, J., Jansen, B. J., Zhang, M., & Hoffmann, P. et al. (2013). Keyword-Based Sentiment Mining using Twitter. *International Journal of Ambient Computing and Intelligence*, 5(2), 56–69. doi:10.4018/jaci.2013040104

Bhatt, C., Dey, N., & Ashour, A. S. (2017). *Internet of Things and Big Data Technologies for Next Generation Healthcare*. Springer-Verlag New York Inc. doi:10.1007/978-3-319-49736-5

Brewer, E. A. (2000). Towards robust distributed systems. In *Proceedings of the nineteenth annual ACM symposium on Principles of distributed computing - PODC '00* (p. 7). http://doi.org/ doi:10.1145/343477.343502

Cloud Security Alliance. (2013). *Cloud Computing Vulnerability Incidents: A Statistical Overview : Cloud Security Alliance*. Retrieved June 17, 2015, from https://cloudsecurityalliance.org/download/cloud-computing-vulnerability-incidents-a-statistical-overview/

Codd, E. F. (1970). A relational model of data for large shared data banks. *Communications of the ACM*, 13(6), 377–387. doi:10.1145/362384.362685

Crockford, D. (2006). *IETF JSON RFC 4627*. Retrieved April 20, 2015, from http://tools.ietf.org/html/rfc4627

DataNucleus. (2016). *DataNucleus Website*. Retrieved October 1, 2016, from http://www.datanucleus.com/

Dey, N., & Santhi, V. (Eds.). (2017). *Intelligent Techniques in Signal Processing for Multimedia Security* (Vol. 660). Cham: Springer International Publishing. doi:10.1007/978-3-319-44790-2_16

Edlich, S., Friedland, A., Hampe, J., Brauer, B., & Brückner, M. (2011). *NoSQL (2nd ed.)*. Hanser Publishing. doi:10.3139/9783446428553

Furht, B., Escalante, A., Jin, H., Ibrahim, S., Bell, T., Gao, W., ... Wu, S. (2010). Handbook of cloud computing. In B. Furht & A. Escalante (Eds.), Handbook of Cloud Computing (pp. 3–19). Springer US. http://doi.org/ doi:10.1007/978-1-4419-6524-0

Gens, F., & Shirer, M. (2013). *IDC Forecasts Worldwide Public IT Cloud Services Spending to Reach Nearly $108 Billion by 2017 as Focus Shifts from Savings to Innovation*. Retrieved February 1, 2016, from http://www.idc.com/getdoc.jsp?containerId=prUS24298013

Gilbert, S., & Lynch, N. (2002). Brewers conjecture and the feasibility of consistent, available, partition-tolerant web services. *ACM SIGACT News*, *33*(2), 51–59. doi:10.1145/564585.564601

Impetus. (2016). *Kundera Website*. Retrieved October 1, 2010, from https://github.com/impetus-open-source/Kundera

Ireland, C., Bowers, D., Newton, M., & Waugh, K. (2009). A Classification of Object-Relational Impedance Mismatch. In *2009 First International Conference on Advances in Databases, Knowledge, and Data Applications* (pp. 36-43). IEEE. doi:10.1109/DBKDA.2009.11

Jain, A., Bhatnagar, V., Al-Jarrah, O. Y., Yoo, P. D., Muhaidat, S., Karagiannidis, G. K., & Misra, R. K. et al. (2016). Olympics Big Data Prognostications. *International Journal of Rough Sets and Data Analysis*, *3*(4), 32–45. doi:10.4018/IJRSDA.2016100103

Jain, A., Bhatnagar, V., Chen, M., Mao, S., Liu, Y., Frings, S., & Santhi, V. et al. (2016). Movie Analytics for Effective Recommendation System using Pig with Hadoop. *International Journal of Rough Sets and Data Analysis*, *3*(2), 82–100. doi:10.4018/IJRSDA.2016040106

Juels, A., & Oprea, A. (2013). New approaches to security and availability for cloud data. *Communications of the ACM*, *56*(2), 64–64. doi:10.1145/2408776.2408793

Kohler, J., Simov, K., Fiech, A., & Specht, T. (2015). On The Performance Of Query Rewriting In Vertically Distributed Cloud Databases.*Proceedings of The International Conference Advanced Computing for Innovation ACOMIN 2015.*

Kohler, J., Simov, K., & Specht, T. (2015a). Analysis of the Join Performance in Vertically Distributed Cloud Databases. *International Journal of Adaptive, Resilient and Autonomic Systems*, *1*(2). doi:10.4018/IJARAS

Kohler, J., Simov, K., & Specht, T. (2015b). Analysis of the Join Performance in Vertically Distributed Cloud Databases. *International Journal of Adaptive, Resilient and Autonomic Systems*, *6*(2), 65–87. doi:10.4018/IJARAS.2015070104

Kohler, J., & Specht, T. (2012). SeDiCo - Towards a Framework for a Secure and Distributed Datastore in the Cloud.*Proceedings of Chip-to-Cloud Security Forum 2012.*

Kohler, J., & Specht, T. (2015a). Analysis of Cache Implementations in a Vertically Distributed Cloud Data Store.*Proceedings of the 3rd IEEE World Conference on Complex System*. doi:10.1109/ ICoCS.2015.7483294

Kohler, J., & Specht, T. (2015b). Performance Analysis of Vertically Partitioned Data in Clouds Through a Client-Based In-Memory Key-Value Store Cache. In *Proceedings of the 8th International Conference on Computational Intelligence in Security for Information Systems*. Burgos, Spain: Springer. doi:10.1007/978-3-319-19713-5_1

Lakshman, A., & Malik, P. (2010). Cassandra: A decentralized structured storage system. *Operating Systems Review, 44*(2), 35. doi:10.1145/1773912.1773922

Mason, C., Benson, H., Lehmann, J., Malhotra, M., Goldman, R., Hopkins, J., & Ochsner, K. N. et al. (2015). Engineering Kindness. *International Journal of Synthetic Emotions, 6*(1), 1–23. doi:10.4018/ IJSE.2015010101

Mell, P., & Grance, T. (2011, September). *The NIST Definition of Cloud Computing*. Retrieved February 1, 2016, from http://csrc.nist.gov/publications/nistpubs/800-145/SP800-145.pdf

Mohanpurkar, A. A., Joshi, M. S., Agrawal, R., Haas, P., Kiernan, J., Blayer, O., & Waghmode, V. V. et al. (2016). A Traitor Identification Technique for Numeric Relational Databases with Distortion Minimization and Collusion Avoidance. *International Journal of Ambient Computing and Intelligence, 7*(2), 114–137. doi:10.4018/IJACI.2016070106

MongoDB. (2016a). *MongoDB Documentation*. Retrieved January 3, 2017, from https://docs.mongodb. com/

MongoDB. (2016b). *MongoDB Website*. Retrieved October 1, 2016, from https://www.mongodb.org/

Moniruzzaman, B. M., & Hossain, S. A. (2013). NoSQL Database: New Era of Databases for Big data Analytics - Classification, Characteristics and Comparison. *CoRR, 6*(4), 14.

Neo4j. (2016). *Neo4j Documentation*. Retrieved January 3, 2017, from https://neo4j.com/docs/

Neo Technology Incorporation. (2016). *Neo4J Website*. Retrieved October 1, 2016, from https://neo4j.com/

Neves, B. A., Correia, M. P., Bruno, Q., Fernando, A., & Paulo, S. (2013). DepSky: Dependable and secure storage in a cloud-of-clouds. *ACM Transactions on Storage, 9*(4), 31–46. doi:10.1145/2535929

NoSQL Archive. (2016). *NoSQL Archive Website*. Retrieved February 1, 2016, from http://nosql-databases.org/

Odella, F., Adamic, L., Adar, E., Adkins, B., Smith, D., Barnett, K., & Wigg, J. M. et al. (2016). Technology Studies and the Sociological Debate on Monitoring of Social Interactions. *International Journal of Ambient Computing and Intelligence, 7*(1), 1–26. doi:10.4018/IJACI.2016010101

Oracle. (2014). *JSR 221: JDBCTM 4.0 API Specification*. Retrieved February 1, 2016, from https://jcp. org/en/jsr/detail?id=221

Pettey, C., & Goasduff, L. (2011). *Gartner Says Solving "Big Data" Challenge Involves More Than Just Managing Volumes of Data*. Retrieved from http://www.gartner.com/newsroom/id/1731916

RedHat. (2015). *Getting started with Hibernate OGM*. Retrieved February 1, 2016, from http://hibernate. org/ogm/documentation/getting-started/

RedHat. (2016a). *Hibernate OGM Documentation*. Retrieved October 1, 2016, from http://hibernate. org/ogm/documentation/

RedHat. (2016b). *ORM Hibernate Documentation*. Retrieved February 1, 2016, from http://hibernate. org/orm/documentation/5.0/

Redislab. (2016). *Redis Website*. Retrieved October 1, 2016, from http://redis.io/

Ripon, S., Kamal, S., Hossain, S., Dey, N., Abraham, H. O. A., Ashrafi, M., & Gao, W. et al. (2016). Theoretical Analysis of Different Classifiers under Reduction Rough Data Set. *International Journal of Rough Sets and Data Analysis*, *3*(3), 1–20. doi:10.4018/IJRSDA.2016070101

Saleh, E., & Meinel, C. (2013). HPISecure: Towards data confidentiality in cloud applications. In *Proceedings - 13th IEEE/ACM International Symposium on Cluster, Cloud, and Grid Computing, CCGrid 2013* (pp. 605–609). http://doi.org/ doi:10.1109/CCGrid.2013.109

Saleh, M. A., Awada, A., Belnap, N., Perloff, M., Bonnefon, J.-F., Longin, D., & Casacuberta, D. et al. (2016). A Logical Model for Narcissistic Personality Disorder. *International Journal of Synthetic Emotions*, *7*(1), 69–87. doi:10.4018/IJSE.2016010106

Sang, T. (2013). A log-based approach to make digital forensics easier on cloud computing. In *Proceedings of the 2013 3rd International Conference on Intelligent System Design and Engineering Applications, ISDEA 2013* (pp. 91–94). http://doi.org/ doi:10.1109/ISDEA.2012.29

Sood, S. K. (2012). A combined approach to ensure data security in cloud computing. *Journal of Network and Computer Applications*, *35*(6), 1831–1838. doi:10.1016/j.jnca.2012.07.007

Tchepnda, C., Moustafa, H., Labiod, H., & Bourdon, G. (2009). Vehicular Networks Security. *International Journal of Ambient Computing and Intelligence*, *1*(1), 39–52. doi:10.4018/jaci.2009010104

TPC. (2003). *TPC Benchmark W (Web Commerce) Specification Version 2.0r*. Retrieved February 1, 2016, from http://www.tpc.org/tpcw/default.asp

Wang, B., Chow, S. S. M., Li, M., & Li, H. (2013). Storing shared data on the cloud via security-mediator. In *Proceedings - International Conference on Distributed Computing Systems* (pp. 124–133). http://doi. org/ doi:10.1109/ICDCS.2013.60

Wang, C., Chow, S. S. M., Wang, Q., Ren, K., & Lou, W. (2013). Privacy-preserving public auditing for secure cloud storage. *IEEE Transactions on Computers*, *62*(2), 362–375. doi:10.1109/TC.2011.245

Yildiz, M., Abawajy, J., Ercan, T., & Bernoth, A. (2009). A layered security approach for cloud computing infrastructure. In *I-SPAN 2009 - The 10th International Symposium on Pervasive Systems, Algorithms, and Networks* (pp. 763–767). http://doi.org/ doi:10.1109/I-SPAN.2009.157

Zappi, P., Lombriser, C., Benini, L., Tröster, G., Baldauf, M., Dustdar, S., & Starner, T. E. et al. (2010). Collecting Datasets from Ambient Intelligence Environments. *International Journal of Ambient Computing and Intelligence*, *2*(2), 42–56. doi:10.4018/jaci.2010040103

KEY TERMS AND DEFINITIONS

JDO: Java Data Objects is a commonly known persistence framework that abstracts from an implementation-specific database dialect such that concrete database systems can be exchanged without modifying the application logic.

JPA: Java Persistence Application Programming Interface is a commonly known persistence framework that abstracts from an implementation-specific database dialect such that concrete database systems can be exchanged without modifying the application logic.

JSON: Java Script Object Notation is a key:value notation that is used as a successor to XML as a meta and description language.

Security-By-Distribution: Aims at establishing a certain level of security and privacy with the separation of logically coherent data and their storage at different locations.

Chapter 6
Selective Data Consistency Model in No-SQL Data Store

Shraddha Pankaj Phansalkar
Symbiosis International University, India

Ajay Dani
G. H. Raisoni Institute of Technology, India

ABSTRACT

Contemporary web-applications are deployed on the cloud data-stores for realizing requirements like low latency and high scalability. Although cloud-based database applications exhibit high performance with these features, they compromise on the weaker consistency levels. Rationing the consistency guarantees of an application is a necessity to achieve the augmented metrics of application performance. The proposed work is a paradigm shift from monotonic transaction consistency to selective data consistency in web database applications. The selective data consistency model leverages consistency of critical data-objects and leaves consistency of non-critical data-objects to underlying cloud data-store; it is called selective consistency and it results in better performance of the cloud-based applications. The consistency of the underlying data-object is defined from user-perspective with a user-friendly consistency metric called Consistency Index (CI). The selective data consistency model is implemented on a cloud data-store with OLTP workload and the performance is gauged.

INTRODUCTION

Commercial big data stores and big data analytics have become popular among enterprises because of their assurance of providing unlimited scalability and availability. Their application is from areas like emotion and sentiment analysis (Alvandi, 2011) to daily monitoring of urban traffic (Meier and Lee, 2009). Database applications in the cloud environment are required to be available 24x7 to serve the demands of the users across the globe. The databases of such applications are simulated across the world to guarantee high accessibility of data, low latency time and cost of accessibility. The CAP theorem (Brewer, 2000) states that the provision of strong consistency plus high scalability simultaneously, is improbable in the existence of network partitioning. The state-of-the-art web applications compromise

DOI: 10.4018/978-1-5225-2486-1.ch006

data consistencies to a definite level and thus attain high performance and availability. The design of the databases of these web applications can be considered as an optimization problem (Redding et al., 2009), where the desired performance level is achieved with optimized levels of consistency. This work introduces user perspective of data consistency and measures it by a comprehensive quantitative metric known as Consistency Index (CI). Any user can realize his consistency requirements objectively, if consistency is quantitatively measured and indexed (by some index measure). It must be a simple, flexible metric that is independent of application. It is supposed to be such, which can have applicability to database objects with different granularity from attributes (i.e. database fields) and database rows (objects) to database tables (collection). This metric realizes the user perspective of consistency. CI can be used to develop intelligent transaction scheduling strategies which can optimize the performance of applications.

No-SQL data stores offer the augmented metrics of performance with different levels of consistency and lower isolation levels. Table 1 shows the summary of the popular No-SQL data stores with respect to consistency, replication, availability, fault tolerance and scalability guarantees.

Consistency of data is the consensus of the data across multiple copies (replicas) in the system in the replicated databases (Padhye, 2014). This is the database perspective of the data consistency problem. However, in contemporary web applications, maintaining strict consistency throughout the database is difficult, if requirements like low query response time and high availability of data are to be achieved with higher priority. Besides these, security and privacy of huge data sets against intrusive threats is elucidated in works by Mohanpurkar and Joshi (2016), Fouad et al. (2016) and Odella (2016) which poses a new challenge to big data world. The articles like Curran et al. (2014) also emphasize on related techniques and tools to carry location based tracking of objects in different environments

CAP theorem by Brewer (2000) states that consistency and availability are inversely proportional in a partitioned system. Hence consistency needs to be rationed to weaker levels in case of web applications with high availability requirements. The positive impact of consistency rationing (accepting weaker levels of consistency) on the system performance has been studied in Koroush (1995).

The idea of tradeoff between consistency, response time and high availability has been proposed in (Redding et al., 2009). All the levels of consistency like sequential, serializable, eventual, release consistency are discussed for replicated distributed database systems in transactional as well as non-transactional context. The researchers have planned different approaches to ration consistency and progress the performance of web-based functions in transactional or non-transactional circumstance.

Use of replicated data stores is mandatory for improving application performance with respect to availability and reliability. Consistency rationing is thus highly desirable in replicated data stores.

In Olston and Widom (2000), the authors have proposed a replicated system which works on a combination of thresholds in cache and server data to deliver an answer in tolerable limit. Here a transaction query is attributed with the bounds of staleness to which the system must abide.

Haifeng and Vahdat, in 2002 developed a consistency model to describe data consistency in replicated objects using a new metric called conit which is a combination of three measures viz value error, sequence error and correctness for the replicated data. In this work, a middleware layer that managed consistency bounds among replicated data objects was built with these metrics.

Zhang and Zhang (2003) propose Window Based Quantitative Model, which expresses inconsistency as the proportion of non-consensus in writes. The system specifies the tolerable number of missed updates as the consistency rationing mechanism.

A probabilistic approach uses subset of replicas to find threshold limit of inconsistency with respect to both version number of the replicas and physical time, this is provided by the theory of Probabilisti-

Table 1. Performance of No-SQL data stores

NOSQL Data Store	Consistency	Replication System	Availability	Fault Tolerance	Scalability
MongoDB Open Source Document Oriented	All writes and reads happen through primary by default. Default consistency level is higher. "Read-concern" and "write concern" levels are used to adapt the levels of consistency and availability	Default Replication Factor: 3 Primary-Secondary Architecture	3 replica set of any data in the cluster exists to guarantee availability	There is automatic fail over mechanism where the secondary takes over when the primary fails	Data partitioning (sharding)
Amazon SimpleDB Document oriented	Eventual consistency by default	Replication Factor: 3 Truly distributed replication system	Auto replication to 3 replicas of *domains*	Higher as even if one replica fails, data can be fetched from distant replica	Poor
Apache Cassandra Open source Key value data store	Tunable consistency, Quorum based consensus with Paxos algorithm	Tunable replication factor. Multiple nodes that contain the replicated data in the cluster	Highly available with multiple replicas	Fault tolerant within the data center	Higher with horizontal scalability with cheaper commodity hardware
Apache HBase Column oriented key value data store	Strong read-write consistency	Hadoop replication system in terms of block replication	Highly available for read operations	Highly fault tolerant with Hadoop architecture	Highly Scalable

cally Bounded Staleness (PBS). This has been projected in Bailis et al. (2012). The proportion of non-agreed updates on a replicated data object is used to measure inconsistency as proposed by Kraska et al. (2009). This work also applies consistency to the data attributes individually and presents how biased data consistency applied to an online web application helps to improve the performance with respect to cost. Our work proposes a novel concept to database administrators to define the consistency guarantees on the data than at transaction level. It advocates a consistency rationing model where consistency is selectively enforced on data.

On the similar lines, the proposed work is a paradigm shift from transaction consistency to data consistency, treating critical data with strict consistency and less critical data with weak consistency.

Many data stores ranging from relational SQL databases to No-SQL data stores like Cassandra (2016), Amazon SimpleDB (2016), allow the user to apply these consistency constraints to transactions. In No-SQL data stores, the data is granulized as entity groups like Megastore (Baker et al., 2011), htables in HBase (George, 2011), domains in Simple DB (Amazon SimpleDB, 2016). The consistency constraints are applied to the data groups. This can be exploited for selectivity of consistency protocol where critical data groups are strictly observed. This is a paradigm shift of looking at data consistency. In this shift, consistency is characteristic of data and not of a database transaction.

Consistency as a Service (Wang and Wu, 2014) has been presented in a strategy of auditing cloud consistency across multiple replicated data objects with an extra layer of audit cloud, which monitors the consistency guarantees over the cloud data. The audit process is done at local node level as well as globally across all the nodes. The local audit aims to promise the consistency at the customer-centric consistency level that is specified and is either monotonic reads, read-your own-writes and so on. The global audit is an expensive process and carried out offline periodically using graph based methods of tracing dependency.

Ogunyadeka et al. (2016) proposed multi key transaction model for big data stores. This system claims support to standard transaction and high level of consistency in No-SQL environment. The working model of this system has an extra layer in architecture to manage the data transactions. The prototype is validated using MongoDB and results into stronger consistency and good performance with Transaction Processing Engine (TPE), Data Management Store (DMS) and Time-Stamp Manager (TSM) to evaluate as transaction overhead and consistency.

Marcos K. Aguilera and Douglas B Terry (2016) brief about two types of consistencies as state consistency which is concerned about the state of the database which is affected by operations, failures, faults and so on whereas operation consistency which gives properties that operation returns correct results or not. Operation consistency is achieved at many levels of consistency from read your write level to the strongest level of Serializability. The paper is an exhaustive survey of the levels of consistency that many research works and their models guarantee.

The use of predictive data analytics is proposed in many recent research works like (Jain and Bhatnagar, 2016 a) and (Jain and Bhatnagar, 2016b) in the fields of entertainment. Many significant works like (Ripon et al.,2016) and (Baumgarten, 2013) propose statistical methods for classifying large rough data sets. The work (Kausar et al.,2016) presents the role of optimized data mining and classification algorithms in the accurate diagnosis of diseases like cardiac strokes and cancer. The role of statistical approaches and genetic algorithm to classify the larger number of abstracts in Mediline have been elucidated in (Karaa et al., 2016) and a comprehensive classification of mining algorithms in image processing is represented in (Dey et al.,2015).

The data consistency is described from user perspective and the work develops the definition of consistency index.

CONSISTENCY IN REPLICATED DATA-STORE: DATA CHARACTERISTIC AND FUNCTION OF DATA CRITICALITY

It is observed that not all data attributes have same consistency requirements. Their criticality and importance to the business may be different and their cost of inconsistency may also be different. As an example one can consider banking transactions. A customer's address will not change as frequently as the balance in his account. The consistency requirement of account balance is more stringent compared to customer address data. In case of withdrawal transaction at any instant of time t, the latest updated and correct balance amount should be available. If this does not happen, it can pose serious problems to the bank (like possible legal action by customer or compensating customer for any loss etc.). In case of account balance, the balance has to change immediately and the next transaction may occur immediately. The change of address transaction and any subsequent queries on customer address, can possibly read non-updated data. An incorrect read on account balance may lead to catastrophic results. Thus there is a scope of need of a consistency model which discriminates the data on the basis of its criticality. Secondly consistency is costly affair. Maintaining stringent levels of consistency (like serializable isolation level) for all the data objects causes substantial loss in performance (Brewer, 2000).

Criticality of data can be formulated in different ways. It is generally a function of frequency of its access as well as frequency of updates as described in the legendary works by (Chu and Leong, 1993) to the recent works by (Huang and Lai, 2016). It is also defined as the frequency of conflicted access to the data objects (Kraska et al., 2009). However for this work, the criticality of every data object is stated by the application developer.

In cloud or web-based transactional applications, a large number of transactions occur simultaneously and the replicated data-store gets updated frequently. Maintaining higher levels of consistency of a critical data object is a challenge when response time and scalability are to be achieved. Selective data consistency treats these data objects effectively while allowing lower levels of consistency to work on the not-so-critical data-objects.

The traditional levels of consistency in SQL are reviewed to further map our perspective with these levels.

Isolation Levels of Consistency in Relational Databases

In Relational Database Management System (RDBMS), transaction integrity is referred by the concept of Isolation (Tanenbaum and Van, 2007). Data isolation in RDBMS is all about transactions. The queries retrieve data consistency and its correctness. As per the necessity of consistency in RDBMS, there are four levels of isolation as given below:

Relational databases are transactional in nature and the SQL isolation levels tune the degree to which one transaction must be isolated from data modifications made by other transactions.

- Read Uncommitted is the first isolation level. In this level, read is permitted on a row with or without write lock. There is no guarantee that concurrent transaction will not modify a row or roll back changes done to a row. It allows dirty reads, non-repeatable reads, and phantom reads.
- Read Committed is the second Isolation level. Read is only permitted on committed data. Write lock is acquired and held for read on current row only, but released when cursor moves off the row. There is no guarantee that data will remain unchanged during transaction. It prevents dirty reads and allows non-repeatable reads and phantom reads.
- Repeatable read is the third isolation level. There is row lock acquired as each row in the result set is read and held until transaction ends. It prevents dirty reads and non-repeatable reads and allows phantom reads.
- Serializable is the strongest isolation level and transactions occur in a completely isolated fashion. There is table lock which prevents from dirty reads, non–repeatable reads and phantom reads.

The read phenomena consistency with these isolation levels is depicted in the Table 2.

Table 2. SQL Isolation levels and read phenomena

Isolation Level	Read (Uncommitted)	Read (Committed)	Read (Repeatable)	Serializable
Consistency	Dirty read	Non repeatable reads, phantom read	Phantom read	No
Response time	Less	Standard	Standard	Higher

Client Centric Levels of Consistency

Processor centric consistency is usually difficult to perceive. In database applications where there is less conflict, client-centric consistency models (Padhye, 2014) are used to describe the requirements of consistency.

1. **Eventual Consistency:** This level of consistency is a weaker consistency model in the system where there is lesser number of updates. It states that all the replicas will eventually converge.
2. **Monotonic Read Consistency:** If a process p reads the value of a data item x, a read operation on x by that p will always return that same value or a more recent value of x.
3. **Monotonic Write Consistency:** A final update must be agreed upon. All writes on X must follow an order of occurrence.
4. **Read-Your-Write Consistency:** A value written by a process on a data item X will be always available to a successive read operation performed by the same process on data item X.
5. **Writes-Follows-Reads Consistency:** In writes-follow-reads consistency, updates are propagated after performing the previous read operations. A write operation by a process on a data item x following a previous read operation on x by the same process is guaranteed to take place on the same or a more recent value of x that was read.

Data Validation in No-SQL Data Stores

In No-SQL data stores, enforcing data validation rules is an overhead on application development. Although the relational SQL databases offer higher data integrity with data validation, they are equally expensive when availability, replication and scalability are important. Some No-SQL databases offer limited data validation mechanisms. Some of them automatically append the _id in the document which offers uniqueness feature like primary key constraint in the relational databases. PostgreSQL (PostgreSQL, 2016) offers the validation constraints on the data fields in the JSON data structure. Even MongoDB offers data validation for uniqueness in the name space, correctness of data within a collection with validate function (MongoDB, 2016). RethinkDB (RethinkDB, 2016) is JSON database where validate. js offers data validation on strings to find its correctness and completeness.

Application Level Security in No-SQL Data Stores

No-SQL data stores are used to build scalable applications and hence deployed on cloud. As the cloud applications allow usage through internet, they are not built to make applications secure. Kerberos authentication is available for securing the data stores with access control techniques. Encrypting critical data, keeping non-encrypted data in a controlled environment, authentication techniques also foster the data store security. MongoDB supports the security with authentication, authorization with encryption as the standard security measures (MongoDB, 2016). Apache Cassandra offers encryption in network communication although the data at rest is unencrypted. Cassandra Query Language (CQL) can be also used to manage user accounts. Some service providers like Cloudera and Datastax offer the secured variants of their offered No-SQL data-stores. However security of the applications on No-SQL data stores opens a wide area of research problems.

User Perspective of Selective Data Consistency Model

The No-SQL data stores guarantee client centric data consistency models as they are less costly to maintain. Amazon SimpleDB (Amazon SimpleDB, 2016) guarantees eventual consistency level whereas MongoDB (MongoDB, 2016) guarantees stronger levels of consistency by default. This is because MongoDB is a single-master system and all reads and updates go to the primary by default. However, the user is interested to know; if his queries are answered with the most updated and agreed upon values within specified performance limits. That is, the user does not encounter stale reads. As well as the reads on any replica should return a data that is agreed upon by all (majority) of the replicas, which ensures stricter levels of consistency.

A close look at the anatomy of update operation in replicated database suggests that in case of replicated databases, an update transaction occurring on one replica, at an instant of time, would get propagated to other replicas (Tanenbaum and Van, 2007). This update transaction will be reflected on all other replicas after some time gap that is at instance (t+d). Once the update transaction is propagated to all other replicas, the database will be in consistent state. The update will propagate to other replicas at different instances of time during time interval [t, t+d]. During this interval a read operation on the replica where the update transaction has propagated will read the most updated data. It will read stale data, if it occurs on replica, where the update transaction has not propagated. In case of the user reading the data at any instant of time t, a read is a "fresh read" if it reads the most updated data, whereas a read is "stale read" if it reads the stale data. Now a fresh read may rollback if it is an uncommitted read that is dirty read. Thus a fresh read which is agreed upon by all (majority) of the replicas is a correct read. Every other read is incorrect read. This is the user perspective of consistency.

Detection of Incorrectness in Read

Let there be n replicas R1, R2, R3… Rn (where n ∈ I, n>1) of databases in case of web based or cloud application. A sequence of read and update transactions (in any order) occur in such applications. An update transaction can add a new object in one or more collection of data objects (insert operation) or may change value/values of one or more elements in data objects (update operation). It may also result in deletion of one or more objects from the data objects' collection. A read operation will retrieve data from one or more data objects. A close look at the anatomy of reads and writes on databases, shows that generally an object in the database will be read first and then updated. It is argued that an update/insert/delete operation in database is always preceded by read operation.

Suppose that a sequence of transactions ST (t1,t2)={TR1, TR2,TR3,…,TRm} occurs in a web based cloud applications consisting of n database replicas between time interval [t1,t2]. TRi (i=1, 2,..,m) can be a read (R) or update transaction (U). As explained before, it is a realistic assumption that a read and update transaction can occur at any instant of time with equal probability. In a fully replicated distributed system (like cloud or web based applications), a read and update transactions TRi (i = 1,2,..,m) should occur simultaneously on any replica Rj (j = 1,2,3,…n) to make certain not only high availability but also quick response time. While another replica Rj is updated, the modification (an insert, delete or change of values of attributes) is propagated to all other replicas Ri (i= 1, 2, 3…, n and i ≠ j) in the system. After the update is propagated on the other (n-1) replicas, the database will be in consistent state. This will be called as convergence of replicas. The update to the replicas may be propagated immediately (atomicity) or with some time delay (no-atomicity).

Suppose that a transaction TRi from sequence ST (t1,t2) occurs at an instant of time t (where t1 $\leq$ t<t2). At time instant (t+d), it is propagated to all the n replicas (d>0). In other words, d is the time required for update to propagate to all other (n-1) replicas. Then a read occurring on replica Ri (i=1, 2, 3,…,n) at instant of time t + tr (where tr<d) can be an stale or fresh read. It will be a fresh read if it occurs on replica Ri, where the update has propagated and will be stale read, in case the update has not propagated to the replica Rj (j≠i). This time interval (t, t+d) is defined as unsafe period.

This period is an unsafe period because a read occurring in this period will be an incorrect read (by our definition). Our approach finds out the number of incorrect reads by enumerating the occurrence of the reads in the unsafe period.

Correct Read and Incorrect Read

Suppose that the latest update transaction (U) has occurred on replicated data object at replica Rj (j = 1, 2, 3…M). After U, a read transaction (R) on the replicated data object at any other replica R_k (k=1, 2, 3… M and k≠j) occurs such that no other update transaction occurs between U and R. Thus the Time stamp (U) <Time stamp(R).

Then R will be a correct read if all of the following occur:

- R reads what is written by U that is fresh read.
- Time Stamp(R) > t+d where d is the period of convergence for the M- replicated data object that is the read is committed read.

Suppose that the latest update transaction (U) has occurred on replicated data object at replica Rj (j = 1, 2, 3…M). After U, a read transaction (R) on the replicated data object at any other replica Rk (k=1, 2, 3… M and k≠j) occurs such that no other update transaction occurs between U and R. Thus the Time stamp (U) <Time stamp(R).

Then R will be a correct read if any one or all of the following occur:

1. R does not read what is written by U that is stale read.
2. Time Stamp(R) <= t+d where d is the period of convergence for the M-replicated data object that is the read is uncommitted read.

Statistical Read Classifier: Incorrect/Correct Read

A read operation is defined as incorrect read if it falls in the unsafe period. "d" is the value of time-gap amid read operation and the prior update operation.

Here a problem of finding the threshold value (T_g) of d for a M-replicated data object is presented so that Time-Gap must be interspersed in the read and the previous update so as to assure its correctness. The classifier can be constructed with the output as either correct read /incorrect read.

The output (O) of the read on a data object implies that the read on a data object is in one of the states: correct read (1) state or incorrect read (0) state. For a data object D_o, it is predicted with the parameters as follows:

1.   Replication factor (R_p) of D_o.
2.   The latency period (T_g) between the preceding read and successive update on the data-object D_o.

In the work by (Kamal et al., 2016) statistical methods and data mining techniques are used to draw inferences/ relations for distributed system based applications.

A statistical read classifier for the data object is built and the results of the read classifier on all the nine data objects from Transaction Processing Benchmark –C (TPCC) are presented here. As a sample case, the results of stock data object are presented here.

Data-store Amazon SimpleDB (Amazon SimpleDB, 2016) is used and every data-object is mapped to a domain in SimpleDB. Every data-object is replicated with R_p replicas (1 to 10).A read operation on the stock-item is sent to the stock domain after varying the values of Time-gap (T_g) connecting a read and a previous update. The yield of a read request is observed (0/1) by changeable R_p and T_g of the stock data object. The training data set is consequently formed by the triplet (R_p, T_g, O). Then a classifier predicts the correctness of an incoming read request for a specified value of time-gap (T_g) along with replication factor (R_p) of a simulated data object using Logistic Regressive Classifier and Neural Network Classifier depicted as follows:

Workload Read Classifier With Logistic Regression

In Logistic Regression, the yield of read is definite that is updated value (1) or stale value (0). For this reason it is recommended to make use of Logistic Regressive Classifier. The Regression analysis was run on the data set collected as explained over. R_p is represented as a covariate as the classifier exhibited a distinctive performance in the O over the group of data sets with common value of replication factor with change in latency. The test statistic is X2 with G-2 degrees of freedom where G is number of groups. Therefore (dof) degree of freedom in Table 3 is 8 which is 2 less than the number of groups. The p-statistic is revealed to be 0.00. Hence the significance of statistical inferences is revealed. In this model fit, the key factor is pseudo R^2 which is an estimate of correlation explicated by the model. It is 0.54 in the results. Nagelkerke's R^2 is 0.79 in the results which means considerable goodness of fit.

Table 3. CI for stock: model summary of logistic regressive read classifier

Step		-2 Log Likelihood	Cox and Snell R Square	Repeatable Read
		74.892	0.592	0.790
Hosmer and Lemeshow Test				
		Chi-square	Number of groups	Significance.
		54.346	8	0.000
Classification Table				
		Predicted Output		Correct Percentage
Experimental Output		0	1	
	0	152	18	89.4
	1	18	171	90.5
General percentage				90.0

The correctness of this regression model is shown by the classification table. The predictive model has given the classification rate as 90% with this classification model, which means that the read operation in the workload is classified into correct read (1) or Incorrect read category (0) is classified to 90% after the application R_p and T_g. The classification model is made statistically significant by this.

Workload Read Classifier Using Radial Basis Function Neural Network (RBFNN)

The recent research works (Kamal et al., 2016) have proved that neural networks outperform other prediction models with efficient removal of redundant data. Radial Basis Functions are always proven better than neural networks like multilayer perceptron layer. Besides being robust in their architecture, RBFNN offer quicker training times. They also offer better accuracy over other neural networks when the input data is susceptible to uncertainties and adversible errors. Being non-linear classification of data, they are built with three layers and typically one hidden layer and offer non-linear activation functions and Gaussian distribution. Other feedforward networks are susceptible to the problem of local minima as against RBFNN adds bias to the weights.

The (RBFNN) Radial Basis Function Neural Network (Schalkoff, 1997) performs prediction and classification in two stages using clustering methods and uses least square regression method to minimize the sum-of-squares error. Radial Basis Function is utilized to model the relationship of correct read with the same predictor variables as planned in the commencement of this section. The data set is also retained. The latency in the read-update pair (T_g) is applied as predictor and the replication factor (R_p) as covariate. The input workload is offered as 60% data for training the model and 40% for testing the model. The error (SSE) of data is 1.953 and the percent incorrect predictions of test data is 8.3%. The efficiency of classification is found as 91.7%. The Mean-Squared Error (MSE) is calculated with sum of square error, degree of freedom and the number of cases. MSE is reached to 0.22. The readings of (RBF) Radial Basis Function based output predictor is revealed in the Table 4.

With the statistical read classifier, every incoming read on a data-object can be classified into "correct"/ "incorrect" read.

Table 4. CI for stock: model summary of RBFNN read classifier

Training	SSE total		9.748	
	Percent Incorrectness		37%	
Testing	SSE total		1.953	
	Percent Incorrectness		8.3%	
Categorization				
Model	**Actual**		**Predicted**	
Training	0	0	1	Percent Correct
	1	11	9	55.0%
	Percent	7	16	69.6%
Testing	0	4	0	100.0%
	1	1	7	87.5%
	Percent	41.7%	58.3%	**91.7%**

Consistency Index

A quantitative metric is presented to describe the correctness of operations carried out by a user on a data-object. Consistency Index (CI (O, t)) of a n- replicated data object O for time period t is defined as the ratio of number of correct reads on data object O during time period t across all n replicas to the entire number of reads on data object O during period t across all n replicas. It can be expressed as follows

$$CI\left(O,t\right) = \frac{Number\ of\ Correct\ Reads\ on\ O\ during\ time\ period\ t}{Total\ number\ of\ Reads\left(R\right)\ on\ O\ during\ time\ period\ t} \tag{1}$$

CI is a ratio of correct reads on a data object to total number of reads. It is a value between [0, 1] where 0 implies incorrect reads and thus guarantees no consistency. The value one implies correct reads and thus the strongest level of consistency. The values which are closer to one imply higher consistency in the observed time period.

Properties of Consistency Index

CI offers many advantages over existing metrics of consistency. It is an application independent metric that requires no reference for comparison. It does not require inter-replica communication and can be periodically calculated by a central data manager which can be implemented at data access object or data access interface. CI (O, t) is a property of data object O and not of an application, hence can be applied to the selected data. Its properties are as follows:

1. It can be defined on data objects like data attribute, row, set of rows in a database table, a column of database, set of columns of database table and database tables. It will be the ratio of correct reads to the total number of reads for corresponding data object during the specified time period.
2. The time period t can be a cumulative that is $0 < t < t_1$, the number of reads occurred till time instant t_1) time interval or it can be the time interval between two time instants (i.e. $t_1 \leq t \leq t_2$).
3. Its value will lie in interval [0, 1]. The value of 0 indicates that there was no correct read during time period t and that of 1 will indicate all correct reads. The value close to one will indicate higher level of consistency and close to zero will indicate lower level of consistency.
4. The CI values for any two different data objects for the same time period t are comparable. Let O_1 and O_2 be two data objects. If condition CI (O_1, t) > CI (O_2, t) is satisfied, then it indicates that O_1 is more consistent than O_2 during time period t.
5. The CI can be defined for two or more data objects. If O_1 and O_2 are two data objects, the joint CI (O_1, O_2, t) can be defined as the ratio of number of correct reads on O_1 and O_2 across all replicas during time period t to total number of reads on O_1 and O_2 across all replicas during time period t. In this case, it is taken into account, the read transactions which read both the data objects and can be defined for more than two data objects in a similar manner.
6. Changes in CI values of different data attributes over different time intervals can possibly indicate changes in workload patterns over period of time. It is possible to obtain CI values for data attributes for different time intervals. If the value of CI changes significantly over time period (when there is no significant decrease in number of reads), it will indicate the changes in workload patterns.

The decrease in the value of CI over two time periods for a data attributes, when number of read transactions do not change significantly, will indicate increase in number of updates. So CI values will also be useful to designers to adopt their applications for dynamic environments.

The selective data consistency is implemented in an application using these properties of CI. In forthcoming section, the application of CI-based selective consistency to an online shopping web application is presented.

SQL Isolation Levels and Their Relation With CI

CI is a consistency metric of a data-object and the SQL isolation levels refer to the isolations of the transactions. Thus the effect of choosing an isolation level of the transaction is observed on the CI of the accessed data-objects. CI is presented and the latency of a read on the stock_item data-object in TPCC schema. The stock_item is accessed by semantic transactions like New_order and Stock_Level transactions which require read and update operations on the stock_item object.

The time-gap in the write-through replication policy (Padhye, 2014) are the critical factors that affect the consistency guarantees in replicated system. Hence, time-gap is varied and the number of replicas of candidate data objects. CI is observed and the resultant latency in read operations in different isolation levels.

Strong levels of isolation are implemented using locking primitives of semaphore like mutex (Tanenbaum and Van, 2007) to lock the data objects. The locking of data-objects at different levels of granularities is carried out with individual data objects or entire SimpleDB domain.

The workload is simulated using an input series of read and update operations on the candidate data-object and is generated in random manner. The workload is scheduled with the time-gap between the operations so that its effect on CI is isolated. The number of replicas of data-objects (stock_item) is varied from one to ten and the effect of replication factor of data object is observed on its CI and response time of a read.

Read Uncommitted Isolation Level

Read uncommitted level is devoid of locks, larger in incorrect reads and lower in CI.

Referring Table 5, it is observed that by means of the increase in the number of replicas, Consistency Index (CI) decreases. The correctness is at stake because of the increase in availability. It is also observed that CI increases with increase in the time-gap for a given number of replicas. It is examined that with the increase in the number of replicas, the average response time increases.

Read Committed Isolation Level

The data access synchronizes through 'acquire' and 'release' lock. The read-committed isolation level is implemented by placing the acquire lock before WRITE operation and releasing it after WRITE operation. Read operation thereby cannot simultaneously execute on the data-object. A concurrent shared lock is allowed. The granularity of the locked data item is entire replicated set of the data-object. Thus

Table 5. CI for read uncommitted level

Replication Factor	Time Gap (ms)	Average Response Time (ms)	CI
5	3000	11829	0.1
7	3000	8506	0.14
7	4000	12290	0.1
7	1000	12686	0.07
10	5000	14340	0.1
10	4000	13098	0.05

only simultaneous read-read are permitted. The users were unable to read the uncommitted data. Higher CI is observed as shown in Table 6. Although dirty reads are prevented non-repeatable and phantom reads are probable.

Repeatable Read

Repeatable read consistency anomaly is simulated with an update query on a row of stock item and synchronized insert query for a new row in stock item table (domain). The effect of this simultaneous change is prevalent when one of the queries was an aggregation of the entire table and the other query inserted a new row in the table. Although this scenario is rare to occur, the value of CI is higher. CI is measured for every data object and that is an individual row of stock item. The upshot of time-gap on the individual data-object is not significant and the CI values continue to remain higher. The effect of this isolation level on response time is adverse because all the affected rows of the table are locked in shared/ exclusive mode. The concurrency is thus very low.

Serializable Read

A lock on entire relation table (domain) has the implementation of serializable read. It thus forces serial execution of input requests so that work will be completed serially by each domain. This leads to the highest value of CI (CI=1). However it adversely affects the response time of the transactions.

Table 6. CI in read-committed level

Replication Factor	Time Gap (ms)	Standard Response Time (ms)	CI
5	3000	11829	0.5
7	4390	12352	0.9
7	4000	12382	0.6
7	5000	13254	0.9
10	5000	15822	0.9
10	4390	12352	0.9

ARCHITECTURE OF THE APPLICATION IMPLEMENTING SELECTIVE DATA CONSISTENCY MODEL

Figure 1 shows the architecture of the application of implementing selective data consistency model. In the recent works like (Grünerbl et al., 2013), challenges for deployment of real time monitoring systems on the big data sets are described. We learn from the challenges and propose the architecture.

Application Layer: The Transaction Manager(TM)

Transaction Manager (TM) manages the transactions. It has the business logic of a transaction. A TM implements a business transaction. The TM further accesses distributed data-objects on the cloud data store. Thus a transaction is divided into sub-transaction such that every sub-transaction accesses a data-object. This not only improves scalability and throughput of the application but also supports the underlying CI-based consistency model. Every sub-transaction of a transaction accesses single data-object, which is tuned to, a desired consistency level with CI. This leads to distributed transactions and consistency overhead and can be handled efficiently with an appropriate data partitioning schemes (Navathe, 1984) to the recent works using clustering based data partitioning like Huang and Lai, 2016.

This work presents a data consistency model, which is selective at data level. Hence this consistency protocol operates at Data Manager (DM) level. As distributed TM allocates a sub-transaction to a data-object, every sub-transaction as an independent request is received by Data Manager (DM) for the accessibility or revision of the underlying data-object.

Figure 1. Architecture of CI-based selective consistency model on TPCC

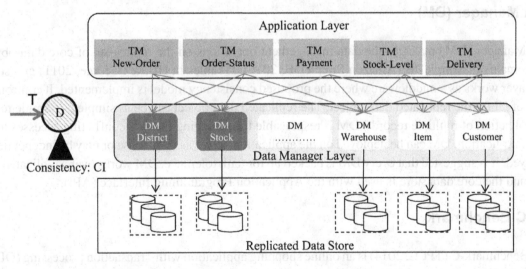

TPCC Data Objects:

1. District	4. Warehouse	7. Orders	10. New Order
2. Stock	5. History	8. Customer Name	
3. Item	6. Customer	9. Order Line	

Data Store

The data store which supports replication, can be a minor distributed file system otherwise a virtualized No-SQL data store. A data-object may be replicated to N copies. A group of N-replica for a data-object is controlled by a Data Manager (DM) of that object. The DM sets and manages the value of CI for the replicated group.

Every No-SQL data stores has different data model. Data model defines the unit of replication as well as unit of consistency enforcement. Hadoop HDFS (George, 2011) has data blocks, SimpleDB (Amazon SimpleDB, 2016) has domains, MongoDB (MongoDB, 2016) has mongo-shards.

Secondly, every commercial data store has default consistency guarantee, which is determined by synchronization techniques of replicas. Hadoop HDFS implements a Master/Slave architecture and is fit for write once and read many files. SimpleDB (Amazon SimpleDB, 2016) implements eventual consistency as well as configurable stricter levels of consistency. Cassandra (2016) implements configurable number of replicas in the read/update quorum. Most of the No-SQL data-stores have a default weaker level of consistency. This consistency model would be supplementing the existing default consistency guarantees of a data-store with A-P guarantees. The supplementary consistency guarantee is applied selectively to the critical data which can be user-defined as per the business requirements.

The proposed consistency model is tested on (Amazon SimpleDB), which has non-relational data store with high availability and flexibility. In SimpleDB, the part of replication is a domain. Default consistency level for SimpleDB (Amazon SimpleDB, 2016), is eventual consistency. This implies that change to one of the replicas will be eventually made to other replicas. An access request is also generally directed to the nearest replica. Thus in a web-application, user-request may be directed to any replica and thus read operations possibly will drop in the insecure period. These are specified as incorrect reads.

Data Manager (DM)

Data Manager (DM) manages the data management operations on the replica-set of core data-objects like domains in SimpleDB (Amazon SimpleDB, 2016), HTables in HBase (George, 2011) and so on. This layer works as a middleware where the proposed consistency model is implemented. It controls the value of CI for the replicated data-object. The replicated data-object can be as simple as a single record or a collection of multiple records. DM is responsible for managing the non-conflicting accesses to the unit of replication. DM can be deployed on the application server as in our case or may be independently deployed. It is suggested that every DM is backed up for fault tolerance. DM works over a replicated data store and the core data store is used with the Application Programming Interface (API).

TPCC Benchmark

TPC Benchmark-C (TPCC, 2014) is an online shopping application with Transaction processing (OLTP) workload. It is a mixture of read-only and update intensive transactions that simulate the activities found in complex OLTP application environments. TPC-C benchmark is an Online Transaction Processing (OLTP) workload. It replicates absolute computing environment where population of users implements transaction next to database. Due to this reason TPCC has been selected to deploy consistency model and establish the statistical relationship between CI and the set of independent variables.

It is characterized by the simultaneous execution of multiple transaction types that span a breadth of complexity working on databases consisting of many tables with a wide variety of sizes, attributes, and relationships where there is a contention on data access and update. The performance of this application is measured with "throughput" which refers to number of transactions completed per unit time.

Database Entities, Relationships, and Characteristics

Figure 2 shows the components of the TPCC database which consist of nine separate and individual data-objects. The relationships among these objects are defined in the entity-relationship diagram as shown below in Figure 2. Every data-object has attributes which completely describe the working of all its relevant characteristics.

TPCC Transactions

TPCC workload is a combination of read only along with updates thorough transactions for electronic commerce.

- New-order operation.
- Payment operation.
- Order-status operation.
- Delivery operation.
- Stock level operation.

Amazon SimpleDB

Amazon SimpleDB (2016), is a data store with high availability and flexibility. It is No-SQL document acquainted data store with a very uncomplicated and supple schema. Amazon SimpleDB is optimized

Figure 2. TPCC object diagram

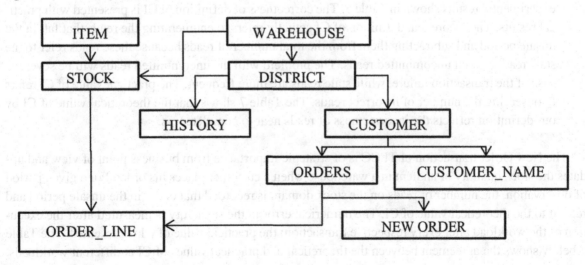

for the provision of high availability and flexibility (A-P), with weaker consistency guarantees. The data is organized in *domains* within which data can be put, obtained or queries can be run.

Amazon SimpleDB keeps multiple copies of each domain. Amazon SimpleDB offers two read-consistency levels: eventually consistent read and consistent read. An eventually consistent read is the default read mode where the update to all replicas is not guaranteed. The stronger level of consistency across all copies of the data is achieved within the second mode where the succeeding read is presented after a short time to return the most updated data. A consistent read returns a result that reflects latest committed write prior to the read. By default, all read APIs offer an eventually consistent read.

TPCC Workload and Transaction Management

TPCC workload is a blend of read only and updates intensive transactions for e-commerce. Every normalized table in TPCC is plotted on a domain taken apart in SimpleDB. TPCC puts into practice the five transactions as mentioned in the earlier sections. A separate Transaction Manager (TM) administers each operation for scalability.

In distributed system, an operation is subdivided into sub-transactions. The division of the transaction to sub-transaction generally depends on the locality of reference of data accessed. A transaction in TPCC is a complex transaction whereas every sub-transaction of a transaction agrees with data access from single domain to perk up throughput with equivalence. The workload on a data-object is hence a stream of the read-write requests from sub-operations of diverse operations with diverse time stamp. This is followed by observing the consistency guarantees of the individual domains in isolation. The transactional load is simulated using multi-threaded requests at a constant transaction arrival rate.

Results and Performance

The work puts forth two important contributions:

1. Measuring consistency with a new metric CI: This metric finds the correctness of a read operation by determining stale reads and uncommitted reads that is, CI = 1 is a consistency guarantee comparable to the read committed isolation level of SQL by theory. That is supported by our experimental results shown in Table 5. The correctness of definition of CI is presented with practical results. The theoretical definition of CI actually refers to enumerating the reads that fall in the unsafe period and subtracting them from the total number of reads because these reads refer to the stale reads as well uncommitted reads. The problem with the uncommitted reads will be severe in case of the transaction failure, while stale reads are more frequent. The practical value of CI refers to observing the number of incorrect reads. The Table 7 shows that the theoretical value of CI by our definition reflects the incorrectness of reads near to completeness.

The New Order transaction of TPCC is of strategic importance from business point of view and updates the stock quantity of an item in a warehouse when a customer places his order. For a given period of observation, the number of reads on the stock domain is recorded that occur in the unsafe period and refer it to the theoretical value of CI. The numerical error in the stock_qty is measured after the execution of the workload after every respective transaction; the practical value of CI is presented. The Table 7 below shows the agreement between the theoretical and practical values of CI at different workloads.

The average time-gap in the transactions of the incoming workload is used to control the system. With the increase in the time-gap it is observed that there is a stronger agreement in the practical and the theoretical values of CI in Table 7.

2. Rationing consistency guarantees with selective data consistency:

The proposed selective data consistency model supplements the default weaker levels of consistency guarantees of the underlying data store with A-P guarantees. The consistency level can be tuned with selection of critical data items and the levels of consistency are measured for the replica set of data-object. The metric used here is Consistency Index (CI).

As the model is selective towards critical data, this work compares the selective consistency guarantees of our model to default consistency guarantees of the underlying data store. As the default guarantees are measured with CI, they assure a common metric for comparison. Default consistency level implies that this model does not impose any consistency restrictions at the application level and allow the transactions to run with the default consistency guarantees of the underlying data store. The next section demonstrates the results quantitatively.

Assured Consistency Guarantees

This work compares the consistency guarantees of the default level of consistency (eventual consistency) of SimpleDB with proposed selective data consistency using consistency measure CI. Further this work observes that the consistency guarantees of observed critical data with default level of SimpleDB results in unpredictable and unassured values of CI. As against this selective consistency model gives assured selective strict consistency of critical data. Figure 3 shows the assured consistency guarantees of selective data model. As against, selective data consistency will assure a CI of value one for the selected data-objects that is all the reads made to the replicated stock or district data-object assure 100 percent correctness.

Response Time

Secondly, this work compares the selective consistency model in SimpleDB with consistent read model of SimpleDB. Strict consistency guarantee in SimpleDB is implemented by setting the flag ConsistentRead = true which is set for the get APIs. Monotonic strict consistency guarantees on a transaction implies that every single data-object in that transaction are rigorously observed. The transactions are penalized by this by originating latency in their execution.

Table 7. CI: comparison of theoretical and practical value with average time gap =100ms

Number of Transactions in the Random Workload	CI: Theoretical Value	CI: Practical Value
10	1.0	1.0
100	0.92	0.98
500	0.780	0.800
1000	0.800	0.890

Figure 3. Selective consistency: Assured consistency guarantees

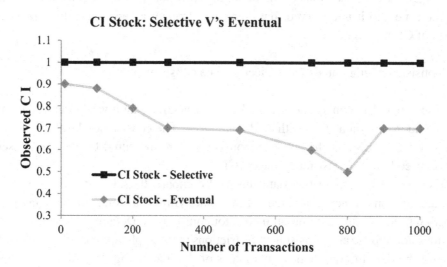

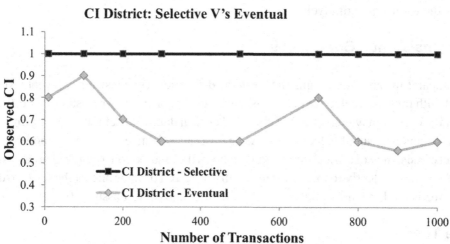

In case of selective consistency, an object O is chosen by an application developer and is strictly observed for consistency. The effect of choosing selective data consistency is observed on the response time of the transactions. The performance of a transaction is observed with selective strict consistency guarantees, against the transactions with monotonic strict guarantees.

In our experiments, the consistency constraints are enforced on all the 9 data-objects (domains in SimpleDB) of TPCC. Initially strict consistency guarantees are levied on all the data domains with no bias and the performance of all the transactions in terms of response time is observed.

Then strict consistency enforcements (CI = 1) are selectively applied on few domains. It is observed that the stock_qty in stock domain and the d_next_o_id from district domain are critical data attributes. SimpleDB works at domain level of data granularity for consistency. Hence this work applies strict consistency guarantees to stock and district domain of TPCC. The consistency guarantees of the remaining domains are left to the default consistency guarantees of the underlying data store. The performance of the transactions is observed in terms of response time. Here it should be noted that the transaction arrival

Figure 4. Selective consistency: responsive application for new-order transaction

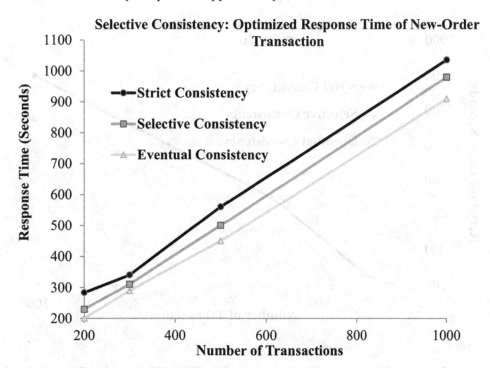

rate is also critical determinant of the correctness of read operation. This is obvious with earlier discussions on correct reads and unsafe period. They are kept constant in a set of observations to isolate their effect on selective data consistency guarantees and the consequent performance of transactions. Then the performance of data selectivity for consistency is observed at the varying transaction arrival rate.

The New-Order transaction is highly frequent, complicated and critical transaction in any online shopping application. Hence the results of New-Order transaction are presented here. Figure 4 shows the responsive application by selective consistency model with New-Order Transaction. Figure 5 shows the responsive application with selective consistency for Payment Transaction. The experiments are run with the increased workload but at different transaction arrival rate. The selective application of strong consistency guarantees on the selected objects leads to a better response time in New-Order transaction than the monotonic strongly consistent transactions. Similarly the performance of Payment transaction is observed with similar results.

CONCLUSION

This work perceives consistency as a data characteristic with user perspective. In the process of making consistency an attribute of data, it is discriminatory with the data. (CI) Consistency Index metric allows the user to express the consistency guarantees quantitatively and in user perceivable manner. The work also helps users of transaction-based databases to realize their consistency requirements with CI and relates CI to the conventional SQL isolation levels.

Figure 5. Selective consistency: responsive application for payment transaction

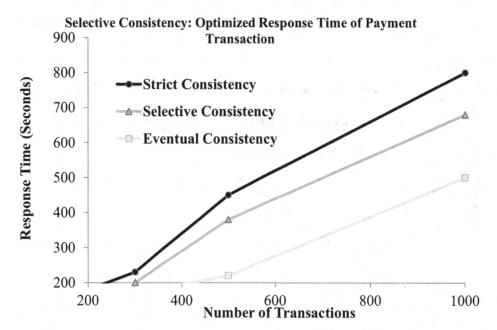

Commercial NO-SQL data store guarantees a default eventual consistency. Applications implement higher levels of consistency over existing guarantees when required. This is selective data consistency model which optimizes the consistency guarantees for better performance. It not only leverages the default consistency of the critical data with assured and stable consistency guarantee but also performs better than the monolithic strict consistency of the data stores.

This work is further extended to find the predictive guarantees (Phansalkar and Dani, 2015a) of our consistency model with known database and workload parameters. The work is also enhanced by exploring the tunable guarantees of CI (Phansalkar and Dani, 2015b) through effective control on the configurable parameters to ensure desired consistency level in update-intensive web-based big-data applications. An important future work can extend CI to develop intelligent scheduling strategies to obtain tradeoff between required level of consistency and performance. The data criticality can be analyzed with usage patterns and can be mined with criticality analyzer.

REFERENCES

Aguilera, M. K., & Terry, D. B. (2016). The many faces of consistency. *Data Engineering*, 3.

Alvandi, E. O. (2011). Emotions and Information Processing: A Theoretical Approach. *International Journal of Synthetic Emotions*, *2*(1), 1–14. doi:10.4018/jse.2011010101

Amazon Simple D. B. Documentation. (2014). Available online at: http://aws.amazon.com/ Simpledb/

Apache Cassandra Documentation. (n.d.). *Configuring Data Consistency*. Available online at: www. datastax.com

Bailis, P., Venkataraman, S., Franklin, M., Hellerstein, M., & Stoica, I. (2012, April). Probabilistically Bounded Staleness for Practical Partial Quorums. *Proceedings of the VLDB Endowment, 5*(8), 776–787. doi:10.14778/2212351.2212359

Baker, J., Bond, C., Corbett, J., Furman, J., Khorlin, A., Larson, J., & Yushprakh, V. (2011, January). Megastore. *Providing Scalable, Highly Available Storage for Interactive Services, In CIDR, 11*, 223–234.

Baumgarten, M., Mulvenna, M., Rooney, N., & Reid, J. (2013). Keyword-Based Sentiment Mining using Twitter. *International Journal of Ambient Computing and Intelligence, 5*(2), 5. doi:10.4018/jaci.2013040104

Brewer, E. (July2000), Towards Robust Distributed Systems. *Proceedings of the 19th ACM Symposium on Principles of Distributed Computing*, 7–10.

Chu, W. W., & Leong, I. T. (1993). A transaction-based approach to vertical partitioning for relational database systems. *IEEE Transactions on Software Engineering, 19*(8), 804–812. doi:10.1109/32.238583

Curran, K., & Norrby, S. (2009). RFID-enabled location determination within indoor environments. *International Journal of Ambient Computing and Intelligence, 1*(4), 63–86. doi:10.4018/jaci.2009062205

Dey, N., & Kar, Á. (2015). Image mining framework and techniques: A review. *International Journal of Image Mining, 1*(1), 45–64. doi:10.1504/IJIM.2015.070028

Fouad, K. M., Hassan, B. M., & Hassan, M. F. (2016). User Authentication based on Dynamic Keystroke Recognition. *International Journal of Ambient Computing and Intelligence, 7*(2), 1–32. doi:10.4018/IJACI.2016070101

George, L. (2011). *HBase: The Definitive Guide*. Sebastopol, CA: O'Reilly Media Inc.

Gray, J., & Lamport, L. (2006, March). Consensus On Transaction Commit. *ACM Transactions on Database Systems, 31*(1), 133–160. doi:10.1145/1132863.1132867

Grünerbl, A., Bahle, G., Hanser, F., & Lukowicz, P. (2013). UWB indoor location for monitoring dementia patients: The challenges and perception of a real-life deployment. *International Journal of Ambient Computing and Intelligence, 5*(4), 45–59. doi:10.4018/ijaci.2013100104

Haifeng, Y., & Vahdat, A. (2002, August). Design and Evaluation of a Conit-Based Continuous Consistency Model for Replicated Services. *ACM Transactions on Computer Systems, 20*(3), 239–282. doi:10.1145/566340.566342

Hosmer, J., & Lemeshow, S. (2004). *Applied Logistic Regression*. Hoboken, NJ: John Wiley& Sons.

Huang, Y. F., & Lai, C. J. (2016). Integrating frequent pattern clustering and branch-and-bound approaches for data partitioning. *Information Sciences, 328*, 288–301. doi:10.1016/j.ins.2015.08.047

Jain, A., & Bhatnagar, V. (2016). Movie Analytics for Effective Recommendation System using Pig with Hadoop. *International Journal of Rough Sets and Data Analysis, 3*(2), 82–100. doi:10.4018/IJRSDA.2016040106

Jain, A., & Bhatnagar, V. (2016). Olympics Big Data Prognostications. *International Journal of Rough Sets and Data Analysis, 3*(4), 32–45. doi:10.4018/IJRSDA.2016100103

Kamal, S., Ripon, S. H., Dey, N., Ashour, A. S., & Santhi, V. (2016). A MapReduce approach to diminish imbalance parameters for big deoxyribonucleic acid dataset. *Computer Methods and Programs in Biomedicine, 131*, 191–206. doi:10.1016/j.cmpb.2016.04.005 PMID:27265059

Karaa, W. B. A., Ashour, A. S., Sassi, D. B., Roy, P., Kausar, N., & Dey, N. (2016). Medline Text Mining: An Enhancement Genetic Algorithm Based Approach for Document Clustering. In Applications of Intelligent Optimization in Biology and Medicine (pp. 267-287). Springer International Publishing.

Kausar, N., Palaniappan, S., Samir, B. B., Abdullah, A., & Dey, N. (2016). Systematic analysis of applied data mining based optimization algorithms in clinical attribute extraction and classification for diagnosis of cardiac patients. In *Applications of Intelligent Optimization in Biology and Medicine* (pp. 217–231). Springer International Publishing. doi:10.1007/978-3-319-21212-8_9

Kourosh, G. (1995), *Memory Consistency Models for Shared memory Multiprocessors* (PhD thesis). Tech. Report CSL-TR-95-685, Stanford University.

Kraska, T., Hentschel, M., Alonso, G., & Kossmann, D. (2009, August). Consistency Rationing in the Cloud: Pay only When it Matters. *Proceedings of VLDB, 2*(1), 253–264. doi:10.14778/1687627.1687657

Liu, Q., Wang, G., & Wu, J. (2014). Consistency as a service: Auditing cloud consistency. *IEEE eTransactions on Network and Service Management, 11*(1), 25–35. doi:10.1109/TNSM.2013.122613.130411

Meier, R., & Lee, D. (2009). Context-aware services for ambient environments. *International Journal of Ambient Computing and Intelligence, 1*(1), 1–14. doi:10.4018/jaci.2009010101

Mohanpurkar, A. A., & Joshi, M. S. (2016). A Traitor Identification Technique for Numeric Relational Databases with Distortion Minimization and Collusion Avoidance. *International Journal of Ambient Computing and Intelligence, 7*(2), 114–137. doi:10.4018/IJACI.2016070106

MongoDB Tutorial. (2016). Available online at: http://www.tutorialspoint.com/mongodb/

Navathe, S., Ceri, S., Wiederhold, G., & Dou, J. (1984, December). Vertical Partitioning Algorithms for Database Design. *ACM Transactions on Database Systems, 9*(4), 680–710. doi:10.1145/1994.2209

Odella, F. (2016). Technology Studies and the Sociological Debate on Monitoring of Social Interactions. *International Journal of Ambient Computing and Intelligence, 7*(1), 1–26. doi:10.4018/IJACI.2016010101

Ogunyadeka, A., Younas, M., Zhu, H., & Aldea, A. (2016, March). A Multi-key Transactions Model for NoSQL Cloud Database Systems. In *2016 IEEE Second International Conference on Big Data Computing Service and Applications(Big Data Service)* (pp. 24-27). IEEE. doi:10.1109/BigDataService.2016.32

Olston, C., & Widom, J. (2000). Offering a Precision-Performance Tradeoff for Aggregation Queries over Replicated Data. *Proceedings of the 26th International Conference on Very Large Data Bases*, 144-155.

Padhye, V. (2014). *Transaction and Data Consistency Models for Cloud Applications* (Thesis). University of Minnesota.

Panda, S. K., Mishra, S., & Das, S. (2017). An Efficient Intra-Server and Inter-Server Load Balancing Algorithm for Internet Distributed Systems. *International Journal of Rough Sets and Data Analysis, 4*(1), 1–18. doi:10.4018/IJRSDA.2017010101

Phansalkar, S., & Dani, A. (2015a). Predictive models for consistency index of a data object in a replicated distributed database System'. *WSEAS Transactions on Computers*, *14*, 395–401.

Phansalkar, S. P., & Dani, A. R. (2015b). Tunable consistency guarantees of selective data consistency model. *Journal of Cloud Computing*, *4*(1), 1.

Postgre, S. Q. L. (2016). *The world's most advanced open source database*. Available online at https://www.postgresql.org/

Redding, D., Florescu, D., & Kossmann, D. (2009, March). Rethinking Cost and Performance of Database Systems. *SIGMOD Record*, *38*(1), 43–48. doi:10.1145/1558334.1558339

RethinkDB. (n.d.). *The open-source database for the realtime web*. Available online at: https://www.rethinkdb.com/

Ripon, S. H., Kamal, S., Hossain, S., & Dey, N. (2016). Theoretical Analysis of Different Classifiers under Reduction Rough Data Set: A Brief Proposal. *International Journal of Rough Sets and Data Analysis*, *3*(3), 1–20. doi:10.4018/IJRSDA.2016070101

Schalkoff, R. (1997). *Artificial Neural Networks* (1st ed.). New York: McGraw-Hill.

Silberschatz, A., Korth, H., & Sudarshan, S. (1997). *Database System Concepts* (Vol. 4). Singapore: McGraw Hill.

Tanenbaum, A., & Van, M. (2007). *Distributed System* (2nd ed.). Pearson Prentice Hall.

Transaction Processing Performance Council. (n.d.). *TPC benchmark C standard specification, revision 5.11*. Available online at: http://www.tpc.org/tpcc/

Zhang, C., & Zhang, Z. (2003). Trading Replication Consistency for Performance and Availability: an Adaptive Approach. *Proceedings of the 23rd International Conference on Distributed Computing Systems*, 687-695.

KEY TERMS AND DEFINITIONS

CI: A ratio of correct read to total number of reads.

Consistency Rationing: Permitting data consistency at lower levels.

Correct Read: A fresh read which is agreed upon by all (majority) of the replicas is a correct read.

DM: Manager Module of the data object of different granularity which manages replication strategy and consistency guaranty.

Incorrect Read: A read other than correct read.

Read Classifier: Statistical classification module for categorizing incoming workload read operation into correct/incorrect read.

Selective Consistency: Selecting higher levels of consistency for critical data.

Time-Gap: Delay between an update and succeeding read operation on the same data-object.

User-Perspective: Relevant to the user (here the context is consistency).

Section 4
Data Mining

Chapter 7

Educational Data Mining Review:
Teaching Enhancement

Rashmi Agrawal
Manav Rachna International University, India

Neha Gupta
Manav Rachna International University, India

ABSTRACT

In today's era, educational data mining is a discipline of high importance for teaching enhancement. EDM techniques can reveal useful information to educators to help them design or modify the structure of courses. EDM techniques majorly include machine learning and data mining techniques. In this chapter of the book, we will deliberate upon various data mining techniques that will help in identifying at-risk students, identifying priority learning needs for different groups of students, increasing graduation rates, effectively assessing institutional performance, maximizing campus resources, optimizing subject curriculum renewal. Various applications of data mining are also discussed by quoting example of various case studies. Analysis of social networks in educational field to understand student network formation in classrooms and the types of impact these networks have on student is also discussed.

INTRODUCTION TO EDUCATIONAL DATA MINING

Educational data mining or "EDM" is an emerging multidisciplinary area of scientific research which centers on the development of methods and techniques for exploring the data that originates from various educational information systems. These methods and techniques will help to better understand students and the environment which they learn in.

The availability and use of big data has created a subtle difference in the information we use in our daily lives. Education has always been high on all agendas. With advent increase of data science in the education sector, the transformative developments have been done to understand the learning patterns of students. This can dramatically expand the process of teaching and learning procedures.

DOI: 10.4018/978-1-5225-2486-1.ch007

Educational Data Mining focuses on designing new algorithms and tools for discovering and analyzing educational data patterns. The various algorithms are decision tree, Naïve Bayes, k-nearest neighbour (using classification technique), Apriori algorithm (using association rule mining), K-means, K-mode (using clustering techniques). The various methods and techniques used by Educational Data Mining are from statistics, machine learning and from data mining (DM). These methods help in analyzing the data collected during teaching and learning processes.

EDM helps in identification of students learning patterns and the environment in which they learn. It enables data driven decisions that helps in improving the current educational practices. Educational data mining (EDM) covers DM methods with respect to the structure of educational data. EDM deals with the analysis of study-related data as to understand student behavior. These techniques are usually applied to provide more effective learning environment.

EDM techniques can reveal useful information to educators to help them design or modify the structure of courses. Students can also facilitate their studies using the discovered knowledge

EDM is rooted in general data mining, however the EDM methods are different from data mining methods due to multidisciplinary hierarchy of educational data and the inter dependence of different variables of educational data. Because of multidisciplinary hierarchy and the inter dependence of data variables, various psychometric techniques along with machine learning methods are integrated for analysis of data.

Computer-supported interactive learning methods and tools—intelligent tutoring systems, simulations, games—have opened up the doors to collect and analyze student data to discover patterns and trends in these data, and to make new discoveries and test hypotheses about how students learn. Data collected from online learning systems can be aggregated over large numbers of students and may contain many variables that data mining algorithms can explore for model building.

CYCLIC APPLICATION OF DATA MINING IN EDUCATIONAL SYSTEMS

Data mining techniques are useful in discovering useful information that can assist educators in formative evaluation of educational systems when designing or modifying an environment or teaching approach. Below is the cyclic graph showing the application of data mining in any educational system.

In Figure 1, educators are responsible for designing, planning, building and maintaining of educational systems. The educational systems may belong to traditional classrooms, web based systems, adaptive systems or e-learning systems. These educational systems provide academic and interactive data about students, their usage patterns, course information etc. Various data mining techniques like clustering, classification, text mining and pattern recognition are applied on these systems to mine the useful information that helps in improving the teaching-learning process. This discovered knowledge is useful for both educators and students. The mined knowledge helps educators in better designing and maintenance of educational systems and helps the educators to evaluate the instructional design in a formative manner.

This mined knowledge helps the educators, students and the educational systems to guide facilitate and enhance learning as a whole.

Figure 1. Cyclic application of data mining in educational systems

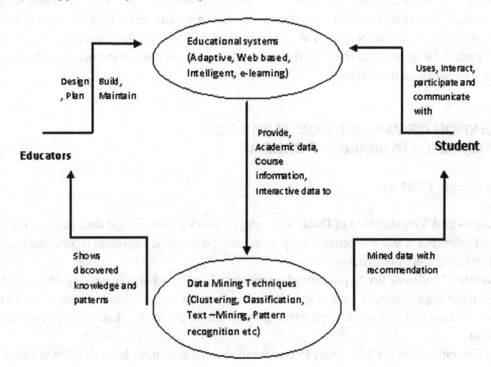

DATA MINING IN EDUCATIONAL DOMAIN

Data mining in educational domain is an emerging research field that concerns with the development of techniques such as decision trees, classification, neural networks, naïve bayes etc to discover methods that are used to discover the knowledge from the data belongs to educational environments.

Data mining on educational domain uses much the knowledge that can be used for the prediction and analysis of overall performance of the student. Data mining techniques can be very useful for any educational system as these techniques can help in discovering and analyzing the following area of educational domain.

1. At-risk students.
2. Identifying priority learning needs for different groups of students.
3. Increasing graduation rates.
4. Effectively assessing institutional performance.
5. Maximizing campus resources.
6. Optimizing subject curriculum renewal.

Use of technology in educational system has made a large amount of data available for analysis and interpretation. Data mining techniques helps in analyzing the educational data and to solve various educational issues. Now days the scope of educational domain is very vast and include data from a variety of resources like academic institutions, web, multimedia etc.

Therefore, data mining techniques are used to interpret, analyze and categorize these data sets to better understand the settings and the environment in which a student learn. EDM has classified the task of mining into two broad categories: a) Web Mining and b) Statistics and visualization. Web mining is used to extract the useful patterns from the web and statistics is used to mathematically evaluate the patterns and to conclude the results.

ASSOCIATION OF VARIOUS EDM TASKS TO TRADITIONAL DATA MINING PROBLEMS

The basic goals of EDM are:

1. **Analysis and Visualization of Data:** The analysis and visualization of data helps in highlighting useful information and also provide support in taking decisions. Two main techniques are statistics and visualization of information.
2. **Providing Feedback for Supporting Instructors:** Feedback helps in making decisions that will help in the improvement of learning behavior of students and will enable instructors to take appropriate remedial action. Most common technique used for feedback analysis is association rule mining.
3. **Recommendations for Students:** Recommendation models have been developed using various data mining techniques like clustering, sequential pattern mining etc. to make recommendations directly to the students with respect to their personalized activities.
4. **Predicting Student Performance:** Prediction is a process to estimate the unknown value of a variable that will describe the student. In EDM, prediction will help in estimating the performance, marks and knowledge of student or a learner. Techniques of prediction can be regression analysis, classification, neural networks and soon. The predictive value can be applied on numerical, discrete or categorical variables etc.
5. **Student Modeling:** Student modeling is a technique that helps in development of cognitive models of students to understand their skills, knowledge, motivations and attitude. Techniques used are naïve bayes, decision trees, clustering, classification etc.
6. **Detecting Undesirable Student Behavior:** EDM helps in detecting the undesirable behavior of those students who have unusual behavior like low motivation, cheating, academic failure etc. Classification and clustering techniques are used to detect such undesirable behaviors.
7. **Grouping Students:** In this task, students are grouped according to their characteristics, features, needs, skills etc. These groups can then be used by educators to develop a personalized learning system in order to promote effective learning or to provide adaptive contents. The data mining techniques used for such tasks are classification for supervised learning and clustering for unsupervised learning.
8. **Social Network Analysis:** Social network analysis is a technique used to study relationship among individuals. Social networks are usually designed to group people, who can connect to each other by social relationships like friendship, cooperative relations or for information exchange. Collaborative filtering is the most common data mining technique used to mine social networks in education

domain. Collaborative filtering helps in predicting the interest of a user by collecting preferences from many users. The social network data can also be mined to find useful information related to education domain.

TECHNIQUES OF EDM

Following are the techniques of EDM:

Prediction

Prediction is a method to infer one aspect of the data from different combinations of other aspects of data. Inferred aspect of data is predicted variable and combination of data are predictor variable. Prediction requires labeling the output variables considering the degree of approximation for these labels. The most common types of prediction models used in EDM are classifiers and regressors. Both classifiers and regressors are emerged from the research field of data mining and artificial intelligence and have used various models like user modeling, psychometrics etc.

In EDM, prediction can have two key uses:

1.   To study the features that are important for prediction by giving information about the underlying construct.
2.   To predict the output value in context where it is not necessary to directly obtain a label for that context.

The first method can be used to predict educational outcomes of the student without predicting intermediate or mediating factors. The second method can be used to predict the success of interactive learning environment by exploiting the features of a system.

Prediction can be broadly classified into three categories:

*   Classification.
*   Regression.
*   Density estimation.

Table 1 highlights the characteristics of all three methods of prediction.

Table 1. Characteristics of prediction

	Classification	Regression	Density Estimation
Predicted Variable	Binary or Categorical	Continuous	Probability Density Function
Popular Methods	Decision Trees, Logistic Regression	Linear Regression, Neural Networks	Kernel Functions, Gaussian Functions
Measuring Goodness of a Predictor	Linear Correlation	Cohen's Kappa	'A' Method
Validation method used	Cross Validation	Latent Knowledge Estimation	Q-Matrix Approached

Clustering

Clustering is used to find the data points that can be grouped together by splitting the entire data set into a set of clusters. Clustering helps in identifying the categories that are not very common within the dataset. Clusters can be created with different grain-sizes like in EDM different schools can be grouped to form a cluster to identify and analyze the similarities and differences among them. Similarly actions of students can be clustered together to identify and analyze their behavior patterns.

Clustering algorithms are classified into two categories:

1.   **Non-Hierarchical Clustering:** Algorithm for clusters having no prior hypothesis, e.g. K-mean algorithm, Gaussian mixture modeling.
2.   **Hierarchical Clustering:** Algorithm for clusters having specific hypothesis, e.g. expectation maximization algorithm, HAC (Hierarchical Agglomerative Clustering)

Relationship Mining

Relationship mining is a data mining technique used to identify and discover the relationship among variables within a dataset having very large number of variables. Relationship mining helps in finding out the association of variables that are strongly associated with a single variable o a particular interest or to discover the strongest relationships between any two variables. For example, relationship mining helps in finding the relationship of student with their performance. Relationship mining is broadly classified into four categories:

1.   Correlation mining.
2.   Association rule mining.
3.   Casual data mining.
4.   Sequential pattern mining.

To find linear correlation among variables, correlation mining is used. It means to identify the relationship impact of one variable (Positive or negative) on another variable. For example, finding the impact of instructor/teacher on student.

Association rule mining works on if-then-else principle where variable value of one data set will impact the variable value of another data set like the relationship of student performance with his ability and zeal to learn. Association rule mining is a subfield of data mining particularly from the Market Basket analysis which is used to mine the business data.

Casual data mining is identifying the cause and effect of an event. It is used to analyze the co-variance of two events by observing whether one event was the cause of other event and so-on.

Sequential pattern mining helps in identifying the temporal associations among events. It is a subfield emerged from bioinformatics community. Two aspects of sequential pattern mining are:

1.   **Classical Sequential Pattern Mining:** Which is considered as the special case of association rules mining.
2.   **Motif Analysis:** A method commonly used in bioinformatics to find general patterns.

Discovery With Models

Discovery with models is a process of developing a model using various data mining techniques like clustering, prediction or with knowledge engineering. The model developed can then be used as a component in any other analysis using either prediction or relationship mining. The model developed using prediction technique uses predictor variable which in turn is used to predict new variables. For example- (Baker et.al, 2008) have analyzed the complex constructs like gaming the system for online learning environments which are dependent on the assessment of the probability that the current knowledge component which has to be learnt by the student or is already known by the student.

Similarly the models developed using relationship mining techniques are used to identify and analyze the relationships among complex latent construct and observable constructs. Discovery with models helps in forming a prediction model that is validated and generalized for various constructs. For example- (Baker, 2007) used an educational software for one year to analyze the performance of the students using the game based educational software to predict student behavior.

Distillation of Data for Human Judgment

Another recent trend that fascinates the data mining techniques are distillation of data for human judgment. In this method, data is distillated on the basis of the inferences made by human beings. The process of distillation of data is beyond the scope of various automated data mining methods. EDM uses various information visualization methods that are entirely different from the methods of solving problem of information visualization. For Example: Data can be meaningfully organized into two categories:

1. Learning material that consist of skills, lesson plans, problem solving, etc.
2. Learning settings such as arrangement of classes, appointment of teachers, selection of students, etc.

Distillation of data for human judgment solves two key purposes.

1. **Identification:** In this method, data is distilled to display in a form that can easily identify well known patterns that are not very difficult to express. For example- representing the performance of a student in relation to his skill on a graph having x-axis and y-axis.
2. **Classification:** In this method, data is distilled for human labeling which can later be used for the developing a prediction model. The sub-section of a data set are labeled by human coders and are displayed either in visual format (in the form of tables or graphs) or in text format. These labels are used for the developing a predictor. Classification approach is used to model complex phenomena where the task needs several iterations.

EDM Techniques and Their Key Applications

Table 2 shows the various EDM Techniques and their key applications.

Table 2. EDM techniques and their key applications

Category	Technique	Key Applications
Prediction	• Classification • Regression • Density Estimation	• Identify at-risk students • Understanding student educational outcomes
Clustering	• K-mean • Gaussian Mixture Modeling • HAC • Expectation Maximization	• Categorizing student behavior • Finding similarities and differences between students or schools
Relationship mining	• Correlation Mining • Association Rule Mining • Casual Data Mining • Sequential Pattern Mining	• Finding the relationship between parents education level and students' drop out level from school • Discovery of pedagogical strategies that can lead to robust learning
Discovery with Models	• Prediction Techniques • Relationship Mining Techniques	• Discovery of relationships between student's behavior and student characteristics. • Analysis of research questions on wide variety of contexts.
Distillation of Data with Human Judgment	• Identification • Classification	• Identification of human patterns in student learning, and behavior • Labeling of student data for use in development of prediction model.

GOALS OF EDUCATIONAL DATA MINING

Improving Student Models

One of the important goals of EDM is to improve student models by providing detailed information about various parameters related to a student like knowledge of a student, motivation to participate or to study, met cognition, student's attitude towards various situations. These parameters vary from student to student. Student modeling enable softwares to identify and respond to these differences which is the key research area in education domain. These student data models have been explored and expanded using various educational data mining tools and techniques and helped the researchers to expand the student models for better understanding. Particularly, educational data mining methods have enabled researchers to make higher-level inferences about students' behavior, such as

1. During game playing by the student.
2. When a student makes error despite the skills.
3. When a student is engaged in self-explanation (Shih, Koedinger, & Scheines, 2008).

Student modeling is supplemented by behavior analysis of students and also allows performance prediction, recommendation generation, providing sufficient information to educators, to improve content and learning environment. These student models are useful in two fashions.

1. Such models have increased the ability to predict student knowledge on future performance such as incorporating models of guessing and slipping into predictions of student future performance has increased the accuracy of these predictions by up to 48% (Baker, Corbett, & Aleven, 2008).
2. Using these models researchers are enabled to study what factors will lead students to make specific choice in a particular learning environment.

Discovery Models of the Knowledge Domain

Another goal of EDM is to discover or improve models of the knowledge domain. In EDM, methods have been created for fast discovery of accurate domain models directly from data. These methods have combined psychometric modeling frameworks with advanced space-searching algorithms, and these are offered as prediction problems for the purpose of model discovery (for example, predicting whether individual actions will be right or wrong. This is done using different domain models. Barnes, Bitzer, & Vouk (2005) had given algorithms for automatic discovery of Q-Matrix from data. Cen, Koedinger, & Junker (2006) developed algorithms for using domain knowledge to identify differences between items for driving automated search for IRT models. Pavlik et al. (2008) gave algorithms for finding partial order knowledge structure models

Pedagogical Support Provided by Learning Software

Third goal of EDM is to study the pedagogical support provided by learning software. Modern educational software gives various types of pedagogical support to students like online notes, PowerPoint presentations, tutorials, web based learning, adaptive learning, mobile based learning etc. Discovering the effectiveness of the pedagogical support is a key area of interest for the educational data miners. Researchers are constantly working on models to identify which kind of pedagogical support is most effective for student.

Identifying the effectiveness of learning software helps the educators and the students in better designing and up gradation of these software. Learning decomposition (Beck & Mostow, 2008), is a type of relationship mining that fits learning curve to performance data to find out the amount and type of pedagogical support that a student has received. For support the weight is assigned and this weight tells the effectiveness of each type of pedagogical support.

Scientific Discovery About Learning and Learners

Another important goal of EDM is to provide scientific discovery about learning and learners. This is of several types. The application of EDM in answering questions in the previously discussed models like student models, domain models and pedagogical support have scientific benefits. Apart from these above-mentioned areas, few other analyses are also aimed towards scientific discovery. One such key method is discovery with models. A prominent example of this was given by Baker,2007 to find out that either state or trait factors are predictors for identifying that, whether a student would game the session or not.

APPLICATIONS OF EDUCATIONAL DATA MINING

Modeling Student Performance in Higher Education Using Data Mining

Identifying students' behavior and performance is the most important aspect in higher education and it has become more challenging day by day due to large volumes of data. To address this, issue the traditional methods are not sufficient to predict the performance of students in efficient manner. Therefore, a systematic and efficient technique is required which could bring the benefits and impacts to educators, students and academic institutions. Educational Data Mining (EDM) extracts useful pattern and information from a voluminous educational database and provides a platform where educators can monitor their students' performance and students could also improve their learning and also educational institutions improves the overall system performance. Hence, by applying the data mining techniques in education specific needs with different entities is fulfilled.

Generally, predictive modeling can be used to predict student performance in EDM. Amongst the various techniques, classification is the most popular technique and various algorithm of classification technique like- Artificial Neural Network, Naïve Bayes, k-Nearest Neighbor (k-NN) and support vector machines are used.

Most of the researchers have used the technique of decision tree in EDM due to its simplicity and comprehensibility to identify small or large data structures. Romero et al. (2008), Mayilvagan and Kalpana Devi (2014), Gray et al. (2014) applied the decision tree for predicting students' performance in their study.

Neural Network, which is also a popular technique in Educational Data Mining, has the ability to detect all possible interactions between predictor variables. Table 3 represents the work done by the researchers in EDM using Neural Network.

Naïve Bayes and k-Nearest Neighbor methods are also a good option for researchers when it comes to the ease of understanding and implementation. Bigdoli et al. (2003) has applied k-Nearest Neighbor for finding the student performance in internal assessment and gave 82% accuracy in results whereas Gray et al. (2014) applied k-NN on psychometric factors and achieved 69% accuracy in results.

Detecting Personality of a Player in an Educational Game

In computer based learning environments personality traits of an individual have a great significance as different students might have different personality traits. These personality traits may affect the moods of an individual which in turn will affect the result or outcome of an event. Fredrik Vaassen and Walter described *delearyous*, a serious gaming project for developing an environment to improve the communication skills of users through natural language processing. They used several machine learning algorithms for emotion classification task.

To characterize a unique individual personality behavioral, temperamental, emotional and mental attributes makes it whole. Typically, personality of an individual is assessed by five dimensions known as big five. These are: 1) Extraversion vs Introversion, 2) Emotional Stability vs Neuroticism 3) Agreeableness vs Disagreeable 4) Conscientiousness vs Unconscientious and 5) Openness to experience. Norman (1963), Peabody and Goldberg (1989) have obtained these five personality traits by using the factor analysis on the basis of lexical hypothesis given by Allport and Odbert (1936).

Table 3. Major work done by researchers in EDM using neural networks

Authors	Domain	Results
Gray et al., 2014	Psychometric factors	69%
Wang and Mirovic, 2002	Internal Assessment	81%
Oladokun et al. (2008)	External assessment, Student Demographic, High school background	72%

Read et al. gave a technique using neural network to bridge the gap between dynamic and structural approaches to personality. This technique was able to provide an account of personality dynamics and person–situation interactions. In addition, it suggests how dynamic processing approaches and dispositional, structural approaches can be integrated in a common framework.

A virtual learning internship, *Land Science*, created by researchers at University of Wisconsin-Madison provides a platform in which students' acts as a virtual intern at a fabricated urban firm. Students are placed in project teams and they propose land-use changes by using their research studies, stake holder assessments and various professional tools. In this simulation, learners are expected to perform the tasks that urban planners do in their training. All activities are done in real time and learners communicate with their team mates as well.

Predicting Student Performance From Combined Data Sources

In distance education where students do not meet face to face and interact with learning material on a virtual learning environment (VLE), machine learning methods are applied to combine data sources of students which allow the educators to judge the required assistance per student. Although VLE techniques are being used in the past to deliver the course material but their use at a large scale is a recent phenomenon. Kabra and Bichkar (2011) choose decision tree over other methods to predict the failing engineering students. Bhardwaj and Pal (2012) also used decision tree to predict the student performance outcome combined with other information such as attendance. To produce the instantly available information upon which learners and educators can take action to produce the learning outcome, real time predictive analysis of large data sets of students is required. If we incorporate the VLE data while also considering the existing static students' demographic data, past history of students, their behavioral data and assessment data in the datasets, the predictive analytics from VLE data will become more relevant and efficient with the emergence of recent massive open online courses such as provided by Future Learn and Coursera and Big Data University. Such open online website providers are able to make use of virtual learning environment with the educational data mining techniques.

Predicting Learners Answer Correctness Through Eye Movement

Bayazit, Askar and Cosgun gave a data mining technique, Random Forests, to predict learners' result. As a teacher, it is feasible to know the learners' cognitive processes in the period of test and it can be predicted that whether he/she will answer the question correctly or not. For such kind of information eye tracking technology is used. In cognitive psychology, distinctive objects are recognized at 50 ms which is known as 'salience effect'. In general, attention selectively filters the inputs of a system and hence the work load of system is reduced. In human brain, the data received by the eyes is filtered in many levels which constructs the visual attention system. Visual attention mechanism also considers the following events-

1. Identifying an area of interest.
2. Identifying the characteristics/value of interest.
3. Controlling the information.
4. Shifting to one area to another.

Random Forests (RF), also known as Random Decision Forests, are an ensemble learning method which is greatly used for classification and regression. Random Forests are preferred over decision trees as they overcome the decision trees' habit of overfitting of the training data. As RF gives importance to variables hence the researchers used RF as a feature selector. During the question solving it is very useful for the instructors to understand the reasons of blank, right and wrong answers.

To predict the learners' answer correctness through eye movement, eye tracker device was used to record eye movement. And total fixation duration, first fixation duration, fixation count, visit duration, mouse click count and time from first fixation to next mouse click were recorded. Total Fixation Duration metric measures the time in seconds as the sum of the time of all fixations within an area of interest. First Fixation Duration metric also measures time of first fixation in seconds. Fixation count is a count metric which counts the number of times the participants fix on an area of interest. Other metric also measures the mouse click, visit duration etc. These metrics are used predicting the learners' answer correctness through eye movement.

Text Mining for Educational Applications

Text Mining or Text Data Mining is the analysis of data which is confined in natural language text for some useful purpose. Typical text mining applications help organizations in getting insight into their business from text based contents. Mining of such unstructured data is quite challenging with the technique of natural language processing, statistical modeling and machine learning.

Text mining also has educational applications and currently it is required to integrate different tools for education focused text mining. In education sector, following can be the area of interest where educational data mining related to text documents can be applied:

1. Extracting graphs from text data representing relevant terms.
2. Helping instructor to evaluate student article qualitatively.
3. Helping teachers/ instructors to find relevant text from students' discussion forums.
4. Text Categorization, where a set of documents can be classified into a particular category based on some keywords.
5. Providing editorial support in publishing services.

Sobek is a popular text mining tool which was developed to support educational applications. Sobek was initiated in 2003 by Schenker and later modified by GTech.edu research group. Sobek is very useful tool which is easy to use and understand. Sobek is able to perform analysis of any type of text but in reality, its growth was originally encouraged by the requirement of university teachers who work with distant learning and needs to read lot of texts written by students. The text mining tool Sobek, empowers the teachers to complete their work speedily and allowing educators to concentrate on specific problems. This tool is also able to analyze text even in different file formats.

EDM AND LEARNING ANALYTICS

Extraction of useful information from large data sets is termed as Analytics or Data Mining. The same concept and techniques when applied to educational domain is called Learning Analytics or sometimes

Educational Data Mining. Both the communities have considerable overlap in terms of research and researchers but both the communities conduct research that benefit learners and helps in enhancing the learning sciences.

Learning analytics have a greater focus on human interpretation of data and visualization whereas EDM has greater focus on automated tools to discover knowledge.

Few prominent differences between EDM and Learning Analytics are (see Table 4).

The various types of analytics that can be obtained from EDM are:

1. Quality of text.
2. Richness of content.
3. Similarity of content.
4. Content with respect to some benchmark text.
5. Recommending suitable learning objects.
6. Facilitating reasoning about the educational process.

SOCIAL NETWORK ANALYSIS IN THE EDUCATIONAL FIELD

The process of analyzing and investigating social structures using network and graph theories is called social network analysis. Network structure is characterized in terms of nodes and edges or links. Nodes are the individual actors or people within the network and edges are the relationships among the nodes. Due to the increasing popularity of the social network services like Facebook, Twitter, Instagram etc. Social network analysis has emerged as a popular research field now days. Students of all age groups are using social networking sites and analyzing the impact of their usage can inform educators in a unique way to improve educational reform.

In any learning context which uses social network as the base for education promotion, teachers, educators and students can act as main nodes among which different relationships can be defined. For example, even student and teacher can participate in different blogs together to put forward their views.

Social network analysis plays a major role in understanding student network formation in classrooms and the types of impact these networks have on student. SNA even helps in formulating the techniques to improve the student learning patterns and also in transforming the learning outcomes based on student behavior and skills.

Table 4. Differences between EDM and learning analytics

EDM	Learning Analytics
Focuses on Latent Technology Estimation	Focuses on Classical approaches of classification and regression
Emphasized on Domain Structure Discovery Algorithm	Emphasized on Social Network Analysis
Relationship Mining methods are more commonly used to interpret data	Relationship mining methods are less commonly used although these methods support interpretation of data by analyst.
Discovery with model is a prominent method in EDM	Least commonly used due to differences in research question in focus.
Uses Biclustering and frequent pattern mining	Uses Collaborative filtering and Visual analytics

Social network analysis helps in gathering the information about

1. Group Cohesion.
2. Participation in Collaborative Activities.
3. Connection among subjects.
4. Student behavior profile.
5. Performance and dropout patterns.

Although to analyze and predict the student performance and behavior, a lot of data mining tools are available but to uncover the patterns of people interaction by understanding the psychology of people and implementing the techniques to improve educator's outcome using these patterns is an unexplored area. Hence classification techniques of data mining are popularly used in SNA to forecast student performance and to predict student behavior.

SNA aims to understand and measure the social relationships and is suitable for interpreting and analyzing the structure and relations in collaborative tasks and interactions with communication tools (Rabbany et al., 2008).

FUTURE RESEARCH AREAS

In the past few years, researchers are paying their attention to investigate that how data mining can facilitate education. Throughout the chapter, various key application of educational data mining like modeling student performance in higher education, detecting personality of players in educational game, predicting student performance etc have been discussed in detail. Research in educational data mining is the need of the current era and still there is lot of future scope in this field for the researchers. Currently, most of the researchers are focusing on e-learning like Moodle but it would be beneficial if the researchers pay attention towards the use of social networking tools as these are gaining high popularity among students these days. Researchers also need to focus on integrating Google Analytics with blog data environment and using the blog data for educational mining.

Another area of research is to relate interdisciplinary fields such as artificial intelligence in education. A lot of scope to the researchers and software developers in EDM is in the discovery with models. Another recommendation is to create a strong collaboration between research, educational sector and their commercial use. Commercial organization may provide support to the researchers in producing fast data which will be careful for research.

Finally, to make the complete use of EDM, it is necessary that EDM tools must be freely available to be used by a wider population and educators and institutions should develop a culture of making instructional decisions and improving instructions with the use of EDM so that results from research of EDM can be used in the narrow context of specific research problem.

REFERENCES

Allport, G. W., & Odbert, H. S. (1936). Trait names: a psycho-lexical study. *Psychological Monographs, 47*(1), 171–220.

Baker, R. S. J. d. (2007). Is Gaming the System State-or-Trait? Educational Data Mining Through the Multi-Contextual Application of a Validated Behavioral Model. *Proceedings of the Workshop on Data Mining for User Modeling at the 11th International Conference on User Modeling 2007*, 76-80.

Baker, R. S. J. d., & de Carvalho, A. M. J. A. (2008). Labeling Student Behavior Faster and More Precisely with Text Replays.*Proceedings of the First International Conference on Educational Data Mining*, 38-47.

Barnes, T., Bitzer, D., & Vouk, M. (2005). Experimental Analysis of the Q-Matrix Method in Knowledge Discovery. Lecture Notes in Computer Science: Vol. 3488. Foundations of Intelligent Systems (pp. 603-611). Springer. doi:10.1007/11425274_62

Beck, J. E., & Mostow, J. (2008). How who should practice: Using learning decomposition to evaluate the efficacy of different types of practice for different types of students. *Proceedings of the 9th International Conference on Intelligent Tutoring Systems*, 353-362. doi:10.1007/978-3-540-69132-7_39

Bhardwaj, B. K., & Pal, S. (2012). *Data Mining: A prediction for performance improvement using classification*. arXiv preprint arXiv:1201.3418

Bidgoli, B. M., Kashy, D., Kortemeyer, G., & Punch, W. (2003). Predicting student performance: An application of data mining methods with the educational web-based system lon-capa. *Proceedings of ASEE/IEEE frontiers in education conference*.

Cen, H., Koedinger, K., & Junker, B. (2006). Learning Factors Analysis - A General Method for Cognitive Model Evaluation and Improvement. *Proceedings of the 8th International Conference on Intelligent Tutoring Systems*, 12-19. doi:10.1007/11774303_17

Desmarais, M. C., Maluf, A., & Liu, J. (1996). User-expertise modeling with empirically derived probabilistic implication networks. *User Modeling and User-Adapted Interaction*, *5*(3-4), 283–315. doi:10.1007/BF01126113

Gray, G., McGuinness, C., & Owende, P. (2014). An application of classification models to predict learner progression in tertiary education. Advance Computing Conference (IACC),2014IEEE International, 549–554. doi:10.1109/IAdCC.2014.6779384

Kabra & Bichkar. (2011). Performance prediction of engineering students using decision trees. *International Journal of Computer Applications, 36*(11).

Mayilvaganan, M., & Kalpanadevi, D. (2014). Comparison of classification techniques for predicting the performance of students academic environment. *Communication and Network Technologies (ICCNT), 2014International Conference on*, 113–118. doi:10.1109/CNT.2014.7062736

Norman, W. T. (1963). Toward an adequate taxonomy of personality attributes: Replicated factor structure in peer nomination personality rating. *Journal of Abnormal and Social Psychology*, *66*(6), 574–583. doi:10.1037/h0040291 PMID:13938947

Oladokun, V., Adebanjo, A., & Charles-Owaba, O. (2008). Predicting students academic performance using artificial neural network: A case study of an engineering course. *The Pacific Journal of Science and Technology*, *9*(1), 72–79.

Pavlik, P., Cen, H., Wu, L., & Koedinger, K. (2008). Using Item-Type Performance Covariance to Improve the Skill Model of an Existing Tutor. *Proceedings of the First International Conference on Educational Data Mining*, 77-86.

Peabody, D., & Goldberg, L. R. (1989). Some determinants of factor structures from personality-trait descriptor. *Journal of Personality and Social Psychology, 57*(3), 552–567. doi:10.1037/0022-3514.57.3.552 PMID:2778639

Rabbany, R., Takaffoli, M., & Zaıane, O. R. (2011). Social network analysis and mining to support the assessment of on-line student participation. *SIGKDD Explorations, 13*(2), 20–29. doi:10.1145/2207243.2207247

Read, S. J., Monroe, B. M., Brownstein, A. L., Yang, Y., Chopra, G., & Miller, L. C. (2010). A neural network model of the structure and dynamics of human personality. *Psychological Review, 117*(1), 61–92. doi:10.1037/a0018131 PMID:20063964

Romero, C., Ventura, S., Espejo, P. G., & Hervas, C. (2008). Data mining algorithms to classify students in Educational Data Mining. *Transactions on Educational Data Mining, 22*, 122–130.

Schenker, A. (2003). *Graph-Theoretic Techniques for Web Content Mining* (PhD thesis). University of South Florida.

Shih, B., Koedinger, K. R., & Scheines, R. (2008). A Response-Time Model for Bottom-Out Hints as Worked Examples. *Proceedings of the First International Conference on Educational Data Mining*, 117-126.

Vaassen & Daelemans. (2010). Emotion classification in a serious game for training communication skills. *LOT Occasional Series, 16*, 155-168.

Wang, T., & Mitrovic, A. (2002). Using neural networks to predict student's performance. *Computers in Education, 2002. Proceedings. International Conference on*, 969–973. doi:10.1109/CIE.2002.1186127

ADDITIONAL READING

Agrawal, R. (2014). K-Nearest Neighbor for Uncertain Data. *International Journal of Computers and Applications, 5*(11), 13–17.

Agrawal, R. (2016). A Modified K-Nearest Neighbor Algorithm Using Feature Optimization. *IACSIT International Journal of Engineering and Technology, 8*(1), 28–37.

Bienkowski, M., Feng, M., & Means, B. (2012). Enhancing teaching and learning through educational data mining and learning analytics: an issue brief. In *Tech republic*. Washington, D.C.: Office of Educational Technology, U.S. Department of Education.

Dawson, S., Tan, J. P. L., & McWilliam, E. (2011). Measuring creative potential: Using social network analysis to monitor a learners creative capacity. *Australasian Journal of Educational Technology, 27*(6), 924–942. doi:10.14742/ajet.921

Lin, C. C., & Tsai, C. C. (2012). Participatory learning through behavioral and cognitive engagements in an online collective information searching activity, I. J. *Computer-Supported Collaborative Learning*, 7(4), 543–566. doi:10.1007/s11412-012-9160-1

Macfadyen, L. P., & Dawson, S. (2010). Mining fLMSg data to develop an early warning system for educators: A proof of concept. *Computers & Education*, 54(2), 588–599. http://www.sciencedirect.com/science/article/pii/S0360131509002486 doi:10.1016/j.compedu.2009.09.008

Section 5
Big Data Privacy and Security

Chapter 8
Privacy Preserving Data Mining on Unstructured Data

Trupti Vishwambhar Kenekar
G. H. Raisoni Institute of Engineering and Technology, India

Ajay R. Dani
G. H. Raisoni Institute of Engineering and Technology, India

ABSTRACT

As Big Data is group of structured, unstructured and semi-structure data collected from various sources, it is important to mine and provide privacy to individual data. Differential Privacy is one the best measure which provides strong privacy guarantee. The chapter proposed differentially private frequent item set mining using map reduce requires less time for privately mining large dataset. The chapter discussed problem of preserving data privacy, different challenges to preserving data privacy in big data environment, Data privacy techniques and their applications to unstructured data. The analyses of experimental results on structured and unstructured data set are also presented.

INTRODUCTION

It is estimated that on an average around 1.09 billion users accessed popular social networking site "Facebook" every day in the month of March 2016 (Anonymous,2016) As per statistics published on site Internet Live statistics state that search engine "Google" carries out 40000 search queries every second(Anonymous,2016). The number of internet users in the world is estimated to be around 3.17 billion (Statista, 2016). Apart from using social networking sites internet users carry out other activities like electronic fund transfers, online purchases, reservations etc. These activities carried out over internet by different users generate large volume of electronic data every day. In last few years volume of electronic data is growing rapidly because of usage number of different devices like smart phones, video recordings in different offices and locations (e.g. Close Circuit Television (CCTV) recordings), mobile phones with cameras, wireless sensor networks etc. All of these have resulted in serious challenges to data privacy.

DOI: 10.4018/978-1-5225-2486-1.ch008

In order to use "Facebook" user needs to create his profile, which consists of information like name, date of birth etc. (also called as data attributes). These data attributes can be categorized into two categories as follows.

1. **Identifying Attributes (IA):** These are attributes which can identify individuals uniquely or help in their identification. The examples of such attributes are Permanent Account Number (PAN) allotted by Income Tax Department of Government of India, Social Security Number (SSN) in USA, Name and Date of Birth etc.
2. **Sensitive Attributes (SA):** These attributes represent sensitive and private information about individuals like medical history, salary details, web browsing history etc. It is expected that only authorized users should be able to view sensitive and private information of users.

When an individual can be identified from the data (e.g. published frequent item sets) the data privacy is said to be violated. When unauthorized users are able to view sensitive information of individuals (say his medical records or financial status) individual's privacy is violated. The privacy violation is more serious in case unauthorized user is able to link sensitive and private information to individual's identity. In the webpage (Adrienne Felt, 2016) of Computer Science Department of University of Virginia, USA the problem of privacy violation with "Facebook" Platform has been described by researcher Adrienne Felt and it is stated that "Facebook" platform allows any "Facebook" user to add different gadgets to his profile. After adding gadgets user can run external third party applications without leaving "Facebook" site. Any data which can be accessed by the user can be accessed by the owners of these applications. The owner of the application can collect data about user's friends and network and sensitive information like birthdays and can violate data privacy.

The problem of releasing privately held data without identifying individuals is not a new problem (Sweency, 2002). The main purposes of releasing such information can be making data available to researchers, public (for information and other proposes) or can be purely commercial. However in last decade computing environment has changed significantly posing serious data privacy challenges. The main reasons are as follows.

1. In last decade large number organizations (e.g. social networking sites) having private and sensitive information of individuals has emerged. Many of these organizations are willing to share at least part of this information with other companies for commercial purposes. There are many companies who have commercial interest in mining such data.
2. The user profile on social networking site and his network can be commercially useful to many companies.
3. Increasing web activity and usage of different electronic devices and gadgets generate large volume of electronic data (big data environment).The mining of such massive data sets can provide commercially valuable information to many companies.
4. Increase and availability of cheap computing power has made it possible to apply data mining algorithms on very large data sets (big data mining).
5. In addition to this there is emergence of cloud computing platform (Saurabh K.) has also increases data privacy challenge. The popular service models in cloud computing environment (Saurabh K.) are as follows.
    a. Infrastructure as a service (IaaS).

b.   Platform as a service (PaaS).
c.   Data as a service (DaaS).
d.   Software as a service (SaaS).

Depending upon their requirements enterprises can adopt any of these service models in their operations. In case of SaaS or DaaS model, organization's database is externally stored on the server provided by cloud service provider (Saurabh K.). The cloud services are accessed over public network like internet and cloud service providers cannot be completely trusted. The cloud service provider can potentially get access to the stored data and can get access to the data when it is queried by the users. This can result in violation of data privacy. Many organizations have commercial interests in collecting the private information and cloud databases are good source to provide such information. Due to these reasons there is increasing threat to data privacy. The importance of maintaining privacy of data can be imagined from the fact that multinational giant company named "Sony" was charged with fine of £250000 by Information Commissioners Office of Great Britain (John Glenday,2013), when it was discovered that the company did not use the latest version of data security software on its "Play Station" network. This act of omission on the part of "Sony" allowed hackers to break into its online store. As a result of this private and sensitive information like date of birth and credit card details were exposed to criminals. In another case "Google" was warned by Dutch data protection agency that the company could be fined for 15 million Euros in case it continued violating the privacy of Internet users in Netherlands (Dutch data protection agency, 2014).

The most of the data in the world today is in unstructured text format. The healthcare data of individuals can be considered as sensitive data in unstructured format. Mining of such data can affect data privacy. However the problem of preserving privacy in such environment is not widely studied. In this chapter authors have extended the concept of differential privacy to handle large volume of unstructured data sets. An attempt is made to develop differentially private frequent pattern mining algorithms on large volume of unstructured data. The chapter is organized as follows.

In section 2, different aspects of data privacy are discussed. The data privacy challenges in big data environment are discussed in section 3. Different data privacy techniques like K-anonymity (Sweency, 2002) and differential privacy (Dwork, 2006) and their applications are discussed in section 4. In section 5, the design and architecture of our system is presented. Finally authors conclude in section 6. The experimental results demonstrate the effectiveness of proposed algorithms on unstructured data set.

DATA PRIVACY

In this section, the concept of data privacy is explained with an example from banking domain. An organization like bank or insurance company collects private information about its customer during its operations. If a customer wants to open an account with bank or purchase an insurance policy he needs to complete an application form prescribed by the bank or the insurance company and submit it. Once an account is open customer can carry out different banking transactions. The snapshot of data collected by "State Bank of India" the largest public sector banks can be seen at online (Anonymous, 2015). The bank will collect private information like Passport Details or PAN number, name, address, date of birth, father's name; city of birth etc. (which either identify individual or can help to uniquely identify individuals) and store it in electronic format. The amount of balance in the customer account or amount of loan taken by customer represents the private and sensitive information. Apart from the customer, this information should only be known to the authorized employees of bank. In this case it is necessary for the bank to keep this information away from employees of bank who need not know the customer transactions or details, other customers of bank, any unauthorized person and outside world. In his book Solove (2010) has stated that privacy is a fundamental right, essential for freedom, democracy, psychological well-being, individuality and creativity. The other examples of such private and sensitive data are the data attributes included in medical records, name, date of birth, contact details disease etc. The entities or organization have an obligation to protect individual's private data when they collect, store, use and delete or destroy that data in digital form or any other format(Safe Computing,2016).

Data Security and Privacy are closely related terms. The term data security (Stinson, 2005) is used to mean confidentiality, availability and integrity. The term data privacy (Solove, 2010) means that the entities that collect private and sensitive data of individuals must use it for the purposes for which it was collected. It also means that entities cannot sell, disclose or outsource data for processing without following specified legal procedure (Federal Trade Commission, 2014). The data privacy violations occur when unauthorized users are able to view private and sensitive information or identify individuals from the data available from different sources. The examples of data privacy violations stated in earlier section ("Sony" or "Facebook" examples) occurred because unauthorized users were able to get access to the sensitive and private information by exploiting the flaws in the security system. However such violations can occur even without exploiting any security flaws. The concept of privacy preserving data mining (Malik, Gazi, & Ali, 2012), which attempts to protect the privacy of individuals without sacrificing the utility of the data, has been proposed to overcome the challenges of data privacy arising out of mining sensitive data from different sources in big data environment. In next section authors discuss different challenges do data privacy as result of emergence of big data.

PRIVACY CHALLENGES IN BIG DATA ENVIRONMENT

The traditional data life cycle consists of following phases.

1. **Data Creation:** In this phase data gets created due to many different activities like accessing websites, internet transactions etc.
2. **Data Maintenance:** In this phase the created data is stored in different storage devices and used for analysis and reporting.
3. **Data Sharing:** The stored may be shared with different entities.
4. **Data Archival:** The older stored data (e.g. Data created about year back) is copied and archived for safe keeping and for reusing the storage space.
5. **Data Retention:** The data holders need to retain data for specific period of time as per legal requirements.
6. **Data Deletion:** In some cases the data can be deleted from different storage devices.

The cost of storing such data has decreased over period of time. In big data environment different privacy challenges arise because this data can be correlated with the data sets released for different purposes or available for querying. The main privacy and security challenges in big data environment are to provide guarantee that the private data of individuals will be protected from misuse by users who view that data, the entities who have collected private and sensitive data called as big data holders or the entities like third party cloud service provider. The large volume of data that is available will be useful only if it can provide new insights, help to discover knowledge and can be used invention purpose (i.e. data utility). Some of the data privacy and security challenges in big data environment are as summarized follows (Simo, 2015).

Increased Risk of Capturing Significant of Sensitive Data

The risk of privacy breaches has increased significantly in Big Data environment as data containing some sensitive and private attributes is publicly available, can be accessed using internet, can be shared with other users and organizations. The emergence of Big Data has thrown new privacy challenges about how to access, how to store and manage user related private and sensitive data. In last 3 years, there are many documented series of prominent data security violation incidents where data privacy breaches were caused by users who have gained access to sensitive datasets legally and by the unauthorized users.

It can be seen that the unauthorized users (also called as adversary) who access data can be interested in either gaining access to large volume of private and sensitive data (like financial and identity data) to misuse it or to alter such data so that its analysis can give misleading results. In order to breach data privacy attackers can exploit software and/or hardware design flaws in the infrastructures behind Big Data platforms. Such data breaches may result in damages to the brand names of organizations, loss of customers, loss of trust or loyalty of the partners. It can also cause loss of intellectual property and loss of market share. In case, organizations do not comply with privacy regulations they can be subjected to possible legal penalties.

Loss of Individual Control Over Personal Data

Unlike traditional online environment, information technology (IT) organization used to collect; store and process data is not under control of single individual. As compared to traditional online environment it is difficult to maintain control over personnel information flows in big data environment. In such distributed environment where many autonomous entities control the data it is harder to maintain control over flow of personnel information from diverse sources. In some countries there are regulatory privacy requirements which state requirements like data binding and data minimization. It can be seen that these requirements are challenging to achieve in big data environment.

The ownership of data emerging in big data environment and knowledge that can be inferred through it by applying data mining algorithms is still being debated in different forums. This debate is similar to that of ownership of data that is with e-commerce companies and social media. In recent incidents telecommunications giants like Verizon and Orange and Simo (2015) were about to start the process of selling the data of their consumers to the entities who wanted to use it for marketing purposes or managing financial risk. It is stated in (Simo, 2015) that the compliance with different laws related to privacy using different data anonymization techniques is not sufficient to protect personnel data. The challenge in this respect is similar to that of releasing statistical information by different entities (Sweency, 2002).

There is another important aspect about the data explicitly and implicitly created or disclosed by internet users (data subject), during web activities. In big data environment the doubt is raised about the complete implementation of the control of internet users over data created by them. There are reasonable doubts about whether internet users can have any control over data created by them during its life cycle and feasibility of such controls.

Long Period Availability of Sensitive Datasets

The cost of storing data is continuously decreasing over years. It is possible to store large volume of data on small portable devices. The regulatory requirements stipulate the preservation of data for certain time period. At the same time there are business requirements to retain data, as the knowledge gained from such data can be commercially useful. The researchers also find it easy to build large data sets as such data sets are useful for research purposes. Due to these reasons government, business and researchers have built large data sets of almost permanent nature. The identity attributes in such data sets do not change significantly over time. Apart from identity attributes these data sets contain records of behavioral patterns of individuals, details of their lifestyles, their world views and messages and reactions to events sent to others at different points times (emotional state). In reality such world views and life style can change during once lifetime. Digitized information is stored in cross-linked databases which can be searched electronically. The deletion of such information may not lead to deletion from all sources. Big data sets and the knowledge gained from them may contain lasting records of all the exposes and mistakes the data subject has ever constructed on the web and dislike anyone to recall that them years thereafter (Simo, 2015).

Data Quality/Integrity and Provenance Issues

In many cases quality and integrity of data in big data environment is questionable (Simo, 2015). This happens because data can be collected from diverse sources which may not be trustworthy. In many cases the background knowledge and knowledge of history of changes in data may be required to correctly analyze such data and interpret results. The analyst who analyzes data in big data environment by applying different data mining algorithms will not be able to achieve business optimization or effectively run any valuable data-driven process/operation without taking into account quality, integrity and the background context in which the data was collected. It has been stated in the 2011 survey report of Gartner (Friedman, & Smith, 2011, October 10) that about 40% of initiatives of business fail because of poor quality of data used.

Unwanted Data Correlation and Inferences

Due to availability of low cost computing power it is possible to analyze large data sets collected from different sources. It is also possible to aggregate large data sets from different sources as well cross link them. Due to this there is additional risk of privacy breaches. While analyzing data to identify hidden pattern, correlation of information from diverse sources is usually carried out and this may raise the risk of identification / de-anonymization.

A data set independently may not contain any information which can identify the data subject (e.g. health care information without any identity of person). In many circumstances such data sets can be considered as not enclosed by present data protection rules as they do not contain identifiable information. In some cases it may be possible for researcher to find new suggestions or find out new sets of sensitive information even in cases where data substance has disagreed to share such information. This can be done by correlating data set which may anonymized with openly or other confidentially existing data sets. The privacy challenges arising out of correlating different publicly available data sets have been discussed earlier (Sweency, 2002). In this work an anonymous database of Massachusetts state member of staff health insurance entitlements is linked with an openly available voter registration database of the same state and sensitive information has been inferred by correlating these two data sets.

In research paper (Acquisti & Gross, 2011) it is demonstrated it is possible to accurately guess an individual's social security number by using simply data which is publicly available. In this paper authors use freely available U.S. Social Security Administration's Death Master File, personal data from available from several sources like data brokers, profiles on social networking to predict social security number. In newspaper article (Charle Duhigg, 2012) described how statisticians working in company named "Target" are able to predict whether a female customer is pregnant or not with 87% confidence. This prediction is done by identifying the patterns in their behavior by using history of customers' purchases. The insights gained from this analysis was used to assist those customers recognized as expectant parents with personalized advertisements about new born related goods. In (Kosinski, Stillwell, & Graepl, 2013), exposed that using "Facebook Likes", it is possible to automatically and perfectly draw inferences about sensitive identity attributes of social media users like age, sex, ethnicity, religious and political views and other personality traits. In next section the overview of different privacy preserving techniques is presented.

PRIVACY PRESERVING TECHNIQUES AND RELATED WORK

In this section different privacy preserving techniques used in data mining applications are briefly reviewed. The technique of anonymization (Cox, 1980; Dalenius, 1986) has been proposed for protecting privacy in the perspective of statistical disclosure control. In this technique the sensitive data values of customers like customer identification number, contact number are either removed or replaced by random mapping or encryption mechanism in database. The dataset without any information is released. In today's big data environment the individual information is stored in multiple databases with different entities. The k-Anonymity technique has been projected to overcome the problem privacy breaches arising out of correlating different datasets (Sweency, 2002).

The three most common techniques for privacy preserving data mining are follows.

1. k-Anonymity
2. l-Diversity
3. t-Closeness

The concept of k-Anonymity was introduced by L. Sweency in 2002. In this work it is assumed that an organization has structured data set containing private and sensitive data and an approach to prepare a release of data with precise guarantees that the subjects cannot be re-identified from the release of data and the release remains useful for data analysis and research purposes has been proposed. A release of data satisfies k-anonymity (k>1) property (Sweency, 2002), if the records of an individual contained in the release cannot be distinguished from at least (k−1) individuals whose information also appear in the release. In such case the probability of correct identification of an individual will be (1/k).

Let there be a table of n rows and m columns consisting of private, sensitive and identity data of individuals. A snapshot of disease information table of eleven individuals is indicated in Table 1. The table has 6 columns and 11 rows. The individuals in the table can be identified by their names and age. The combination of attributes like "Name", "Age", "Sex" and "State of Domicile" can be used to identify individuals. It contains private and sensitive information about disease. The data set is not anonymized.

The common methods for achieving k-anonymity for any value of k briefly described below.

1. Suppression In this method, the values of identifying attributes in all or some of the rows are replaced by "*" symbol. In case "Name" attribute is suppressed the person viewing table will know the disease but will not the person who has that disease.

2. Generalization: In this method the values of attributes are substituted by range or broader category. As an example consider "Age" attribute, if the age individual is 18 years, it can be replaced by "$15<Age\leq20$" or can also be replaced by categorical variable "Young".

The table obtained after application of these two steps indicated in Table 2. In Table 2, all values of attributes "Name" and "Religion" are replaced by "*". All the values of "Age" attributes are replaced by range. The data in this table has 2-anonymity property with respect to the attributes "Age", "Sex" and "State of Domicile". The table has at least 2 rows where attribute values for "Age", "Sex" and "State of Domicile" are the (e.g. Age ="$30<Age\leq40$", State="Kerala", Sex="Female" – 2 rows) same. The attributes "Age", "Sex" and "State of Domicile" are called as quasi-identifiers (Aggarwal & Yu, 2008). Each "quasi-identifier" row occurs in at least k records for a dataset with k-anonymity (Aggarwal, & Yu, 2008). The time complexity of rendering k-anonymized data set with minimum amount of information that is released is studied in (Meyerson, & Williams, 2004) and it shown that this optimization problem is NP-Hard (Meyerson, & Williams, 2004). An approach to reduce time complexity of anonymization by discovering the space of possible anonymization that suppresses the combinatorics of the problem is presented in (Bayardo & Agarwal, 2005).

The k-anonymity is simple and easy to implement. The act of identifying individuals using background information from anonymized data set is called as an attack. The authors have shown in (Narayanan, &

Table 1. Medical record of individuals

Name	Age	Sex	State	Religion	Disease
Sarika	38	Female	Maharashtra	Hindu	Cancer
Padama	33	Female	Goa	Hindu	Viral infection
Salima	37	Female	Maharashtra	Muslim	TB
Monty	36	Male	Punjab	Parsi	No illness
Anna	33	Female	Goa	Christian	Heart-problem
Ranvir	32	Male	Punjab	Buddhist	TB
Rakesh	28	Male	Goa	Hindu	Cancer
Aakash	38	Male	Punjab	Hindu	Heart problem
Jon	26	Male	Goa	Christian	Heart-problem
Faiz	28	Male	Goa	Christian	Viral infection

Table 2. Anonymized Table 1

Name	Age	Sex	State	Religion	Disease
*	30<Age ≤ 40	Female	Maharashtra	*	Cancer
*	30<Age ≤ 40	Female	Goa	*	Viral infection
*	30<Age ≤ 40	Female	Maharashtra	*	TB
*	30<Age ≤ 40	Male	Punjab	*	Heart Problem
*	30<Age ≤ 40	Female	Goa	*	Heart-problem
*	30<Age ≤ 40	Male	Punjab	*	TB
*	Age ≤ 30	Male	Goa	*	Cancer
*	30< Age ≤ 40	Male	Punjab	*	Heart-problem
*	Age ≤ 30	Male	Goa	*	Heart-problem
*	Age ≤30	Male	Goa	*	Viral infection

Shmatikov, 2008) if certain information about "Netflix" subscriber is known (background knowledge), it is possible to identify corresponding record and sensitive information from the anonymized dataset. The two most common attacks on k-anonymity are as follows.

1. **Homogeneity Attack:** This attack can occur in instance all the values for a sensitive attributes within a data set of k records are identical. An example of such case can be where the value of "Disease" attribute is identical for a combination of "Age", "Sex" and "State".
2. **Background Knowledge Attack:** In this case the prior knowledge of association between one or more values of quasi-identifier attributes is used to decrease the set of possible values for sensitive attribute. It has been shown in (Machanavajjhala, Kifer, Gehrke & Venkitasubramaniam, 2007) that the background information about rate of occurrence of heart attacks in Japanese patients can be used to narrow the range of values for a sensitive attribute like patient's disease.

L-Diversity

A stronger notion of privacy called as L-diversity has been proposed in (Machanavajjhala, Kifer, Gehrke, & Venkitasubramaniam, 2007) to overcome weaknesses of k-Anonymity model. It has been shown in (Machanavajjhala, Kifer, Gehrke, & Venkitasubramaniam, 2007) that l-diversity can provide data privacy even if data publisher does not know about the type of background knowledge attacker has. The *l*-diversity model can be considered as an extension of *k*-anonymity model and can provide protection against the attacks on k-anonymity described above. The main idea behind l-diversity is that the values of sensitive attributes are well represented in a group. It has been shown that the existing algorithms k-anonymity can be extended to obtain data sets with l-diversity property (Machanavajjhala, Kifer, Gehrke, & Venkitasubramaniam, 2007).

In l-diversity model the techniques of generalization and suppression (Liu & Wang, 2010) is used to reduce the granularity of data representation. The granularity is reduced in such a way that that it is possible to map any given record in the data to at least *k* other records. The reduction in granularity is a tradeoff which can result in certain amount of loss of effectiveness in the results of data mining algorithms in order to achieve some privacy.

Attacks on *l*-Diversity

The *l*-diversity technique is useful because it effectively prevents the attacker from using his background knowledge or information to infer information about sensitive data values in many cases. In some cases an attacker can use the knowledge of a rare positive indicator for a disease to infer values. Such indicator can provide more information than a common negative indicator. In some cases sensitive information can be inferred from the anonymized data set satisfying l-diversity property because l-diversity property confirms "diversity" of sensitive attribute values in each group but these values can be semantically close. As an example one can consider a table satisfying l-diversity, where a group of may consist of individuals with different types of stomach diseases. An attacker can infer that individual has some type of stomach disease.

T-Closeness

The *t*-closeness model extends the *l*-diversity model by taking into account the distribution of sensitive attribute in the table and in a class (N. Li, T. Li, & Venkatsubranmanian, 2007). The property of t-closeness involves that the distribution of a sensitive attribute in any equivalence class is close to the distribution of a sensitive attribute in the overall table. This property can provide protection against the disclosure of the value of sensitive attribute but not against identity disclosure.

Other Methods for Protecting Privacy

In order to design any privacy mechanism the utility and privacy trade-off has to be considered. It is common practice to provide data sets where individual specific data is hidden for data mining. The hiding of individual specific data may result in certain loss in the utility of the data. It can be seen that data set which does not reveal any private information may not be useful for research purposes. So utility and privacy tradeoff has to be achieved. The objective of designing data privacy mechanism is to allow data set to remain useful and protect the privacy of individuals. In order to design privacy preserving mechanism list of different types of data mining algorithms and statistical reports which will be generated on the data set has to be prepared. Then the output has to be has to be transformed in such a way that no private information is revealed. Another aspect that is required to be considered is how different data mining algorithms will be applied. There two ways to apply such data mining algorithms. In first case data set (which will not reveal any private information) is released and data mining algorithms may be applied. In second case data set may be available for interactive queries and analysis and perturbed results are returned. It should not be possible to attacker to deduce the answer even if he knows the privacy preserving method used. Suppose that the age of an individual is x, and the reported answer is y, then it should not be possible for attacker to deduce value of x from y. Few important types of data privacy protection methods are presented in next three paragraphs.

Aggregation

In this technique the granularity of data is reduced and aggregation may be carried with respect to different attributes. This technique is be used to reduce disclosure risks by turning potentially sensitive records (which have high risk of disclosure) into the records with lower risk of disclosure. As an example, consider a case where there is only one person with a particular combination of demographic features in a city, but many people with those characteristics in a state. In such case data can be released at state level rather than at city level. This will reduce the risk of disclosure.

Suppression

The organizations releasing data can delete sensitive values from the released data set. If the values of particular attributes are suppressed the data set with missing values will be created. In some cases it may not be possible to analyze such data set. As an example cone can consider a case where income vales above certain threshold values are suppressed. Then any estimates of the income distribution based on the released data will be biased and the average and median values will be much lower than actual values.

Data Swapping

In this technique the organizations releasing data sets swap data values for certain selected records and then release data sets. A data set can be released after switching values of the attributes like age, race and sex for the records with higher level of disclosure risk with the corresponding values of records with lower level of disclosure risk. Any user who matches the data from released data set with any other known data set will not get the correct results. The organizations using this technique do not reveal the number of swapped values and the algorithms used. The swapping at high levels can destroy relationships among different variables in data.

Adding Random Noise

The technique of adding random noise to numeric data is widely used by many organizations. Adding random noise to numeric data values can decrease the possibilities of perfect matching on the perturbed data and protect privacy. The degree of confidentiality protection offered by adding random noise depends on the nature of the noise distribution. If random numbers drawn from a distribution with large variance are added then higher level of protection can be provided. Adding random noise with large variance can introduce errors in the data and answers to queries. It can distort different statistical measures like regression coefficients. The strong privacy guarantees like differential privacy (Dwork, 2006) can be provided by adding random noise from heavy tailed distribution like a Laplace distribution to the query answers

Synthetic Data

In this technique the actual data values which have higher risk of disclosure or identification are replaced by the values simulated from probability distributions. The organizations using this technique ensure that probability distributions match closely with the actual data distribution. An attempt is also made to reproduce as many of the relationships in the original data as possible. In this technique either all values of variable in data can be replaced by simulated values (full) or subset of values can be replaced (partial). In order to create synthetic data a detailed model of the data is created, or the data is transformed into different space (e.g. Fourier). The alternate representation of the obtained data is perturbed. The synthetic data set is created from the perturbed data. US census bureau (Census Bureau's, 2015) releases the data sets by using synthetic data generation technique in order to ensure that no private or sensitive information gets released.

Frequent item set mining (FIM) is one of the most fundamental problems in data mining (Sweency, 2002). Two efficient algorithms to discover k-frequent patterns from sensitive transactional data have been presented in (Bhaskar, Laxman, Smith, & Thakurta, 2010). The concept of differential privacy (Dwork, 2006) which provides strong theoretical guarantees has been used by many researchers to propose data mining algorithms which can preserve data privacy. An Apriori based differentially private algorithm with precise quantification of utility trade-off is presented in (Zeng, Naughton, & Cai, 2012). The approach of truncating long transactions has been proposed in this work. A differentially private FIM (called as PFP-Growth) algorithm which is highly efficient, achieves high data utility and high degree of privacy is proposed in (Su, Xu, Ceng, Li, & Wang, 2015). These privacy preserving algorithms have been developed for transactional databases.

Differential Privacy

The idea of differential privacy has been proposed in (Dwork, 2006) to overcome some of the limitations of the data privacy techniques discussed earlier. Differential privacy provides strong privacy preserving guarantees. The main principal is that small changes in the database should not be visible to attackers. In this technique the actual results of any query executed on database are returned after adding suitable random noise. It has been studied by researcher in different domains such as FIM (Li, Qardaji, Su, & Cao, 2012), geospatial data (Qardaji, Yang, & Li, 2013), and spatial crowd sourcing (To, Ghinita, & Shahabi, 2014) etc.

A randomized function f (algorithm) satisfies ϵ differential privacy (Dwork, 2006) if for any two input sets (databases) D_x and D_y with symmetric difference of one record or row (also called as neighboring databases), and for any set of outcomes $S \subseteq Range(f)$, the following condition is satisfied

$$\Pr[f(D_x) \in S] \leq e^{\epsilon} \times \Pr[f(D_y) \in S] \tag{1}$$

The term ϵ is the privacy parameter (also called as privacy budget) which states the privacy level of the mechanism. The higher values of ϵ provide lower level of privacy, while the smaller values provide higher level or stronger privacy guarantee.

In differentially private algorithms the concept of global sensitivity (Dwork, McSherry, Nissim & Smith, 2006) is used. The global sensitivity GS of function $f : D \rightarrow R^n$ denoted by $GS(f)$ is defined as is defined as

$$GS(f) = \max_{D_x, D_y} \| f(D_x) - f(D_y) \| \tag{2}$$

So the value of $GS(f)$ defines the upper bound on differences between outputs of function f for any two databases which differ in one record. In order to achieve differential privacy random noise $r(GS(f))$ is added to the output of $f(D_x)$. So the answer $f(D_x) + r(GS(f)/\epsilon)$ will be returned to the user.

The differential privacy has achieved by two well established techniques. The first technique is based on Laplace Mechanism (Dwork, McSherry, Nissim, & Smith, 2006) and the second is based on Exponential Mechanism (McSherry & Talwar, 2007, October).

In case Laplace mechanism is used the noise is generated from a distribution with probability density function $pdf(x \mid \lambda) = \dfrac{1}{2\lambda} e^{-|x|/\lambda}$ where the parameter λ is determined by$\in$ and $GS(f)$.

The authors proposed two phase algorithm in (Bonomi & Xiong, 2013) for privately mining prefixes and substring patterns and the work is based on the assumption large number of frequent patterns can be captured by short strings. In paper (Shen & Yu, 2013), authors have shown that the techniques used in differentially private algorithms cannot be used in mining frequent graph patterns due to the complexity of handling structural information in graphs and have addressed this challenge by proposing a Markov Chain Monte Carlo (MCMC) sampling based algorithm to mine frequent graph patterns. PrivBasis approach proposed in (Li, Qardaji, Su, & Cao, 2012) performs FIM on transactional databases while satisfying differential privacy. In this paper, the concept of basis set (Li, Qardaji, Su, & Cao, 2012) is constructed privately and used to find most frequent itemsets. An approach to limit the length of transaction and improving utility privacy tradeoff has been proposed in (Zeng, Naughton, & Cai, 2012). An Apriori based differentially private frequent item set mining algorithm is proposed in this work (Zeng, Naughton, & Cai, 2012). A mechanism to release set valued data under differential privacy with guaranteed utility using context-free taxonomy trees is proposed in (Chen, Mohammed, Fung, Desai, & Xiong, 2011). A probabilistic top-down partitioning algorithm to generate a differentially private release which can scale linearly with the input data size is also developed in this work (Chen, Mohammed, Fung, Desai, & Xiong, 2011).

The issue of releasing differentially private set valued data in dynamic environment is addressed in (Zhang, Meng, & Chen, 2013). In this paper, an efficient algorithm, called *IncTDPart*, to incrementally generate a series of differentially private releases is proposed. The proposed algorithm is based on top-down partitioning model (Zhang, Meng, & Chen, 2013) with the help of item-free taxonomy tree and update-bounded mechanism. In this work extensive experiments are conducted on real datasets and the results demonstrate that the approach presented keeps high utility and scalability for counting query. A differentially private transit data sanitization approach has been proposed for transit data publication in (Chen, Fung, Desai, & Sossou, 2012). The approach presented in this paper (Chen, Fung, Desai, & Sossou, 2012), is based on hybrid-granularity prefix tree structure. This approach is used to sanitize data which is gathered from automatic fare collecting machines of transportation system in Montreal before release (Chen, Fung, Desai, & Sossou, 2012).In this work in post processing step the inherent consistency constraints of a prefix tree (Chen, Fung, Desai, & Sossou, 2012) are used to conduct constrained inferences. As a result of this better utility is obtained. The approach used in this work (Chen, Fung, Desai, & Sossou, 2012) can be used for sequential data, and can be extended to trajectory data. A variable length model n-gram which extracts required information from sequential database is proposed in (Chen, Acs, & Castelluccia, 2012). In this work authors have designed (Chen, Acs, & Castelluccia, 2012) exploration tree structure and a set of novel techniques based on the Markov assumption. Using these techniques the magnitude of noise required to be added is reduced. Then n-grams can be published and differential privacy is guaranteed (Chen, Acs, & Castelluccia, 2012). In next section the architecture and design of proposed system is discussed.

SYSTEM DESIGN AND ARCHITECTURE

In this section design, architecture and implementation of Privacy Preserving Data Mining (PDPM) System implemented in phases is presented. In first phase PDPM algorithms are implemented for FIM from structured and unstructured data. In subsequent phases it is planned to implement differential privacy on numeric queries and in interactive settings. In case of unstructured data the FIM is applied to identify association between different words or phrases. If the input data is healthcare data then unstructured words and phrases can represent medical terms. So FIM can identify patterns and associations. In first phase the developed system works on count queries on unstructured and structured data. The input to system is structured or unstructured data set. The output is frequent items sets. The random noise is added in such a way that persons cannot be recognized. The phases in Figure 1 present the process flow of the system. Main processing steps in system are as follows.

1. **Data Preprocessing:** In this step preprocessing steps like data normalization and removal of unwanted data are applied on numeric data and steps like stop word removal, stemming and root word identification are carried out for unstructured data.
2. In next step any FIM algorithm is run and frequent sets are generated.
3. The random noise (Laplace or Exponential) is added and results are returned.

In case of big data, the task the complexity of generating FIM increases because of huge volume of unstructured data from different sources. It has been estimated by Gartner that 80% of enterprise data is in unstructured format. Differential Privacy concept is widely used by many researchers to provide privacy guarantees while mining sensitive data. However these techniques have been widely applied on count data. In this chapter the performance of differential privacy on unstructured data is also examined.

Figure 1. Process flow of the system

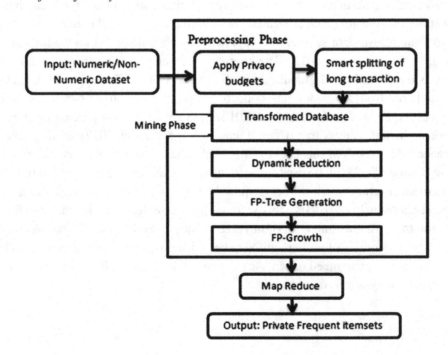

Privacy preserving FIM techniques or algorithms (Shen & Yu, 2013) was earlier applied on numeric dataset. In many cases these techniques are required to be applied on unstructured and non-numeric datasets. In case of such applications, there would be requirement to find FIM from non-numeric dataset while preserving privacy of an individual data. In case of non-numeric data set it is first converted into numeric data set. The conversion algorithm is as follows.

ALGORITHM

1. Algorithm for Preprocessing Non-Numeric Dataset

```
Input:  Nonnumeric dataset   D
Step 1: take dataset D = {pt₁, pt₂, pt₃,..., ptₙ}
Step 2: apply extract word process EWᵢ for D and extract words
Step 3: For each EWᵢ;
              Stop Word (SWᵢ) = EWᵢ;
    //Stop word elimination process
        Stemming(Sᵢ) = SWᵢ        ;
                    // find exact word
Step 4:  For eachSᵢ;
Freq_Count(WCᵢ) = Sᵢ;
//for the total no. of occurrences of each Stem
Return  Sᵢ;
Step 5: Tokens  (Sᵢ) will be passed to system.
Step 6: word categorization and selection
End
Output: Tokens, count (i.e..word, count)
```

After implementation of preprocessing algorithm on non-numeric dataset, FIM is performed using FP and PFP growth algorithms which are implemented using Hadoop Map Reduce platform. The algorithms are as follows.

2. FP Growth Algorithm

```
Input: database   D; the minimum support count threshold min sup.
Method:
First the database D  is scan once then the set of frequent items F and
their support counts are found. Then, support count of F is sorted in de-
scending order as L, the list of frequent items.
Second, create the root of an FP-tree, and tag it as null.
The FP-tree is mined by calling FPgrowth(FPtree, null), which is implemented
```

using method $FPgrowth(Tree, \alpha)$

Output: The complete set of frequent patterns.

3. PFP Growth Algorithm

Authors use PFP growth algorithm (Su, Xu, Ceng, Li, & Wang, 2015) for providing privacy for non-numeric dataset. PFP algorithm consists of two phases preprocessing phase and mining phase. In pre-processing phase smart transaction splitting technique is used for dividing long transactions into multiple sub-transactions to improve utility for numeric data set. In case of non-numeric data set transaction splitting is not carried out. In mining phase information loss due to splitting transaction is computed using run time estimation method for numeric data sets only.

OVERVIEW OF SYSTEM ARCHITECTURE

The system architecture is specifically designed for the Big Data. System is able to deal with huge data with the help of Hadoop Platform. The system is organized into three components.

UI Component

This component provides user interface of the system. It is used to accept input like data set, its type, privacy parameter, maximum number of items in a transaction (L_m) etc. It also provides system output and visualizations.

Preprocessor

This component carries out set of processing steps depending upon the type of input data set. In case of structured data preprocessing steps like data normalization, data categorization, data reduction etc. are carried out. In case of non-numeric or unstructured data set preprocessing algorithm described earlier is applied. The output of this component is input to data mining component. In order to speed up the process this component is also developed using Hadoop Map Reduce Platform. In case of numeric data set maximum length constraint L_m is enforced. Then smart splitting method is applied to split transactions which violate this constraint. After splitting the input data set will be called as transformed data set. This method is not applied to unstructured data set.

Data Miner

This component applies different data mining algorithms on preprocessed data and generates support or counts for different words or items. At present FP algorithm has been applied to find frequent item sets. In next phase other algorithms will be implemented. This component also implements data mining algorithms using Map-reduce platform.

Noise Adder

This component adds the random noise to the output of Data Miner and sends output to UI. Let ∇f defines the global sensitivity of the input query. As already stated for numeric data set the output is of count types. The global sensitivity is always 1 for numeric data set. In case of unstructured data the global sensitivity can exceed 1. In case of numeric data set the noise from Laplace distribution with mean 0 and scale parameter is added. In case non numeric data set the random noise from Laplace or exponential distribution is added. In case non numeric data set has global sensitivity of 1, then noise from Laplace distribution is added otherwise adds noise from Exponential distribution. The Figure 2 presents the system architecture.

Let Y be the amount of noise added Noise adder.

Let f be the output of Data Miner. Then the response returned is $f + Y$. It can be seen that due to addition of random noise some infrequent item sets can become frequent and vice versa.

The level of privacy provided by above algorithm depends upon the value of $\in$. Higher level of security can be guaranteed for lower values of $\in$. Author use value $\in = 2$ for numeric data set. This value is proposed in Dwork (2006). The lower value for $\in$ can be used if the sensitivity of input data set is higher. The values of 0.1, 0.2 or 1 can be used. In case of non-numeric data set lower values are used $(\in = 1, 0.1, 0.2)$. The privacy budget is used determine if the query is to be allowed at any instant of time. The successive application of data mining queries can result in privacy leak, so after generating frequent item sets the privacy budget is reduced. If the privacy budget is below user defined limit then queries are prevented for certain period of time.

In the experimental work publicly available real numeric and nonnumeric data sets are used. Authors used Retail dataset for numeric dataset and publicly available text mining dataset as non-numeric dataset. Authors have implemented PFP algorithm for numeric dataset in JAVA and all experiments are conducted on PC with Intel(R) Core (Tm) 2 Duo. In case of non-numeric dataset authors apply text mining techniques to covert it in numeric data set, extract frequent word and its count so that same PFP algorithm can be used to find frequent item sets.

Figure 2. System architecture

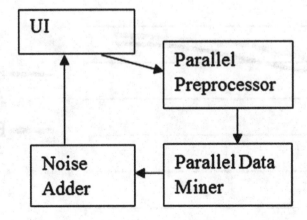

Advantages

The advantages of system are as follow

1. This system reduces the time complexity with the help of Hadoop Map Reduce for finding FIM as compared with existing system.
2. This system is capable of handling non-numeric dataset while preserving privacy.
3. It improves the accuracy as compared to existing algorithms for frequent item sets for unstructured data.

EXPERIMENTAL RESULT

A result of the system is shown by comparing existing system performance. The graph in Figure 3 presents the result for FIM by considering different threshold values and the graph in Figure 4 presents when frequent item set mining for non-numeric dataset implemented on Hadoop Map reduce.

Frequent Item Set Mining Graph

The F-score (Su, Xu, Ceng, Li, & Wang, 2015, July) calculated to measure the utility of generated frequent item set defined as follow

$$F - score = 2 \times \frac{precision \times recall}{precision + recall}$$

Figure 3. The graph for FIM in which X-axis shows different threshold values and Y-axis shows F-score calculated

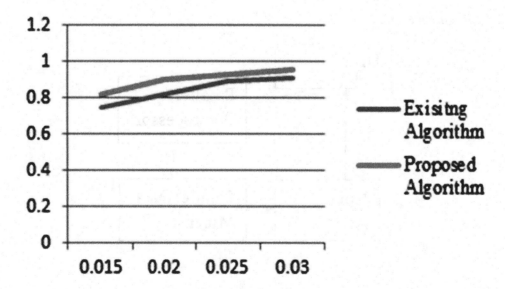

where $precision = \left|U_p \cap U_c\right| / \left|U_p\right|$, $recall = \left|U_p \cap U_c\right| / \left|U_c\right|$, U_p is the frequent item sets generated by a private algorithm and U_c is the actual frequent item sets.

Graph for Frequent Item Set Mining

The comparison graph for frequent item set mining on Hadoop platform and without Hadoop Platform is presented in Figure 4.

The difference in FIM with and without differential privacy is indicated in Table 3. Two runs of algorithms were carried out for retail and Accident data sets which are publicly available. In the executions constraints were imposed on the maximum number of items in item sets. It can be seen from the table that even though there are 23 frequent item set in retail data set the outcome FIM algorithm with differential privacy is different. In first run only 21 item sets are generated and in second case only 17 are generated. In case of accident data set additional item set is generated.

Figure 4. The graph for FIM on Hadoop platform and without Hadoop platform is shown. In this graph x-axis shows different threshold values and y-axis shows time in milliseconds.

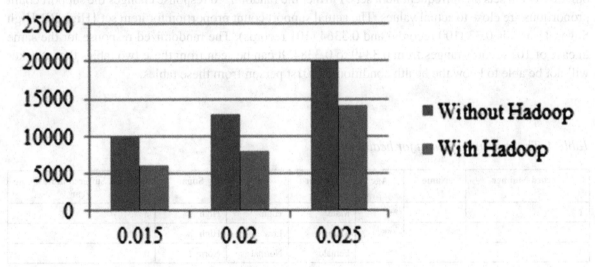

Table 3. The difference in FIM with and without differential privacy

Dataset	Maximum Threshold Constraint L_m	Frequent Item Set Count Using PFP-Growth	Frequent Item Set Count Using FP-Growth
Retail(1st time execution)	3	21	23
Retail(2nd time)	3	17	23
Accident(1)	5	7	7
Accident(2)	5	8	7

The working of proposed system is described with the help of a simple example. A sample of 101 anonymized health care records was collected. These records were in unstructured format. A snapshot of record was as follows.

"A **** Aged ** address *** has high BP and sugar and has suffered viral infection in **".

In the first step these health care records were converted by system into structured format. The snapshot of the structured format is as follows (Table 4).

Then the FIM algorithm was run on these 101 records. The frequent item sets of length 3 were obtained. The threshold for support proportion was set at 0.3. The following 5 item sets were obtained by FIM algorithm (Table 5), when it is run without differential privacy for 100 records.

Suppose that 101st person has High BP, High Sugar and Heart condition, and then applying FIM algorithm without implementing differential privacy will change support proportion of second row to 0.3364. All the proportions in other rows of the table will remain unchanged. The attacker can come to know the health condition of new person easily with little background information.

In next step FIM algorithm using differential privacy was run on the same data set for 100 and 101 records. The value of privacy parameter ϵ was set at 0.1(ϵ=0.1). The output of two runs of the system is presented in Table 6 and Table 7.

It can be seen from Table 6 and Table 7, that differentially private FIM only 3 frequent item sets. The other two item sets are infrequent item sets. Further the randomized response changes the support count proportions are close to actual values. The actual support count proportion for item set {High BP, High Sugar, Heart} is 0.33 (100 records) and 0.3364 (101 records). The randomized response for the same in case of 101 records ranges from 0.3349 to 0.3384. It can be seen from these two tables that attacker will not be able to know the health condition of 101st person from these tables.

Table 4. The structured format for health care

Record Number	Name	Age	Gender	BP	Sugar	Infection Suffered in Last One Year
1	***	***	Male	High	High	3
2	***	***	Male	Low	High	1
3	***	***	Female	Normal	Normal	0

Table 5. Item sets obtained by FIM algorithm

Sr. No.	Item Set	Support Proportion (Support Count/n)
1	High BP, High Sugar, Infection	0.31
2	High BP, High Sugar, Heart	0.33
3	High BP, High Sugar, Vision Problems	0.31
4	High BP, High Sugar, Joint Pains	0.30
5	High BP, High Sugar, high Cholesterol	0.34

Table 6. Output of run 1 (FIM with differential privacy)

Sr. No.	Item Set	Support Proportion (Support Count/n) +Random Noise (100 Records)	Support Proportion (Support Count/n) +Random Noise (101 Records)
1	High BP, High Sugar, Infection	0.3123	0.3121
2	High BP, High Sugar, Heart	0.3354	0.3349
3	Low BP, High Sugar, Infection	0.3117	0.3089
4	High BP, High Sugar, Stroke	0.3486	0.3499
5	High BP, High Cholesterol, Heart	0.3367	0.3365

Table 7. Output of run 2 (FIM with differential privacy)

Sr. No.	Item Set	Support Proportion (Support Count/n) +Random Noise (100 Records)	Support Proportion (Support Count/n) +Random Noise (101 Records)
1	High BP, High Sugar, Heart	0.3319	0.3382
2	High BP, High Sugar, High Cholesterol	0.3408	0.3429
3	High BP, Heart, Kidney	0.3117	03089
4	High BP, High Sugar, Infection	0.3029	0.3053
5	High Sugar, High Cholesterol, Heart	0.3367	0.3365

CONCLUSION

In current era of information, massive amount of data is collected, created, stored and processed to get knowledge for decision making purposes. It is not only important to acquire knowledge but also provide privacy. Differential Privacy technique provides strong privacy guarantee. Differentially private FIM using map reduce requires less time for privately mining large dataset. Map Reduce is used here which can efficiently handle large datasets. The differentially private FIM algorithm for non-numeric dataset which can achieve tradeoff between utility and privacy are implemented.

REFERENCES

Acquisti, A., & Gross, R. (2011). Predicting Social Security numbers from public data, *Proceedings of the National Academy of Sciences of the United States of America*. (Vol. 110, No 15, pp 10975–10980). doi:10.1073/pnas.0904891106

Aggarwal, C. C., & Yu, P. S. (2008). *A General Survey of Privacy Privacy-Preserving Data Mining – Models and Algorithms, Advances in database Systems* (Vol. 34). Springer.

Bayardo, R. J., & Agarwal, R. (2005). Data privacy through optimal k-anonymization. *Proceedings of 21st IEEE International Conference on Data Engineering (ICDE) 2005*, 217-228. doi:10.1109/ICDE.2005.42

Bhaskar, R., Laxman, S., Smith, A., & Thakurta, A. (2010). Discovering frequent patterns in sensitive data.*Proceedings of KDD*, 503-512.

Bonomi, L., & Xiong, L. (2013). A two-phase algorithm for mining sequential patterns with differential privacy.*Proceedings of 22nd ACM Conference on Information and Knowledge Management (CIKM 2013),*269-278. doi:10.1145/2505515.2505553

Census Bureau. (2016). *United States Census Bureau*. Retrieved from www.census.gov

Chen, R., Acs, G., & Castelluccia, C. (2012). Differentially Private Sequential Data Publication via variable length n-grams.*Proceedings of 19th ACM Conference of Computer and Communications Security*.

Chen, R., Fung, B. C. M., Desai, B. C., & Sossou, N. (2012). Differentially private transit data publication: a case study on the Montreal transportation system.*Proceedings of 18th ACM SIGKDD international conference on Knowledge discovery and data mining (KDD 2012),*213-221. doi:10.1145/2339530.2339564

Chen, R., Mohammed, N., Fung, B. C. M., Desai, B. C., & Xiong, L. (2011). Publishing set valued data via differential privacy. *Proceedings of VLDB Endowment, 4*(11), 1087–1098.

Cox, L. H. (1980). Suppression Methodology and Statistical Disclosure Control. *Journal of the American Statistical Association, 75*(370), 377–385. doi:10.1080/01621459.1980.10477481

Dalenius, T. (1986). Finding a needle in a haystack or identifying anonymous census records. *Journal of Official Statistics, 2*(3), 329–336.

Duhigg. (2012). *How Companies Learn Your Secrets*. Retrieved May 11, 2016 from http://www.nytimes.com/2012/02/19/magazine/shoppinghabits.html?pagewanted=1&_r=0

Dutch Data Protection Agency. (2014). *Google faces $18 million fine for web privacy violations: Dutch watchdog*. Retrieved from http://www.reuters.com/article/us-privacy-google-dutch-idUSKBN-0JT1TG20141215

Dwork, C. (2006). Differential privacy.*Proceedings of ICALP*, 1-12.

Dwork, C., McSherry, F., Nissim, K., & Smith, A. (2006). Calibrating noise to sensitivity in private data analysis.*Proceedings of 3rd International Conference on Theory of Cryptography (TCC 06),*265-284. doi:10.1007/11681878

Federal Trade Commission. (2014). *Enforcing Privacy Promises*. Retrieved from https://www.ftc.gov/news-events/media-resources/protecting-consumer-privacy/enforcing-privacy-promises

Friedman, T., & Smith, M. (2011, October 10). *Measuring the Business Value of Data Quality*. Gartner Report.

Glenday. (2016). *Sony fined £250k over 'serious' Data Protection Act breach*. Retrieved May 2, 2016 from http://www.thedrum.com/news/2013/01/24/sony-fined-250k-over-serious-data-protection-act-breach

Google Search Statistics-Internet Live Stats. (2016). Retrieved from http://www.internetlivestats.com/google-search-statistics/

Kosinski, M., Stillwell, D., & Graepl, T. (2013). Private traits and attributes are predictable from digital records of human behavior.*Proceedings of the National Academy of Sciences of the United States of America*. doi:10.1073/pnas.1218772110

Li, N., Li, T., & Venkatsubranmanian, S. (2007). t-Closeness: Privacy beyond k-Annonymity and l-Diversity.*Proceedings of 23rd International Conference on Data Engineering (ICDE),*106-115. doi:10.1109/ICDE.2007.367856

Li, N., Qardaji, W., Su, D., & Cao, J. (2012). Privbasis: Frequent item sets mining with differential privacy. *Proceedings of VLDB, 5*(11), 1340–1351.

Liu, J., & Wang, K. (2010). Anonymizing Transaction Data by Integrating Suppression and Generalization. *Proceedings of 14th Pacific-Asia Conference (PKDD) Advances in Knowledge Discovery and Data Mining,* 171-180. doi:10.1007/978-3-642-13657-3_20

Machanavajjhala, A., Kifer, D., Gehrke, J., & Venkitasubramaniam, M. (2007). l-Diversity: Privacy Beyond k-Anonymity. *ACM Transactions on Knowledge Discovery from Data, 1*(1), 1–47. doi:10.1145/1217299.1217302

Malik, M. B., Gazi, M. A., & Ali, R. (2012). Privacy Preserving Data Mining Techniques: Current Scenario and Future Prospects.*Proceedings of IEEE International Conference on Computer and Communication Technology (ICCCT 2012),* 26-32. doi:10.1109/ICCCT.2012.15

McSherry, F., & Talwar, K. (2007, October). Mechanism design via differential privacy.*Proceedings of 48th Annual IEEE Symposium on Foundations of Computer Science (FOCS 07),*94-103. doi:10.1109/FOCS.2007.41

Meyerson, A., & Williams, R. (2004). On the Complexity of Optimal k-annonymity.*Proceedings of Twenty Third ACM SIGMOD-SIGACT-SIGART Symposium on Principles of Database Systems,* 223-228. doi:10.1145/1055558.1055591

Narayanan, A., & Shmatikov. (2008). Robust De-anonymization of Large Sparse Datasets. *Proceedings of 2008 IEEE Symposium on Security and Privacy,* 111-125. doi:10.1109/SP.2008.33

Nuaimi, Al Neyadi, Mohamed, & Al-Jaroodi. (2015). Applications of big data to smart cities. *Journal of Internet Services Applications,* 6-25.

Privacy Protection for Social Networking APIs. (2016). Retrieved April 10, 2016 from https://www.cs.virginia.edu/felt/privacy/

Qardaji, W., Yang, W., & Li, N. (2013). Differentially private grids for geospatial data.*Proceedings of 29th IEEE International Conference on Data Engineering (ICDE 2013),*757-768. doi:10.1109/ICDE.2013.6544872

Saurabh, K. (2016). *Safe computing: University of Michigan sensitive data guide and Personally Identifiable Information (PII).* Retrieved from http://safecomputing.umich.edu/dataguide/?q=node/89

Shen, E., & Yu, T. (2013). Mining frequent graph patterns with differential privacy.*Proceedings of 12th ACM SIGKDD International Conference on Knowledge Discovery and Data Mining (KDD 2013),* 545-553. doi:10.1145/2487575.2487601

Simo, H. (2015). *Big Data: Opportunities and Privacy Challenges*. Cornell University Library. arXiv:1502.00823v1

Solove, D. J. (2010). *Understanding Privacy*. Harvard University Press.

Statista. (2016). *The statistics portal*. Retrieved May 2, 2016 from http://www.statista.com/ statistics/273018/number-of-internet-users-worldwide/

Stinson, D. R. (2005). *Cryptography Theory and Practice* (3rd ed.). CRC Press.

Su, S., Xu, S., Ceng, X., Li, Z., & Wang, F. (2015, July). Differentially private frequent item set mining via transaction splitting. *IEEE Transactions on Knowledge and Data Engineering, 27*(7), 1875–1891. doi:10.1109/TKDE.2015.2399310

Supplementary Account Opening Form by SBI. (2015). Retrieved May 5, 2016 from https://oaa.onlinesbi. com/sbijava/pdf/Supplimentary Form.pdf

Sweency, L. (2002). K-Anonymity: A Model for protecting privacy. *International Journal of Uncertainty, Fuzziness and Knowledge-based Systems, 10*(5), 557–570. doi:10.1142/S0218488502001648

The Top 20 Valuable Facebook Statistics. (2016). Retrieved March 2016 from https://zephoria.com / top-15-valuable-facebook-statistics/

To, H., Ghinita, G., & Shahabi, C. (2014). A framework for protecting worker location privacy in spatial crowd sourcing. *Proceedings of VLDB Endowment, 7*(10), 919–930. doi:10.14778/2732951.2732966

Zeng, C., Naughton, J. R., & Cai, J. V. (2012). On differentially private frequent item set mining. *Proceedings of VLDB, 6*(1), 26–36.

Zhang, X., Meng, X., & Chen, R. (2013). Differentially Private Set-Valued Data Release against Incremental Updates.*Proceedings of 18th International Conference Database Systems for Advanced Applications*, 392-406.

Chapter 9
Differential Privacy Approach for Big Data Privacy in Healthcare

Marmar Moussa
University of Connecticut, USA

Steven A. Demurjian
University of Connecticut, USA

ABSTRACT

This chapter presents a survey of the most important security and privacy issues related to large-scale data sharing and mining in big data with focus on differential privacy as a promising approach for achieving privacy especially in statistical databases often used in healthcare. A case study is presented utilizing differential privacy in healthcare domain, the chapter analyzes and compares the major differentially private data release strategies and noise mechanisms such as the Laplace and the exponential mechanisms. The background section discusses several security and privacy approaches in big data including authentication and encryption protocols, and privacy preserving techniques such as k-anonymity. Next, the chapter introduces the differential privacy concepts used in the interactive and non-interactive data sharing models and the various noise mechanisms used. An instrumental case study is then presented to examine the effect of applying differential privacy in analytics. The chapter then explores the future trends and finally, provides a conclusion.

INTRODUCTION

Big Data analysis influences most aspects of our modern society, such as mobile services, retail, manufacturing, financial services, medicine and life sciences, as well as physical sciences to name a few (Bertino et al., 2011). Scientific research is being revolutionized by Big Data everyday, for instance in bioinformatics with Next Generation Sequencing increasing the size and number of experimental data sets exponentially. In healthcare, Big Data with transforming patient care towards prevention with substantial home-based and continuous form of monitoring available to patients is definitely personalizing

DOI: 10.4018/978-1-5225-2486-1.ch009

Copyright © 2017, IGI Global. Copying or distributing in print or electronic forms without written permission of IGI Global is prohibited.

healthcare to the benefit of patients. While the potential benefits of Big Data are real and significant, there remain several considerable technical challenges. However, in this broad range of application areas, data is being collected at an unprecedented scale. The emergence and ever increasing emphasis on the big data era means that more and more information on an individual's health, financials, location, and online activity are continuously being harvested, collected, and processed in the cloud and stored in big data repositories. This results in increased concerns regarding the privacy of these large sets of personal data and the loss of an individual's control over his/her sensitive data (Boyd & Crawford, 2012).

The impact of privacy concerns on a big data application is particularly evident in the healthcare domain which has a long established history in requiring that health information technology must comply with the Health Insurance Portability and Accountability Act (HIPAA) for most importantly release of a patient's medical information as well as security and availability as well. HIPAA must also apply to big-data applications for healthcare. This is strongly tied to a movement towards patient controlled access to their medical information with patients able to define the privacy to determine who can see what information at which times. This is evidenced by work that has emphasized granularity and patient control (Sujansky et al., 2010) and a lifetime electronic health record with complete information available anywhere (Caine, 2013). In healthcare there is a need to distinguish levels of security based on the confidentiality and privacy of the data itself and the way that a patient would seek to make such data available to stakeholders. All of these security and privacy concerns must be addressed within big data applications for healthcare as well as in other domains.

This chapter explores the issues related to the security in general and privacy in specific for big data applications, particularly given that the usage of state-of-the-art analytics has explicitly led to growing privacy concerns. As a result, protecting privacy becomes quite harder as information is processed multiple times and shared among multiple diverse entities in the cloud. One example of this problem involves de-identification and anonymization techniques that have been utilized under the false assumption that they allow organizations to reap the benefits of analytics while preserving individuals' privacy. This relies on the assumption that removing certain personal information from a data set would ensure the identity of the users participating in that data set to remain anonymous. However, this has proved to be a misconception as demonstrated by several re-identification and linkage attacks that different data sources harmfully leak private information when combined and when adversaries are able to use some background knowledge, this will be further discussed in the section "Big Data Security and Privacy Issues".

The first focus of this chapter is to explore the utilization of differential privacy to addresses the aforementioned problems in privacy in order to provide confidence to users that their data is carefully controlled. Differential privacy (DWork, 2006) is defined as the application of noise functions of certain characteristics to datasets or query results so that no specifics of individual records present in the original dataset are revealed, while simultaneously allowing the dataset to provide typical big data analytical insights. This constraint allows the various big data analytics mechanisms to behave almost identically on any two datasets that are sufficiently close but only differ by the applied noise mechanism. A formal differential privacy model (DWork, 2006) defined differential privacy as: "the risk to one's privacy should not substantially increase as a result of participating in a statistical database." Differential privacy has recently received increased attention as a general pipeline for the protection of personal information, especially in the fields of big data analytics. The appeal of differential privacy is that there are usually little or no pre-assumptions about a potential attackers pre-existing background knowledge and offers a solid mathematical formulation of the notion of privacy. In contrast to the aforementioned anonymization techniques, the privacy guarantees of differential privacy are rather strong, but can come at the expense of accuracy. This degradation in accuracy would be problematic in a big data application for healthcare if the underlying patient and/or genomic data is incorrect. In addition, there is increased complexity for designing and implementing a differentially private version of nearly every algorithm utilized for a complex task (e.g., data mining) that overshadows the wide application of differential privacy in practice, it is hence of utmost importance to carefully study the gains and costs of applying differential privacy in healthcare.

The second focus of this chapter highlights the issues related to security and privacy for big data applications by presenting a survey and analysis of the most important security and privacy issues in large-scale data processing associated with big data as well as presenting an case study utilizing differential privacy in the healthcare domain. This chapter will summarize several security challenges for big data from four different perspectives (Inukollu et al., 2014): architecture and network related issues such as network protocol security and node validations; authentication and authorization related issues such as node authentication and access control protocols; data related issues such as encryption, key management and data privacy issues; and, general issues such as logging (Peleg et al., 2008). To understand the case study of differential privacy in healthcare, the chapter includes a comprehensive survey of privacy challenges when sharing or releasing big data for analytics. Our work in this chapter will further present the most promising technologies for preserving privacy in big data applications, such as various k-anonymity (Clifton, 2013) and differential privacy techniques. This chapter will also present a theoretical and empirical comparison with respect to the two major differential privacy settings (DWork, 2010): interactive settings where a dataset owner provides a set of differentially private data querying algorithms for a data requester to interact with vs. non-interactive settings where a differentially private data set is released once and the data requester interactions are directly focused on that released privacy preserving dataset. As part of the discussion, this chapter analyzes and compares the major differentially private data release strategies and noise mechanisms such as the Laplace mechanism and the exponential mechanism (DWork, 2014).

This chapter has five sections additional to the introduction. The *Background* section provides general background on characteristics of big data applications, big data challenges, big data processing technologies, and big data analysis techniques. The *Big Data Security and Data Privacy Issue* section discusses the security and privacy challenges and techniques for big data including: architecture-level node authentication protocols, data-encryption protocols, and privacy preserving techniques such as k-anonymity and differential privacy it also introduces and surveys the differential privacy concepts by explaining the interactive and non-interactive models for differential privacy and the various noise mechanisms used in releasing differentially private data. Then, the *Differential Privacy Case Study in Healthcare Data Mining* section presents a case study of applying an approach for differential privacy in big data analytics that can be particularly useful for a domain such as healthcare. The *Future Trends* section explores the potential directions of differential privacy in applying privacy-by-design principles to different data domains and ensuring privacy-aware data usage. Finally, the *Conclusion* section summarizes the contributions of the chapter.

BACKGROUND

This section provides background information on four areas: characteristics of big data applications, big data challenges, big data processing technologies, and big data analysis techniques. To begin, the term

Big Data started as a nebulous term, used by Computer Science researches to describe the exponential rate in data acquisition and recording in the internet age. Big Data is considered a Framework of utilities and characteristics common to all NoSQL platforms. Gartner Research's definition of Big Data is widely adopted; the three Vs of Big Data consists of Volume, Variety and Velocity. A 4th V was also added to make it: variety, volume, velocity and value. Big Data differs from a data warehouse in architecture in that it follows a distributed approach, a data warehouse on the other hand follows a centralized one (Lane, 2013). The major characteristics of big data are: very large data sets (Volume), extremely fast insertion (Velocity), and multiple data types (Variety). Corresponding characteristics (Lane, 2013) include: distributed parallel processing, clustered deployments, providing data analysis capabilities, distributed and redundant data storage, modular design, inexpensive, hardware agnostic, easy to use (relatively), available (commercial or open source), and extensible can be augmented or altered In big data applications, the time from data acquisition to meaningful information realization is critical to extract value from various data sources, including mobile devices, the web and a growing list of automated sensory technologies. Application that can realize this goal would have a huge advantage to organizations that would benefit from speed, capacity, and scalability of cloud storage (Cheung, 2013). Organizations that in addition to benefiting from these big data characteristics also combine predictive analytics with big data have opportunity to explore further benefits in application areas including: digital marketing optimization such as web analytics for online advertisement, context-based recommendations etc.; data exploration and discovery such as statistics, data science, exploring new markets, etc.; fraud detection and prevention and network monitoring and security analysis; social network and relationship analysis with the ultimate goal to influence relevant markets; machine generated analysis for instance remote sensing; data retention and archiving to insure survivability; and, data visualization to present information suitable for users (Arpaia, 2013).

The next background area is Big Data significant challenges further than the analysis phase that occurs in multiple phases (Brown, 2011). In *Data Acquisition and Recording* phase, the *data volume* challenge puts pressure on capacity. The use of data reduction mechanisms can smartly process raw data while defining filters that help to not accidently discard useful information in the process. The general *correct metadata challenge* can alleviate the overhead imposed by the necessity of recording metadata. For example, a processing error at a prerequisite step can render depending analysis erroneous. However, with suitable provenance, one can easily identify all depending subsequent processing steps. This is reflected in the *data preparing and cleaning challenge* in order to effectively extract meaningful information from often noisy data and expressing the data in a form suitable for analysis is often application dependent and is a continuous technical challenge. This is true in healthcare which must combine: electronic health records (EHR) from databases in hospitals (Kendall, 2015); transcribed dictations from several physicians; data structured and collected from biosensors and other modern fitness devices and various –sometime uncertain- measurements; and, medical imaging data such as x-ray, CT, MRI, etc. *Data Integration, Aggregation, and Representation challenges* have led to novel strategies emerged that involve storing unstructured data in distributed NoSQL databases such as the Apache Hadoop Distributed File System (HDFS) (Borthakur, 2007), a single logical file system distributed across many data servers and it is able to scale on demand based on required capacity and was designed to run on commodity hardware and hence be highly scalable and available. HDFS contains MapReduce, a programming model and an associated implementation for effectively processing and querying large data sets with a parallel, distributed algorithm on a cluster of nodes across the disparate data servers. The *Data Modeling and Analysis challenge* must deal with data that is often noisy and dynamic, almost always heterogeneous, and could also sometimes be untrustworthy. "Mining requires integrated, cleaned, trustworthy, and efficiently accessible data, declarative query and mining interfaces, scalable mining algorithms, and big-data computing environments" (Cyril, 2015). The final *result interpretation challenge* involves the need to provide a rich palette of visualizations for results of data analysis. A user needs to be able to not only view and understand the results from the analysis phase, but be able to test the data model and deploy it into the real world and conclude predictive as well as prescriptive results from it for final decision support (Tene, 2012).

The third background area reviews big data processing technologies that are needed to address, volume, variety and velocity utilizing a divide and conquer approach to provide for these characteristics and handle semi-structured and sometimes unstructured data in a distributed environment. NoSQL commercially available systems (e.g., MongoDB, Apache Casandra, etc.) can be leveraged. Existing NoSQL implementations can be classified as: a Key-Value Store where the content of the data is represented as a collection of individual key and value pairs; a Graph Database that represents the data in graph objects utilizing Graph Theory; or a Document Stores that organizes the data in a container object per document (e.g., XML or JSON) to encapsulate all attributes for a given object. These implementations do not necessarily satisfy core concepts (e.g., atomicity, consistency, isolation or durability (ACID)); the very same set of properties that are present in almost all relational database management systems today to guarantee that relational database transactions are processed reliably. One dominant approach as previously mentioned is Hadoop Distributed File System(HDFS). HDFS provides built-in support for data fault-tolerance via data replication and load-balancing using MapReduce which can benefit of the locality of data. MapReduce has three functions to manage the local data, its writes to temporary storage, moving data for downstream processing, and redistributing data based on outputs.

The final background area is big data analysis techniques that are utilized used to generate numerous and also more insightful results than when applied to smaller less diverse sets. Advantages and issues are present for each of the techniques based on its individual characteristics. Analysis techniques include: crowd sourcing, data mining, genetic algorithms, data fusion and integration, machine learning, NLP, neural networks and simulation, pattern recognition, predictive modeling, semantic and sentiment analysis, and statistics. Two techniques of increasing interest are predictive analysis and descriptive analysis. Predictive Analytics applies mathematics, statistics and probability theory in conjunction with the overarching computer science discipline of machine learning, data modeling and algorithm development. From clinical analytics in Clinical Decision Support System (CDSS) to business analytics in Operations Research (OR), Predictive Analytics aids decision makers to make choices and solve problems that have long lasting impacts. Predictive Analytics relies on Descriptive Analytics to provide the descriptive information as well as a foundational framework for such applications. Descriptive analytics, however, only describes the present conditions, whereas predictive analysis is a model-driven and data-driven approach for generating what-if scenarios exploiting the meanings of underlying data.

BIG DATA SECURITY AND DATA PRIVACY ISSUES

This section explores issues in big data security and privacy organized into a five-part discussion to set the context for the chapter in order to support the presentation of the healthcare case study in the next section. In part one, big data security is reviewed with the objective to provide a general background about the current security challenges to which differential privacy is one of the potential answers. In part two, the concepts of differential privacy are reviewed including different approaches, models, and algorithms. Part three of this section reviews the critical properties of differentially private algorithms that are utilized to design differentially private data sharing models. Part four of this section explains a select subset of the noise mechanisms that are the core part of implementing sound differentially private algorithms. The fifth and final part of the section details models of releasing sensitive data with differential privacy that can be leveraged to sharing sensitive datasets in domains like healthcare or other domains with potentially sensitive individual's data.

In the first part of this section, we explore security. Big data have similar vulnerabilities similar to traditional web applications and most data warehouses including: vetting of nodes and client applications before they join into a cluster, protecting data at rest, ensuring network privacy and communications, and also node management; most of these are lacking in the NoSQL platforms utilized for big data. Security controls for big data can be considered from four different levels: architecture/network, authentication and authorization, and data. In the architecture/network level security the challenges are network protocols and network security for distributed nodes validation and internode communication to verify security consistency across a highly distributed cluster of heterogenous platforms. A set of pre-configuration tools has emerged as one possible solution that validate and 'fix' node issues before adding them back to the cluster to ensure a form of baseline security. For authentication and authorization level, the challenges are on authentication methods to manage administrative rights for nodes and authentication of applications and nodes and to ensure that secure administrative passwords are being used correctly and that application users also are being correctly and securely authenticated before gaining access to the cluster. For the data level security the challenges are data encryption to protect the integrity of data at rest as we need to ensure administrators or other unauthorized application processes cannot gain direct access to files while at the same time preventing information leakage or exposure (Chaudhuri, 2012).

In the second part of this section, we explore differential privacy. In the past, various ad-hoc approaches to anonymizing public records have failed when researchers successfully identified personal information by linking several seemingly separate databases (Barbaro, 2006). Two well-known instances of successful "Linkage Attacks" have been the Netflix Database (Bennett, 2007) and the Massachusetts Group Insurance Commission (GIC) medical encounter database (Dankar, 2012). The objective in the general case is for a statistical database where: "a trusted party holds a dataset of sensitive information (e.g. medical records, voter registration information, email usage) with the goal of providing global, statistical information about the data publicly available, while preserving the privacy of the users whose information the data set contains" (Dwork, 2004). The notion of indistinguishability, later termed Differential Privacy (Dwork, 2006), formalizes the exact notion of "privacy" in statistical databases. Informally, differential privacy can be defined to stipulate that any individual has a very small influence on the distribution of the outcome of the computation. As a result, an attacker cannot learn anything about an individual's report to the database, even in the presence of any auxiliary information she may have.

Differential privacy applied to datasets or query results is making a promise to not reveal the specifics of individual records present in the original dataset and achieves this constraint by requiring the mechanism that is to be considered differentially private to behave almost in an identical manner on any two given datasets that are considered sufficiently close. Based on Dwork's work (Dwork, 2004): "imagine a dataset A whose records are members of some abstract domain D, and which can be described as a function from D to the natural numbers N, with $F(x)$ indicating the frequency (number of occurrences) for x in the dataset. $|| A - B ||$ is used to indicate the sum of the absolute values of difference in frequencies (i.e., the total number of records that would have to be added and removed to change A into another dataset B)". This leads to a definition:

Definition 1: Differential Privacy: "A mechanism M mapping datasets to distributions over an output space R provides (ε, δ) - differential privacy if for every S $\subseteq R$ and for all data sets A, B where $\| A - B \| \leq 1$,

$$Pr[M(A) \in S] \leq e^{\varepsilon} Pr[M(B) \in S] + \delta. \text{"}$$ (1)

For $\delta = 0$ in (1) M is said to provide ε -differential privacy. Prior to the field of differential privacy being defined by Dwork between 2004 and 2006, the privacy protection schemes proposed in research mainly included: data distortion methods, data encryption techniques, and restrictive release of only partial or selected group of records. However, these methods failed to offer quantifiable guarantee for user's privacy and did not clearly discuss the extent of an adversary's ability for which they offer protection (De Montjoye, 2015).

To substitute for these failed methods, de-identification and anonymization privacy algorithms were used under the false assumption that removing certain personal information from a data set would ensure the identity of the users participating in that data set to remain anonymous. However, several re-identification and linkage attacks demonstrated that different data sources are harmfully leaking private information when combined, especially given some background knowledge of adversaries. This lack of actual privacy guarantee is one of the reasons anonymization techniques do not satisfy most of the privacy requirements of sensitive data releases. Some of the most interesting examples for such shortcomings were the Netflix Prize related attack presented in (Bennett, 2007) as mentioned before the most recent attack of the credit card metadata re-identification in (De Montjoye, 2015). Anonymity models based on restrictive release of sensitive data were also proposed in part to guarantee user privacy in healthcare application, among such techniques is k-anonymity introduced by Sweeney in 2002 and some of its variations like l-diversity (Sweeney, 2002). It is simply suggesting a property that each record is considered indistinguishable from at least l other records to insure privacy. Although k anonymity and its variants do provide stronger privacy guarantees, there are several points that hinder its wide use for privacy like the high computational cost as k-anonymity is considered np-hard.

Another important facet in differential privacy is global sensitivity and its relation to noise-based privacy to provide protection for sensitive data sharing. For example, using Definition 1, one can derive that when two datasets A and B differ only in the data of one individual, then the gap where $\| A - B \|$ is maximum can be utilized obscure in order to make it difficult to an attacker to infer whether or not a specific individual information is in fact present in one of the dataset versions under consideration. Differential privacy proposes adding noise to the original data set A to cover this gap. In other words, the mechanism for differential privacy $M(f, A) = f(A) + noise$. The difference that this noise must obscure can be calculated as follows: given that A and B are two data sets that differ in exactly one individual's data, and $F(A) = x$ is a deterministic, non-privatized function over data set A, which returns a vector X of k real number results, then, the global sensitivity of F is then defined as:

$$\Delta f = max_{A,B} \mid f(A) - f(B) \mid \qquad\qquad (2)$$

Intuitively, the global sensitivity represents the sum of the worst case difference in answers that can be caused by adding or removing an individual's information from a data set. An example of the noise that can be added to the results of F so as to cover the sensitivity represented in (2) are the random values taken from a Laplacian Distribution with standard deviation that is large enough to cover this gap.

The final aspect of differential privacy is the privacy budget which is utilized to control and regulate the loss in privacy when querying the altered data sets. As noted in (Dwork, 2010), setting a value for ε is not always an easy task and has not been adequately covered in the differential privacy literature. Non-specialist data holders have difficulty measuring the privacy protection of a dataset provided from a specific ε value. What exactly it means to have an information gain of $\varepsilon = 0.01$ is not always intuitive to the data owner. To our knowledge there is still no generalized experimental evaluation to guide the user on choosing an appropriate ε value. In (Dwork, 2010), the recommended values of 0.01, or 0.1, and sometimes ln2, and ln3 can be used as starting values for tuning the best parameter value for each data set. One effort (Dankar, 2013) has suggested that ε cannot be defined in general but will always depend on the dataset under consideration.

In the third part of this section, we review the critical properties of differentially private algorithms and results, namely: data types' invariance, parallel and sequential composition, post-processing invariance, and quantifiable privacy. Data types invariance relies on the assumption that records form our data sets are invariant (Dwork, 2014) and works best when there are few records for each participant. Data types' invariance requires no assumptions about the type of data of the data sets' records. Different from other privacy methods, the privacy guarantees provided by differential privacy do not rely on classifying attributes as sensitive or not, nor perturbing the source data, nor suppressing values that are scarce or sensitive. Independence of data type is an important property that removes the need to customize privacy guarantees for different domains, misclassifying attributes as insensitive, or overlooking sensitive combinations of insensitive attributes. Meaningful guarantees for unstructured data can be provided, like free text and binary data that have previously vexed sensitivity classification. Even mutable records can be supported, replacing each record with a time-line of its contents. Furthermore, by ignoring entirely the records semantics one can provide guarantees for arbitrary functions of them. This property allows analysts to write their own tailored analyses, rather than choose from a set of predefined computations over limited declassified attributes.

The next property, parallel and sequential composition (McSherry, 2009) can be performed over structurally disjoint subsets of the data, where the same sequence of analyses provides $max_i\ \varepsilon_i$-differential privacy. An example of such a sequence of analyses is the grouping of results for horizontally distributed datasets analysis, where each record is guaranteed to participate in at most one aggregation. This means that while general sequences of queries accumulate privacy costs additively, when the queries are applied to disjoint subsets of the data, the bound can be improved. Specifically, if the domain of input records is partitioned into disjoint sets, independent of the actual data, and the restrictions of the input data to each part are subjected to differentially private analysis, the ultimate privacy guarantee depends only on the worst of the guarantees of each analysis, not the sum. The Sequential Composition Theorem for differential privacy states that the sequence of $M_i(X)$ ($\sum_i$)-differential privacy provides, if each M_i ε_i-differential privacy provides. This defines the privacy guarantees degrade as more information is exposed. Sequential composition is crucial for any privacy platform that expects to process more than one query. Privacy definitions that are not robust to sequential composition are usually hard to implement in practice.

The third property, post-processing invariance follows the sequential composition property of differentially private algorithms, but it can run independently so that subsequent computations can consider and incorporate the resulting outcomes of any preceding computations. The final property, quantifiable privacy differs from the previous properties which allow a designer of a differentially private mechanism to bind the privacy implications of arbitrary sequences of arbitrary queries composed of permitted transformations and aggregations leading to quantifiable privacy whose value can be calculated as the needed operations are designed or executed. Queries which arrive in sequence have their epsilon values accumulate; queries applied in parallel require us to track only the maximum (McSherry, 2009). Note that the privacy guarantees degrade as more information is exposed and more accuracy is required, however this decrease in privacy guarantee is somewhat well-controlled and not as drastically deteriorating as in the case of k-anonymity for instance (McSherry, 2009).

In the fourth part of this section, we explore differential privacy noise mechanisms which are utilized to support the analysis when a worst-case of data sets is present and to produce a similar distribution of privatized results, noise is added to span over the sensitivity gap. Adding Laplacian Noise is not the only way, but as suggested in (Dwork, 2008), was proposed that differential privacy can be achieved by adding random noise drawn from the Laplace distribution to the result of an algorithm. Following from the definition of global sensitivity and given a dataset D and the function $F : D \rightarrow R^d$, global sensitivity is ΔF; random algorithm $A(D) = F(D) + noise$ satisfies ε-differential privacy if the noise obeys the Laplace distribution; that is, $noise : Lap(\Delta F / \varepsilon)$; note that the location parameter of the Laplace Distribution in this case is 0 and the scale parameter is $(\Delta F / \varepsilon)$. While the Laplace mechanism is used when the output is numerical, the exponential mechanism presents another possible scheme to control security and achieve differential privacy when the outputs are non-numerical. The exponential mechanism satisfies the constraint that the change of a single database record does not affect the outcome of a pre-defined score function. The exponential mechanism can output non-numerical results according to their values of that score function. The output probability as shown in Figure 1, refers to privacy budget. The highest scored result is shown with higher probability when ε is larger; meanwhile, when the difference between the output probabilities grows, the offered privacy becomes less and vice versa, the smaller ε is, the higher the privacy will be; this can be inferred from equation (3) below. A formal definition of the mechanism is given in (Dwork, 2006) as follows: Let D denote the input dataset, $r \in R$ denotes a potential result, given a score function $u : DxR \rightarrow R$; if a random algorithm A selects an answer based on the following probability:

$$A(D, u) = r :| Pr[r \in R]\alpha \exp(\frac{\varepsilon u(D, r)}{2\Delta u}) \tag{3}$$

where Δu defines the sensitivity of the score function u, then algorithm A is said to satisfy ε-differential privacy.

In the fifth and final part of this section, we review alternative models of releasing sensitive data with differential privacy with a focus on the two strategies for incorporating differential privacy mechanisms when releasing sensitive information or data sets: the interactive and the non-interactive strategies

Figure 1. Probabilities of dp-mechanism A for D and D'

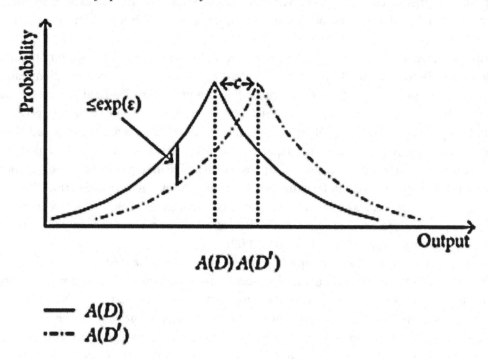

(El Emam, 2011). In the interactive model as shown in Figure 2; a data owner provides a data querying algorithm or tool based on the concepts of differential privacy. Then, the application or user requesting the data sends their query request to that tool/algorithm. When the query algorithm receives this request, the un-sanitized data is recovered from the original database and a privatizing process is performed over the raw data with the sanitized data finally submitted to the requesting party. In this model, the permitted number of queries is restricted by privacy budget ε; so more queries essentially leads to a potentially smaller budget for each query if total budget ε is a constant and a larger noise is added to the query result; this could render the query results to becomes unusable. As a result, the key to the model, is to design the query algorithm to provide the maximum number of queries permitted under limited budget ε that makes sense.

Figure 2. Interactive data release model

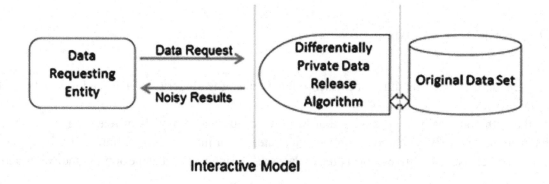

In the non-interactive model shown in Figure 3, the data owner is a trusted party and releases an already differentially private dataset, and data requesting party sends a query request. When the sanitized dataset receives the query request, the noisy result is returned to the requesting party. In this model, the number of permitted queries is unrestricted by privacy budget ε, so how to design the release algorithm with high efficiency to enhance the accuracy of a possible query over the data set at hand is the key to this model.

The interactive and the non-interactive models require histogram release, tree-structure release, and/or time series data algorithms to ensure privacy guarantee and simultaneously provide high utilization of the data and results. In support of the *histogram release algorithm*, a histogram is constructed by splitting the input dataset into mutually disjoint subsets named buckets or sometimes bins that depend on a set of properties. The only access to the original data set is performed through the differential privacy interface when users send their data queries, and the differential privacy histogram is directly utilized to answer those queries. The most straightforward and simple method is to add Laplace noise to each of the histogram buckets. In order to reduce the potential query errors, multiple buckets are possibly merged into one partition; this can be achieved when the number of tuples that fall into each partition or bin is the average value of the number of tuples in these buckets (Sarathy et al., 2011). The noise should be added to each bucket before merging, and the total noise after merging the relevant bins becomes smaller than the value before the merging. However, merge operation can introduce an error caused by approximation as the number of tuples in the partition is the average value of the number of tuples in multiple buckets. Therefore, we need to make the smallest possible number of partitions to minimize the noise error and to make the number of tuples in a partition the same as much as possible in order to reduce the approximation error. In general, a finer-grained partitioning mechanism introduces smaller approximation error but could cause larger noise error, so finding the right balance between approximation error and noise error is an important task.

The *tree-structure data release algorithms* were proposed (Wang, 2015) to support a differential privacy budgeting strategy and reduce the query error, a series of methods based on tree-structure data split. As private spatial decompositions, these algorithms divide the geospatial data into smaller regions and for each of these regions, statistics are obtained on the points within. The approach is called data-dependent decomposition if the partition discloses the sensitive information during spatial decomposition, otherwise, the approach is called data-independent decomposition. For data-dependent decomposition,

Figure 3. Non-interactive data release models

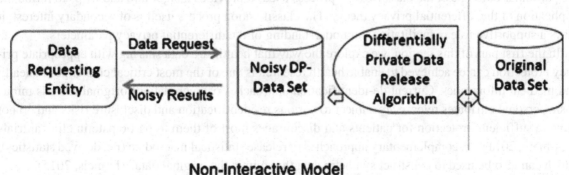

Non-Interactive Model

the noise is added to the node in order to hide the real values when a node is disclosed during splitting. For data-independent decomposition, algorithms based on quadtree were proposed which recursively divide the data space into equal quadrants without disclosure of node data information.

Lastly, the *time series data release algorithm* is an example of methods used for applications with data such as MHR or GPS data. As explained in (Wang 2015): "The real time data with higher correlation between time stamps has a timescale, if the length of the time series is T and the noise $noise_t$ is added to the data x_t at time k, $noise : Lap(T / \varepsilon)$, when T is large, the added noise gets large and leads to poor utility of the data." As for time series data, and for the purpose of reducing the error, the algorithm DFT was proposed based on discrete Fourier transform. In (Mohammed, 2011): " For time series D, DFT first executes the discrete Fourier transform, that is, $F = DFT(D)$, and retains only the first k coefficients; then the Laplace noise is added to those coefficients and the inverse Fourier transform is executed on the noisy coefficients F', that is $D* = IDET(F')$. Finally, the perturbed data $D *$ is released."

DIFFERENTIAL PRIVACY CASE STUDY IN HEALTHCARE DATA MINING

This section discusses privacy-preserving healthcare data sharing and the way to transform raw healthcare data or related querying results into a version that is immunized against privacy attacks to support healthcare data mining. The intent is to illustrate the way that differential privacy can support effective big data typical analytics and mining tasks like for instance k-means clustering (classification) or logistic regression of healthcare data. In order to achieve this, this section discuss a simple design for secure healthcare data releasing and sharing using differential privacy concepts and conduct comprehensive experiments of applying differentially private algorithms to healthcare data sets released for data mining and study the impact of enforcing differential privacy on the results quality. In the process, we evaluate the impact of differential privacy on the data mining tasks by comparing the performance metrics of k-means clustering (classification) with and without the application of differential privacy. In the remainder of this section, a case study of a specific problem in healthcare is presented in three parts. In part one, background on healthcare data sharing and the challenges of the usage of differential privacy is motivated. In part two, we explore the design and implementation of the case study for healthcare data mining that also includes a description of the data set utilized. Part three reviews and discusses the results of the case study. It is important to note that this case study is an instrumental case study used to accomplish a better understanding of the differential privacy in data mining rather than understanding the particular outcome of the classification process used. It provides insight into and helps to refine the application of the differential privacy theory. The classification process itself is of secondary interest; it plays a supportive role in facilitating our understanding of the differential privacy parameters.

In the first part of this section, we explore the way that healthcare data sharing with appropriate privacy protection can be achieved to enable health research is one of the most critical challenges in health and medical informatics. Current de-identification approaches or microdata of original records minus basic personal attributes release are subject to various re-identification and disclosure risks and do not provide sufficient protection for patients and discourages most of them to participate in clinical trials (El Emam, 2011). "A complementary approach is to release statistical macrodata (i.e. derived statistics), which can also be used to construct synthetic data that mimic the original data" (Francis, 2015).

While differential privacy has emerged as one of the stronger provable privacy guarantees for statistical data release, there is still and open question as to whether or not differential privacy can efficiently and effectively release a dataset while guaranteeing practicality and data usefulness for health applications. "Applying differential privacy to healthcare data presents additional new challenges due to the high dimensionality, high correlation, and cross-institution distribution in healthcare datasets that are necessary to support cross-sectional, longitudinal, and cross-institutional studies." (El Emam, 2013). Healthcare data often contains categorical data (e.g., diagnosis, procedure codes, drugs dispensed, laboratory tests, etc.) as well as numeric data (e.g., age, length of stay in hospital, and time since last visit). As a result, both types, numeric and categorical, are addressed by the use of privacy mechanisms similar to both the Laplace and the Exponential mechanisms at the same time to the same data set release (Cormode et al., 2012).

Note that a non-interactive mechanism of differential privacy allows the computation of statistics without having to publish the original data set would be quite suitable for several healthcare data publishing contexts, such as in public health. In public health, ongoing monitoring of some data variables for a epidemic, product recall, etc., often relies on the computation of a well defined and previously known set of statistics at almost regular intervals. Another example also from the public health domain is performance or safety reporting (e.g., the number of eligible patients that received certain screening and the occurrence rate of surgical site infections) which also involves the computation of well-defined statistics. Therefore, for such reporting purposes, differentially private statistic analyses are a good match to the process. A basic and simple design for the way to share data among horizontally divided healthcare data sets is shown in Figure 4. These distributed data sets, in the case of healthcare, would be gathered from different health information technology systems. For example, surgical site infections would be gathered from hospitals and surgical centers for the infections documented on patients.

The goal of differential privacy in this problem domain is to provide enough accuracy in the shared result set between research groups or institutions to help retain statistical significance of potential analyses

Figure 4. Sharing data using differential privacy in horizontally distributed data sets

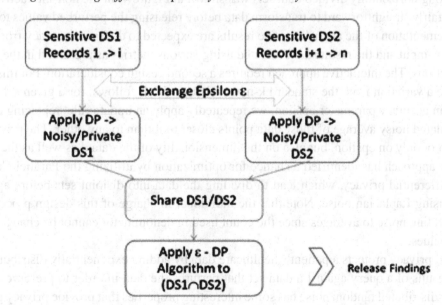

while still ensuring enough noise has been added to provide the aspired privacy guarantees; the solution has to also provide a mechanism that can prevent researchers from possibly exploiting some weaknesses of the system by asking too many high accuracy questions. The querying researcher could ask a mixture of questions both with high accuracy (low privacy) and low accuracy (high privacy) epsilon values to meet the desired goals of statistical significance and patient privacy within an allowed total value of accuracy (a 'privacy budget') (Lee, 2008). This challenge forces us to take a closer look at several design considerations like calculating the sensitivity function for each algorithm, the way to determine and control the allowed accuracy, and identifying possible optimization options for the applied techniques. Other challenges also emerge from the nature of the data set, so appropriate values of epsilon specifically for healthcare datasets need to be evaluated to balance this tradeoff between the desired privacy guarantees and the required statistical accuracy.

In the second part of this section, we explore the design and implementation of the case study for healthcare data mining. To serve as a basis for the case study, the medical data set from the Breast Cancer Wisconsin data sets from the Machine Learning Repository of University of California Irvine Lichman (2013) has been utilized. The data set consists of several groups each with multiple instances of breast tissue cells and the related attributes. The authors use the data as one group for the purpose of this case study. Attributes have been used to describe cell instances such as: radius which is the mean of distances from center to points on the perimeter; texture which is the standard deviation of gray-scale values; perimeter which is the perimeter of the cell; area which is the surface area of the cell; smoothness which indicates the local variation in radius lengths; clump thickness which measures the thickness of the clump formed by the cancer cells since these tend to group in multilayers; uniformity of cell size and shape which indicates whether or not the size and shape are uniform; etc. Each instance has one of two possible classes: benign or malignant given as ground truth. There are 699 cell instances from the Breast Cancer Wisconsin data set from UCI where 458 are benign and 241 malignant used as ground truth.

Given the data, we proceed to a discussion of the design considerations and steps in our case study. The first design consideration is to decide on the location to add the noise when implementing a differentially private version of our k-means clustering algorithm. A basic and simple design for the way to share data among horizontally divided data sets was shown in Figure 4. In the non-interactive scenario, the process is fairly straightforward to transform data before releasing the perturbed values to a standard k-means implementation of the algorithm. The results are expected to differ in accuracy from the original data used as input and the results are evaluated using various metrics as presented in the results and discussion sections. The interactive approach requires a second design consideration. For this approach, one can utilize a variation from the standard k-means that works as follows: for a given set of k points in space and an accuracy parameter epsilon, we repeatedly apply an update rule, replacing each center with the calculated noisy average of those data points closer to it than to any other. The privacy budget then depends not only on epsilon, but also on the dimensionality of the data d as well as the number of centers k. Our approach has identified a chance for optimization by utilizing the Parallel Composition property of differential privacy, which lead to dividing the data into disjoint sets before applying the perturbation using Laplacian noise. Note that the individual in charge of this design process must be careful with adding noise to averages since the count used in denominator cannot be changed, but only the summed values.

Differential privacy protects a patient's healthcare data by adding exponentially distributed random noise to the results of a query against a data set that perturbs the data in order to preserve anonymity. Exponentially distributed random noise has some interesting properties that provide privacy guarantees.

For the case study, the differential privacy noise mechanisms can be applied to specify the amount of accuracy (ε) desired, and translate this to the privacy 'budget' that it can guarantee. For example, in the aforementioned breast cancer data set, noise can be added to every numeric variable. The concern, especially within healthcare datasets, is that the addition of random noise, while providing privacy guarantees, will significantly reduce statistical accuracy. In the case of the breast cancer data set, there must be guarantees that the noise doesn't impact the information on the cells. By applying differential privacy against the used dataset, one should be able to either alleviate or confirm the concern. The expectation given the current popularity of differential privacy in research is that one will be able to determine the range of candidate epsilon values to achieve practicality and guarantee an acceptable level of privacy.

In order to observe the effect of the level of noise introduced on the learning performance of the privacy preserving learning algorithm, the case study in this paper varied ε and performed several runs of k-means classification algorithm on the data set. This results in a number of privacy settings that are explained as follows: The first setting utilizes the original data with no differential privacy applied, where the results of this run are considered to be the new ground truth or base line that is utilized in comparing the results before and after applying differential privacy settings. Several program runs were then performed with both interactive and non-interactive settings and with different DP algorithms applied. The interactive implementation utilized C# as programming language and explicit implementation of k-means was utilized to include the noise adding functions in different steps of the algorithm. This implementation also utilized the PINQ package for querying the data set. Note that since our clustering results are binary in terms of benign or malignant designations of cancer cells, one can view the clustering in this case as a binary classifier for the sake of evaluation. The non-interactive setting was implemented in the R programming language and was applied by adding the noise adding functions in compact, well defined steps before 'releasing' the data set for evaluation. The aforementioned implementations were run with a number of ε_i values applied to the data set, analyzed each result set and averaged errors, and relied on two comparison techniques to judge the algorithms comparisons before and after applying differential privacy noise. This is accomplished by first defining the similarity Jaccard index of clustering results, and second, using the original classifier results as the ground truth/baseline in order to compare with the new version of the dp-classifier.

In the last part of this section, we review and discuss our results. Figure 5 shows the relation between different values of ε and the average query error calculated for an intermediate counting step of the algorithm. To study the classifier performance with and without differential privacy applied, we review the silhouette plots of Figure 6. Note the decrease in the average silhouette width, which the actual mislabeled records are 3 out of 699 data records, which can be considered acceptable for clustering or classification applications such as the case in our dataset, especially considering that $\varepsilon = 0.1$ for these results. In addition, for the non-interactive setting, we evaluated for $\varepsilon = 0.1$ in the similarity of the clustering algorithm before and after applying DP in terms of the contingency table with the co-membership of the observations, using Jaccard coefficient similarity statistic as shown in Figure 7. The similarity coefficient with a value of Cluster Similarity = 0.9306204 indicated high similarity which translates to high accuracy. This result is quite encouraging in general and for this data set, achieved with an acceptable privacy loss of $\varepsilon = 0.1$. Figure 8 shows the silhouette plot for $\varepsilon = 0.05$, which translates to better privacy guarantee than $\varepsilon = 0.1$ of the previous plot, a cluster similarity index of only 0.52 and a decreased accuracy in label prediction. These results can be further fine-tuned to project the desired tradeoff between privacy loss and accuracy based on the application and the end goal of the data

Figure 5. Results of 33 runs using incremental values of epsilon

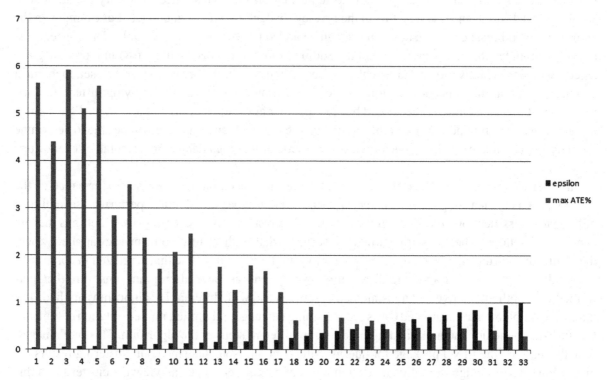

Figure 6. Silhouette plot with no DP applied on the left and with ε -DP applied in non-interactive setting

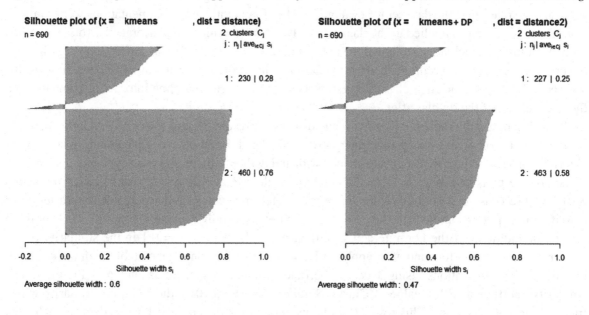

sharing process. In particular, if the breast cancer data set is shared for the benign-malignant classifier model, then fitting is recommended to ensure a high privacy loss in favor of enhanced accuracy. In this case, a more strict privacy parameter could be applied when utilizing this data set as a test set rather than a training set for such a model.

Figure 7. Contingency table with the comembership of the observations

		Truth data			
		Class 1	**Class 2**	**Classification overall**	**Precision**
Classifier results	**Class 1**	126945	4960	131905	96.24%
	Class 2	4504	101296	105800	95.743%
	Truth overall	131449	106256	237705	
	Recall	96.574%	95.332%		

Overall accuracy (OA): 96.019%

Figure 8. Silhouette plot with $\varepsilon = 0.05$

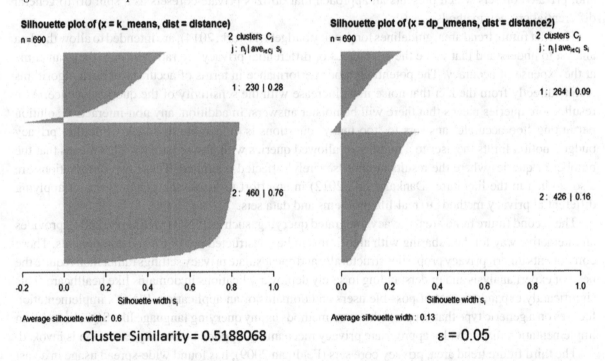

Silhouette plot of (x = k_means, dist = distance)

n = 690

2 clusters C_j
j: n_j | ave$_{i \in C_j}$ s_i

1: 230 | 0.28

2: 460 | 0.76

Silhouette width s_i

-0.2   0.0   0.2   0.4   0.6   0.8   1.0

Average silhouette width: 0.6

Cluster Similarity = 0.5188068

Silhouette plot of (x = dp_kmeans, dist = distance2)

n = 690

2 clusters C_j
j: n_j | ave$_{i \in C_j}$ s_i

1: 264 | 0.09

2: 426 | 0.16

Silhouette width s_i

0.0   0.2   0.4   0.6   0.8   1.0

Average silhouette width: 0.13

$\varepsilon = 0.05$

As for the interactive setting experiment, the results were in general less encouraging. Note that the analysis of the values and optimization ways is a subject of future work. To summarize, our results showed that without much sacrificing privacy $\varepsilon = 0.1$ a 93% similarity was achieved and 96% accuracy relevant to the original clustering performance. In our settings, the non-interactive setting resulted in better metrics than interactive, but this may not occur generally. Specifically, for the breast cancer data set and similar health care data sets, we observe that the non-interactive setting is in fact the more desirable approach when releasing such sensitive health records for research purposes. Cluster similarity when comparing the ground truth with resulting clusters varied from a ratio of 1 to less than 50% depending on ε values (higher ε means better similarity). Using a synthetic set, created from dp-values of original data enhanced the overall performance and this result needs further evaluation in future work. Finally, as expected, higher ε values lead to a deterioration of privacy. Note that any numeric data can actually be utilized to test, which is one of the strengths of DP and as a result, can applied regardless of what the data actually represents.

FUTURE RESEARCH DIRECTIONS

This section explores future trends in there different areas: guidelines for privacy budgets which explores the way that guidelines can be established to assist in the choice of privacy budgets based on data sets' nature and application domain accuracy and privacy loss tolerance; privacy integrated querying which examines a variation of the data sharing setting models discussed in this chapter that utilizes an interactive design of differentially private mechanisms that can be used in horizontally distributed data; and, private coresets which presents an approach that utilizes private coresets as a spin off to general differential privacy methods.

The first future trend area, guidelines for privacy budgets (Dwork, 2014), are intended to allow the data analyst to understand that while the guarantees of differential privacy are rather strong, they can come at the expense of accuracy. The potentially poor performance in terms of accuracy of such algorithms results directly from the fact that noise must increase with the sensitivity of the query sequence. As a result, more queries means that there will be noisier answers. In addition, any non-interactive solution permitting 'too accurate' answers to 'too many' questions is vulnerable to attack while the 'privacy budget' notion limits the user to a number of allowed queries with low sensitivity. This means that the number of queries where the results are not 'severely' affected is limited. These two observations are also studied in the literature (Dankar et al., 2012) in an effort to assess the practicalities of applying differential privacy methods to real-life problems and data sets.

The second future trend area, privacy integrated querying, such as PINQ (McSherry, 2009), provides an interactive way for data sharing with algorithms to be constructed out of trusted components. These components inherit privacy properties structurally and encapsulate privacy settings rather than require the need of expert analysis and understanding to safely deploy applications in domains like healthcare. This significantly expands the set of possible users and domains of an application. PINQ's implementation focuses on a generic type that supports the same methods as any querying language like SQL, but with an implementation that provides appropriate privacy mechanisms applied before any execution is invoked.

The third future trend area, privacy core sets (Feldman 2009), has found wide-spread usage in a vast host of settings involving very large data sets, with the potential future applicability to differential privacy. "A coreset of a point set P is a small weighted set of points that captures the properties of P." (Feldman 2009). A link is forged between coresets and differentially privacy in the sense that if f a small coreset with low generalized sensitivity in fact does exist (i.e., replacing a single point in the original point set slightly affects the quality of the coreset) this in turn implies the existence of a private coreset for the same set of queries. This is particularly helpful in settings where the data set to be shared is particularly large and when the main purpose of the data release is to extract general models describing a data set properties.

CONCLUSION

This chapter explored big data privacy and security techniques and policies with a specific focus on differential privacy as utilized for a case study of healthcare data mining. To support the discussion, the *Background* section reviewed big data applications, big data challenges, big data processing technologies, and big data analysis techniques. This was supplemented by the *Big Data Security and Data Privacy Issue* section that focused on differential privacy with a focus on: big data security, differential privacy, properties of differential private algorithms, the impact of noise mechanisms, and models of releasing sensitive data with differential privacy. Using this as a basis, the *Differential Privacy Case Study in Healthcare Data Mining* section presented a case study and: motivated healthcare data sharing and the challenges of the usage of differential privacy; explored the design and implementation; and reviewed and discussed results. To complete the chapter, the *Future Trends* section explored emerging areas including: *guidelines for privacy budgets* for domain accuracy and privacy loss tolerance, *privacy integrated querying* a variant of data sharing, and, *privacy coresets* to augment general differential privacy methods. Overall, this chapter has provided an in-depth examination on big data privacy, big data analytic methods, and recent tools/technologies for privacy preserving big data applications utilizing a real-world scenario in achieving privacy in big data analytics in the domain of healthcare to securely manage the privacy of patient data.

REFERENCES

Arpaia, M. (2013). Leveraging big data to create more secure web applications. *Code as Craft*. Retrieved from http://codeascraft.com/2013/06/04/leveraging-big-data-to-create-more-secure-web-applications/

Barbaro, M., Zeller, T., & Hansell, S. (2006). A face is exposed for aol searcher no. 4417749. *New York Times, 9.*

Bennett, J., & Lanning, S. (2007). The Netflix prize.*Proceedings of KDD cup and workshop.* 35.

Bertino, E., Bernstein, P., Agrawal, D., Davidson, S., Dayal, U., Franklin, M.,... Jadadish, H. V. (2011). *Challenges and Opportunities with Big Data.* Academic Press.

Borthakur, D. (2007). The Hadoop distributed file system: Architecture and design. *Hadoop Project Website, 11,* 21.

Boyd, D., & Crawford, K. (2012). Critical questions for big data: Provocations for a cultural, technological, and scholarly phenomenon. *Information Communication and Society, 15*(5), 662–679. doi:10.108 0/1369118X.2012.678878

Brown, B., Michael, C., & Manyika, J. (2011). Are you ready for the era of 'big data'. *The McKinsey Quarterly, 4*(1), 24–35.

Caine, K., & Hanania, R. (2013). Patients want granular privacy control over health information in electronic medical records. *Journal of the American Medical Informatics Association, 20*(1), 7–15. doi:10.1136/amiajnl-2012-001023 PMID:23184192

Chaudhuri, S. (2012). What next? A half-dozen data management research goals for big data and the cloud. *Proceedings of the 31st Symposium on Principles of Database Systems*, 1-4. doi:10.1145/2213556.2213558

Cheung, S. (2013). Developing a big data application for data exploration and discovery. *IBM Developerworks*. Retrieved from http://www.ibm.com/developerworks/library/bd-exploration/

Clifton, C., & Tassa, T. (2013). On syntactic anonymity and differential privacy. *IEEE 29th International Conference on Data Engineering Workshops (ICDEW)*, 88–93. doi:10.1109/ICDEW.2013.6547433

Cormode, G., Procopiuc, C., Srivastava, D., Shen, E., & Yu, T. (2012). Differentially private spatial decompositions. *Data Engineering (ICDE), 2012 IEEE 28th International Conference on*, 20–31. doi:10.1109/ICDE.2012.16

Cyril, N., & Soman, A. (2015). *Big Data Analysis using Hadoop*. Academic Press.

Dankar, F. K., & El Emam, K. (2012). The application of differential privacy to health data. *Proceedings of the 2012 Joint EDBT/ICDT Workshops*, 158–166. doi:10.1145/2320765.2320816

Dankar, F. K., & El Emam, K. (2013). Practicing differential privacy in health care: A review. *Transactions on Data Privacy, 6*(1), 35–67.

De Montjoye, Y. A., Radaelli, L., Singh, V. K., & Pentland, A. S. (2015). Unique in the shopping mall: On the reidentifiability of credit card metadata. *Science, 347*(6221), 536–539. doi:10.1126/science.1256297 PMID:25635097

Dwork, C. (2006). Differential privacy. *Proceedings of 33rd International Colloquium*, 1-12. doi:10.1007/11787006_1

Dwork, C. (2006). Differential privacy. In *Automata, languages and programming* (pp. 1–12). Springer. doi:10.1007/11787006_1

Dwork, C. (2008). An ad omnia approach to defining and achieving private data analysis. In Privacy, Security, and Trust in KDD, PinKDD 2007, (pp. 1–13). Springer. doi:10.1007/978-3-540-78478-4_1

Dwork, C. (2008). Differential privacy: A survey of results. In *Theory and applications of models of computation* (pp. 1–19). Springer. doi:10.1007/978-3-540-79228-4_1

Dwork, C., Feldman, V., Hardt, M., Pitassi, T., Reingold, O., & Roth, A. (2015). The reusable holdout: Preserving validity in adaptive data analysis. *Science, 349*(6248), 636–638. doi:10.1126/science.aaa9375 PMID:26250683

Dwork, C., Feldman, V., Hardt, M., Pitassi, T., Reingold, O., & Roth, A. L. (2015): Preserving statistical validity in adaptive data analysis. *Proceedings of the Forty-Seventh Annual ACM on Symposium on Theory of Computing*, 117–126. doi:10.1145/2746539.2746580

Dwork, C., McSherry, F., Nissim, K., & Smith, A. (2006). Calibrating noise to sensitivity in private data analysis. In *Theory of cryptography* (pp. 265–284). Springer. doi:10.1007/11681878_14

Dwork, C., & Nissim, K. (2004). Privacy-preserving datamining on vertically partitioned databases. In Advances in Cryptology–CRYPTO 2004 (pp. 528–544). Springer. doi:10.1007/978-3-540-28628-8_32

Dwork, C., & Roth, A. (2014). The algorithmic foundations of differential privacy. *Foundations and Trends in Theoretical Computer Science*, *9*(3-4), 211–407. doi:10.1561/0400000042

Dwork, C., & Roth, A. (2014). The algorithmic foundations of differential privacy. *Foundations and Trends in Theoretical Computer Science*, *9*(3-4), 211–407. doi:10.1561/0400000042

Dwork, C., & Smith, A. (2010). Differential privacy for statistics: What we know and what we want to learn. *Journal of Privacy and Confidentiality*, *1*(2), 2.

El Emam, K., Mercer, J., Moreau, K., Grava-Gubins, I., Buckeridge, D., & Jonker, E. (2011). Physician privacy concerns when disclosing patient data for public health purposes during a pandemic influenza outbreak. *BMC Public Health*, *11*(1), 454. doi:10.1186/1471-2458-11-454 PMID:21658256

Feldman, D., Fiat, A., Kaplan, H., & Nissim, K. (2009). Private coresets. In *Proceedings of the forty-first annual ACM symposium on Theory of computing* (pp. 361-370). ACM.

Francis, T., Madiajagan, M., & Kumar, V. (2015). Privacy issues and techniques in e-health systems. *Proceedings of the 2015 ACM SIGMIS Conference on Computers and People Research*,113–115.

Health Insurance Portability and Accountability Act. (n.d.). Retrieved from http://www.hhs.gov/ocr/hipaa

Inukollu, V., Arsi, S., & Ravuri, R. (2014). Security issues associated with big data in cloud computing. *International Journal of Network Security & Its Applications*, *6*(3), 45–56. doi:10.5121/ijnsa.2014.6304

Kendall, D., & Quill, E. (2015). A Lifetime Electronic Health Record for Every American. Washington, DC: Third Way. Available at http://www.thirdway.org/report/a-lifetime-electronic-health-record-for-every-american

Lane, A. (2012). *Securing Big Data: Security Recommendations for Hadoop and NoSQL Environments*. Securosis, LLC. Retrieved from https://securosis.com/assets/library/reports/SecuringBigData_FINAL.pdf

Lane, A. (2013). *Security Implications Of Big Data Strategies*. Dark Reading's Database Security Tech Center Report. Retrieved from http://www.darkreading.com/risk/security-implications-of-big-data-strategies/d/d-id/1139379

Lee, D. G. Y. (2008). *Protecting patient data confidentiality using differential privacy*. Academic Press.

Lichman, M. (2013). *UCI Machine Learning Repository*. Irvine, CA: University of California, School of Information and Computer Science.

McSherry, F. (2009). Privacy integrated queries: an extensible platform for privacy-preserving data analysis. *Proceedings of the 2009 ACM SIGMOD International Conference on Management of data*, 19–30. doi:10.1145/1559845.1559850

Mohammed, N., Chen, R., Fung, B., & Yu, P. (2011). Differentially private data release for data mining. *Proceedings of the 17th ACM SIGKDD international conference on Knowledge discovery and data mining*, 493–501. doi:10.1145/2020408.2020487

Peleg, M., Beimel, D., Dori, D., & Denekamp, Y. (2008, December). Situation-Based Access Control: Privacy management via modeling of patient data access scenarios. *Journal of Biomedical Informatics*, *41*(6), 1028–1040. doi:10.1016/j.jbi.2008.03.014 PMID:18511349

Sarathy, R., & Muralidhar, K. (2011). Evaluating Laplace noise addition to satisfy differential privacy for numeric data. *Transactions on Data Privacy.*, *4*(1), 1–17.

Sujansky, V., Faus, S. A., Stone, E., & Brennan, P. F. (2010). A method to implement fine-grained access control for personal health records through standard relational database queries. *Journal of Biomedical Informatics*, *43*(5Suppl), S46–S50. doi:10.1016/j.jbi.2010.08.001 PMID:20696276

Sweeney. (2002). k-anonymity: A model for protecting privacy. *International Journal of Uncertainty, Fuzziness and Knowledge-Based Systems*, *10*(5), 557–570.

Tene, O., & Polonetsky, J. (2012). Response: Privacy in the Age of Big Data: A Time for Big Decisions. *Stanford Law Review*. Retrieved from http://www.stanfordlawreview.org/online/privacy-paradox/big-data

Vu, D., & Slavkovi, A. (2009). Differential privacy for clinical trial data: Preliminary evaluations. *Data Mining Workshops, 2009. ICDMW'09. IEEE International Conference on*, 138–143.

Wang, J., Liu, S., & Li, Y. (2015). A review of differential privacy in individual data release. *International Journal of Distributed Sensor Networks*, *2015*, 1. doi:10.1155/2015/743160

Yadav, C., Wang, S., & Kumar, M. (2013). *Algorithm and approaches to handle large data-a survey*. arXiv preprint arXiv:1307.5437

ADDITIONAL READING

Kamal, S., Dey, N., Nimmy, S. F., Ripon, S. H., Ali, N. Y., Ashour, A. S., & Shi, F. et al. (2016). Evolutionary framework for coding area selection from cancer data. *Neural Computing & Applications*, 1–23.

Mason, C. (2015). Engineering Kindness: Building a Machine with Compassionate Intelligence. *International Journal of Synthetic Emotions*, *6*(1), 1–23. doi:10.4018/IJSE.2015010101

Odella, F. (2016). Technology Studies and the Sociological Debate on Monitoring of Social Interactions. *International Journal of Ambient Computing and Intelligence*, *7*(1), 1–26. doi:10.4018/IJACI.2016010101

Panda, S. K., Mishra, S., & Das, S. (2017). An Efficient Intra-Server and Inter-Server Load Balancing Algorithm for Internet Distributed Systems. *International Journal of Rough Sets and Data Analysis*, *4*(1), 1–18. doi:10.4018/IJRSDA.2017010101

Ripon, S. H., Kamal, S., Hossain, S., & Dey, N. (2016). Theoretical Analysis of Different Classifiers under Reduction Rough Data Set: A Brief Proposal. *International Journal of Rough Sets and Data Analysis*, *3*(3), 1–20. doi:10.4018/IJRSDA.2016070101

Vallverdú, J., Shah, H., & Casacuberta, D. (2010). Chatterbox challenge as a test-bed for synthetic emotions. Creating Synthetic Emotions through Technological and Robotic Advancements, 118-144.

Zappi, P., Lombriser, C., Benini, L., & Tröster, G. (2012). Collecting datasets from ambient intelligence environments. Innovative Applications of Ambient Intelligence: Advances in Smart Systems: Advances in Smart Systems, 113.

KEY TERMS AND DEFINITIONS

Big Data Applications: Data storage, processing, and analysis technologies that are characterized by high velocity, volume and variety.

Differential Privacy: A privacy mechanism that allows statistical databases to be used for analysis without individual records being vulnerable for privacy risks.

Interactive Data Release Model: A data sharing model, where the user interacts with a differentially private version of an algorithm to query a confidential data set.

K-Means Clustering: A clustering algorithm that aims to partition observations into k clusters where each observation is assigned to the cluster with the nearest mean.

Laplace Noise: Random noise generating functions that follow the Laplace distribution and it is the simplest noise model to be used in differential privacy.

Non-Interactive Data Release Model: A data sharing model, where the data is transformed via differential privacy noise perturbation before being released to users.

Sensitivity Gap: Represents the sum of the worst case difference in answers that can be caused by adding or removing an individual's information from a data set and that needs to be reflected in the global sensitivity setting in a differential privacy algorithm.

Section 6
Is IoT Driving a Big Data?

Chapter 10
Internet of Things in Real Life:
Applications

Abhijeet Chandrakant Dabre
Smt. Kashibai Navale College of Engineering, India

Sandesh Shivaji Mahamure
Smt. Kashibai Navale College of Engineering, India

Snehal Pandurang Wadibhasme
Smt. Kashibai Navale College of Engineering, India

ABSTRACT

This chapter specifically with Internet of Things (IoT), initially presents what exactly it is? It's just a smart route to improving daily life activities by connecting devices to widely used Internet. Then gradually put a view on history, which closely talked about traditional ways of communication mechanisms, moving forward it touches the current ideology of IoT. Further in this chapter authors discussed different aspects of IoT which was explained by different philosophers and it clears the idea of how to introduce, how to learn and how to launch IoT in different sectors (such as education, power generation, water management, road safety, automobiles etc). The practicality of the knowledge explains the usefulness of IoT and also explains how it impacts on the overall growth of the country and why every individual attracted towards this smart network of things. At the end, this chapter accomplished with the need of IoT in developing countries, how IoT provides efficient solutions to overcome upcoming challenges and finally briefs about why it is recommended.

INTRODUCTION

Internet of Things (IoT) is not an updated version of Internet and not the technology which is developed for the small span of time. Basically, IoT is same as the Internet with modification in the communication where Human-Human, Human-Things, and Things-Things have easily occurred. In other words, IoT is a network of anything and now onwards actual things came into the picture. The thing is any object or entity which has Sensing, Computation, and Communication facilities enabled with it. Sensing considers

DOI: 10.4018/978-1-5225-2486-1.ch010

information which will obtain in a similar fashion as it from human/animals body sensors. There are five well-organized sensors named as sight, smell, hear, taste and touch. Don't you think that these sensing capabilities will establish inside a non-living object? The answer is obviously Yes! Because skies will not always the limit, there is something beyond it and for sure that is IoT. Nowadays, things capture sensing capabilities in them which ultimately helps to reach the future goals with ease shown by Rhee S. (2016, April). Hence such things are popularly called as 'smart things'. It is possible to connect each with every (EwE) using IoT. IoT also works on the same framework on which Internet is working with a little modification in the connectivity protocol. After the birth of IoT, the World connects each other very closely and it is reflected in Figure 1. Information sharing between things makes everyone's life easy.

In India, public access Internet was launched by Videsh Sanchar Nigam Limited (VSNL) on 15th August 1995 same the day of Independence. During the process of building ERNET (Education and Research Network) Nakajima T. et.al. Team (2002, August) works passionately and an Internet brought to the India. According to TRAI (Telecom Regulatory Authority of India) recently there are 302.35 million Internet subscribers in India. Figure 2 states pie chart and statistics data provided by TRAI on 15th August 2015, in the relation with information of last 2 decades Internet made 31% population of India as Internet-friendly. Then it is much obvious that IoT will encrust remaining 69% population in very less number of years. IoT is networks of smart things, where things make everything happen in less amount of time for the human. The impact was so immediate hence, more and more people curious about IoT and indulge with developers to create platforms for IoT enable devices to access it in real life. IoT acting as a third way of communication system because things can communicate with each other depending on the surrounding situations.

Consider an example; someone wants to go for a long drive with friends but don't know where he puts the keys (keys of the car is a smart thing). Then, instead of looking each every place as it requires a large amount of time. Simply search the keys using smarter way i.e., track the location of keys on a smartphone. The idea behind this work is sensor attached to the keys notifies its location on web applica-

Figure 1. Layered communication

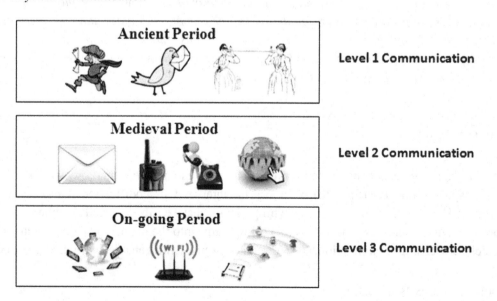

Figure 2. BI statistics

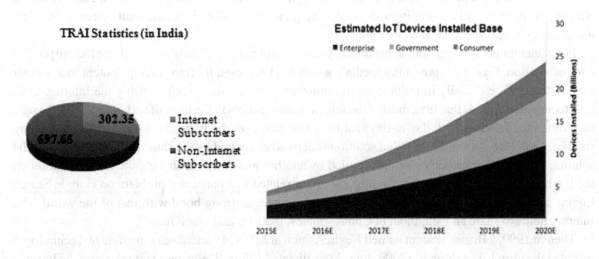

tion and that is installed as an application program on the phone. Just think what if there is no provision of such highly materialized network? Or what if there is no Internet at all. It means human beings are still lives in the ancient period. This network of smart things will able to reduce the limited parameter 'Time' and also speed-up the working scenario.

BACKGROUND

History of IoT

The communication mechanism in an ancient time shown in Figure 3a. has done by using letters and symbolic notations. After that manual effort turns into a new generation of communication known as

Figure 3. History and current standing of communication mechanism

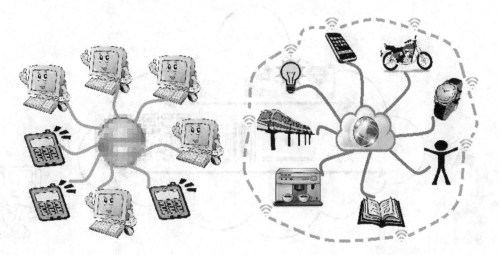

the Internet where peoples are able to connect through standardize TCP/IP protocols and communicate with each other via e-mails, sending videos, sharing pictures etc. The electronic mail system is trending like a professional way of communication.

In an ancient period, sign and convention system is utilized completely for fulfilling the purpose of communication. Figure 4 represents a media's which has been used for transferring content in a simpler way. After 1995, especially in India users of computer system liaise to others using the Internet as an interfacing platform. At that time most of the information transfers in the form of text, image, video, voice recording etc. Tackling with day-to-day real time situation everybody needs an efficient and effective solution on it. But, it's not the case that solution is derived & applied by the same person. Sometimes the solution derived by somebody else and applied by another just done via sharing the needy solution on the Internet. Exactly it is similar to finding a solution related to a particular problem on Google Search Engine and that everyone does nowadays. Hence, it creates a strong bond with rest of the world. The Internet helps to share an idea, thoughts, philosophies, theories and much more.

Then in 1999, a British student named Kevin Ashton at MIT (Massachusetts Institute of Technology) invented the term IoT. Ashton K. (2009, June 22nd), dictated IoT as "Describe a system where the Internet is connected to the physical world via ubiquitous sensors". As mentioned earlier IoT is a network of smart sensors stacked with computing and communicable hardware device. Sensors are also called as things have collects data by sensing surrounding environment. That collected data transferred to appropriate device/end-user using wireless media over the Internet states by Fouad, K. M., Hassan, B. M., & Hassan, M. F. (2016, June). IoT is a big-picture of embedded system. It mainly based on sensor technology, computing system, and communication mechanism.

Current Ideology of IoT

Things showed in Figure 3b. help to capture data more precisely it is a bit-oriented data. Till now any type of system or a technology uses a bit-oriented data which is also called as digital data for executing a task (or running its own work). Computing of digital data done using advanced computing frameworks

Figure 4. Different media used for information exchange

(such as multi-core systems, cloud systems, information retrieval systems etc) and at the end displays computed result in the form of the digital format to the end user or node device by using appropriate communication mechanism.

Core parts of IoT shown in Figure 5 elaborated separately in the following sections are as follows:

Sensor (Having Sensing Capability)

- It is a physical device which response by detecting a situation (like sensible, electronic, physical, chemical or biological) and used for the measurement purpose.
- In the 19th century, there was an explorer named as Nain Singh Rawat lived in India explores head of Indian territory i.e., the Himalayas using a compass as a sensor. It shows that practical applications of sensor technology have been in use in those days. e.g., thermometer, pressure sensor, light sensor, touch-sensitive elevator buttons etc.
- In IoT sensors work on optical and electrical signals in the form of digitized data. Valued information collected from different sensors is called as sensor data.

Computation System

- The computer is a combination of hardware unit as well as a software application, in which hardware is mainly used to perform an action(s) depend on the précised input and at the same time software applications is used as editor moreover represents an output.
- The basic computation system architecture has given by Isaac Von-Neumann in 1945 and still it in use to perform the calculative task.

Figure 5. Iot categorization-main

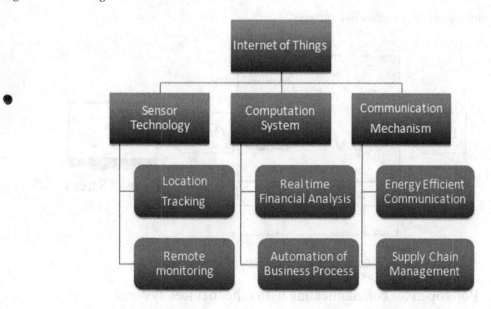

- A sensor through which sensor data is accepted has one more advantage of the computing unit. Computing unit retains extra cost and time, simply by performing execution activity on the sensor. Hence no need to search for availability of computation environment.
- Thus, it leads to time and cost efficient operations. Figure 6 represents a traditional approach to computation.

1. The client gives an input to central processing unit (CPU) and obviously, it is in the form of instructions, so it goes into memory.
2. Depend on the sequence of instructions now available to the main memory control unit (CU) assigned them to arithmetic logic unit (ALU) for execution.
3. Either the computed result returned as an output to the client.
4. Or the computed result sends using ports present with the system bus to other devices for further processing.
5. But in IoT enable network system, traditional client replaced by smart things.

Communication Mechanism

- **Wired Communication:** It specifies connection-oriented communication which gives the status of data whether it is reached at receiving end or not and because of this it slow in nature.
  - e.g., TCP Communication.
- **Wireless Communication:** Dey, N., Dey, G., Chakraborty, S., & Chaudhuri, S. S. (2014, September) specifies connectionless communication in which data loss can occur and it is fast in nature.
  - e.g., UDP Communication.

Figure 6. Traditional model of computation systems

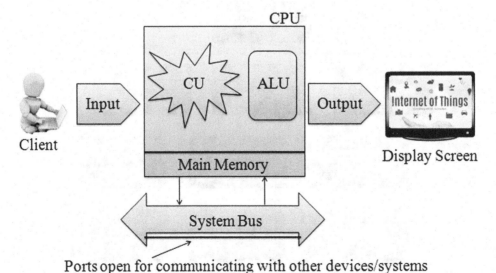

TERMS RELATED WITH IOT

Computer Network

Two or more computers cooperatively connected together using network cables for information sharing and resource allocation. Devices involved in network creation can be attached together via wired/wireless media and there are various topologies (such as star, Ring, Bus, Mesh etc.) already defined and implement them as per the user or enterprise requirements. Weiser M. (1991, September) explains that the constraint of distance holds on wired connectivity but wireless media establishes an attachment between them using basic computer network i.e., the Internet. The core elements of a computer network are as follows…

1. Network Nodes.
2. Transmission Channel.
3. Connectivity Protocol.

Formation of computer network initiated by the host which is also known as a network node and this network node is responsible for the exchange of information as well as the allocation of resource(s). But before actual exchange and allocation procedure begins the type of connection need to be addressed whether it is connection-oriented (TCP) or connectionless (UDP). Transmission channel divided into two type's Physical (wired) medium and Logical (wireless) medium and selection of this medium may base on connectivity protocol.

Bluetooth

A personal area network where data exchange occurs over short distances using small-range radio waves in a non-wired way. Bluetooth uses frequency hopping spread spectrum technique and follows a master-slave strategy for communication in the form packet based protocols. The structure established during communication is called as Piconet (special form is a point to multipoint piconet). Nusser R. & Pelz R. M. (2000, September 28th) shows that it is designed with a consideration of low power consumption and low-cost microchips; hence it is advisable for each device and becomes universal standard to switch-on IoT. Bluetooth acts as a mediator between user and devices by connecting devices together which further linked with application programs installed in handheld devices. For enabling IoT Bluetooth low energy protocol (like GATT) plays an outlandish role. (e.g., Wireless Audio Headsets).

Near Field Communication (NFC)

The transmission of small-sized data within short range using radio waves either by enabling Bluetooth or Wi-Fi. NFC is working on radio waves but there is 2-way communication possible between sender and receiver, not like RFID. The best real time example is Credit Card which is activated with NFC chip and it is easier to add parental controls to it. The usage of NFC in daily life explains by Ozdenizci, B., Aydin, M. N., Coskun, V., & Ok, K. (2010, June) using the following scenario…
Scenario: Daily Bus Journey

1. Passenger check-in at bus stop using the NFC-enabled smartphone.
2. After reaching destination passenger so check-out.
3. Fare details displayed on a smartphone which is based on total distance covered.

But due to continuous transmission of radio signals thief can steal data for their own use. Hence security to data or protection to confidentiality becomes a major challenge for NFC-enable devices.

Radio Frequency Identification (RFID)

An identification technique describes by Mohanpurkar, & Joshi, (2016) based on electromagnetic fields uses tags which contain electronic information are linked with any physical object. Information available with real time objects tracks digitally using a tag which is also called as an antenna. Maximum 2000 bytes of information stores on small chip present inside the tag and scan this information via RFID reader by Weinstein (2005, August). Depending on the power source RFID tags categorize in two types- a. Passive Tags: This tag doesn't contain any power source hence connect with nearest RFID reader. b. Active Tags: This tag contains a local power source (like a battery) and hence connects with a respective tag within the range of 100 meters. A unique ID is assigned to each RFID tag to avoid misleading during reading information from tags. It mainly helps to make our daily life easier by tracking and controlling the physical objects using RFID technology.

Internet Protocol Version 4

The standardize internetworking method used for directing an Internet traffic under packet-switched network. Basically, it provides a 32-bit addressing scheme which was initially used in ARPANET in 1983. This large but limited numbers of addresses divided into various classes of the network (such as Class A, Class B, Class C, Class D and Class E) and allocated to the system depending on network identifier as well as a host identifier. IPv4 represented using dotted decimal notation in which four 8-bit octets join by periods (i.e., dots). This connectionless mechanism used for communication and it uses user datagram packets (UDP) to transfer information from one network to another as described on Wikipedia (2016). Security of information present in the packets maintain through encryption methodologies. By default, communication through IPv4 occurs in public network, but for the private network, the network administrator needs to provide either IP Tunnel or Virtual Private Network (VPN) mechanism which makes possible to transfer IP packets through the public network.

1. **Internet Protocol Version 6:** To overcome a limited address space problem in IPv4 it is best to design a long-term solution and that is IPv6 which uses 128-bit addressing scheme. This 128-bit address contains 8-blocks each carries 16-bytes each which next converted into same 8-blocks in the form of 4-digit hexadecimal numbers and separated by ':' (colon). Internet protocols act as a building block for the smooth functioning of Internet. To access the aggressively growing services for a meet up the requirements desktop computers or mobile devices are widely connected together. The transition from IP version 4 to IP version 6 possesses with new challenges for network engineers (like the development of dual stack mechanism). Deering S. E. (1998, December) suggested that users are able to use both versions of IP at the same time through Dual Stack.

2. **6LoWPAN:** 6LoWPAN is an open standard defined in RFC 6282 and support IEEE 802.15.4 for low-power non-wired networks. It is abbreviated as IPv6 over *L*ow p*O*wer *W*ireless *P*ersonal *A*rea *N*etwork. This concept came into existence when each physical thing tries to connect to the Internet. Shelby Z. & Bormann C. (2011) for transferring the information associated with those physical things Internet Protocol plays a role of mediator, but it is complex to install IP stack mechanism over low power devices called as hosting nodes and this complexity resolved using the concept of 6LoWPAN. The IP-based low power nodes form a mesh network for providing accessibility to various services of IoT applications to the end user. 6LoWPAN works as adaptation layer that qualifies IPvy6 Packets carried efficiently into link layer frames. This technology quite advanced to the world and hence there is huge scope in designing and deployment of IoT application.

3. **Arduino:** Arduino is an open source electronic platform to develop applications with the hardware interface. The major requirements to develop an application with this microcontroller are Arduino programming language and Arduino IDE. This circuit is used by wide variety of users like students, professionals, artists etc. The design and development of Arduino are done at Ivera Interaction Design Institute. The motivation of this tool is to develop fast prototyping of student projects who don't have programming and electronics background as stated by Arduino AC (2016). It's easy to user feature makes it popular in the world.

4. **Raspberry Pi:** Raspberry is the microcontroller with Broadcom chip and that contains ARM central processing unit. There are 40 pins are present among which 27 are GPIO pins. It is like a mini computer which is having its own processing power. The raspberry circuits come into various versions currently raspberry pi 3 is present in the market. It needs separate monitor interface given by Odella, F. (2016). The USB port and LAN port is also present on the circuit. From small scale projects to the complex project can be developed by a large variety of users. Currently, a Raspbian operating system widely used in this circuit. According to McManus S. (2014), Raspberry can be used as an interface, gateway as well as middleware for IoT projects. It has inbuild python environment for development.

5. **Big Data:** The name itself describe it in general, Big refers to Large or Huge and jointly it describes the amount of data collect through online as well as offline media. The data grows rapidly because of more and more connectedness existing in between devices. The main source availability of data is smart phones, smart aerial monitoring devices, cameras, NFC chips, RFID tags, sensors enabled smart homes, industries, transportation and many more applications which are tremendously used in the daily routine by human beings. The data captures through these media is large rather highly composite and hence need to evolve data processing techniques freshly. Due to vast generation of data recently in use processing techniques are not suitable for dealing with big data. An actual use of IoT-based applications in day to day life generates a large quantity of data in the various forms as text, image, video, voice recordings etc. For handling this large size of data generated through sensor enable component requires high-performance computing environments (like massively parallel processor system, Cloud).

TECHNICAL ASPECTS

There is some selected description about IoT written and were published by renowned authors are as follows…

1. **Kevin Ashton (Co-founder of Auto-ID Center at MIT):** "The network of connecting objects in the physical world of an Internet".
    a. The 20th-century computer has brains but no sense, they always hold a human's little like a baby. On the other hand, computers of the 21st century can possibly sense surrounding scenarios with the help of smart things.
    b. Real-time application of such smart network of the sensor is GPS based location tracker.
2. **CISCO (Multinational Corporation Technology):** "Internet of Things (IoT) is increasing the connectedness of people and things on a scale that once was unimaginable" devised by CISCO.
    a. IoT connected every, in fact, all objects to people and these objects shares an information using the platform of Internet. Hence it becomes Internet of Everything (IoE).
3. **European Commission:** "Internet of Things represents the next step towards the digitization of society and economy where people are interconnected through communication networks and report about their status and the surrounding environment" explains by Atzori L. (2010).
    a. When everything linked then it is easy to communicate with anyone, it looks similar to the one-to-many or broadcast mechanism and defined action will perform on the basis of status.
    b. It really helps to a common man to get an educated and prosperous life.

Figure 7. IoT scenario by Cisco
Source: Enabling the Internet of everything Cisco IoT architecture on www.slideshare.com

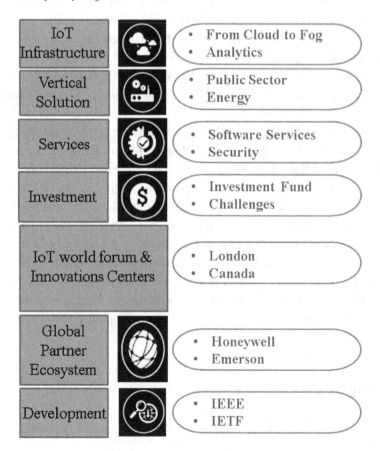

4. **Dr. Parikshit N. Mahalle (HOD Computer Department at SKNCOE):** Mahalle P. et. al. (2010, July) states "IoT is a service oriented network with resource constraints and is a mandatory subset of Future Internet (FI). IoT is a convergence of sensor nodes, RFID objects, and smart devices. IoT connects object around us to provide seamless communication and contextual services provided by them".

   a. Today world of communication heading towards S-things (such as Smart-home, Smart-cars (driverless), Smart-hospitals (telemedicine), Smart-agriculture).

   b. IoT is basically a communication network of every smart object which is accessible from anywhere.

5. **GISFI:** Chen Y. K. (2012, January) shows in his research that "IoT describes a world-wide network of intercommunicating devices. It integrates the ubiquitous communication, pervasive computing, and ambient intelligence."

   a. IoT devices are responsible for connecting people of same as well as remote locations by sharing the available resources via the platform of Internet.

   b. Everything is connected, will connect everybody.

6. **Proposed Definition of IoT**: "Internet of Thing (IoT) is defined as an automated intelligent computing system of the smart sensor which communicates with the world for the purpose of information exchange. IoT is comprised of 3C's connects, computes and communicates"

   a. IoT is a bigger picture of an embedded system that allows to connects various domains (like machine learning, information retrieval, data mining, business intelligence etc.) together.

   b. Learned or trained objects in day to day life acts to execute tasks to improve the constraints (as time, cost and performance) and provides a statistical report.

   c. Till now everyone says that "Every dog has his day" but this phrase changed and now onwards people start saying that "There is time for everything".

Today every human being tries to take at least the pure and good quality of water for drinking. Smart Water-Purifier systems resolve some needy and basic doubts, those are as follows…

How IoT maintains purity and quality of water? What are the steps to enhance or implement IoT mechanism in water-purification center? What are the advantages and disadvantages of such system? All these doubts need to clear for designing IoT-enabled Water-Purifier system shown in Figure 8.

The typical contents present in water are Chlorine, Fluorine compounds, Methane compounds, salt percentage, Nitrates, Pesticides etc. and any of these chemical presents above the threshold then it will be cautious for human health. Depending on the percentage of available contents in water purification method is adopted or either needs to be evolved shows Mason, C. (2015). There are some hazardous methods (such as Fluoridation) used for filtration and purification banned in European countries, but these methods are still in existence and hence it is really necessary to include IoT enable the system in daily life.

WORLD OF IOT

Technology affects the growth of each and every living species on the Earth in the way it relates to an entire life journey of the person. There is more and more physical entities use for running through daily situations. And it increases when that physical entity becomes smart and the term known as smart

Figure 8. Smart water purifier

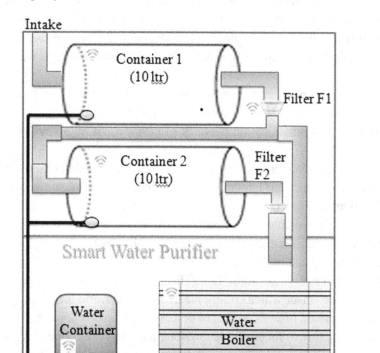

things. The communication networks of smart things (i.e., IoT) are now able to connect with each other for information exchange. Various market leaders predict estimation about connected devices by 2020 which clears scope and challenges of IoT shown in Figure 9.

1. **Internet of Things in North America:** The Northern region of America involves total 23 republic states in which 4.9% of world's population lives. Still, the only United States and Canada adopted the usage recent trends and technologies on large scale. Internet world stat Grünerbl, A., Bahle, G., Hanser, F., & Lukowicz, P. (2013) reports there are nearly 313 million users existed on the Internet and hence these two countries has played a major contribution in the development of upcoming technologies. Near about 70% of the market, sector captured by IT companies in North America. According to the global survey of World Bank, there are more than 700 million Internet users spread all over the world which maintains connectivity with each other. There is a high possibility of adaptation of IoT enable devices in developed regions of North America (such as USA and Canada) and take part in research and development of IoT-related innovations. The Internet is the best platform to access services and functionalities present on a cloud narrated by Panda et. al. in a cost-efficient way.

Figure 9. World population and connected devices

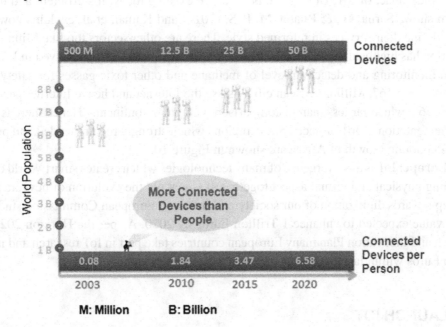

2. **Internet of Things in South America:** In comparison with developing countries Latin American regions effectively grown the usage of Internet and overcome the economic and political challenges. Future of Internet i.e., IoT runs Industries and Business growth in an exponential manner. Hence 8.5% population gets an opportunity to take part in the evolution of technology and reached an advanced level. Cisco's VNI statistics shows that IP traffic increased by 25% in Latin America and this is good news for researchers. Currently, 22% of the region executed under completely developed IoT projects and surprisingly developers plan to engage 60% of the region for development. There is around 74% population of Latin America uses the mobile application in their daily life (such as purchasing vegetables, public transport, e-health etc) and remaining will soon adapting this enormous change. Ripon, S. H., Kamal, S., Hossain, S., & Dey, N. (2016) shows it looks like a prediction will become true about worldwide connected devices through the Internet by 2020. From the survey of 578 apps in California, it is found that 79% of the developers work under the IoT domain utilizes their 25% of the time on analytics and 42% of the time on Big Data states by Jain, A., & Bhatnagar, V. (2016). IoT is the new mainstream for data generation and this will lead to a prime sector which booms into the market known as Data Science.

3. **IoT in Africa:** It is true that African countries do not much take part into evergreen World market of technology and a simple reason behind lag in the growth of the country is not updating lifestyle or trend in comparison with the rest of World. There is very less literacy rate in most of the African countries which bind them against Economical and Technological growth. Now, an African country needs to grow by 7% in each year to reduce their own poverty to 50%. In the upcoming year report of World Development strongly mention Africa arranges its countries into 4 cells to imply governance and development policies. A chief Investment officer at Business Connexion said IoT is present in daily routine which cannot be ignored. It brings out the transformation in business strategies, changes the functioning and makes capable to strong place into World market of technology.

To view the impact of IoT, Uber is the best source existing today. It's efficient and user-friendly platform shows Sarna, G., & Bhatia, M. P. S. (2016) and Kamal, et.al. explains how IoT allows Uber to define their services in reformed style. There are other sectors too like Mining and Power Generation has highly affected because of IoT. In Mining smart sensors evolved in IoT Ecosystem perform monitoring and detecting level of methane and other toxic gasses for safety. Out of the total population 167, Million African citizens use the Internet and hence Internet penetration rate becomes 16% which far less than in comparison with other continents. Hence there is huge scope for implementation of IoT projects. Some regions which strongly recommended and put the major part in Economic growth of Africa are shown in Figure 10.

4. **IoT in Europe:** IoT is a convergence of many technologies which creates smart World of Things by combining physical and virtual aspect together. It is just not the evolution of new era but actually next step towards digitization of our society and Industry. European Commission study states the market value expected to enhance 1 Trillion Euros by 2020. As per the Horizon 2020 European Research and Innovation Plan many European countries take part in IoT research and invested 192 Million Euros within last 2 years.

HOW TO LAUNCH IOT

Authors tried to answer every query regarding the concept of Internet of Things through following use cases. These use cases are familiar to everyone on this planet because knowingly or unknowingly they went through it at least once in a life, but the strategy used for these cases are might be different. Most of the people daily running through either one of them and hence author explains and suggested the idea of smartness behind it.

Education

Education is the process of sharing information (known and proved facts) from expert to no voice. Learning becomes easier after vast use of Internet in day to day working. Through the Internet, it is possible to sharing resources online with each other by simply connecting and putting a contribution in learning. In the 21st century when social networking sites (like facebook, twitter, vk etc) capturing everyone's attention, Experts/Professionals establishes an open page or group to connect with rest of the world and communicate with each other for a good reason. In the research of Baumgarten, M., Mulvenna, M.,

Figure 10. Economical growth sectors

Rooney, N., & Reid, J. (2013) it clears such social networking platform uses keyword dependent sentiment analysis. According to George Siemens, of late in the field of education blogging turns into a new medium for connecting and interacting with the world. Resources are present right here like EduBlog, youtube, TEDTalk, Qwiki etc. The best reason behind memorizing the things is visual learning and most of the humans do not forget the visuals than the theory and this is done through mind mapping. Also, the huge size of information stored freely on Internet space, no need for flash drives (e.g., Dropbox). Speedy changes in technology and upcoming ideas has modified education field in a different way. The Internet connects students together for education, but smarter things existed in surrounding made them hyper-connected and by learning to establish new standards and challenges current approach of teaching. This rapid growth in communication network increases learning style, access to the resources, quality in theories and transparency in Education given by Bureš, V., Tučník, P., Mikulecký, P., Mls, K., & Blecha, P. (2016). Usage of IoT in real life grabs students in the virtual classroom either in real-time or via video lectures. Leading companies in the world hired suck skilled IoT student to secure their own place in the competition. The impact of this is global there will be around 2 million or may be more than 2 million unfilled information and communication technology (ICT) related jobs in coming decade. To fulfill this rift learning institutions will need to create more and more technical graduates. It helps educators to involve IoT in the curriculum to prepare students for gainful employment and undeniably it encrust following key points:

1. Provide limitless learning.
2. Wealth of information available on Zero cost.
3. Quality education and Increase worldwide literacy rate.
4. Creates digital students.

Use Case 1: School Student

A school bus driver named John; check out all pickup points coming on his route towards the school. His daily work is to pick up students in his route and drops on time to all of them at school. Active RFID tags present with each student notifies the RFID reader to attach on Bus hence it is quite easy for John to pick a particular student in optimum time. It works because of proper authentication techniques applied in wireless communication between RFID chips which is stated by Dey, N., Mukhopadhyay, S., Das, A., & Chaudhuri, S. S. (2012) in his research. From here the journey starts but the actual journey begins when John gets ready and started driving the bus. Bus already equipped with smart sensors and wireless connectivity. As soon as student boarded the bus a temporary auto responder notification sends to his/her parent's registered mobile number. Same activity done from John's mobile auto responding notification sends to respective teacher guardian's mobile and it helps them to take daily attendance. This set of actions followed for all remaining students. There is the provision of occupancy sensors present inside the bus and it continuously monitors every student activity. In the case of medical emergency, this sensor modifies the on-going schedule and set status from normal to an emergency. Every on-boarded student of the bus can check real time tracking and estimated time of arrival to school.

Parents can also check real-time running status of the bus sitting from home through GPS tracking. When the distance is less than 100 meter and time for reaching to school is less than 10 sec, again an alert blinks on each student mobile to they will ready to get down from the bus. After reaching to their respected classroom a schedule of the current program displayed on the classroom panel and this is an efficient way to inform all students. During the class, teachers can execute data analytical program to check grasping percentage and status of the student and accordingly improvise their own teaching methods. At the end of school john finally, has to drop each student to their respective places from where they boarded in the morning. This way the world changes and soon IoT become everyone's 4th basic need for living (like food, clothes, and shelter). In Japan, if any public transport like bus/train will not arrive on its defined time then conductor of the bus/trains provides an apology receipt to every passenger of bus/train so they can submit to their workplace as a consideration of allowance, Yes this happens in real time. Hence technology and Internet of Things plays a vital role in Education.

Smart Food Restro

Equipment = {T_i, D_i, C_i, AC_i, S_i, CA_i, TV_i, M_i, W.Display, W. Area, Order Panel, Feedback Panel}

where,

T_i – Number of tables in the restro.

D_i – Number of sensor devices

D_1 – Customer check_in facility (Registration: Mobile number and E-mail address) and Table Allocation as per customer requirement.

D_2 – Count the number of customers visited and sends a notification to machine1 and details to the customer on registered mobile number and e-mail address.

D_3 – To check whether the required area is available or occupied.

D_4 – Sensors connected on each table allows customers to access inline Wi-Fi to place the order, also notifies similar to order panel and machine 2 for billing.

C_i (C_1 to C_{13}) – Camera for surveillance, it mainly associates with machine 2 to indulge the available resources properly.

AC_i (AC_1 to AC_2) – Air conditioner to On/Off according to the occupancy of the customer, it also manages to temperature level inside the cafeteria.

S_i (S_1 to S_{12}) – Slot sensor checks the occupancy and informs the details to the machine 2 and it contacted with order panel in the kitchen room for ordering a food.

CA_i (C_1 to C_3) – it is a cooking area used to notify the status of the work to machine 2 and helps the owner to take entry of food item ordered.

TV_i (TV_1 – TV_2) – Television On/Off provision and displays waiting time to customers.

M_i (M_1 and M_2) – Machine 1 used to make entry of customer, provide them each facility of the restro and finally generate a bill from order list. Similarly, machine 2 monitors each on-going activity and controls the services.

W. Display – Displays the current waiting status on LED screen.

W. Area – Shows status of washing area on machine 2 and helps a manager to control working manpower.

Order Panel – Shows ordered item name, respective table number and depending on the item ordered chef can update required time to make that dish.

Feedback Panel – This is an optional part of the restro customers could write their valuable comments and suggestion regarding quality and service.

Figure 11. Smart food restaurant

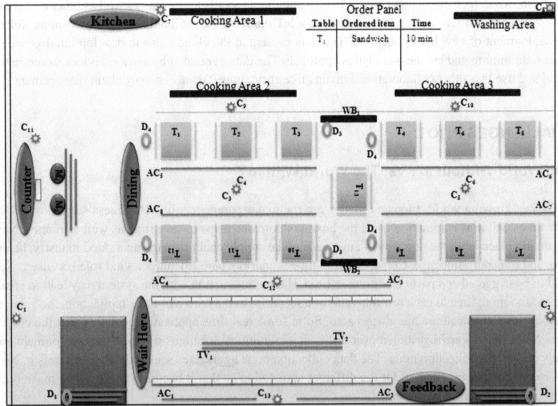

BIG DATA WITH IOT

What is big data? Is it really huge amount of data? How to define that huge amount? Big data comes with two subproblems first is storage and another one is processing. In IoT, there is little bit modification requires the definition of big data. Big data is the data which is followed 5V properties i.e. *Velocity, Volume, Variety, Variability, Veracity*. If data coming into the system at receiving end is greater than systems processing power, then in simple words it is referred as big data. If data is coming to the system is 2kbps and processing power of the system is 1kbps for this system 2kb data is actually known as big data. This description of big data changes from system to system. In near future, millions and trillions of devices are going to be connected to the Internet and these devices will generate a huge amount of data. Is it really challenging task to storage and processing of this data? Cloud could be the best option to store the data and Hadoop will be the best solution to the processing data given by Zappi, P., Lombriser, C., Benini, L., & Tröster, G. (2012). In IoT architecture at the physical layer sensor devices are present. The data collection node collects data from the sensor node. Data collection node preprocesses the data. This preprocessing of data helps to improve the quality of data which will helpful for efficient decision making and prediction making. This preprocesses data can be sent to the middleware where device authentication, as well as device management, is done. As far as implementation concerns data collection node and middleware considers as a single unit. Now the middleware has limited storage and processing capacity so it forwards data to the cloud. Kamal, S., Ripon, S. H., Dey, N., Ashour, A. S., & Santhi, V. (2016) shown in their study that cloud provides ubiquitous access to the data as well as other resources. Now various cloud service vendors provide new IoT platform that will help to development as well as the deployment of new IoT application. The data present at the cloud helps to develop intelligence by using data mining and business analytics approach. The data generated by sensor devices stored in the cloud and used for other collaborative domains like agriculture, finance, supply chain management etc.

CHALLENGES IN IOT

The World Without IoT vs. The World With IoT

In the fast-growing world, time and money are the major parameters in all business scenarios. IoT or sometimes call it as automation in all the business domains helps to save time as well as money. Now IoT taking place in all the domains of engineering like supply chain management, food industry, health care, and transportation also. Consider a real-time scenario where IoT plays a vital role because events need to be triggered at a particular point in time. Human interaction with the system may lead to errors and require more time to get a result in real time scenario. In the hard real-time application, the value of outcome after the deadline has always zero. So in some real time application, IoT can play the crucial role. When sensors are distributed over different geographical locations it senses the environment and sends to the data collection node. The data collection node aggregates sensor data and process it. Now this collected data can be used for the different application so that it becomes very easy to make decisions and to predict future actions.

Figure 12. IoT challenges

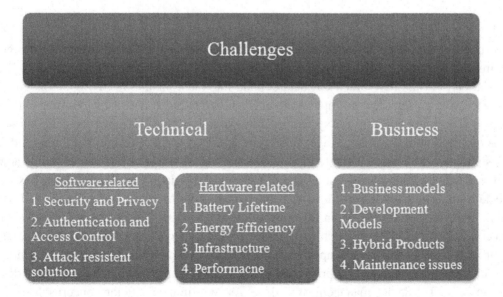

In health care domain previously it became very difficult to provide treatment to the patient who is present at the remote location. IoT brings lots of changes in a healthcare application shows in Dey, N., Dey, M., Mahata, S. K., Das, A., & Chaudhuri, S. S. (2015). The special drone has been designed to give treatment to the patient at the remote location. There are lots of applications present in the market. E-wall is one of the best health monitoring applications specially designed for independently living adult. This project is funded by EU and designed under the FP7 program. In this particular application, the sensors are placed over walls of the home and on the body of an adult person. These sensors continuously monitor the activity of the person. If any doubtful behavior found the notification is sent to the doctors and family members. There are many other projects are developing under EU framework program presented by Kamal, S et.al (2016, August).

Now the world is facing various problems related to natural resources. There should be proper management of such resources like water, electricity coal or petroleum etc. IoT will be helpful to manage and monitor usage of these resources. Actually, one of the motivations of IoT is to optimum utilization natural resources. Consider a simple application like smart home. If a person forgets to switch off home appliances and went out of the house. In such condition occupancy, sensor existed in the house detects that there is no one in the house and resources are unnecessarily using electricity. By using intelligence O'Shaughnessy, S., & Gray, G. (2012) shows it switches off all the home appliances and sends notification on mobile of the house owner.

Now transportation and logistics domain are also highly transformed by IoT. Recently the big companies introduce driverless car. In logistics previously there is no provision for tracking an object for shipment. Now we can track the exact location of the object and the same with the vehicle also. RFID and GPS help to find out location and position of the object. IoT brings betterment in human life.

IoT also brings huge transformation in agriculture domain. In countries like India still, most of the farmers are using the traditional method of farming to cultivating the crops. In traditional farming, there are lots of such barriers which brings down income sometimes its due wrong information or due to getting late information. The traditional method of farming using today is also one of the major issues for the failure of agriculture in developing countries. IoT has the potential to connect all the stakeholders of agriculture domain. IoT brings transformation in agriculture due to its right information at right time characteristic. The new information can easily share over the internet.

Consider a real life scenario in which a person wants to buy some things from the market and he went to the mall. The person does shopping in mall and collects products into the cart and at the end, he needs to pay the bill. For paying bill, he waits in the queue. Now this scenario can be changed with IoT. Consider if all the products are having RFID tag over it. When the user picks a product and put it into cart RFID reader reads the RFID tag. The RFID tags have all the information related to the product. At the end, the user gets notification of final estimation of the bill. He just swipes the card and pays the bill. In this process, the user can save his significance amount of time. And the owner has no need to take care of checking all products from the customer describe by Warwick, K., & Shah, H. (2014). These simple applications make most of the process easier for the user.

The well-known fact is "Change is the only permanent thing in this world" and IoT has that much potential to bring positive change in human life. Hopefully, IoT will bring positive changes in every individual's life in near future.

CONCLUSION

An entire universe consisting of the tremendous amount of physical entities attached with smart sensors connected digitally with the platform of Internet. In IoT sensors act as fetching media and Internet used to perform computation on the fetch data and shares with other available devices or peoples connected with the Internet. Also, it should be an intelligent system of many heterogeneous networks of smart things which design the new golden edge to the upcoming period. In future, it may happen smart things updated to Intelligent things and becomes an essential part of everyone's life. The devices which have computing, communication and sensing capability in them can take part into IoT. The author finally concludes with some key features are as follows:

- Information generated from IoT goes beyond decimal number system.
- IoT is the new and major source of Big Data.
- IoT is things-based functionalities activated through IT based services.
- There is need of light-weight algorithms and protocols to manage sensor generated data at the middleware.
- Also, there is requirement of privacy preservation algorithm for IoT
- For providing end-end communication, researchers need to put more focus on the generic framework.

The big data leads to the problem of processing and storage and these problems can be solved by the technologies like Hadoop, Spark etc. To store and process data, the cloud is one of the best options which can manage both problems as well as privacy and at the same time user's privacy should not be compromised.

REFERENCES

Arduino. (n.d.). Retrieved September 18, 2016, from https://www.arduino.cc/en/Guide/Introduction

Ashton, K. (2009, June22). That 'internet of things' thing. *RFiD Journal*, *22*(7), 97–114.

Atzori, L., Iera, A., & Morabito, G. (2010). The internet of things: A survey. *Computer Networks*, *54*(15), 2787–2805. doi:10.1016/j.comnet.2010.05.010

Baumgarten, M., Mulvenna, M., Rooney, N., & Reid, J. (2013). Keyword-Based Sentiment Mining using Twitter. *International Journal of Ambient Computing and Intelligence*, *5*(2), 56–69. doi:10.4018/jaci.2013040104

Bureš, V., Tučník, P., Mikulecký, P., Mls, K., & Blecha, P. (2016). Application of Ambient Intelligence in Educational Institutions: Visions and Architectures. *International Journal of Ambient Computing and Intelligence*, *7*(1), 94–120. doi:10.4018/IJACI.2016010105

Chen, Y. K. (2012, January). Challenges and opportunities of the internet of things. In *17th Asia and South Pacific Design Automation Conference* (pp. 383-388). IEEE. doi:10.1109/ASPDAC.2012.6164978

Deering, S. E. (1998, December). *Internet protocol, version 6 (IPv6) specification*. Academic Press.

Dey, N., Dey, G., Chakraborty, S., & Chaudhuri, S. S. (2014, September). Feature analysis of blind watermarked electromyogram signal in wireless telemonitoring. In *Concepts and Trends in Healthcare Information Systems* (pp. 205–229). Springer International Publishing. doi:10.1007/978-3-319-06844-2_13

Dey, N., Dey, M., Mahata, S. K., Das, A., & Chaudhuri, S. S. (2015). Tamper detection of an electro-cardiographic signal using watermarked bio–hash code in wireless cardiology. *International Journal of Signal and Imaging Systems Engineering*, 8(1-2), 46–58. doi:10.1504/IJSISE.2015.067069

Dey, N., Mukhopadhyay, S., Das, A., & Chaudhuri, S. S. (2012). Using DWT analysis of P, QRS and T components and cardiac output modified by blind watermarking technique within the electrocardiogram signal for authentication in the wireless telecardiology. *IJ Image, Graphics and Signal Processing*.

European Countries Banning the Use of Fluoride. (n.d.). Retrieved from http://www.ecomall.com/greenshopping/fluoride4

Fouad, K. M., Hassan, B. M., & Hassan, M. F. (2016, June). User Authentication based on Dynamic Keystroke Recognition. *International Journal of Ambient Computing and Intelligence*, 7(2), 1–32. doi:10.4018/IJACI.2016070101

Gantz, J., & Reinsel, D. (2012). The digital universe in 2020: Big data, bigger digital shadows, and biggest growth in the far east. *IDC iView: IDC Analyze the future, 2007*, 1-16.

Grünerbl, A., Bahle, G., Hanser, F., & Lukowicz, P. (2013). Uwb indoor location for monitoring dementia patients: The challenges and perception of a real-life deployment. *International Journal of Ambient Computing and Intelligence*, 5(4), 45–59. doi:10.4018/ijaci.2013100104

Internet of Things. (n.d.). Retrieved from http://www.cisco.com/c/en_in/solutions/internet-of-things/

Internet Protocol Version 4. (n.d.). Retrieved from https://en.wikipedia.org/wiki/IPv4

Jain, A., & Bhatnagar, V. (2016). Olympics Big Data Prognostications. *International Journal of Rough Sets and Data Analysis*, 3(4), 32–45. doi:10.4018/IJRSDA.2016100103

Jain, A., & Bhatnagar, V. (2016). Movie Analytics for Effective Recommendation System using Pig with Hadoop. *International Journal of Rough Sets and Data Analysis*, 3(2), 82–100. doi:10.4018/IJRSDA.2016040106

Kamal, S., Dey, N., Nimmy, S. F., Ripon, S. H., Ali, N. Y., Ashour, A. S., & Shi, F. Evolutionary framework for coding area selection from cancer data. *Neural Computing and Applications*, 1-23.

Kamal, S., Ripon, S. H., Dey, N., Ashour, A. S., & Santhi, V. (2016). A MapReduce approach to diminish imbalance parameters for the big deoxyribonucleic acid dataset. *Computer Methods and Programs in Biomedicine*, 131, 191–206. doi:10.1016/j.cmpb.2016.04.005 PMID:27265059

Mahalle, P., Babar, S., Prasad, N. R., & Prasad, R. (2010, July). Identity management framework towards internet of things (IoT): Roadmap and key challenges. In *International Conference on Network Security and Applications* (pp. 430-439). Springer Berlin Heidelberg. doi:10.1007/978-3-642-14478-3_43

Mason, C. (2015). Engineering Kindness: Building a Machine with Compassionate Intelligence. *International Journal of Synthetic Emotions*, 6(1), 1–23. doi:10.4018/IJSE.2015010101

McManus, S. (2014). *Raspberry Pi for dummies*. John Wiley & Sons.

Mohanpurkar, A. A., & Joshi, M. S. (2016). A Traitor Identification Technique for Numeric Relational Databases with Distortion Minimization and Collusion Avoidance. *International Journal of Ambient Computing and Intelligence, 7*(2), 114–137. doi:10.4018/IJACI.2016070106

Nakajima, T., Ishikawa, H., Tokunaga, E., & Stajano, F. (2002, August). Technology challenges for building Internet-scale ubiquitous computing. In *Object-Oriented Real-Time Dependable Systems, 2002 (WORDS 2002)*. Proceedings of the Seventh International Workshop on (pp. 171-179). IEEE.

Nusser, R., & Pelz, R. M. (2000, September28). Bluetooth-based wireless connectivity in an automotive environment. In *Vehicular Technology Conference, 2000. IEEE-VTS Fall VTC 2000. 52nd* (Vol. 4, pp. 1935-1942). IEEE. doi:10.1109/VETECF.2000.886152

O'Shaughnessy, S., & Gray, G. (2012). Development and evaluation of a dataset generator tool for generating synthetic log files containing computer attack signatures. *Pervasive and Ubiquitous Technology Innovations for Ambient Intelligence Environments*, 116.

Odella, F. (2016). Technology Studies and the Sociological Debate on Monitoring of Social Interactions. *International Journal of Ambient Computing and Intelligence, 7*(1), 1–26. doi:10.4018/IJACI.2016010101

Ozdenizci, B., Aydin, M. N., Coskun, V., & Ok, K. (2010, June). *NFC research framework: a literature review and future research directions*. The 14th International Business Information Management Association (IBIMA) Conference, Istanbul, Turkey.

Rhee, S. (2016, April). Catalyzing the Internet of Things and smart cities: Global City Teams Challenge. In *Science of Smart City Operations and Platforms Engineering (SCOPE) in partnership with Global City Teams Challenge (GCTC) (SCOPE-GCTC), 2016 1st International Workshop on* (pp. 1-4). IEEE.

Ripon, S. H., Kamal, S., Hossain, S., & Dey, N. (2016). Theoretical Analysis of Different Classifiers under Reduction Rough Data Set: A Brief Proposal. *International Journal of Rough Sets and Data Analysis, 3*(3), 1–20. doi:10.4018/IJRSDA.2016070101

Sarna, G., & Bhatia, M. P. S. (2016). An Approach to Distinguish Between the Severity of Bullying in Messages in Social Media. *Violence and Society: Breakthroughs in Research and Practice: Breakthroughs in Research and Practice*, 160.

Shelby, Z., & Bormann, C. (2011). *6LoWPAN: The wireless embedded Internet* (Vol. 43). John Wiley & Sons.

Vallverdú, J., Shah, H., & Casacuberta, D. (2010). Chatterbox challenges as a test-bed for synthetic emotions. *Creating Synthetic Emotions through Technological and Robotic Advancements*, 118-144.

Warwick, K., & Shah, H. (2014). Outwitted by the hidden: Unsure emotions. *International Journal of Synthetic Emotions, 5*(1), 46–59. doi:10.4018/ijse.2014010106

Weinstein, R. (2005, August). RFID: A technical overview and its application to the enterprise. *IT Professional, 7*(3), 27–33. doi:10.1109/MITP.2005.69

Weiser, M. (1991, September). The computer for the 21st century. *Scientific American, 265*(3), 94–104. doi:10.1038/scientificamerican0991-94 PMID:1675486

Yang, L., Chen, Y., Zuo, W., Nguyen, T., Gurumani, S., Rupnow, K., & Chen, D. (2015, November). System-level design solutions: Enabling the IoT explosion. In *ASIC (ASICON), 2015 IEEE 11th International Conference on* (pp. 1-4). IEEE.

Zappi, P., Lombriser, C., Benini, L., & Tröster, G. (2012). Collecting datasets from ambient intelligence environments. *Innovative Applications of Ambient Intelligence: Advances in Smart Systems: Advances in Smart Systems, 113.*

Section 7
Big Data Analytics

Chapter 11
Development of Data Analytics in Shipping

Lokukaluge P. Perera
Norwegian Marine Technology Research Institute (MARINTEK), Norway

Brage Mo
Norwegian Marine Technology Research Institute (MARINTEK), Norway

ABSTRACT

Modern vessels are monitored by Onboard Internet of Things (IoT), sensors and data acquisition (DAQ), to observe ship performance and navigation conditions. Such IoT may create various shipping industrial challenges under large-scale data handling situations. These large-scale data handling issues are often categorized as "Big Data" challenges and this chapter discusses various solutions to overcome such challenges. That consists of a data-handling framework with various data analytics under onboard IoT. The basis for such data analytics is under data driven models presented and developed with engine-propeller combinator diagrams of vessels. The respective results on data analytics of data classification, sensor faults detection, data compression and expansion, integrity verification and regression, and visualization and decision support, are presented along the proposed data handling framework of a selected vessel. Finally, the results are useful for energy efficiency and system reliability applications of shipping discussed.

INTRODUCTION

The International Maritime Organization (IMO) and other respective authorities (IMO, 2007) have proposed "e-navigation", a global vision for an international collaborative communication network, to improve the safety and efficiency in the shipping industry (IMO, 2014). The e-navigation framework can facilitate towards standardized ship navigation platforms (i.e. integrated bridge systems (IBSs) to overcome the present emission control based energy efficiency industrial challenges (Rodesth 2011). IMO and other respective maritime authorities have introduced various emission control (i.e. CO_2, SOx, and NOx) regulations to develop more energy efficient ships. It is reasonable to believe that tighter emission control measures will introduce for vessels navigating in designated emission control areas (ECAs)

DOI: 10.4018/978-1-5225-2486-1.ch011

(IMO, 2009) in the future. Hence, there is a need to develop appropriate ship navigation strategies to accommodate not only weather routing but also emission control and energy efficiency type applications (Perera and Guedes Soares, 2017). Furthermore, such navigation strategies can complement with the proposed e-Navigation framework by introducing intelligent decision support capabilities under IBSs. However, such intelligent decision support capabilities should be based on adequate ship performance and navigation data, i.e. "Big data." It is an expectation that the ICT infrastructure and "Big Data" will play an increasingly important role towards digitalization of the shipping industry in the coming decade. Therefore, there is a development need for appropriate data handling frameworks to use onboard vessels and support the ICT infrastructure and "Big Data" applications.

Modern IBSs that should facilitate towards such data-handling framework often consist two separate networks for collecting ship performance and navigation data: navigation and automation systems. Such divisions in IBSs also supports various classification societies' requirements with the navigation safety and reliability considerations. Modern IBSs are equipped with various appropriate sensors and data acquisition (DAQ) systems to collect ship performance and navigation information and that creates onboard Internet of Things (IoT) (Rodseth (2016) and Bhatt and Bhatt (2017)). Ship navigation systems may consist of the following systems: electronic chart display and information system (ECDIS), autopilot system conning, radar, and other respective sensors. Ship automation systems may consist of the following systems: power management architecture for engine and propulsion controls and other systems that relate to various engine room operations. An adequate overview of ship performance and navigation conditions is possible to observe under such IoT and the collected information (i.e. vessel performance and navigation data) and use it towards intelligent decision support capabilities. Such navigation decisions under an appropriate data-handling framework can lead to more energy efficient ships. It is a belief that an appropriate data-handling framework can also play an important role in such IoT, where effective navigation strategies depend accurate ship performance and navigation information.

This study proposes such data-handling framework to organize ship performance and navigation information under IoT (Atzoria et al., 2010). This framework collects large-scale data sets, so called "Big Data", that should be analyzed to evaluate ship performance under various navigation conditions in onboard or shore based data centers. One should note that conventional data analysis tools and techniques might fail to capture actual ship performance and navigation conditions under such large-scale data sets. Therefore, this framework introduces several data handling layers to overcome such challenges in handling large scale-data sets in vessels. Such layers are categorized as "data analytics", where the main contribution of this chapter is to observe ship performance and navigation conditions from the receptive data analytics. Ship performance and navigation information under such data analytics can facilitate to identify optimal vessel operational and navigation conditions, where such analytics and the respective results can also be a part of the ship energy efficiency management plan (SEEMP) (IMO, 2009 & 2012). Furthermore, the proposed data-handling framework under IoT is also an important step towards the proposed digitalization of the shipping industry.

DATA HANDLING FRAMEWORK

This section describes various data analytics to support the proposed data-handling framework under IoT. That is presented in Figure 1 and facilitated by both top down and bottom up approaches. The top

Figure 1. Data handling framework

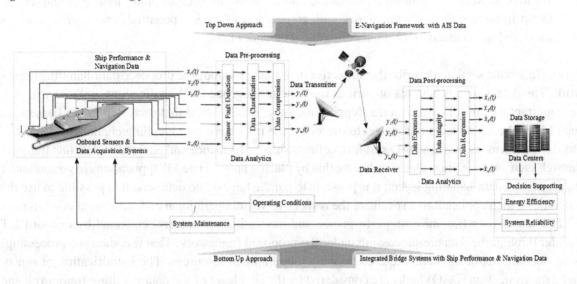

down and bottom up approaches are facilitated by e-navigation and onboard IoT, respectively under the same framework. Furthermore, that orientates towards the proposed industrial digitalization path of the shipping industry. The main objective in this chapter consists of developing various data analytics (i.e. data handling layers) to overcome the respective big data challenges (i.e. sensor faults, large data sets, data integrity and visualization issues). Various machine intelligence (MI) applications are under these data handling layers introduced in both pre and post-processing steps. The life cycle of such data analytics along the data-handling framework can be categorized as:

- **Development Data Driven Models:** Derivation of the next generation data driven models for ship performance and navigation monitoring.
- **Ship On-Board Data Collection With IoT:** Investigation of various available sensors and DAQ systems (i.e. IoT) for ship performance and navigation monitoring and implementation of appropriate modifications to facilitate data driven models.
- **Sensor and DAQ Fault Detection:** Data analytics to identify various sensor and DAQ fault situations and detect responsible sensors and/or DAQ units.
- **Data Compression and Expansion:** Data analytics to compress and expand big data sets.
- **Data Regression and Integrity Verification:** Data analytics to implement data regression and integrity verification for big data sets.
- **Data Visualization and Decision Support:** Data analytics to visualize big data sets for decision support.
- **System Integration and Validation:** Implementation of the proposed data analytics on-board vessel and offline for system level evaluation and verification.
- **Knowledge Creation:** Creation of knowledge on data analytics to use on-board IoT and observe optimal ship performance and navigation conditions.
- **Energy Efficiency and System Reliability:** Reduction of the environmental impact by identifying energy efficient operational and navigation conditions for vessels.

- • **Industrial Recommendation:** Innovation and demonstration of shipping industrial implementation in the proposed data analytics with respect to fuel saving potentials and develop various industrial recommendations on handling big data under IoT.

The following sections describe the respective data analytics along the proposed data-handling framework. The data analytics consists of various machine intelligence (MI) applications and that will play an important role in IoT of the future shipping industry. It is believed that each step of the framework such MI application can be introduced to overcome the respective data handling challenges. IoT, various onboard sensors through DAQ systems, collects ship performance and navigation data that transfers through such data analytics. One should note that by placing appropriate MI applications in groups under the respective data-handling layers; it is possible to handle large-scale data sets. It is possible to use the outcome of such applications to evaluate the respective vessel operational and navigation conditions.

The sensor data (i.e. the ship performance and navigation parameters) collected by onboard IoT transfer through the data pre-processing under the proposed framework. That (i.e. data pre-processing) is an onboard application and requires limited computational resources. The identification of sensor and data acquisition (DAQ) faults are considered by the first layer of the data-handling framework and such erroneous data regions should be isolated from the respective data sets to improve the information quality. The next steps of the data-handling framework consist of the data classification and compression layers implemented to reduce the quantity (i.e. the size) of the data set. The proposed layers are vital to improve the integrity of the respective ship performance and navigation data. Due to the data compression layer, the pre-processed data are communicated in much smaller improved data sets through the transmitters. Such step can reduce the respective transfer costs due to smaller data sets. However, a further reduction in such data sets is possible by considering additional data handling technologies (i.e. various data compression methods).

Shore based data centers receive the respective data sets through data receivers. The same data sets transfer through the data post-processing under the proposed framework. That consists of data expansion, integrity verification and regression layers to improve and extract the ship performance and navigation information from the same data sets. Such data sets accommodate in data storage facilities as required. The outcome of the pre-post processed data visualize appropriately under various decision supporting features in energy efficiency and system reliability applications of shipping. Energy efficiency applications in vessels identify optimal vessel operating and navigation conditions to reduce the respective fuel consumption. Reliability applications identify system health conditions in vessels to improve the availability of onboard systems and develop optimal maintenance actions to reduce the operating costs of vessels.

DATA ANALYTICS

Introduction

The respective data analytics under the pre and post processing steps are described in this section, introducing various MI techniques. In general, hidden data patterns, clusters, correlations and other useful information are possible to extract from the receptive data sets by the proposed data analytics (Perera & Mo, 2017). It is noted that the conventional data analysis methods (i.e. various empirical ship performance and navigation models) (Strasser et al., 2015) often fail to handle big data sets due to various reasons: system-model uncertainties, sensor noise and fault conditions and complex parameter interactions. Such models may have various difficulties in adapting and predicting actual ship performance and navigation behavior under the respective data sets. Therefore, the outcome of such models may challenge the validity of ship performance and navigation behavior. This study purposes to investigation of data driven models facilitated with various data analytics to overcome such difficulties.

The implementation of the proposed data analytics is on a data set (i.e. ship performance and navigation data) of a selected vessel, where the period between two consecutive data points is 15 (min). The vessel consists of following particulars (Perera et al., 2015): ship length: 225 (m), beam: 32.29 (m), gross tonnage: 38.889 (tons), deadweight at max draft: 72.562 (tons), main engine (ME): 2-stroke, maximum continuous rating (MCR) of 7564 (kW) at the shaft rotational speed of 105 (rpm), and propeller: fixed pitch propeller, diameter 6.20 (m) with 4 blades. The respective data set consists of following parameters: STW (speed through water) (Knots), SOG (speed over ground) (Knots), ME (main engine) power (kW), shaft speed (rpm), ME fuel consumption (cons.) (Tons/day), auxiliary (aux.) fuel consumption (cons.) (Tons/day), average (avg.) draft (m), trim (m), and relative (rel.) wind speed (m/s) and direction (deg.). The following section presents the development steps of the respective data analytics along with the proposed data-handling framework.

Data-Driven Models and Data Classification

Other transportation systems present various data driven models to overcome similar data handling challenges (Zhang et al., 2011; Kamal et al., 2016). However, less research studies focus on such models and analytics under the shipping industry. Modern Vessels collect large quantities of ship performance and navigation data these days, therefore the requirements of finding such data driven models and analytics are on the rise. Such requirements are often addressed as "Big Data" solutions (Rodseth et al., 2016), where appropriate data analytics should be developed. Such solutions, often guided by statistical models, capture realistic ship performance and navigation behavior, where MI applications further enhance the same. The combination of statistical models and MI applications creates the basis for data driven models. Such models are developed in a high dimensional data space and often called topological models, in which have the capability of handling large-scale data sets (Perera & Mo, 2016a). Hence, initial statistical data analyses (i.e. histograms) are considered to understand the respective parameter distributions, then various MI applications are used to identify the combined statistical distributions of the same parameters in a high dimensional space (Perera & Mo, 2016b).

Figure 1 presents streaming of ship performance and navigation data as real-time data sets under the proposed framework. The data-handling framework selects a data set at each time of an instant to develop the respective data driven models. This method, categorizing it is an unsupervised learning approach, where the model learns itself from the data sets without external prototypes (Hagan et al., 2014). However, there are some internal supervisions, the domain knowledge, should be given by the initial statistical distributions. This domain knowledge can consist of ship dynamics, hydrodynamics, ship steering, propulsion and engine operating conditions (i.e. the engine-propeller combinator diagrams) and other navigation conditions (i.e. trim and average draft conditions) (Perera & Mo, 2016c). The model learning can be an automated process, where the initial supervision is given by the statistical distributions (i.e. histograms). Furthermore, the MI applications take that information to derive data driven model as several data clusters in a high dimensional space. The data clustering process should initiate on the engine-propeller combinator diagram of the vessel, classifying the respective data sets into several sub-sets under engine operating modes. Therefore, this method is an engine centered data classification approach. One should note that the proposed data driven models always relate to vessel performance and navigation conditions due to the same reasons. Furthermore, it is possible to cluster other parameters in ship performance and navigation data sets along the same classification borders of the engine propeller combinator diagram as required. This data classification approach can visualize ship performance and navigation data, appropriately, because the method derives small data sets that relates to the frequent engine operating regions. Therefore, it is possible to observe ship performance and navigation behavior with respect to such engine operating regions (i.e. engine modes).

A MI algorithm of Gaussian mixture models (GMMs) with an expectation maximization (EM) algorithm are implemented for the data clustering process, where the respective operating regions of the engine is identified by ship performance and navigation data. One should note that such analytics uses the EM algorithm to estimate the respective parameters of the GMMs (Moon, 1996). Multivariate Gaussian distributions with the respective mean and covariance values represent such GMMs. This data classification, under GMMs with the EM algorithm consist, of two iterative levels (Ng, 2015): expectation (E-step) and maximization (M-step). The E-step evaluates the probability that each data point belongs to the respective data cluster (i.e. GMM). Each data point accommodates in the respective data cluster (i.e. GMM) with respect to the highest probability by updating its mean and covariance values in the M-step. The E-step initiates by considering a multivariate GMM and denoted as:

$$p_j(x;\mu_j,\Sigma_j) = \frac{1}{(2\pi)^{\frac{n}{2}}|\Sigma_j|^{\frac{1}{2}}} e^{-\frac{1}{2}(x-\mu_j)^T \Sigma_j^{-1}(x-\mu_j)} \tag{1}$$

where x is the input data set and $p_j(x;\mu_j,\Sigma_j)$ is the PDF of the j-th GMM with, μ_j and Σ_j, the mean and covariance values of the of the j-th data cluster, respectively. One should note that the j-th GMM is a n-dimensional data cluster. The probability of the i-th data point belongs to the j-th cluster can be written as:

$$w_j^{(i)} = p\left(z^{(i)} = j \mid x^{(i)};\varphi,\mu,\Sigma\right) \tag{2}$$

One should note that (2) calculates the "soft guess value" for the parameter, $z^{(i)}$. Considering the Bayes rule and (1), the posterior probability of the parameter, $z^{(i)}$, given the parameter, $x^{(i)}$, can be written as:

$$p\left(z^{(i)} = j \mid x^{(i)};\varphi,\mu,\Sigma\right) = \frac{p\left(x^{(i)} \mid z^{(i)} = j;\mu,\Sigma\right)p\left(z^{(i)} = j;\varphi\right)}{\sum_{l=1}^{k} p\left(x^{(i)} \mid z^{(i)} = l;\mu,\Sigma\right)p\left(z^{(i)} = l;\varphi\right)} \tag{3}$$

where $p\left(z^{(i)} = j; \varphi\right)$ is the prior probability of the j-th data cluster and k is the number of data clusters. One should note that the equal prior probability of each data cluster is assumed, initially and (3) represents a GMM with μ_j and Σ_j are the mean and covariance values, respectively. Hence, the M-step written as:

$$\varphi_j = \frac{1}{n} \sum_{i=1}^{n} w_j^{(i)}$$
$$\mu_j = \sum_{i=1}^{n} w_j^{(i)} x^{(i)'} \Bigg/ \sum_{i=1}^{n} w_j^{(i)} \tag{4}$$
$$\Sigma_j = \sum_{i=1}^{n} w_j^{(i)} \left(x^{(i)} - \mu_j\right)\left(x^{(i)} - \mu_j\right)^T \Bigg/ \sum_{i=1}^{n} w_j^{(i)}$$

This step updates the respective GMM by calculating the new mean and covariance values with respect to each data point. This iterative process should either stop at the end of the training data set or approximately stable prior and posterior mean and covariance values. The respective GMMs of ship performance and navigation data set is implemented the next step. The analytics identifies three specific operating modes (i.e. three GMMs) of the marine engine in this data set. The results (i.e. the respective data clusters) are in Figure 2 presented as an engine power (kW-log scale) and shaft speed (rpm) diagram (i.e. the engine propeller combinator diagram). One should note that the respective data clusters are by Model 1, 2 and 3 denoted. The data clusters relate to three operating modes of the marine engine (i.e. vessel operating points) as mentioned before. It is an expectation that other parameters in ship performance and navigation data should also relate to the same engine operating modes.

As the next step of such data driven models, analytics lookups the hidden structure of each data cluster (i.e. each GMM). A MI algorithm of principal component analysis (PCA) identifies the respective data structures (Jackson, 1980) of each GMM. PCA categorizes as a non-parametric method to extract relevant information from various high dimensional data sets. A linear combination of original ship performance and navigation parameters in the data set derives the new basis for the respective data set. That basis is categorized as the principal components (PCs) for the şame data set. However, such basis transformations may consist for various linear functions. The respective data set with ship performance and navigation parameters can be denoted as $x_1(t), x_2(t), \ldots, x_m(t)$. The sample mean, $\bar{x}$, and variance, S_x, of each ship performance and navigation parameter can be written as:

$$\bar{x} = \frac{1}{n} \sum_{i=1}^{n} x_i$$

$$S_x = \frac{1}{n} \sum_{i=1}^{n} \left(x_i - \bar{x}\right)\left(x_i - \bar{x}\right)^T \tag{5}$$

This data cluster (i.e. GMM) is into a new basis transformed by considering the following steps under PCA and written as:

Figure 2. Marine engine operating region classification

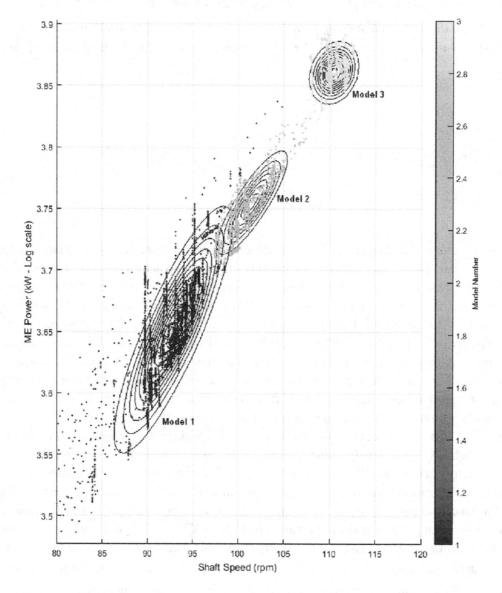

$$\overline{y} = \frac{1}{n} \sum_{i=1}^{n} y_i = u^T \overline{x}$$

$$S_y = \frac{1}{n} \sum_{i=1}^{n} \left(y_i - \overline{y}\right)\left(y_i - \overline{y}\right)^T = u^T S_x u \tag{6}$$

where $\overline{y}$ is the mean and S_y is the respective variance of the transformed basis and u is a unit variance vector that uses to project the old basis into the new basis of the ship performance and navigation data set. Hence, that also satisfies:

$$u^T u = I \tag{7}$$

PCA maximizes the value of each variance direction (i.e. PC direction) of the new basis. Hence, the trace of S_y should be maximal and denoted as:

$$\text{Max.} \quad trace\left(S_y\right) = \text{Max.} \quad trace\left(u^T S_x u\right) \tag{8}$$

The Lagrange multiplier that satisfies (8):

$$L = trace\left(u^T S_x u\right) = \sum_{i=1}^{n}\left[u_i^T S_x u_i + \lambda\left(1 - u_i^T u_i\right)\right] \tag{9}$$

The derivatives of the Lagrange multiplier in (9):

$$S_x u_i = \lambda_i u_i$$

$$u_i^T u_i = 1 \tag{10}$$

where λ_i is the eigen values and u_i is the respective eigenvectors of S_x of the ship performance and navigation data set. Hence, such eigenvalues and eigenvectors represent the respective structure of each GMM. This step completes the derivation of the respective data drive models under ship performance and navigation information. However, the main objective of the proposed mathematical derivation is to identify the hidden structure of the respective data cluster (i.e. a GMM) that is presented by the calculated eigenvectors. The third data cluster (i.e. model 3) presented in Figure 2 is considered for PCA. The calculated PCs are in Figure 3 and the i-th PC is denoted as:

$$Z_i = \begin{bmatrix} z_{i,1} & z_{i,2} & z_{i,3} & z_{i,4} & z_{i,5} & z_{i,6} & z_{i,7} & z_{i,8} & z_{i,9} & z_{i,10} \end{bmatrix} \tag{11}$$

where $z_{i,1}, z_{i,2}, z_{i,3}, ..z_{i,10}$ represent the respective eigenvector components of the i-th PC (i.e. eigenvector). One should note that the top and bottom PCs (i.e. eigenvectors) are Z_1 and Z_{10}, respectively. Hence, the respective vector components of each PC are further in the next step investigated by an appropriate data visualization method and the results are presented in Figure 3. One should note that this figure represents a 10 dimensional vector space, where the respective PCs (i.e. eigenvectors) are in a polar coordinate system demonstrated. Each PC is by a dotted circle presented, where the top and bottom PCs have the largest and smallest radiuses. Each axis that intersects these circles represents a parameter from the ship performance and navigation data set. The respective vector components of each PC are by colored circles presented and the same circle radius represents the significance of that vector component with respect to other components within the same PC. This figure also represents an overview of the relative correlations among the respective ship performance and navigation parameters. One should note that high positive (HP) correlations represented by yellow color large circles and high negative (HN) correlations represented by blue color large circles in the same figure (see the color bar).

The respective PCs with their vector components are in this section further discussed (see Figure 3). The 1st PC represents: when avg. draft (high) increases (HP), STW (medium) decreases, shaft speed (medium) decreases, SOG (high) decreases, and trim (medium) decreases. That means ship resistance has increased due to the draft increments, where STW and SOG of the vessel are also decreased. The same conditions decrease shaft speeds due to high engine loads. Furthermore, the compensation for draft increments performed by trim adjustments of the vessel. In general, when vessel avg. draft increases, then trim increases, STW decreases, and SOG decreases. The 2nd PC represents: when engine power and shaft speed (medium) increases, ME fuel consumption (high) increases, and aux. fuel consumption

Figure 3. PCs for model 3

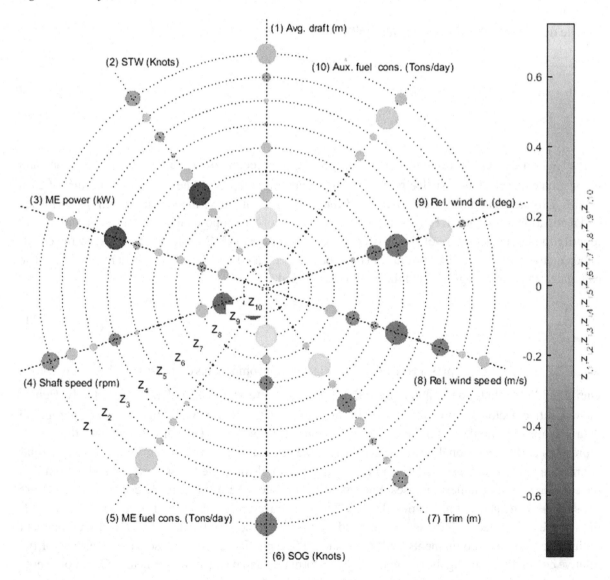

(high) increases. That means a moderate increment in engine shaft speed increases engine power levels, moderately and fuel consumption in both main and auxiliary engines, significantly. These results shows that shaft speed increments beyond the mean operating point in this engine operating region may not increase engine power, considerably but that may increase the respective fuel consumption, significantly. In general, when engine power and shaft speed increases, engine fuel consumption increases, and aux. fuel consumption increases.

The 3rd PC represents: when rel. wind speed (medium) decreases, then rel. wind angle (high) increases. That means when the vessel increases its speed, then rel. wind speed increases and rel. wind angle decreases (i.e. the vessel encounters high head wind conditions with the speed increments). The 4th PC represents: when ME power (high) increases, then shaft speed (medium) increases. That means the shaft speed increments increase engine power. The 5th PC represents: when vessel trim (medium) increases, then relative wind speed (high) and direction (high) increase. That means various trim values are used under calm water conditions, where relative wind speed is higher and angle is higher. One should note that this represents a contradictory relationship with respect to the 3rd PC. Such contradictory relationships show that this data cluster has not been distributed, properly and that may be a combination of additional data clusters. Hence, the vessel trim draft conditions that relates to the same data cluster should be further studied. The 6th PC represents: when STW (high) decreases, then relative wind angle (medium) decreases. That means a positive correlation between STW and relative wind direction of the vessel.

The 7th PC represents: when avg. draft (medium) increases, then SOG (medium) decreases, trim (high) increases, and rel. wind speed (medium) decreases. That means ship resistance increases due to the draft increments, therefore SOG also decreases. The same conditions reduce rel. wind speed, as discussed previously. Furthermore, the compensation for draft increments performed by the trim variations under slow maneuvering conditions of the vessel. The 8th PC represents: when avg. draft (high) increases, then shaft speed (medium) increases. That means ship resistance increases due to the draft increments, therefore shaft speed increases to compensate the speed losses in the vessel. The 9th PC represents: when shaft speed (high) decreases, then SOG (high) increases. The 10th PC represents: when ME fuel consumption (high) decreases, then aux. fuel consumption (high) increases. The bottom PCs, the 9th and 10th PCs, may not represent any useful information about the respective parameter relationships as mentioned before. Therefore, there is no expectation of a proper interpretation for the bottom PCs. Furthermore, that can accumulate erroneous conditions of ship performance and navigation data, therefore such relationships between parameters should be ignored.

The low positive and negative correlations among the respective parameters are from the above discussion ignored. Those effects (i.e. low positive and negative correlations) should incorporate in the respective parameter relationships to see an overall picture of ship performance and navigation data. However, that can complicate the outcome of the respective PCs in some situations. Furthermore, it is important to remove erroneous data regions that may influence the results in some situations. Therefore, the respective tools to identify and remove such data erroneous situations are developed in the next section and that improve the accuracy of the respective PCs. Understanding the high-dimensional structure of ship performance and navigation data can facilitate to find the respective solutions to such erroneous data regions. It is believed that the same data driven models can identify the erroneous data conditions (i.e. sensor and DAQ faults) within the ship performance and navigation data set. Furthermore, the same structure can be used to reduce the dimensions and improve the information visibility of the same ship performance and navigation data set. The same feature improves the data-handling framework by introducing much smaller data sets. Furthermore, the external data sources (i.e. AIS and weather data) can further improve the data-handling framework under data integrity verification and regression layers.

Sensor and DAQ Fault Detection

This layer consists of detecting sensor and DAQ faults and isolating such erroneous regions from ship performance and navigation data. The initial sensor and DAQ faults observed by checking each parameter behavior with respect to its mean and variance values. Each parameter in ship performance and navigation data sets may have its variation region, if the parameter is going beyond that range such situations are sensor and DAQ faults. Complex sensor and DAQ faults are identified by checking the respective covariance values among the ship performance and navigation parameters. However, using advanced relationships among ship performance and navigation parameters identify such faults. Such covariance values, i.e. how much two random variables change together, make the foundation for advanced data driven models in a high dimensional space and represent complex interactions among ship performance and navigation parameters. Hence, the data driven models can extensively identify complex sensor and DAQ fault situations (Perera, 2016a), where the data structure (i.e. linear relationships among the parameters (PCs) of ship performance and navigation data) of such models are to identify sensor and DAQ fault situations. One should note that that the respective outliers of each data cluster in a high dimensional space are observed to capture such erroneous data regions. Any data point that positions beyond such outliers is in the category of sensor and DAQ faults and such outliers are often observed under the bottom PCs. This approach consists of projecting the data set into the bottom PCs and observing such outliers (i.e. such sensor and DAQ faults) from the same (Perera, 2016b).

Figure 4 presents the results of the proposed approach in, where the respective parameters (i.e. 10 parameters) presented in the top 10 plots and the detected faults situations (i.e. fault alarm) are presented in the bottom plot. One should note that the presentation of these plots is with respect to the number (No.) of data points (i.e. sample number). The detection of two sensor faults situations in this data set is framed by two windows. In the first sensor fault situation, several parameters (ME power, ME fuel consumption, STW, shaft speed, and auxiliary engine fuel consumption) with some unusual behavior (i.e. a sudden drop in the parameter value) are detected. In the second sensor fault situation (i.e. a data interval), several parameters (i.e. average draft, trim) with some unusual behavior and the auxiliary engine fuel consumption with considerably higher values are detected.

Data Compression and Expansion

The compression and expansion steps are the last layer in data pre-processing and the first layer in data post-processing, respectively under the same data-handling framework. The third data cluster (i.e. model 3), classified in the engine and propeller combinator diagram, is considered separately for these steps. However, the ship performance and navigation data sets may consist of additional parameters that have not been considered for the data clustering process. Such parameters should along the same engine operating modes be classified, appropriately. Hence, the clustered data set of model 3 with other ship performance and navigation parameters is used for the data compression and expansion steps, where an autoencoder network, another machine learning approach, is proposed (i.e. data compression and expansion) (Lv et al., 2015; Wang et al., 2016). An autoencoder is a feed-forward neural network also relates to a linear version of deep learning (Perera and Mo, 2016d) as an unsupervised learning method. The

Figure 4. Sensor and DAQ fault detection

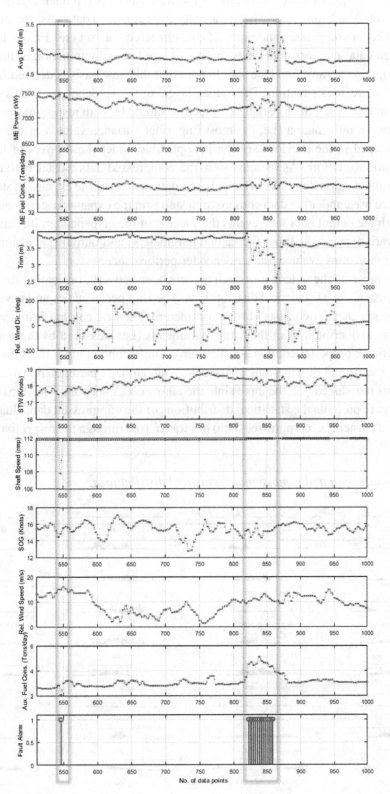

input recreates at the output of the neural network that consists of two hidden layers (i.e. between the input and output layers) and compress/expand the respective clustered data sets. Hence, the first hidden layer of the autoencoder compresses and transmits the clustered data set (see Figure 1).

The compressed data set consists of a new basis that is a linear combination of measured ship performance and navigation parameters. One should note that this new basis is derived from the PCs that are calculated in the previous situation. The hidden layers of the autoencoder relates to the number of parameters in the new data set. Such parameter selection should be with respect to the PCs and that can preserve the important information (i.e. the most important variance values) of the data cluster. The PC structure developed in the previous section is applicable under these layers of the data-handling framework as mentioned before. As the next step, the compressed data cluster is transmitted through the respective communication networks to shore based data centers of the expansion step. Similarly, the same PCA structure used under the data compression step is in the expansion step used. Comparing the input data sets with the output data sets reveals the success of the autoencoder. It is an expectation that some parameter variations on the input (i.e. actual parameters) and output (i.e. estimated parameters) data clusters, such variations evaluate the autoencoder performance.

Figure 5 and 6 presents the outcome of such autoencoder network, presenting the respective input and output data clusters are as statistical distributions. The ship performance and navigation data cluster used under the autoencoder consists of nine parameters. The first column from the left in Figure 5 presents the statistical distributions of the actual parameters (i.e. measured by the onboard vessel and clustered on the engine propeller combinator diagram). The second column from the left in the same figure presents the statistical distributions of the same standardized parameters. One should note that this data cluster has introduced (i.e. the input) into the autoencoder network. The third column from the left in the same figure presents the statistical distributions of the compressed data cluster under the top PCs. The same data cluster (i.e. compressed data) has transferred through the respective communication

Figure 5. Data compression and expansion as statistical distributions

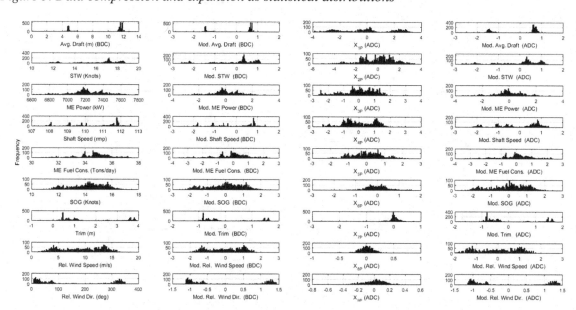

Figure 6. Data compression and expansion with sample number

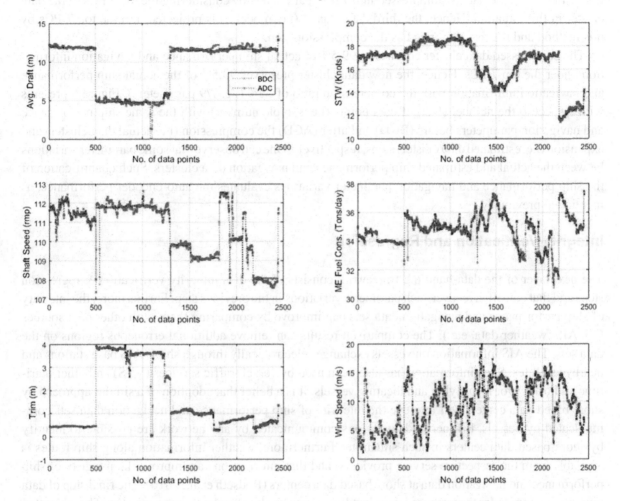

networks to shore based data centers. Even though inclusion of nine new parameters in this new data set, by considering the respective PCs communication needs to use a less number of new parameters. The fourth column from the left in the same figure is the output of the autoencoder network and represents the statistical distributions of the expanded data cluster (i.e. estimated parameters). The following section presents further details on these compression and expansion steps of the autoencoder network with respective to the third data cluster (i.e. model 3).

A comparison of the input and output data clusters of ship performance and navigation parameters evaluates the performance of the autoencoder network. That has been done by comparing the second (i.e. inputs) and forth (i.e. outputs) columns from the left of the same figure. One should note the statistical distributions of the same data clusters are approximately similar in some situations. However, some parameter variations noted in the same statistical distributions due to the data compression and expansion steps of the autoencoder network. It shows that some ship performance and navigation parameters may not recover, completely in some situations. The usage of the knowledge on the PCs can overcome such data recovery situations. The input to the autoencoder network is 9 ship performance and navigation parameters and that has compressed into 7 new parameters by considering the top 7 PCs of the data cluster in this situation. Hence, the third data cluster (i.e. model 3) is projected into the top 7 PCs by this method and that is categorized as the compression step.

The compressed data cluster consists of 99.5% of actual ship performance and navigation information under the top 7 PCs. Hence, the new data cluster preserves 99.5% of the actual ship performance and navigation information with the compression ratio of 22% (i.e. 7/9 parameters). Figure 6 presents with respect to the number (No.) of data points (i.e. sample number) with the same ship performance and navigation parameters before (BCD) and after (ACD) the compression (i.e. actual data cluster) and expansion (i.e. estimated data cluster) steps, respectively. One can observe that some parameter variations between the actual and estimated ship performance and navigation data clusters. Such quantification of the ship performance and navigation parameter variations evaluates the auto-encoder performance, as mentioned previously.

Integrity Verification and Regression

The next layer of the data-handling framework consists of the data integrity verification & regression steps and that can often recover such parameter variations in the previous step. Furthermore, the integrity of ship performance and navigation data sets can improve by comparing them with other data sources (i.e. AIS, weather data, etc.). The comparison results can remove additional erroneous regions on the data sets. The AIS information on vessels exchanges electronically through ships, AIS base stations and nearby satellites. Such information has also been used by vessel traffic services (VTS) and other maritime authorities for identifying and locating vessels. It is a belief that adoption of a similar approach by shore based data centers will improve the integrity of ship performance and navigation data sets communicated by vessels. Erroneous data regions communicated by any network are possible to identify by shore-based data centers in such situations. Furthermore, weather information along ship routes is available from the respective service providers, and that information can improve the integrity of ship performance and navigation data at shore based data centers (Rodseth et al., 2016). The final step of data post-processing under the proposed data-handling framework is the data regression step. The estimated data clusters of ship performance and navigation information may have some parameter variations (see Figure 6) and that is possible to eliminate by various smoothing algorithms under this step. Therefore, the accuracy of estimated ship performance and navigation data can further improve by both steps, to minimize the parameter fluctuations.

Data Visualization and Decision Supporting

The last layer of this data handling framework is data visualization and decision supporting that can be into energy efficiency and system reliability further divided. However, the focus of this study is on ship energy efficiency. Therefore, the respective data visualization analytics on ship energy efficiency are developed. At this layer, appropriate visualization should reveal the improved quality in ship performance and navigation data sets. One should observe less data scattering situations in these situations due to the proposed data cleaning approaches by considering various data handling layers. A better overview of ship speed and power performance information under various weather conditions should be in these results visualized. These data clusters consist of a higher dimensional space, where the respective PCs can also improve data visualization and decision supporting features as also presented in Figure 3.

Therefore, these data clusters may project into the respective combined PCs to improve the visibility of vessel performance and navigation conditions (Perera & Mo, 2016e; Post et al., 2002).

An example of such ship performance and navigation conditions for the same data set is visualized in Figure 7. The same set of ship performance and navigation parameters in Figure 2 presents in the bottom plot of Figure 7. This statistical distribution consists of two parameters of ME power and shaft speeds. One should note that this parameter combination is often identified as the engine propeller combinator diagram as presented in Figure 2. The data driven models (model 1, 2 and 3) identified in Figure 2 are also denoted in the same plot and those are the respective data clusters that relate to engine operating modes. Therefore, the vessel operational data clustered under such engine operating modes create a meaningful structure for ship performance and navigation data as visualized in this figure. One should note that the structure is used to derive the data driven models. The top-left plot of the figure represents the contour plot of the same statistical distribution. The top-right plot of the figure represents the same contour plot with the respective ME fuel consumption of the vessel. One should note that the higher engine power regions coincide with the higher fuel consumption regions in this plot. Therefore, such data visualization approaches can further improve the information visibility of ship performance and navigation data.

CONCLUSION

It is a belief that the required knowledge towards such big data applications under IoT in shipping is still in the preliminary stage. Therefore, that may create additional challenges on various digitalization steps in the shipping industry. However, other transportation systems have already implemented appropriate MI applications with IoT (i.e. various sensors, data acquisition and communication networks) to over-

Figure 7. Marine engine operating regions

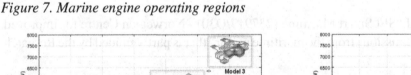

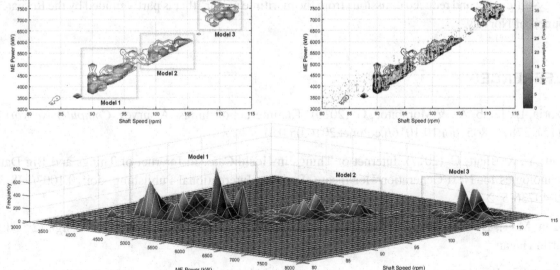

come the similar challenges. Hence, this study proposes a data-handling framework with statistical data analyses based MI applications to overcome such large-scale data handling challenges in shipping. The proposed framework consists of various data handling layers to overcome the respective challenges in the large-scale data sets of ship performance and navigation information under onboard IoT. The framework divides into two main divisions of pre-and post-processing steps. Data pre-processing is in the category of onboard applications consisting sensor faults detection, data classification and data compression steps. Data post-processing is in the category of shore based applications (i.e. in data centers) consisting data expansion, integrity verification and data regression steps. Various MI applications (i.e. PCA, GMMs with an EM algorithm and autoencoders) are included under the data analytics of the proposed data-handling framework. This combination (i.e. statistical data analyses and MI techniques) can lead to identifying the respective structure of ship performance and navigation data sets and that are categories as data driven models. Such data driven models can address the fundamental data handling challenges in the shipping industry as proposed under this framework.

Furthermore, the same framework can improve the quality of ship performance and navigation information under the respective data handling layers. The improved data quality can lead to appropriate visualization of ship performance and navigation conditions. Such visualization methods can identify energy efficient operating conditions of vessels and that information can develop appropriate ship navigation strategies. It is a belief that the shipping industry will demand superior data analytics to preserve the required navigation safety and efficiency levels. Hence, the respective ship performance and navigation data with IoT under the proposed data-handling framework can satisfy such navigation safety and efficiency levels. That resulted in appropriate navigation strategies for vessels under the e-navigation strategy in a global level (i.e. as a shipping fleet) and the SEEMP in a local level (i.e. onboard the vessel).

ACKNOWLEDGMENT

This work is from the project of "SFI Smart Maritime (237917/O30) - Norwegian Centre for improved energy-efficiency and reduced emissions from the maritime sector" that is partly funded by the Research Council of Norway.

REFERENCES

Atzoria, L., Ierab, A., & Morabitoc, G. (2010). The internet of things: A survey. *Computer Networks*, *54*(15), 2787–2805. doi:10.1016/j.comnet.2010.05.010

Bhatt, Y., & Bhatt, C. (2017). Internet of Things in HealthCare. In Internet of Things and Big Data Technologies for Next Generation Healthcare. Springer International Publishing. doi:10.1007/978-3-319-49736-5_2

Hagan, M. T., Demuth, H. B., Beale, M. H., & De Jesus, O. (2014). *Neural Network Design* (2nd ed.). Martin Hagan.

IMO (2007). *Development of an e-Navigation Strategy*. IALA and e-navigation, sub-committee on Safety of Navigation, Report of the Correspondence Group on e-Navigation, NAV/53/13/3.

IMO. (2009a). *Resolution MEPC.1/Circ.683, Guidelines for the development of a ship energy efficiency management plan*. SEEMP.

IMO. (2009b). *Resolution MEPC.1/Cric.684, Guidelines for the voluntary use of the ship energy efficiency operational indicator*. EEOI.

IMO. (2012). Guidelines for the development of a ship energy efficiency management plan. *Resolution MEPC., 213*(63), 2012.

IMO (2014). *Draft E-Navigation Strategy Implementation Plan*. Report to the Maritime Safety Committee, Annex 7, NCSR 1/28.

Jackson, J. E. (1980). Principal components and factor analysis: Part i-principal components. *Journal of Quality Technology, 12*(4), 201–213.

Kamal, S., Ripon, S. H., Dey, N., Ashour, A. S., & Santhi, V. (2016). A MapReduce approach to diminish imbalance parameters for big deoxyribonucleic acid dataset. *Computer Methods and Programs in Biomedicine, 131*, 191–206. doi:10.1016/j.cmpb.2016.04.005 PMID:27265059

Lv, Y., Duan, Y., Kang, W., Li, Z., & Wnag, F. Y. (2015). Traffic flow prediction with big data: A deep learning approach. *IEEE Transactions on Intelligent Transportation Systems, 16*(2), 865–873.

Moon, T. K. (1996). The expectation-maximization algorithm. *Signal Processing Magazine, IEEE, 13*(6), 47–60. doi:10.1109/79.543975

Ng, A. (2015). Mixtures of Gaussians and the EM algorithm. *Lecture Notes on Machine Learning*.

Perera, L. P. (2016a). Marine Engine Centered Localized Models for Sensor Fault Detection under Ship Performance Monitoring. *Proceedings of the 3rd IFAC Workshop on Advanced Maintenance Engineering, Service and Technology (AMEST'16)*. doi:10.1016/j.ifacol.2016.11.016

Perera, L. P. (2016b). Statistical Filter based Sensor and DAQ Fault Detection for Onboard Ship Performance and Navigation Monitoring Systems. *Proceedings of the 8th IFAC Conference on Control Applications in Marine Systems (CAMS 2016)*. doi:10.1016/j.ifacol.2016.10.362

Perera, L.P., & Guedes Soares, C. (2017). Weather Routing and Safe Ship Handling in the Future of Shipping. *Journal of Ocean Engineering*. DOI: 10.1016/j.oceaneng.2016.09.007

Perera, L. P., & Mo, B. (2016a). Data Analytics for Capturing Marine Engine Operating Regions for Ship Performance Monitoring. *Proceedings of the 35th International Conference on Ocean, Offshore and Arctic Engineering (OMAE 2016)*. doi:10.1115/OMAE2016-54168

Perera, L. P., & Mo, B. (2016b). Marine Engine Operating Regions under Principal Component Analysis to evaluate Ship Performance and Navigation Behavior. *Proceedings of the 8th IFAC Conference on Control Applications in Marine Systems (CAMS 2016)*. doi:10.1016/j.ifacol.2016.10.487

Perera, L. P., & Mo, B. (2016c). Data Analytics for Capturing Marine Engine Operating Regions for Ship Performance Monitoring. *Proceedings of the 35th International Conference on Ocean, Offshore and Arctic Engineering (OMAE 2016)*. doi:10.1115/OMAE2016-54168

Perera, L. P., & Mo, B. (2016d). Data Compression of Ship Performance and Navigation Information under Deep Learning. *Proceedings of the 35th International Conference on Ocean, Offshore and Arctic Engineering (OMAE 2016)*. doi:10.1115/OMAE2016-54093

Perera, L. P., & Mo, B. (2016e). Marine Engine Operating Regions under Principal Component Analysis to evaluate Ship Performance and Navigation Behavior. *Proceedings of the 8th IFAC Conference on Control Applications in Marine Systems (CAMS 2016)*. doi:10.1016/j.ifacol.2016.10.487

Perera, L. P., & Mo, B. (2017). Marine Engine Centered Data Analytics for Ship Performance Monitoring. *Journal of Offshore Mechanics and Arctic Engineering-Transactions of The ASME, 2017*. doi:10.1115/1.4034923

Perera, L. P., Mo, B., Kristjansson, L. A., Jonvik, P. C., & Svardal, J. O. (2015). Evaluations on Ship Performance under Varying Operational Conditions. *Proceedings of the 34th International Conference on Ocean, Offshore and Arctic Engineering (OMAE 2015)*. doi:10.1115/OMAE2015-41793

Post, F. H., Nielson, G. M., & Bonneau, G.-P. (2002). *Data Visualization: The State of the Art*. Research paper TU delft.

Rodesth, O. J. (2011). *A maritime ITS architecture for e-navigation and e-maritime: Supporting environment friendly ship transport*. IEEE ITS Conference.

Rodesth, O. J. (2016). *Sustainable and Competitive Cyber-Shipping through Industry 4.0*. Singapore Maritime Sustainability Forum 2016: Smart Maritime Solutions and Overcoming Challenges, Suntec City, Singapore.

Rodseth, O. J., Perera, L. P., & Mo, B. (2016). Big data in shipping - Challenges and opportunities. *Proceedings of the 15th International Conference on Computer Applications and Information Technology in the Maritime Industries (COMPIT 2016)*.

Strasser, G., Takagi, K., Werner, S., Hollenbach, U., Tanaka, T., Yamamoto, K., & Hirota, K. (2015). A verification of the ITTC/ISO speed/power trials analysis. *Journal of Marine Science and Technology, 20*(1), 2–13. doi:10.1007/s00773-015-0304-7

Zhang, J., Wang, F. Y., Wang, K., Lin, W. H., Xu, X., & Chen, C. (2011). Data-Driven Intelligent Transportation Systems: A Survey,. *IEEE Transactions on Intelligent Transportation Systems, 12*(4), 1624–1639.

Wang, X., Gao, L., & Mao, S. (2016). Pandey, S., CSI-based Fingerprinting for Indoor Localization: A Deep Learning Approach. *IEEE Transactions on Vehicular Technology*.

Chapter 12
Big Data Predictive Analysis for Detection of Prostate Cancer on Cloud–Based Platform:
Microsoft Azure

Ritesh Anilkumar Gangwal
Dr. Babasaheb Ambedkar Marathwada University, India

Ratnadeep R. Deshmukh
Dr. Babasaheb Ambedkar Marathwada University, India

M. Emmanuel
Pune Institute of Computer Technology, India

ABSTRACT

BIG DATA AS THE NAME WOULD REFER TO A SUBSEQUENTLY LARGE QUANTITY OF DATA WHICH IS BEING PROCESSED. WITH THE ADVENT OF SOCIAL MEDIA THE DATA PRESENTLY AVAILABLE IS TEXT, IMAGES, AUDIO VIDEO. IN ORDER TO PROCESS THIS DATA BELONGING TO VARIETY OF FORMAT LED TO THE CONCEPT OF BIG DATA PROCESSING. TO OVERCOME THESE CHALLENGES OF DATA, BIG DATA TECHNIQUES EVOLVED. VARIOUS TOOLS ARE AVAILABLE FOR THE BIG DATA NAMING MAP REDUCE, ETC. BUT TO GET THE TASTE OF CLOUD BASED TOOL WE WOULD BE WORKING WITH THE MICROSOFT AZURE. MICROSOFT AZURE IS AN INTEGRATED ENVIRONMENT FOR THE BIG DATA ANALYTICS ALONG WITH THE SAAS CLOUD PLATFORM. FOR THE PURPOSE OF EXPERIMENT, THE PROSTATE CANCER DATA IS USED TO PERFORM THE PREDICTIVE ANALYSIS FOR THE CANCER GROWTH IN THE GLAND. AN EXPERIMENT DEPENDING ON THE SEGMENTATION RESULTS OF PROSTATE MRI SCANS IS USED FOR THE PREDICTIVE ANALYTICS USING THE SVM. PERFORMANCE ANALYSIS WITH THE ROC, ACCURACY AND CONFUSION MATRIX GIVES THE RESULTANT ANALYSIS WITH THE VISUAL ARTIFACTS. WITH THE TRAINED MODEL, THE PROPOSED EXPERIMENT CAN STATISTICALLY PREDICT THE CANCER GROWTH.

DOI: 10.4018/978-1-5225-2486-1.ch012

INTRODUCTION

Big data as the name would refer to a subsequently large quantity of data which is being processed. As per Definition: Big Data is a term for data sets processing that are so large or complex that traditional data processing applications are not adequate".

As per (Fouad, K., Hassan, B., & Hassan, M. (2016)) the current scenarios where the capacity of storage devices is increasing constantly from terabytes to petta-bytes to Zettabytes (43 Trillion Gigabytes) so on, it is become difficult for the relational database systems and query processing system to operate. Now the question might arise, with the advent of huge storage space the primary memory is also multiplying thus counterfeiting the problem of huge data, so why is the need for the additional tool for the Big data.

To define the term in some common words is: "Big Data is not only about huge quantity of data, but it is a way of finding new insights into some existing data, to analyze and get the unknown facts". As per (Dave, P.2016 & Fernández et al., 2014), it can make businesses dynamic and robust, so as to overcome various business hurdles and adapt to the growing challenges.

Big data refers to scenarios preciously with the 3V's.

1. Volume
2. Velocity
3. Variety

Volume

With the advent of transistor, there has been an explosive growth in the data storage device's capacity. Thus the data stored is now just more than text. Currently data is available in various forms may it be conventional text, Video streams, Audio's etc. which is most oftenly found in the social media or News Channels. As the storage capacity grows, the applications and architecture already developed also needs to be evaluated again. Sometimes the same data is examined with respect to multiple dimensions, even though the original data is not altered. The big volume thus represents most usual aspect of Big Data.

Velocity

There has been a huge change in perspective of how we look at the data due to huge data growth and social media. Earlier, data available of yesterday was consider recent, but today with the advent of social media, we reply on them in order to provide update with latest happenings. Sometimes, a few moments old data on social media is considered outdated and rendered useless, thus does not interests users. Such old messages are often discarded and people are diverted to the latest or recent update. The data movement has to be real time and update time needs to be reduced to fraction of seconds. Thus the high velocity plays a critical role to represent big data.

Variety

The data is stored in multiple formats in the data storages may be it in the form of database, excel sheets, comma separated files, text file, images, PDF files, video files etc. example, O'Shaughnessy, S. & Gray, G. (2011). This makes it necessary for the organization to manage and make the data meaningful. It is sometimes easy if the data is in the same format. But most often the data acquired belongs to multiple format, becoming it difficult to manage. This difficulty can be resolved using big data. Thus, the variety of data represents key aspects of Big Data (Figure 1).

Other descriptions of up to 9V's can be also found with respect to big data, adding terms like Veracity, Value, Viability, and Visualization, among others.

Veracity

Veracity in the Big data represents the abnormalities such as biased data and noise. As the data is received from multiple sources, these inconsistencies are common. But the data stored is mostly utilized for the mining or analysis purpose, such abnormalities should be removed. Thus this aspect should be examined before directly using the raw datasets.

Value

Though the Big data systems require huge cost for setup & maintenance, the value imparted by such system to an organization is of tremendous importance.

Viability

Viability refers to the possibility of success of operations in big data. As we know, though the big data has huge volume of data with different varieties of data, it has proved to be viable in long run for any organization. For example, Facebook or Google.

Figure 1. 3 Vs of big data

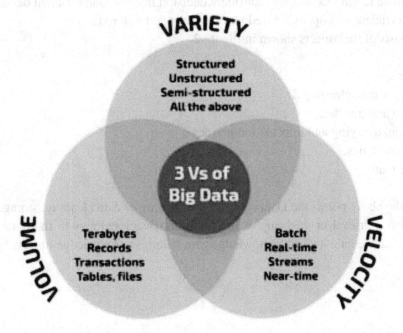

Validity

Similar to the Veracity, Validity is the issue of big data. Validity defines the correctness of the data, thus suitable tools needs to be designed to validate huge chunk of data before processing.

Volatility

As discussed, with the use of social media, the data is moving fast and these data becomes invalid or useless after some time. In this ever growing world one has to monitor the data, to check its validity with respect to time.

Visualization

This refers to the representation of the data in the graphical form, but as the data is huge it cannot be directly represented. Therefore the techniques such as feature extraction and dimensionality reduction needs to be used for size reduction. But these techniques sometimes cannot represent the actual trend in the data, thus an appropriate balance needs to be achieved between features and the size of data to be used.

BIG DATA TECHNOLOGIES

Big Data is a term which is now been used to refer to the challenges and advantages which are derived from collecting and processing huge amounts of data. These challenges include capture & analysis of data, data curation, searching, sharing, storing, transferring, querying & information privacy, data visualization. The ("Big data", 2016) term frequently refers to the use of predictive analytics or few other advanced methods to extract or fetch value from data, and not frequently to a particular size of data. Accuracy in big data might lead to more confident decision making, and efficient decisions, which can result in greater efficiency of operation, reduction of cost and risk reduction.

Big data consists of the aspects shown in Figure 2.

1. Data capture.
2. Data curing or data cleaning
3. Data storage and transfer,
4. Visualization, querying and information privacy
5. Predicative analytics.
6. Knowledge gain

Referring to the above points the Data capture, Data curing or data cleaning, storage, Data transfer, Data Visualization, retrieval or querying & information privacy belongs to the data pre-processing. Whereas the Predicative analytics and Knowledge gain belongs to knowledge discovery.

Figure 2. Information retrieval flow as per ("Data Scientists vs. Data Engineers", 2016)

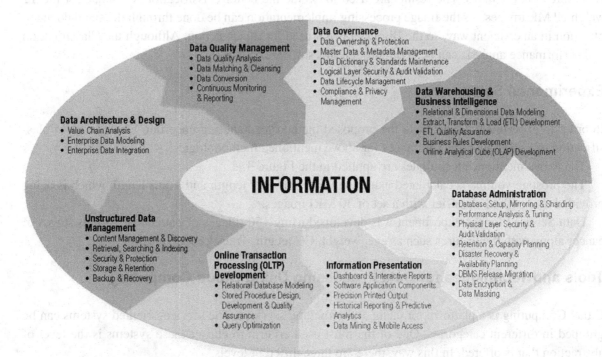

Introduction to Prostate Cancer Detection

As per Gangwal, R. & Deshmukh, R. (2014) Prostate carcinoma is the most widely occurring cancer among men in the world. It is a heterogeneous disease, which ranges from normal gland to rapidly progressive systemic malignancy. The occurrence of prostate cancer is so high that it can be considered a normal age-related phenomenon. Conservative MRI of the prostate relies on morphological changes within the prostate gland to define the presence and extent of cancer. Segmentation of the prostate gland in Magnetic Resonance images is an important task for image guided prostate cancer therapy. Kamal, S., Dey, N., Nimmy, S., Ripon, S., Ali, N., & Ashour, A. et al. (2016) suggested that Prostate cancer patients require a non-invasive detection and staging as the invasive techniques are quite painful. Mortality in patients is often due to the spread of cancer from prostate to bones which happens only in a small number of patients.

Magnetic Resonance Imaging (MRI) as per Dey, N., Dey, M., Mahata, S., Das, A., & Chaudhuri, S. (2015) plays a critical role in prognosis of prostate cancer. MRI is used to support biopsies, radiation therapy, or planning of surgeries. In-order to detect the prostate in MRI scans object detection algorithm is used. Post detection of the prostate gland, determining the particular prostate volume remains the main area of interest. The prostate volume deals with the numeric value which can be applied to the Classification technique.

Machine learning technique such as Support vector classification which is the supervised Learning methods are used to compute the results which are then compared depending upon the Accuracy (Acc),

AUC (area under curve). The results are used to decide the better classification technique for the T2 weighted MR images. As the Image processing implementation can be done through the standalone application in an efficient way, so the Big Data is not used for the detection. Although the Classification and performance analysis can be done through this software.

Experimental Setup

In order to experimentally evaluate the proposed method for handling uncertain labels in SVM classification, we simulate different images for above mentioned methodologies.

The above mentioned techniques are applied in the Figure 3.

The prostate volume is calculated using the CC length, AP length and Trans length which is being provided to the SVM classifier with a set of 30 MRI images.

Data Set used for the experiment was developed using 150 images of patients at various stages of cancer along with the features such as age, weight, CC length, Trans Length, etc.

Tools and Techniques for Data Processing Using Cloud Computing

Cloud Computing is a platform for using and providing services. The service-oriented systems can be grouped in different categories. One of the most used criteria to cluster these systems is the level of abstraction that is offered. In this way, there are three different levels.

Figure 3. Prostate detection and volume calculation

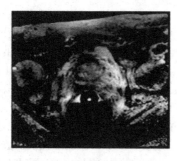

a) Prostate MRI image

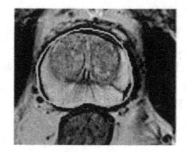

b) Prostate detection

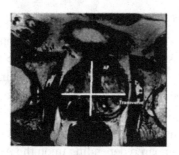

c) Volume detection

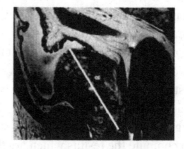

d) Transverse Length for Volume

- Infrastructure as a Service-> IaaS,
- Platform as a Service -> PaaS, and
- Software as a Service -> SaaS.

Cloud Computing provides various features such as scalability with respect to use of resources, reduced effort of administration, price flexibility and the software user mobility. Keeping these assumptions in mind, it is obvious that the Cloud Computing technology benefits projects or organization which are quite huge, such as the ones related with Business Intelligence.

Common tools for Data Processing are:

1. Map Reduce
2. Apache Hadoop Ecosystem
3. Apache Spark framework

Map Reduce

Map reduce as described by Kamal, S., Ripon, S., Dey, N., Ashour, A., & Santhi, V. (2016) is a programing techniques that provides the extensive scalability with respect to data stored at multiple clusters. As the name suggest it consist of two operation, Map and Reduce. The Map function provides the operations such as sorting, searching, filtering etc. on each of the data set assigned, on the other hand Reduce function summarizes the results obtained from multiple Map operations.

Apache Hadoop Ecosystem

Apache Hadoop Ecosystem is a complete package which uses the Map Reduce technique for data processing part, HDFS (Distributed File system) for the file storage, HBASE for the no SQL Database and APACHE DRILL for the mining purpose. It is the complete systems which provides the big data operation to function using multiple individual technique. This system is marked by Apache License 2.0 and is thus open source.

Apache Spark Framework

Apache Spark framework is also an open Source cluster computing platform developed by Apache. It is a platform which competes with the Map Reduce in terms of distributed data processing. It does not have its own Files system and thus uses HDFS for the same.

As the focus of this chapter is to introduce the Predictive analytics using Cloud computing on the research oriented complex data, we would now move to Predictive analytics, the data processing can be done through any of the above tool which serves as the input for the Predictive analysis.

Tools for the Predictive analytics on cloud platforms:

1. Cloud Machine Learning (Google Cloud Platform),
2. Big ML,
3. Microsoft Azure,
4. Amazon Web Services (Machine Learning).

As all the Cloud based tools provide the Software as a Service (SaaS), we would continue with Microsoft Azure as it is one of the leading Machine Learning Tool used in the Software industry.

MICROSOFT AZURE®

Introduction

As per *Azure Tutorial; Be in cloud (Part 1) [Introduction]* (2016)., Microsoft Azure is a cloud computing platform and an IT infrastructure created by Microsoft in order to build, deploy, and manage applications and services through a global network of Microsoft-managed datacenters. It delivers PaaS & IaaS both and supports many different programming languages, tools and frameworks, including software specific to Microsoft and third-party software and systems.

Infrastructure Overhead and Cost

Infrastructure Overhead seems to be the most frightening thing for an organization and for their business. The infrastructure establishment and its keep up may seem to be trivial task, but for any official who runs the business, has to suffer the pain for keeping the office operational and updated with such huge volume of data.

With the advent of cloud based infrastructure, officials don't have to care about updating, maintaining and backing up the data frequently. This technology helps the organization which does not have a full-fledged infrastructure or does not have budget for huge investment or for capable IT support. Due to such technology, issues related to renting the space rent, purchase of servers, electricity charges, hiring of qualified employees and keeping them up to date have significantly reduced.

Agile

Agile services is basic requirement for any cloud based service, so it is next to mandatory for cloud service provider to provide services through agile. Sometimes, requirement comes to you without prior information and in-order to handle this is to have everything at one place. But question arises why an organization would keep everything prepared for such a thing which has the rarest possibility of occurrence. Considering the cost factor involved, most of the companies would never give it importance and when it occurs, its affects very drastically. With the use of agility feature of cloud, one can always have the option to change one's requirement at run time without any delays.

Reliability

Reliability is which you can take for granted with machines. Imagine if some bad virus hits your data center affecting the whole lot of data or any natural calamity hit your region which physically damaged your data centers. Considering the size of business, the loss would be in millions or sometimes in billions due to down time, if such calamity occurs. Most organizations do tie up with multiple vendors for data backup and emergency setup, but have to pay a huge cost for these services. The reliability which is an inbuilt feature of cloud can come to the rescue with much less cost. Microsoft Azure which is a cloud based platform provides reliability of data which keeps the application and services up and running. It is the feature which is guaranteed in Azure, unlike its other competitors.

Scalability

It is yet another feature which is most often required for a business on web. Consider you are running an ecommerce business and the number of hits on the site is in millions on usual days but it considerably increases to billion on one fine with the launch of sale thus the site would not be able to handle the extra load. But without cloud, organizations would have to maintain the infrastructure which could allow the maximum traffic throughout the year. But it would lie idle for most of the year as the load would not be high throughout. However, cloud provide a service 'scalability', which provides infinite limit of resources for an application with a small cost with respect to the complete infrastructure cost.

Availability

The cloud vendors maintain your resources in all possible location without any down time, you are worry free of maintaining your resources which are available round the clock.

S+S Model

Jackson (2016) explained that, Software and Service model is available with cloud, where the software and service is normally added with a restriction of SLA.

Data Lake Used by Microsoft Azure®

As described by Data Lake., 2016, and Jain & Bhatnagar, 2016., Microsoft has provided 3 ways to store data on Azure, which has made the cloud computing platform more supportive to big data analysis.

Azure now has a data warehouse service, named as "data lake" service which stores huge amounts of data, and also has an elastic database that can store data that differ in size. As per "Exploring Azure's Data Lake" (2016), the Azure Data Warehouse has provided a way to enterprises to store huge amount of data so that it can easily be ingested by the programs for data visualization, data orchestration or Machine learning Services.

Unlike the conventional data warehouse systems, Azure cloud service can adjust itself so as to accommodate the quantity of data that needs to be stored. Azure also provides the user with the option to specify the processing power required. Ripon, S., Kamal, S., Hossain, S., & Dey, N. (2016) and Sarna, G. & Bhatia, M. (2016) and Mohanpurkar, A. & Joshi, M. (2016) concluded, that the Azure Data Lake is designed for those enterprises that require to store huge chunks of data, so that it can be analyzed and processed by Hadoop or any other "big data" platforms. This service is most useful for IoT-based systems that mostly uses large amounts of sensor data.

The new services introduced recently would be useful for running software services, where in the amount of database storage needed can vary significantly. Today, most Software-as-a-Service (SaaS) are offering to overprovision their databases to accommodate the potential peak demand.

Key capabilities:

- Dynamic scaling.
- Faster code Development, debugging and smarter optimization using familiar tools.
- U-SQL: powerful and extensible.
- Integrates seamlessly with existing IT infrastructure.
- Cost efficient.

U-SQL Language (SQL + C# = U-SQL)

The "Tutorial: Get started with Azure Data Lake Analytics U-SQL language" (2016) states that, U-SQL is a new data querying language developed by Microsoft that enables user to run queries in a distributed manner. It is built using combination from T-SQL, ANSI-SQL & Hive and a SQL syntax with C# extensibility. U-SQL can query virtually any size of data be it small file or files bigger than an Exabyte. By using an Extract-Transform-Output pattern user can process data and come out with required data. The language also supports other features such using partition tables, using variables in folder paths, these allow user to add the variable to the output data set. Also inline C# statements can be run or call external assemblies from within scripts.

Some frequently used keywords used in the U-SQL:

- **Rowset Variables:** The query which results into a rowset can be assigned to some variable. U-SQL follows the similar naming pattern as T-SQL, for ex., @searchlog in the script. The assignment to a variable does not always results into execution but it names the expression, so that user can build-up more complex expressions.
- **EXTRACT:** It provides user to describe a schema on read and the field name is used to specify the schema. It uses an Extractor, for ex., Extractors.Tsv () can be used to extract.tsv files. Custom extractors can also be developed by end user.
- **OUTPUT:** Uses a rowset and serializes it. The Outputters.Csv () function provides an output in the form of.CSV file into the specified location. Similar to Extractor custom Output can be developed.

Getting Started With the Microsoft Azure Machine Learning

Data Set to be used: The data set we are using for this demo is regarding the predictive analysis of prostate cancer depending on Volume of the prostate gland. The prostate MRI scans were processed to segment the gland and applied with the various algorithms to find the volume of the gland. Considering the patients biological details were used as the attribute.

As we are working on some research oriented data, we would create a simple experiment which would suite our purpose.

Case Study: SVM Using Microsoft Azure ® on Cancer Data Set

Step 1: Go to Microsoft Azure® Login using an Existing Windows id or Register for a new account. For this development, used a Guest account with limited access (Figure 4).
Step 2: Once logged into the System the below screen would be visible. To create a new Learning Model Create a new blank Experiment. Click on the '+' on lower left hand corner (Figure 5 and Figure 6).

Figure 4. Microsoft Azure sign-in (copyright Microsoft Azure®. Reused by permission as per Microsoft policies)

Figure 5. Azure dashboard (copyright Microsoft Azure®. Reused by permission as per Microsoft policies)

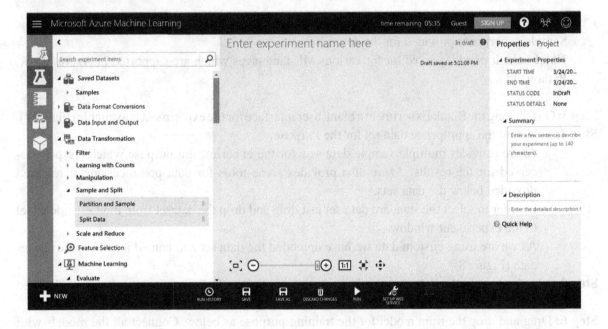

Menu details:

- **Dataset:** Which can be used to upload a new data set from the used.
- **Module:** To upload a custom Zip package.
- **Project:** To add multiple single experiment into one directory named as package.

Figure 6. Azure experiment dashboard (copyright Microsoft Azure®. Reused by permission as per Microsoft policies)

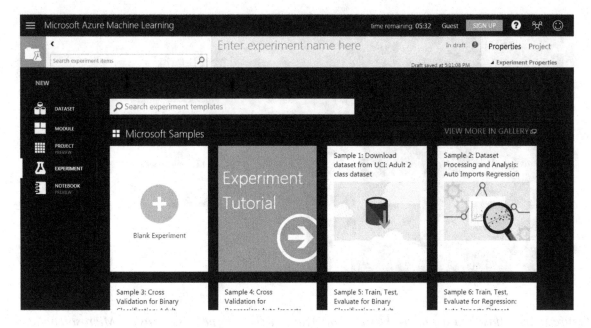

- **Experiment:** It consist of a utility to create a blank experiment for the analytics. There are few Sample experiment provided for the demo.
- **Notebook:** It provides an editor for various ML languages which are supported in Azure like R, Python etc.

Step 3: On Clicking the Blank Experiment a blank user interface for the experiment is available (Figure 7).

Step 4: Selecting the appropriate data set for the Purpose.

- ◦ Azure provides multiple sample data sets for the experimental purpose which are pre-processed for the results. Azure also provides some tools for data preprocessing if required provided below the data sets.
- ◦ In order to select the standard data set just drag and drop the dataset from the Left side panel to the experiment window.
- ◦ As we are using custom data we have uploaded the data set and named it as Prostate cancer data (Figure 8).

Step 5: In order to split the data into the Training set and test set Split data is used. It can be dragged form the left panel (Figure 9).

Step 6: Drag and drop the train model for the training purpose as below. Connect all the models with the connecting link as shown which specifies the logical flow. Specify the column name for which the analysis needs to be done on right hand side (Figure 10).

Step 7: Now select the appropriate algorithm either supervised or unsupervised. For our purpose a two class SVM model is used. If the appropriate model is not available Azure supports the various languages which can be used as a custom build algorithm i.e. other than the standard models. Connect the earlier models as shown. (Figure 11).

Figure 7. Sample data set (copyright Microsoft Azure®. Reused by permission as per Microsoft policies)

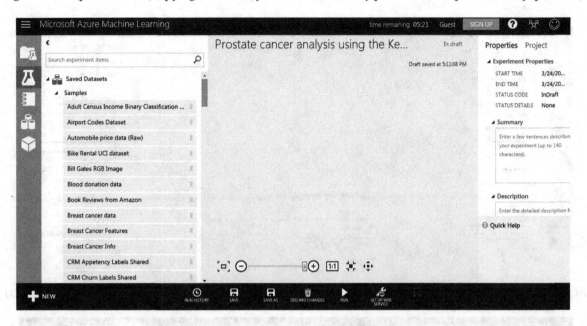

Figure 8. Experiment case study (copyright Microsoft Azure®. Reused by permission as per Microsoft policies)

Step 8: Select a score model and evaluate model for the training and performance evaluation purpose and connect as shown in Figure 12.

Step 9: Now execute the program using the Run Command at the bottom of the screen. If correct each model represents a green tick (Figure 13).

Figure 9. Data split (copyright Microsoft Azure®. Reused by permission as per Microsoft policies)

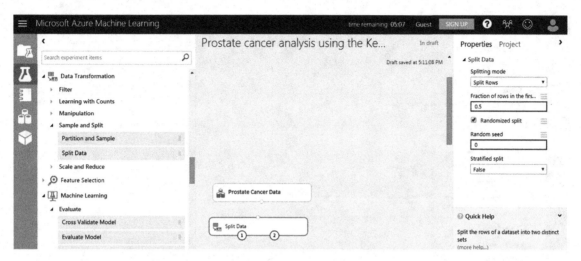

Figure 10. Model training (copyright Microsoft Azure®. Reused by permission as per Microsoft policies)

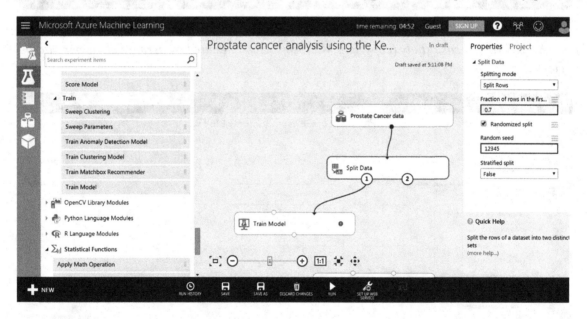

Step 10: To view the result, right click the Evaluate model and select Visualize. The performance analysis in the form of ROC curve, Accuracy, Cumulative AUC is displayed (Figures 14 and 15).

Thus the Microsoft Azure is a convenient tool for the predictive analysis purpose.

Figure 11. Application of SVM (copyright Microsoft Azure®. Reused by permission as per Microsoft policies)

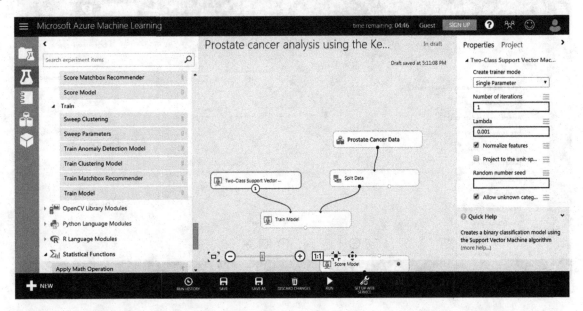

Figure 12. Experiment model (copyright Microsoft Azure®. Reused by permission as per Microsoft policies)

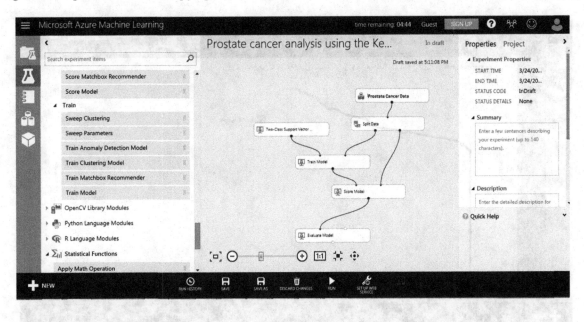

RESULT AND DISCUSSION

Though the result for the SVM are similar to that of any standalone application ML tool compared to the Microsoft Azure. The advantage of Microsoft Azure lies with the seamless availability of data on cloud along with the processing of Machine Learning algorithm on the large data sets at run time.

Figure 13. Test execution (copyright Microsoft Azure®. Reused by permission as per Microsoft policies)

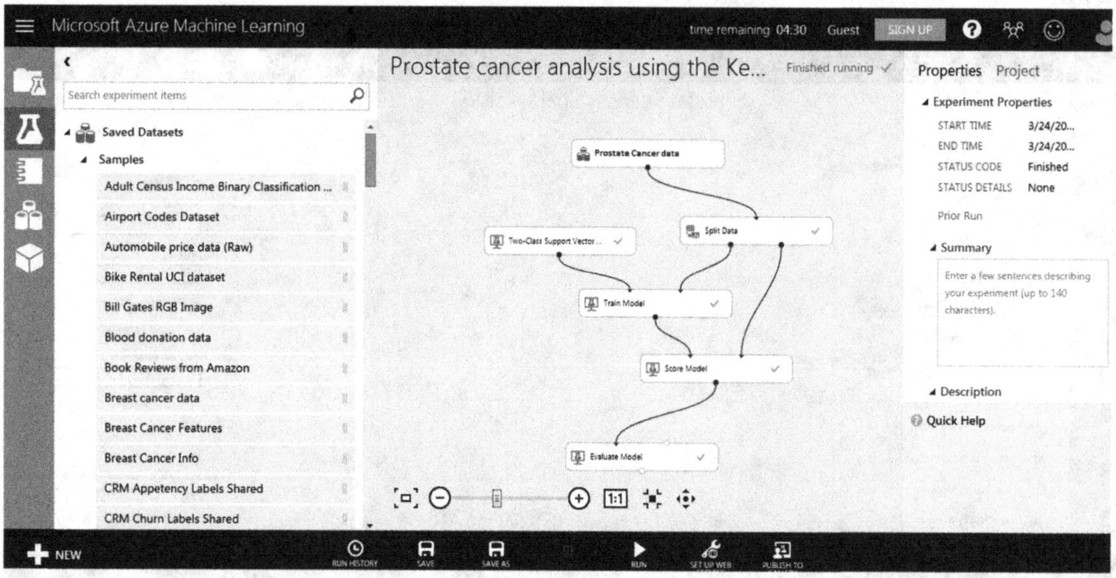

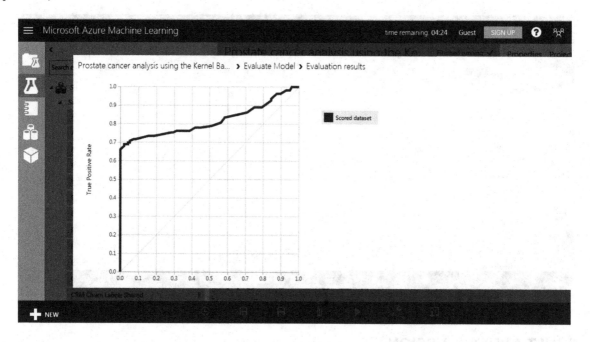

Figure 14. Performance evaluation (copyright Microsoft Azure®. Reused by permission as per Microsoft policies)

Figure 15. Result analysis (copyright Microsoft Azure®. Reused by permission as per Microsoft policies)

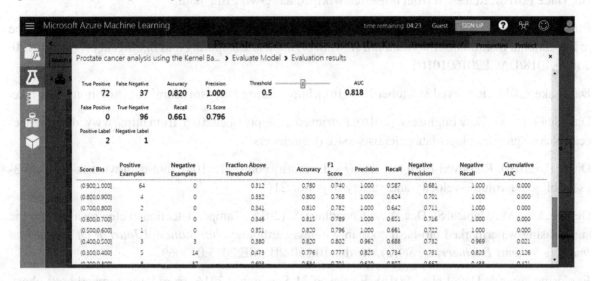

For the current problem data set, the result analysis is carried out on basis of ROC, Accuracy & Precision. As per the above calculation, Accuracy of classification is approx. 82 percentage.

ADVANTAGES

The advantages and disadvantages a technology is mostly with respect to the perspective and necessity of the user. However, let us investigate what are the advantages one would get to enjoy being in cloud. The existing technologies are also having the features which we discussed above but, it's the entire feature set which one would get in a single technology is what makes a difference.

ACKNOWLEDGMENT

All the Microsoft Azure® screen images are used as per intellectual property policies and with permission from Microsoft as described on the portal for intellectual property: https://www.microsoft.com/en-us/legal/intellectualproperty/Permissions/default.aspx.

REFERENCES

Azure Tutorial; Be in cloud (Part 1) [Introduction] - CodeProject. (2016). Retrieved 25 October 2016, from http://www.codeproject.com/Articles/144769/Azure-Tutorial-Be-in-cloud-Part-Introduction

Baumgarten, M., Mulvenna, M., Rooney, N., & Reid, J. (2013). Keyword-Based Sentiment Mining using Twitter. *International Journal of Ambient Computing and Intelligence*, 5(2), 56–69. doi:10.4018/jaci.2013040104

Big Data. (2016). Retrieved from https://en.wikipedia.org/wiki/Big_data

Bureš, V., Tučník, P., Mikulecký, P., Mls, K., & Blecha, P. (2016). Application of Ambient Intelligence in Educational Institutions. *International Journal of Ambient Computing and Intelligence*, 7(1), 94–120. doi:10.4018/IJACI.2016010105

Data Lake. (2016). Retrieved 8 October 2016, from https://azure.microsoft.com/en-in/solutions/data-lake/

Data Scientists vs. Data Engineers. (2016). Retrieved 21 September 2016, from http://www.datascience-central.com/profiles/blogs/data-scientists-vs-data-engineers

Dave, P. (2016). Retrieved from http://blog.sqlauthority.com/2013/10/02/big-data-what-is-big-data-3-vs-of-big-data-volume-velocity-and-variety-day-2-of-21/

Dey, N., Dey, M., Mahata, S., Das, A., & Chaudhuri, S. (2015). Tamper detection of electrocardiographic signal using watermarked bio-hash code in wireless cardiology. *International Journal Of Signal And Imaging Systems Engineering*, 8(1/2), 46. doi:10.1504/IJSISE.2015.067069

Exploring Azure's Data Lake. (2016). Retrieved 21 September 2016, from http://tomkerkhove.ghost.io/2015/10/22/exploring-azures-data-lake/

Fernández, A., del Río, S., López, V., Bawakid, A., del Jesus, M., Benítez, J., & Herrera, F. (2014). Big Data with Cloud Computing: An insight on the computing environment, MapReduce, and programming frameworks. *Wiley Interdisciplinary Reviews: Data Mining and Knowledge Discovery*, 4(5), 380–409. doi:10.1002/widm.1134

Fouad, K., Hassan, B., & Hassan, M. (2016). User Authentication based on Dynamic Keystroke Recognition. *International Journal of Ambient Computing and Intelligence*, 7(2), 1–32. doi:10.4018/IJACI.2016070101

Grünerbl, A., Bahle, G., Hanser, F., & Lukowicz, P. (2013). UWB Indoor Location for Monitoring Dementia Patients. *International Journal of Ambient Computing and Intelligence*, 5(4), 45–59. doi:10.4018/ijaci.2013100104

Jackson, J. (2016). Microsoft to offer three new ways to store big data on Azure. *Computerworld*. Retrieved 11 October 2016, from http://www.computerworld.com/article/2916719/big-data/microsoft-to-offer-three-new-ways-to-store-big-data-on-azure.html

Jain, A., & Bhatnagar, V. (2016). Olympics Big Data Prognostications. *International Journal of Rough Sets and Data Analysis*, 3(4), 32–45. doi:10.4018/IJRSDA.2016100103

Jain, A., & Bhatnagar, V. (2016). Movie Analytics for Effective Recommendation System using Pig with Hadoop. *International Journal of Rough Sets and Data Analysis*, 3(2), 82–100. doi:10.4018/IJRSDA.2016040106

Kamal, S., Dey, N., Nimmy, S., Ripon, S., Ali, N., Ashour, A., & Shi, F. et al. (2016). Evolutionary framework for coding area selection from cancer data. *Neural Computing & Applications*. doi:10.1007/s00521-016-2513-3

Kamal, S., Ripon, S., Dey, N., Ashour, A., & Santhi, V. (2016). A MapReduce approach to diminish imbalance parameters for big deoxyribonucleic acid dataset. *Computer Methods and Programs in Biomedicine*, *131*, 191–206. doi:10.1016/j.cmpb.2016.04.005 PMID:27265059

Mohanpurkar, A., & Joshi, M. (2016). A Traitor Identification Technique for Numeric Relational Databases with Distortion Minimization and Collusion Avoidance. *International Journal of Ambient Computing and Intelligence*, *7*(2), 114–137. doi:10.4018/IJACI.2016070106

Odella, F. (2016). Technology Studies and the Sociological Debate on Monitoring of Social Interactions. *International Journal of Ambient Computing and Intelligence*, *7*(1), 1–26. doi:10.4018/IJACI.2016010101

OShaughnessy, S., & Gray, G. (2011). Development and Evaluation of a Dataset Generator Tool for Generating Synthetic Log Files Containing Computer Attack Signatures. *International Journal of Ambient Computing and Intelligence*, *3*(2), 64–76. doi:10.4018/jaci.2011040105

Panda, S., Mishra, S., & Das, S. (2016). An Efficient Intra-Server and Inter-Server Load Balancing Algorithm for Internet Distributed Systems. *International Journal of Rough Sets and Data Analysis*, *4*(1), 1–18. doi:10.4018/IJRSDA.2017010101

Ripon, S., Kamal, S., Hossain, S., & Dey, N. (2016). Theoretical Analysis of Different Classifiers under Reduction Rough Data Set. *International Journal of Rough Sets and Data Analysis*, *3*(3), 1–20. doi:10.4018/IJRSDA.2016070101

Sarna, G., & Bhatia, M. (2016). An Approach to Distinguish Between the Severity of Bullying in Messages in Social Media. *International Journal of Rough Sets and Data Analysis*, *3*(4), 1–20. doi:10.4018/IJRSDA.2016100101

Tutorial: Get started with Azure Data Lake Analytics U-SQL language. (2016). Retrieved 21 September 2016, from https://azure.microsoft.com/en-in/documentation/articles/data-lake-analytics-u-sql-get-started/

Vallverdú, J., Shah, H., & Casacuberta, D. (2010). Chatterbox Challenge as a Test-Bed for Synthetic Emotions. *International Journal of Synthetic Emotions*, *1*(2), 12–37. doi:10.4018/jse.2010070102

Warwick, K., & Shah, H. (2014). Outwitted by the Hidden. *International Journal of Synthetic Emotions*, *5*(1), 46–59. doi:10.4018/ijse.2014010106

Zappi, P., Lombriser, C., Benini, L., & Tröster, G. (2010). Collecting Datasets from Ambient Intelligence Environments. *International Journal of Ambient Computing and Intelligence*, *2*(2), 42–56. doi:10.4018/jaci.2010040103

KEY TERMS AND DEFINITIONS

AP Length: Horizontal length.

Carcinoma: Cancer which arises in the epithelial or the internal part of the organ.

CC Length: Cephalocaudal means the head to toe length.

Heterogeneous: The cancer occurs in different parts of the Gland and is not located at one location.

T2 Weighted MRI: MRI is a 3-dimesional scan technique and the T2 weighted is the scan along the axis depending on the fat (White matter) and water content of the tissue.

Compilation of References

Acquisti, A., & Gross, R. (2011). Predicting Social Security numbers from public data, *Proceedings of the National Academy of Sciences of the United States of America.* (Vol. 110, No 15, pp 10975–10980). doi:10.1073/pnas.0904891106

Aggarwal, C. C., & Yu, P. S. (2008). *A General Survey of Privacy Privacy-Preserving Data Mining – Models and Algorithms, Advances in database Systems* (Vol. 34). Springer.

Aguilera, M. K., & Terry, D. B. (2016). The many faces of consistency. *Data Engineering*, 3.

Allport, G. W., & Odbert, H. S. (1936). Trait names: a psycho-lexical study. *Psychological Monographs, 47*(1), 171–220.

Alvandi, E. O. (2011). Emotions and Information Processing: A Theoretical Approach. *International Journal of Synthetic Emotions, 2*(1), 1–14. doi:10.4018/jse.2011010101

Amazon Simple D. B. Documentation. (2014). Available online at: http://aws.amazon.com/ Simpledb/

Amedie, A. F. (2013*). Impacts of climate change on plant growth, ecosystem services, biodiversity, and potential adaptation measure* (Master's thesis). Retrieved from http://bioenv.gu.se/digitalAssets/1432/1432197_fantahun.pdf

American Statistical Association. (2016). *Data Science Tops List of Fields with Massive Potential.* Retrieved May 27, 2016, from http://www.amstat.org/

Apache Cassandra Documentation. (n.d.). *Configuring Data Consistency.* Available online at: www.datastax.com

Apache Software Foundation. (2016a). *Apache HBase Website.* Retrieved October 1, 2016, from http://hbase.apache.org/

Apache Software Foundation. (2016b). *Hadoop MapReduce Tutorial.* Retrieved October 1, 2016, from https://hadoop.apache.org/docs/r1.2.1/mapred_tutorial.html

Apache. (2016a). *Apache HBase Reference Guide.* Retrieved January 3, 2017, from https://hbase.apache.org/book.html

Apache. (2016b). *Cassandra Documentation.* Retrieved January 3, 2017, from http://cassandra.apache.org/doc/latest/

Arduino. (n.d.). Retrieved September 18, 2016, from https://www.arduino.cc/en/Guide/Introduction

Arora, R., & Aggarawal, R. (2013). Modeling and Querying Data in MongoDB. *International Journal of Scientific & Engineering Research, 4*(7), 141–144.

Arpaia, M. (2013). Leveraging big data to create more secure web applications. *Code as Craft.* Retrieved from http://codeascraft.com/2013/06/04/leveraging-big-data-to-create-more-secure-web-applications/

Ashton, K. (2009, June22). That 'internet of things' thing. *RFiD Journal, 22*(7), 97–114.

Atzori, L., Iera, A., & Morabito, G. (2010). The internet of things: A survey. *Computer Networks, 54*(15), 2787–2805. doi:10.1016/j.comnet.2010.05.010

Azure Tutorial; Be in cloud (Part 1) [Introduction] - CodeProject. (2016). Retrieved 25 October 2016, from http://www. codeproject.com/Articles/144769/Azure-Tutorial-Be-in-cloud-Part-Introduction

Bailis, P., Venkataraman, S., Franklin, M., Hellerstein, M., & Stoica, I. (2012, April). Probabilistically Bounded Staleness for Practical Partial Quorums. *Proceedings of the VLDB Endowment, 5*(8), 776–787. doi:10.14778/2212351.2212359

Baker, J., Bond, C., Corbett, J., Furman, J., Khorlin, A., Larson, J., & Yushprakh, V. (2011, January). Megastore. *Providing Scalable, Highly Available Storage for Interactive Services, In CIDR, 11*, 223–234.

Baker, R. S. J. d. (2007). Is Gaming the System State-or-Trait? Educational Data Mining Through the Multi-Contextual Application of a Validated Behavioral Model. *Proceedings of the Workshop on Data Mining for User Modeling at the 11th International Conference on User Modeling 2007*, 76-80.

Baker, R. S. J. d., & de Carvalho, A. M. J. A. (2008). Labeling Student Behavior Faster and More Precisely with Text Replays.*Proceedings of the First International Conference on Educational Data Mining*, 38-47.

Banerjee, C., Kundu, A., Basu, M., Deb, P., Nag, D., & Dattagupta, R. (2013). A service based trust management classifier approach for cloud security. *2013 15th International Conference on Advanced Computing Technologies (ICACT)*, 1–5. http://doi.org/ doi:10.1109/ICACT.2013.6710519

Barbaro, M., Zeller, T., & Hansell, S. (2006). A face is exposed for aol searcher no. 4417749. *New York Times, 9.*

Barnes, T., Bitzer, D., & Vouk, M. (2005). Experimental Analysis of the Q-Matrix Method in Knowledge Discovery. Lecture Notes in Computer Science: Vol. 3488. Foundations of Intelligent Systems (pp. 603-611). Springer. doi:10.1007/11425274_62

Baumgarten, M., Mulvenna, M. D., Rooney, N., & Reid, J. (2016). Keyboard-based sentiment mining using twitter. *International Journal of Ambient Computing and Intelligence*, 56–69.

Baumgarten, M., Mulvenna, M. D., Rooney, N., Reid, J., Jansen, B. J., Zhang, M., & Hoffmann, P. et al. (2013). Keyword-Based Sentiment Mining using Twitter. *International Journal of Ambient Computing and Intelligence, 5*(2), 56–69. doi:10.4018/jaci.2013040104

Bayardo, R. J., & Agarwal, R. (2005). Data privacy through optimal k-anonymization. *Proceedings of 21st IEEE International Conference on Data Engineering (ICDE) 2005*, 217-228. doi:10.1109/ICDE.2005.42

Beck, J. E., & Mostow, J. (2008). How who should practice: Using learning decomposition to evaluate the efficacy of different types of practice for different types of students. *Proceedings of the 9th International Conference on Intelligent Tutoring Systems*, 353-362. doi:10.1007/978-3-540-69132-7_39

Bennett, J., & Lanning, S. (2007). The Netflix prize.*Proceedings of KDD cup and workshop.* 35.

Berreis, T. (2016, March 15). *Virtualisierung und Containerisierung.* Retrieved from https://wr.informatik.uni-hamburg. de/_media/teaching/wintersemester_2015_2016/nthr-1516-berreis-virtualization_and_containerization-ausarbeitung.pdf

Bertino, E., Bernstein, P., Agrawal, D., Davidson, S., Dayal, U., Franklin, M., ... Jadadish, H. V. (2011). *Challenges and Opportunities with Big Data.* Academic Press.

Bhardwaj, B. K., & Pal, S. (2012). *Data Mining: A prediction for performance improvement using classification.* arXiv preprint arXiv:1201.3418

Bhaskar, R., Laxman, S., Smith, A., & Thakurta, A. (2010). Discovering frequent patterns in sensitive data.*Proceedings of KDD*, 503-512.

Bhatt, Y., & Bhatt, C. (2017). Internet of Things in HealthCare. In Internet of Things and Big Data Technologies for Next Generation Healthcare. Springer International Publishing. doi:10.1007/978-3-319-49736-5_2

Bhatt, C., Dey, N., & Ashour, A. S. (2017). *Internet of Things and Big Data Technologies for Next Generation Healthcare.* Springer-Verlag New York Inc. doi:10.1007/978-3-319-49736-5

Bhosale, H. S., & Gadekar, D. P. (2014). A Review Paper on Big Data and Hadoop. *International Journal of Scientific and Research Publications, 4*(10), 1–7.

Bidgoli, B. M., Kashy, D., Kortemeyer, G., & Punch, W. (2003). Predicting student performance: An application of data mining methods with the educational web-based system lon-capa. *Proceedings of ASEE/IEEE frontiers in education conference.*

Big Data. (2016). Retrieved from https://en.wikipedia.org/wiki/Big_data

Blazhievsky, S. (2013). *Introduction to Hadoop and MapReduce and HDFC for Big Data Application.* SNIA Education.

Bollier, D. (2010). *The Promise and Peril of Big Data: Aspen Institute.* Washington, DC: Communications and Society Program.

Bonomi, L., & Xiong, L. (2013). A two-phase algorithm for mining sequential patterns with differential privacy. *Proceedings of 22nd ACM Conference on Information and Knowledge Management (CIKM 2013),* 269-278. doi:10.1145/2505515.2505553

Borthakur, D. (2007). The Hadoop distributed file system: Architecture and design. *Hadoop Project Website, 11,* 21.

Boyd, D., & Crawford, K. (2012). Critical questions for big data: Provocations for a cultural, technological, and scholarly phenomenon. *Information Communication and Society, 15*(5), 662–679. doi:10.1080/1369118X.2012.678878

Brewer, E. A. (2000). Towards robust distributed systems. In *Proceedings of the nineteenth annual ACM symposium on Principles of distributed computing - PODC '00* (p. 7). http://doi.org/ doi:10.1145/343477.343502

Brewer, E. (July 2000), Towards Robust Distributed Systems. *Proceedings of the 19th ACM Symposium on Principles of Distributed Computing,* 7–10.

Brown, C. (1970, January 01). *NoSql Tips and Tricks.* Retrieved from http://blog.nosqltips.com/search?q=cap%2Btheorem

Brown, B., Michael, C., & Manyika, J. (2011). Are you ready for the era of 'big data'. *The McKinsey Quarterly, 4*(1), 24–35.

Bures, V., Tucnik, P., Mikulecky, P., Mls, K., & Blecha, P. (2016). Application of ambient intelligence in educational institutions: Visions and architectures. *International Journal of Ambient of Ambient Computing and Intelligence, 7*(1), 94–120. doi:10.4018/IJACI.2016010105

Caine, K., & Hanania, R. (2013). Patients want granular privacy control over health information in electronic medical records. *Journal of the American Medical Informatics Association, 20*(1), 7–15. doi:10.1136/amiajnl-2012-001023 PMID:23184192

Casey, J. (2012, April 5). Google Trends reveals clues about the mentality of richer nations. *Ars Technica.* Retrieved from *http://arstechnica.com/gadgets/2012/04/google-trends-reveals-clues-about-the-mentality-of-richer-nations/*

Cen, H., Koedinger, K., & Junker, B. (2006). Learning Factors Analysis - A General Method for Cognitive Model Evaluation and Improvement. *Proceedings of the 8th International Conference on Intelligent Tutoring Systems,* 12-19. doi:10.1007/11774303_17

Census Bureau. (2016). *United States Census Bureau.* Retrieved from www.census.gov

Changqing, J. (2012). Big data processing in cloud computing environments. *IEEE International Symposium on Pervasive Systems, Algorithms and Networks (ISPAN)*, 17–23. doi:10.1109/I-SPAN.2012.9

Chaudhuri, S. (2012). What next? A half-dozen data management research goals for big data and the cloud. *Proceedings of the 31st Symposium on Principles of Database Systems*, 1-4. doi:10.1145/2213556.2213558

Chen, R., Acs, G., & Castelluccia, C. (2012). Differentially Private Sequential Data Publication via variable length n-grams. *Proceedings of 19th ACM Conference of Computer and Communications Security.*

Chen, R., Fung, B. C. M., Desai, B. C., & Sossou, N. (2012). Differentially private transit data publication: a case study on the Montreal transportation system. *Proceedings of 18th ACM SIGKDD international conference on Knowledge discovery and data mining (KDD 2012)*, 213-221. doi:10.1145/2339530.2339564

Chen, R., Mohammed, N., Fung, B. C. M., Desai, B. C., & Xiong, L. (2011). Publishing set valued data via differential privacy. *Proceedings of VLDB Endowment, 4*(11), 1087–1098.

Chen, Y. K. (2012, January). Challenges and opportunities of the internet of things. In *17th Asia and South Pacific Design Automation Conference* (pp. 383-388). IEEE. doi:10.1109/ASPDAC.2012.6164978

Cheung, S. (2013). Developing a big data application for data exploration and discovery. *IBM Developerworks*. Retrieved from http://www.ibm.com/developerworks/library/bd-exploration/

Chodorow. (2013). *MongoDB: The Definitive Guide*. New York, NY: O'Reilly Media.

Chu, W. W., & Leong, I. T. (1993). A transaction-based approach to vertical partitioning for relational database systems. *IEEE Transactions on Software Engineering, 19*(8), 804–812. doi:10.1109/32.238583

Clifton, C., & Tassa, T. (2013). On syntactic anonymity and differential privacy. *IEEE 29th International Conference on Data Engineering Workshops (ICDEW)*, 88–93. doi:10.1109/ICDEW.2013.6547433

Cloud Security Alliance. (2013). *Cloud Computing Vulnerability Incidents: A Statistical Overview : Cloud Security Alliance*. Retrieved June 17, 2015, from https://cloudsecurityalliance.org/download/cloud-computing-vulnerability-incidents-a-statistical-overview/

Codd, E. F. (1970). A relational model of data for large shared data banks. *Communications of the ACM, 13*(6), 377–387. doi:10.1145/362384.362685

CORDIS. (2012, September 1). *Big data public private forum* [Online forum comment]. Retrieved from http://cordis.europa.eu/project/rcn/105709_en.html

Cormode, G., Procopiuc, C., Srivastava, D., Shen, E., & Yu, T. (2012). Differentially private spatial decompositions. *Data Engineering (ICDE), 2012 IEEE 28th International Conference on*, 20–31. doi:10.1109/ICDE.2012.16

Cox, L. H. (1980). Suppression Methodology and Statistical Disclosure Control. *Journal of the American Statistical Association, 75*(370), 377–385. doi:10.1080/01621459.1980.10477481

Crockford, D. (2006). *IETF JSON RFC 4627*. Retrieved April 20, 2015, from http://tools.ietf.org/html/rfc4627

Curran, K., & Norrby, S. (2009). RFID-enabled location determination within indoor environments. *International Journal of Ambient Computing and Intelligence, 1*(4), 63–86. doi:10.4018/jaci.2009062205

Cyril, N., & Soman, A. (2015). *Big Data Analysis using Hadoop*. Academic Press.

Dalenius, T. (1986). Finding a needle in a haystack or identifying anonymous census records. *Journal of Official Statistics, 2*(3), 329–336.

Dankar, F. K., & El Emam, K. (2012). The application of differential privacy to health data. *Proceedings of the 2012 Joint EDBT/ICDT Workshops*, 158–166. doi:10.1145/2320765.2320816

Dankar, F. K., & El Emam, K. (2013). Practicing differential privacy in health care: A review. *Transactions on Data Privacy*, *6*(1), 35–67.

Data Lake. (2016). Retrieved 8 October 2016, from https://azure.microsoft.com/en-in/solutions/data-lake/

Data Scientists vs. Data Engineers. (2016). Retrieved 21 September 2016, from http://www.datasciencecentral.com/profiles/blogs/data-scientists-vs-data-engineers

DataNucleus. (2016). *DataNucleus Website*. Retrieved October 1, 2016, from http://www.datanucleus.com/

Dave, P. (2016). Retrieved from http://blog.sqlauthority.com/2013/10/02/big-data-what-is-big-data-3-vs-of-big-data-volume-velocity-and-variety-day-2-of-21/

De Montjoye, Y. A., Radaelli, L., Singh, V. K., & Pentland, A. S. (2015). Unique in the shopping mall: On the reidentifiability of credit card metadata. *Science*, *347*(6221), 536–539. doi:10.1126/science.1256297 PMID:25635097

Dean, J., & Ghemawat, S. (2008). MapReduce: Simplified data processing on large clusters. *Communications of the ACM*, *51*(1), 107–113. doi:10.1145/1327452.1327492

Deering, S. E. (1998, December). *Internet protocol, version 6 (IPv6) specification*. Academic Press.

Desmarais, M. C., Maluf, A., & Liu, J. (1996). User-expertise modeling with empirically derived probabilistic implication networks. *User Modeling and User-Adapted Interaction*, *5*(3-4), 283–315. doi:10.1007/BF01126113

Dey, N., Mukhopadhyay, S., Das, A., & Chaudhuri, S. S. (2012). Using DWT analysis of P, QRS and T components and cardiac output modified by blind watermarking technique within the electrocardiogram signal for authentication in the wireless telecardiology. *IJ Image, Graphics and Signal Processing*.

Dey, N., Dey, G., Chakraborty, S., & Chaudhuri, S. S. (2014, September). Feature analysis of blind watermarked electromyogram signal in wireless telemonitoring. In *Concepts and Trends in Healthcare Information Systems* (pp. 205–229). Springer International Publishing. doi:10.1007/978-3-319-06844-2_13

Dey, N., Dey, M., Mahata, S. K., Das, A., & Chaudhuri, S. S. (2015). Tamper detection of an electrocardiographic signal using watermarked bio–hash code in wireless cardiology. *International Journal of Signal and Imaging Systems Engineering*, *8*(1-2), 46–58. doi:10.1504/IJSISE.2015.067069

Dey, N., & Kar, Á. (2015). Image mining framework and techniques: A review. *International Journal of Image Mining*, *1*(1), 45–64. doi:10.1504/IJIM.2015.070028

Dey, N., & Santhi, V. (Eds.). (2017). *Intelligent Techniques in Signal Processing for Multimedia Security* (Vol. 660). Cham: Springer International Publishing. doi:10.1007/978-3-319-44790-2_16

Duhigg. (2012). *How Companies Learn Your Secrets*. Retrieved May 11, 2016 from http://www.nytimes.com/2012/02/19/magazine/shoppinghabits.html?pagewanted=1&_r=0

Dutch Data Protection Agency. (2014). *Google faces $18 million fine for web privacy violations: Dutch watchdog*. Retrieved from http://www.reuters.com/article/us-privacy-google-dutch-idUSKBN0JT1TG20141215

Dwork, C. (2006). Differential privacy. *Proceedings of 33rd International Colloquium*, 1-12. doi:10.1007/11787006_1

Dwork, C. (2008). An ad omnia approach to defining and achieving private data analysis. In Privacy, Security, and Trust in KDD, PinKDD 2007, (pp. 1–13). Springer. doi:10.1007/978-3-540-78478-4_1

Dwork, C., & Nissim, K. (2004). Privacy-preserving datamining on vertically partitioned databases. In Advances in Cryptology–CRYPTO 2004 (pp. 528–544). Springer. doi:10.1007/978-3-540-28628-8_32

Dwork, C. (2006). Differential privacy.*Proceedings of ICALP*, 1-12.

Dwork, C. (2008). Differential privacy: A survey of results. In *Theory and applications of models of computation* (pp. 1–19). Springer. doi:10.1007/978-3-540-79228-4_1

Dwork, C., Feldman, V., Hardt, M., Pitassi, T., Reingold, O., & Roth, A. (2015). The reusable holdout: Preserving validity in adaptive data analysis. *Science, 349*(6248), 636–638. doi:10.1126/science.aaa9375 PMID:26250683

Dwork, C., Feldman, V., Hardt, M., Pitassi, T., Reingold, O., & Roth, A. L. (2015): Preserving statistical validity in adaptive data analysis.*Proceedings of the Forty-Seventh Annual ACM on Symposium on Theory of Computing*, 117–126. doi:10.1145/2746539.2746580

Dwork, C., McSherry, F., Nissim, K., & Smith, A. (2006). Calibrating noise to sensitivity in private data analysis. In *Theory of cryptography* (pp. 265–284). Springer. doi:10.1007/11681878_14

Dwork, C., McSherry, F., Nissim, K., & Smith, A. (2006). Calibrating noise to sensitivity in private data analysis. *Proceedings of 3rd International Conference on Theory of Cryptography (TCC 06),*265-284. doi:10.1007/11681878

Dwork, C., & Roth, A. (2014). The algorithmic foundations of differential privacy. *Foundations and Trends in Theoretical Computer Science, 9*(3-4), 211–407. doi:10.1561/0400000042

Dwork, C., & Smith, A. (2010). Differential privacy for statistics: What we know and what we want to learn. *Journal of Privacy and Confidentiality, 1*(2), 2.

Edlich, S., Friedland, A., Hampe, J., Brauer, B., & Brückner, M. (2011). *NoSQL (2ⁿᵈ ed.)*. Hanser Publishing. doi:10.3139/9783446428553

El Emam, K., Mercer, J., Moreau, K., Grava-Gubins, I., Buckeridge, D., & Jonker, E. (2011). Physician privacy concerns when disclosing patient data for public health purposes during a pandemic influenza outbreak. *BMC Public Health, 11*(1), 454. doi:10.1186/1471-2458-11-454 PMID:21658256

Environmentalscience.org. (2016). *Agricultural science and GIS*. Retrieved from http://www.environmentalscience.org/agriculture-science-gis

European Countries Banning the Use of Fluoride. (n.d.). Retrieved from http://www.ecomall.com/greenshopping/fluoride4

Exploring Azure's Data Lake. (2016). Retrieved 21 September 2016, from http://tomkerkhove.ghost.io/2015/10/22/exploring-azures-data-lake/

Federal Trade Commission. (2014). *Enforcing Privacy Promises*. Retrieved from https://www.ftc.gov/news-events/media-resources/protecting-consumer-privacy/enforcing-privacy-promises

Feldman, D., Fiat, A., Kaplan, H., & Nissim, K. (2009). Private coresets. In *Proceedings of the forty-first annual ACM symposium on Theory of computing* (pp. 361-370). ACM.

Ferdinand, D. (2016). *Flexible Learning Environments: Theories*. Trends, and Issues. doi:10.13140/RG.2.1.3958.2488

Ferdinand, D., & Umachandran, K. (2016). Online assessment: Product development in academic writing. *Maha Journal of Education, 2*(1), 73–78.

Fernández, A., del Río, S., López, V., Bawakid, A., del Jesus, M., Benítez, J., & Herrera, F. (2014). Big Data with Cloud Computing: An insight on the computing environment, MapReduce, and programming frameworks. *Wiley Interdisciplinary Reviews: Data Mining and Knowledge Discovery, 4*(5), 380–409. doi:10.1002/widm.1134

Fouad, K. M., Hassan, B. M., & Hassan, M. F. (2016). User authentication based on dynamic keystroke recognition. In Information Resources Management Association (Ed.), Identity Theft: Breakthroughs in research and practice (pp. 403-437). Information Resources Management Association. doi:10.4018/IJACI.2016070101

Francis, T., Madiajagan, M., & Kumar, V. (2015). Privacy issues and techniques in e-health systems. *Proceedings of the 2015 ACM SIGMIS Conference on Computers and People Research,* 113–115.

Friedman, T., & Smith, M. (2011, October 10). *Measuring the Business Value of Data Quality.* Gartner Report.

Furht, B., Escalante, A., Jin, H., Ibrahim, S., Bell, T., Gao, W., … Wu, S. (2010). Handbook of cloud computing. In B. Furht & A. Escalante (Eds.), Handbook of Cloud Computing (pp. 3–19). Springer US. http://doi.org/ doi:10.1007/978-1-4419-6524-0

Gantz, J., & Reinsel, D. (2012). The digital universe in 2020: Big data, bigger digital shadows, and biggest growth in the far east. *IDC iView: IDC Analyze the future, 2007,* 1-16.

Gens, F., & Shirer, M. (2013). *IDC Forecasts Worldwide Public IT Cloud Services Spending to Reach Nearly $108 Billion by 2017 as Focus Shifts from Savings to Innovation.* Retrieved February 1, 2016, from http://www.idc.com/getdoc.jsp?containerId=prUS24298013

George, L. (2011). *HBase: The Definitive Guide.* Sebastopol, CA: O'Reilly Media Inc.

Gilbert, S., & Lynch, N. (2002). Brewers conjecture and the feasibility of consistent, available, partition-tolerant web services. *ACM SIGACT News, 33*(2), 51–59. doi:10.1145/564585.564601

Glenday. (2016). *Sony fined £250k over 'serious' Data Protection Act breach.* Retrieved May 2, 2016 from http://www.thedrum.com/news/2013/01/24/sony-fined-250k-over-serious-data-protection-act-breach

Google Search Statistics-Internet Live Stats. (2016). Retrieved from http://www.internetlivestats.com/google-search-statistics/

Gray, G., McGuinness, C., & Owende, P. (2014). An application of classification models to predict learner progression in tertiary education. Advance Computing Conference (IACC),2014IEEE International, 549–554. doi:10.1109/IAdCC.2014.6779384

Gray, J., & Lamport, L. (2006, March). Consensus On Transaction Commit. *ACM Transactions on Database Systems, 31*(1), 133–160. doi:10.1145/1132863.1132867

Grunerbl, A., Bahle, G., Hanser, F., & Lukowicz, P. (2013). UWB indoor location for monitoring dementia patients: The challenges and perception of a real-life deployment. *International Journal of Ambient Computing and Intelligence, 5*(4), 45–59. doi:10.4018/ijaci.2013100104

Hagan, M. T., Demuth, H. B., Beale, M. H., & De Jesus, O. (2014). *Neural Network Design* (2nd ed.). Martin Hagan.

Haifeng, Y., & Vahdat, A. (2002, August). Design and Evaluation of a Conit-Based Continuous Consistency Model for Replicated Services. *ACM Transactions on Computer Systems, 20*(3), 239–282. doi:10.1145/566340.566342

Halewood, N. J., & Surya, P. (2012). Mobilizing the agricultural value chain. In World Bank (Ed.), *2012 information and communication development* (pp. 21-43). Retrieved from http://siteresources.worldbank.org/EXTINFORMATION-ANDCOMMUNICATIONANDTECH NOLOGIES/Resources/IC4D-2012-Chapter-2.pdf

Hashem, I. A. T., Yaqoob, I., Anuar, N. B., Mokhtar, S., Gani, A., & Ullah Khan, S. (2015). The rise of big data on cloud computing: Review and open research issues. *Journal of Information Systems, 47*, 98–115. doi:10.1016/j.is.2014.07.006

Hashimoto, Y., & Day, W. (Eds.). (1991). *Mathematical and Control Applications in Agriculture and Horticulture: Conference Proceedings*. Amsterdam, Netherlands: Elsevier Science & Technology.

Health Insurance Portability and Accountability Act. (n.d.). Retrieved from http://www.hhs.gov/ocr/hipaa

Hosmer, J., & Lemeshow, S. (2004). *Applied Logistic Regression*. Hoboken, NJ: John Wiley& Sons.

Huang, Y. F., & Lai, C. J. (2016). Integrating frequent pattern clustering and branch-and-bound approaches for data partitioning. *Information Sciences, 328*, 288–301. doi:10.1016/j.ins.2015.08.047

Hurwitz, Nugent, Halper, & Kaufman. (2013). *Big Data for Dummies*. Wiley.

IBM. (2014). *International Technical Support Organization, Information Governance Principles and Practices for a Big Data Landscape*. University of Illinois.

IMO (2007). *Development of an e-Navigation Strategy*. IALA and e-navigation, sub-committee on Safety of Navigation, Report of the Correspondence Group on e-Navigation, NAV/53/13/3.

IMO (2014). *Draft E-Navigation Strategy Implementation Plan*. Report to the Maritime Safety Committee, Annex 7, NCSR 1/28.

IMO. (2009a). *Resolution MEPC.1/Circ.683, Guidelines for the development of a ship energy efficiency management plan*. SEEMP.

IMO. (2009b). *Resolution MEPC.1/Cric.684, Guidelines for the voluntary use of the ship energy efficiency operational indicator*. EEOI.

IMO. (2012). Guidelines for the development of a ship energy efficiency management plan. *Resolution MEPC., 213*(63), 2012.

Impetus. (2016). *Kundera Website*. Retrieved October 1, 2010, from https://github.com/impetus-opensource/Kundera

Internet of Things. (n.d.). Retrieved from http://www.cisco.com/c/en_in/solutions/internet-of-things/

Internet Protocol Version 4. (n.d.). Retrieved from https://en.wikipedia.org/wiki/IPv4

Inukollu, V., Arsi, S., & Ravuri, R. (2014). Security issues associated with big data in cloud computing. *International Journal of Network Security & Its Applications, 6*(3), 45–56. doi:10.5121/ijnsa.2014.6304

Ireland, C., Bowers, D., Newton, M., & Waugh, K. (2009). A Classification of Object-Relational Impedance Mismatch. In *2009 First International Conference on Advances in Databases, Knowledge, and Data Applications* (pp. 36-43). IEEE. doi:10.1109/DBKDA.2009.11

Jacks, D. (2014). *The learning analytics workgroup: A report on building the field of learning analytics for personalized learning at scale*. Retrieved from https://ed.stanford.edu/sites/default/files/law_report_executivesummary_24-pager_09-02- 2014.pdf

Jackson, J. (2016). Microsoft to offer three new ways to store big data on Azure. *Computerworld*. Retrieved 11 October 2016, from http://www.computerworld.com/article/2916719/big-data/microsoft-to-offer-three-new-ways-to-store-big-data-on-azure.html

Jackson, J. E. (1980). Principal components and factor analysis: Part i-principal components. *Journal of Quality Technology, 12*(4), 201–213.

Jain, A., & Bhatnagar, V. (2016a). Olympics Big Data prognostications. *International Journal of Rough Sets and Data Analysis*, *3*(4), 32–45. doi:10.4018/IJRSDA.2016100103

Jain, A., & Bhatnagar, V. (2016b). Movie analytics for effective recommendation system using Pig and Hadoop. *International Journal of Rough Sets and Data Analysis*, *3*(2), 82–100. doi:10.4018/IJRSDA.2016040106

Jimenez, A. (2013). *Seven big data lessons for farming*. Retrieved from http://www.e-agriculture.org/news/seven-big-data-lessons-farming

Jlassi, A., & Martineau, P. (2016). Benchmarking Hadoop Performance in the Cloud - An in Depth Study of Resource Management and Energy Consumption. *Proceedings of the 6th International Conference on Cloud Computing and Services Science*, 1-12. doi:10.5220/0005861701920201

Juels, A., & Oprea, A. (2013). New approaches to security and availability for cloud data. *Communications of the ACM*, *56*(2), 64–64. doi:10.1145/2408776.2408793

Kabra & Bichkar. (2011). Performance prediction of engineering students using decision trees. *International Journal of Computer Applications, 36*(11).

Kamal, S., Dey, N., Nimmy, S. F., Ripon, S. H., Ali, N. Y., Ashour, A. S., & Shi, F. Evolutionary framework for coding area selection from cancer data. *Neural Computing and Applications*, 1-23.

Kamal, S., Dey, N., Nimmy, S., Ripon, S., Ali, N., Ashour, A., & Shi, F. et al. (2016). Evolutionary framework for coding area selection from cancer data. *Neural Computing & Applications*. doi:10.1007/s00521-016-2513-3

Kamal, S., Ripon, S. H., Dey, N., Ashour, A. S., & Santhi, V. (2016). A MapReduce approach to diminish imbalance parameters for big deoxyribonucleic acid dataset. *Computer Methods and Programs in Biomedicine*, *131*, 191–206. doi:10.1016/j.cmpb.2016.04.005 PMID:27265059

Karaa, W. B. A., Ashour, A. S., Sassi, D. B., Roy, P., Kausar, N., & Dey, N. (2016). Medline Text Mining: An Enhancement Genetic Algorithm Based Approach for Document Clustering. In Applications of Intelligent Optimization in Biology and Medicine (pp. 267-287). Springer International Publishing.

Kausar, N., Palaniappan, S., Belhaouari, S., Abdullah, A., & Dey, N. (2015). Systematic analysis of applied data mining based optimization algorithms in clinical attribute extraction and classification for diagnosis for cardiac patients. In A. Hassanien, C. Grosan, & M. F. Tolba (Eds.), *Applications of intelligent optimization in biology and medicine* (Vol. 96, pp. 217–231). doi:10.1007/978-3-319-21212-8_9

Kendall, D., & Quill, E. (2015). A Lifetime Electronic Health Record for Every American. Washington, DC: Third Way. Available at http://www.thirdway.org/report/a-lifetime-electronic-health-record-for-every-american

Khalil, M., & Ebner, M. (2015). *Learning analytics: Principles and constraints*. Academia. Retrieved from https://www.academia.edu/13200536/Learning_Analytics_Principles_and_Constraints

Khan, M. (2014). Seven V's of Big Data understanding Big Data to extract value. *American Society for Engineering Education (ASEE Zone 1), 2014 Zone 1 Conference of the IEEE*. DOI: 10.1109/ASEEZone1.2014.6820689

Kohler, J., Simov, K., Fiech, A., & Specht, T. (2015). On The Performance Of Query Rewriting In Vertically Distributed Cloud Databases.*Proceedings of The International Conference Advanced Computing for Innovation ACOMIN 2015*.

Kohler, J., Simov, K., & Specht, T. (2015a). Analysis of the Join Performance in Vertically Distributed Cloud Databases. *International Journal of Adaptive, Resilient and Autonomic Systems*, *1*(2). doi:10.4018/IJARAS

Kohler, J., Simov, K., & Specht, T. (2015b). Analysis of the Join Performance in Vertically Distributed Cloud Databases. *International Journal of Adaptive, Resilient and Autonomic Systems*, *6*(2), 65–87. doi:10.4018/IJARAS.2015070104

Kohler, J., & Specht, T. (2012). SeDiCo - Towards a Framework for a Secure and Distributed Datastore in the Cloud. *Proceedings of Chip-to-Cloud Security Forum 2012.*

Kohler, J., & Specht, T. (2015a). Analysis of Cache Implementations in a Vertically Distributed Cloud Data Store.*Proceedings of the 3rd IEEE World Conference on Complex System.* doi:10.1109/ICoCS.2015.7483294

Kohler, J., & Specht, T. (2015b). Performance Analysis of Vertically Partitioned Data in Clouds Through a Client-Based In-Memory Key-Value Store Cache. In *Proceedings of the 8th International Conference on Computational Intelligence in Security for Information Systems*. Burgos, Spain: Springer. doi:10.1007/978-3-319-19713-5_1

Kosinski, M., Stillwell, D., & Graepl, T. (2013). Private traits and attributes are predictable from digital records of human behavior.*Proceedings of the National Academy of Sciences of the United States of America.* doi:10.1073/pnas.1218772110

Kourosh, G. (1995), *Memory Consistency Models for Shared memory Multiprocessors* (PhD thesis). Tech. Report CSL-TR-95-685, Stanford University.

Kraska, T., Hentschel, M., Alonso, G., & Kossmann, D. (2009, August). Consistency Rationing in the Cloud: Pay only When it Matters. *Proceedings of VLDB*, *2*(1), 253–264. doi:10.14778/1687627.1687657

Kreps, J., Narkhede, N. & Rao, J. (2011). *Kafka: A Distributed Messaging System for Log Processing*. Available at http://research.microsoft.com/en-us/um/people/srikanth/netdb11/netdb11papers/netdb11-final12.pdf

Kumar, R., Charu, S., & Bansal, S. (2015). Effective way to handling big data problems using NoSQL Database (MongoDB). *Journal of Advanced Database Management & Systems*, *2*(2), 42–48.

Lakshman, A., & Malik, P. (2010). Cassandra: A decentralized structured storage system. *Operating Systems Review*, *44*(2), 35. doi:10.1145/1773912.1773922

Lane, A. (2012). *Securing Big Data: Security Recommendations for Hadoop and NoSQL Environments*. Securosis, LLC. Retrieved from https://securosis.com/assets/library/reports/SecuringBigData_FINAL.pdf

Lane, A. (2013). *Security Implications Of Big Data Strategies*. Dark Reading's Database Security Tech Center Report. Retrieved from http://www.darkreading.com/risk/security-implications-of-big-data-strategies/d/d-id/1139379

Lee, D. G. Y. (2008). *Protecting patient data confidentiality using differential privacy*. Academic Press.

Lichman, M. (2013). *UCI Machine Learning Repository*. Irvine, CA: University of California, School of Information and Computer Science.

Li, N., Li, T., & Venkatsubranmanian, S. (2007). t-Closeness: Privacy beyond k-Annonymity and l-Diversity.*Proceedings of 23rd International Conference on Data Engineering (ICDE),*106-115. doi:10.1109/ICDE.2007.367856

Li, N., Qardaji, W., Su, D., & Cao, J. (2012). Privbasis: Frequent item sets mining with differential privacy. *Proceedings of VLDB*, *5*(11), 1340–1351.

Liu, J., & Wang, K. (2010). Anonymizing Transaction Data by Integrating Suppression and Generalization. *Proceedings of 14th Pacific-Asia Conference (PKDD) Advances in Knowledge Discovery and Data Mining*, 171-180. doi:10.1007/978-3-642-13657-3_20

Liu, Q., Wang, G., & Wu, J. (2014). Consistency as a service: Auditing cloud consistency. *IEEE eTransactions on Network and Service Management*, *11*(1), 25–35. doi:10.1109/TNSM.2013.122613.130411

Luk, T., Blake, M., & Silberglitt, B. (2016). *Comparing MongoDB GU*. Retrieved September 19, 2016, from https://scalegrid.io/blog/which-is-the-best-mongodb-gui/

Lv, Y., Duan, Y., Kang, W., Li, Z., & Wnag, F. Y. (2015). Traffic flow prediction with big data: A deep learning approach. *IEEE Transactions on Intelligent Transportation Systems, 16*(2), 865–873.

Mac Slocum, A. A. (2012). Big Data Now: Current Perspectives. O'Reilly Media.

Machanavajjhala, A., Kifer, D., Gehrke, J., & Venkitasubramaniam, M. (2007). l-Diversity: Privacy Beyond k-Anonymity. *ACM Transactions on Knowledge Discovery from Data, 1*(1), 1–47. doi:10.1145/1217299.1217302

Magoulas, R., & Lorica, B. (2009). *Big data: Technologies and techniques for large-scale data*. Retrieved from http://assets.en.oreilly.com/1/event/54/mdw_online_bigdata_radar_pdf.pdf

Mahalle, P., Babar, S., Prasad, N. R., & Prasad, R. (2010, July). Identity management framework towards internet of things (IoT): Roadmap and key challenges. In *International Conference on Network Security and Applications* (pp. 430-439). Springer Berlin Heidelberg. doi:10.1007/978-3-642-14478-3_43

Malik, M. B., Gazi, M. A., & Ali, R. (2012). Privacy Preserving Data Mining Techniques: Current Scenario and Future Prospects. *Proceedings of IEEE International Conference on Computer and Communication Technology (ICCCT 2012)*, 26-32. doi:10.1109/ICCCT.2012.15

Marr, B. (2014, March 2). *Big Data: The 5 Vs Everyone Must Know*. Retrieved from http://www.epmchannel.com/2015/02/02/big-data-the-5-vs-everyone-must-know/

Mason, C., Benson, H., Lehmann, J., Malhotra, M., Goldman, R., Hopkins, J., & Ochsner, K. N. et al. (2015). Engineering Kindness. *International Journal of Synthetic Emotions, 6*(1), 1–23. doi:10.4018/IJSE.2015010101

Mather, T., Kumaraswamy, S., & Latif, S. (2009). *Cloud Security and Privacy, An Enterprise Perspective on Risks and Compliance*. O'Reilly.

Mayilvaganan, M., & Kalpanadevi, D. (2014). Comparison of classification techniques for predicting the performance of students academic environment. *Communication and Network Technologies (ICCNT), 2014 International Conference on*, 113–118. doi:10.1109/CNT.2014.7062736

McManus, S. (2014). *Raspberry Pi for dummies*. John Wiley & Sons.

McSherry, F. (2009). Privacy integrated queries: an extensible platform for privacy-preserving data analysis. *Proceedings of the 2009 ACM SIGMOD International Conference on Management of data*, 19–30. doi:10.1145/1559845.1559850

McSherry, F., & Talwar, K. (2007, October). Mechanism design via differential privacy. *Proceedings of 48th Annual IEEE Symposium on Foundations of Computer Science (FOCS 07)*, 94-103. doi:10.1109/FOCS.2007.41

Meier, R., & Lee, D. (2009). Context-aware services for ambient environments. *International Journal of Ambient Computing and Intelligence, 1*(1), 1–14. doi:10.4018/jaci.2009010101

Mell, P., & Grance, T. (2011, September). *The NIST Definition of Cloud Computing*. Retrieved February 1, 2016, from http://csrc.nist.gov/publications/nistpubs/800-145/SP800-145.pdf

Meo, P. D. O. (2014, December 15). *Hadoop Lab*. SuperComputing Applications and Innovation Department. Retrieved from https://hpcforge.cineca.it/files/CoursesDev /public/2014/Tools_Techniques_Data_Analysis/presentations/Docker_NGS_lab_v1.1.pdf

Meyerson, A., & Williams, R. (2004). On the Complexity of Optimal k-annonymity. *Proceedings of Twenty Third ACM SIGMOD-SIGACT-SIGART Symposium on Principles of Database Systems*, 223-228. doi:10.1145/1055558.1055591

Miller, H.E. (2013). Big-data in cloud computing: a taxonomy of risks. *Information Research, 18*(1), paper 571. Available at http://InformationR.net/ir/18-1/paper571.html

Mohammed, N., Chen, R., Fung, B., & Yu, P. (2011). Differentially private data release for data mining. *Proceedings of the 17th ACM SIGKDD international conference on Knowledge discovery and data mining*, 493–501. doi:10.1145/2020408.2020487

Mohanpurkar, A. A., & Madhuri, S. J. (2016). A traitor identification technique for numeric relational databases with distortion minimization and collusion avoidance. *International Journal of Ambient Computing and Intelligence, 7*(2), 114–137. doi:10.4018/IJACI.2016070106

MongoDB Tutorial. (2016). Available online at: http://www.tutorialspoint.com/mongodb/

MongoDB. (2016a). *MongoDB Documentation*. Retrieved January 3, 2017, from https://docs.mongodb.com/

MongoDB. (2016b). *MongoDB Website*. Retrieved October 1, 2016, from https://www.mongodb.org/

Moniruzzaman, A. B. M., & Hossain, S. A. (2013). NoSQL Database: New Era of Databases for Big data Analytics Classification, Characteristics and Comparison. *International Journal of Database Theory and Application, 6*(4), 1–13.

Moniruzzaman, B. M., & Hossain, S. A. (2013). NoSQL Database: New Era of Databases for Big data Analytics - Classification, Characteristics and Comparison. *CoRR, 6*(4), 14.

Moon, T. K. (1996). The expectation-maximization algorithm. *Signal Processing Magazine, IEEE, 13*(6), 47–60. doi:10.1109/79.543975

Morel, G., Valckenaers, P., Faure, J., Pereira, C., & Diedrich, C. (2007). *Manufacturing plant control challenges and issues*. Retrieved from https://hal.archives-ouvertes.fr/hal-00147431/document

Nakajima, T., Ishikawa, H., Tokunaga, E., & Stajano, F. (2002, August). Technology challenges for building Internet-scale ubiquitous computing. In *Object-Oriented Real-Time Dependable Systems, 2002 (WORDS 2002)*. Proceedings of the Seventh International Workshop on (pp. 171-179). IEEE.

Narayanan, A., & Shmatikov. (2008). Robust De-anonymization of Large Sparse Datasets. *Proceedings of 2008 IEEE Symposium on Security and Privacy,* 111-125. doi:10.1109/SP.2008.33

National Science Foundation. (2012). *NSF leads federal efforts in big data*. Retrieved from http://www.nsf.gov/news/news_summ.jsp?cntn_id=123607

Navathe, S., Ceri, S., Wiederhold, G., & Dou, J. (1984, December). Vertical Partitioning Algorithms for Database Design. *ACM Transactions on Database Systems, 9*(4), 680–710. doi:10.1145/1994.2209

Nazim, M., & Mukherjee, B. (2011). Implementing knowledge management in Indian academic libraries. *Journal of Knowledge Management Practice, 12*(3). Retrieved from http://www.tlainc.com/articl269.htm

Neo Technology Incorporation. (2016). *Neo4J Website*. Retrieved October 1, 2016, from https://neo4j.com/

Neo4j. (2016). *Neo4j Documentation*. Retrieved January 3, 2017, from https://neo4j.com/docs/

Neves, B. A., Correia, M. P., Bruno, Q., Fernando, A., & Paulo, S. (2013). DepSky: Dependable and secure storage in a cloud-of-clouds. *ACM Transactions on Storage, 9*(4), 31–46. doi:10.1145/2535929

Ng, A. (2015). Mixtures of Gaussians and the EM algorithm. *Lecture Notes on Machine Learning*.

Norman, W. T. (1963). Toward an adequate taxonomy of personality attributes: Replicated factor structure in peer nomination personality rating. *Journal of Abnormal and Social Psychology, 66*(6), 574–583. doi:10.1037/h0040291 PMID:13938947

Norwig, C. (2015). *Learning Analytics can shape the future of adult learning.* Retrieved from https://ec.europa.eu/epale/en/blog/learning-analytics-can-shape-future-adult-learning

NoSQL Archive. (2016). *NoSQL Archive Website.* Retrieved February 1, 2016, from http://nosql-databases.org/

Nuaimi, Al Neyadi, Mohamed, & Al-Jaroodi. (2015). Applications of big data to smart cities. *Journal of Internet Services Applications,* 6-25.

Nusser, R., & Pelz, R. M. (2000, September28). Bluetooth-based wireless connectivity in an automotive environment. In *Vehicular Technology Conference, 2000. IEEE-VTS Fall VTC 2000. 52nd* (Vol. 4, pp. 1935-1942). IEEE. doi:10.1109/VETECF.2000.886152

O'Shaughnessy, S., & Gray, G. (2012). Development and evaluation of a dataset generator tool for generating synthetic log files containing computer attack signatures. *Pervasive and Ubiquitous Technology Innovations for Ambient Intelligence Environments,* 116.

O'Shaughnessy, S., & Gray, G. (2013). Development and evaluation of a dataset generator tool for generating synthetic log files containing computer attack signatures. In I. G. L. Global (Ed.), *Pervasive and ubiquitous technology innovations for ambient intelligence environments* (pp. 116–127). IGI Global. doi:10.4018/978-1-4666-2041-4.ch011

Odella, F. (2017). Technology studies and the sociological debate on monitoring or social interactions. In I. G. L. Global (Ed.), *Biometrics: Concepts, methodologies, and applications* (pp. 529–558). IGI Global. doi:10.4018/978-1-5225-0983-7.ch022

Odella, F., Adamic, L., Adar, E., Adkins, B., Smith, D., Barnett, K., & Wigg, J. M. et al. (2016). Technology Studies and the Sociological Debate on Monitoring of Social Interactions. *International Journal of Ambient Computing and Intelligence, 7*(1), 1–26. doi:10.4018/IJACI.2016010101

Ogunyadeka, A., Younas, M., Zhu, H., & Aldea, A. (2016, March). A Multi-key Transactions Model for NoSQL Cloud Database Systems. In *2016 IEEE Second International Conference on Big Data Computing Service and Applications (Big Data Service)* (pp. 24-27). IEEE. doi:10.1109/BigDataService.2016.32

OHSU Library. (2012). *Recommended file formats for long term data preservation.* Retrieved from http://www.ohsu.edu/xd/education/library/data/plan-and-organize/file-formats.cfm

Oladokun, V., Adebanjo, A., & Charles-Owaba, O. (2008). Predicting students academic performance using artificial neural network: A case study of an engineering course. *The Pacific Journal of Science and Technology, 9*(1), 72–79.

Olston, C., & Widom, J. (2000). Offering a Precision-Performance Tradeoff for Aggregation Queries over Replicated Data. *Proceedings of the 26th International Conference on Very Large Data Bases,* 144-155.

Oracle. (2014). *JSR 221: JDBCTM 4.0 API Specification.* Retrieved February 1, 2016, from https://jcp.org/en/jsr/detail?id=221

OShaughnessy, S., & Gray, G. (2011). Development and Evaluation of a Dataset Generator Tool for Generating Synthetic Log Files Containing Computer Attack Signatures. *International Journal of Ambient Computing and Intelligence, 3*(2), 64–76. doi:10.4018/jaci.2011040105

Oussous, A., Benjelloun, F. Z., Lahcen, A., & Belfkih, S. (2015). *Comparison and Classification of NoSQL Databases for Big Data.* Paper presented at International conference on Big Data, Cloud and Applications, Tetuan, Morocco.

Ozdenizci, B., Aydin, M. N., Coskun, V., & Ok, K. (2010, June). *NFC research framework: a literature review and future research directions.* The 14th International Business Information Management Association (IBIMA) Conference, Istanbul, Turkey.

Padhye, V. (2014). *Transaction and Data Consistency Models for Cloud Applications* (Thesis). University of Minnesota.

Panda, S. P., Mishra, S., & Das, S. (2017). An efficient intra-server and inter-server load balancing algorithm for internet distributed systems. *International Journal of Rough Sets and Data Analysis*, *4*(1), 1–18. doi:10.4018/IJRSDA.2017010101

Pavlik, P., Cen, H., Wu, L., & Koedinger, K. (2008). Using Item-Type Performance Covariance to Improve the Skill Model of an Existing Tutor. *Proceedings of the First International Conference on Educational Data Mining*, 77-86.

Peabody, D., & Goldberg, L. R. (1989). Some determinants of factor structures from personality-trait descriptor. *Journal of Personality and Social Psychology*, *57*(3), 552–567. doi:10.1037/0022-3514.57.3.552 PMID:2778639

Peleg, M., Beimel, D., Dori, D., & Denekamp, Y. (2008, December). Situation-Based Access Control: Privacy management via modeling of patient data access scenarios. *Journal of Biomedical Informatics*, *41*(6), 1028–1040. doi:10.1016/j.jbi.2008.03.014 PMID:18511349

Perera, L.P., & Guedes Soares, C. (2017). Weather Routing and Safe Ship Handling in the Future of Shipping. *Journal of Ocean Engineering*. DOI: 10.1016/j.oceaneng.2016.09.007

Perera, L. P. (2016a). Marine Engine Centered Localized Models for Sensor Fault Detection under Ship Performance Monitoring. *Proceedings of the 3rd IFAC Workshop on Advanced Maintenance Engineering, Service and Technology (AMEST'16)*. doi:10.1016/j.ifacol.2016.11.016

Perera, L. P. (2016b). Statistical Filter based Sensor and DAQ Fault Detection for Onboard Ship Performance and Navigation Monitoring Systems. *Proceedings of the 8th IFAC Conference on Control Applications in Marine Systems (CAMS 2016)*. doi:10.1016/j.ifacol.2016.10.362

Perera, L. P., & Mo, B. (2016a). Data Analytics for Capturing Marine Engine Operating Regions for Ship Performance Monitoring. *Proceedings of the 35th International Conference on Ocean, Offshore and Arctic Engineering (OMAE 2016)*. doi:10.1115/OMAE2016-54168

Perera, L. P., & Mo, B. (2016b). Marine Engine Operating Regions under Principal Component Analysis to evaluate Ship Performance and Navigation Behavior. *Proceedings of the 8th IFAC Conference on Control Applications in Marine Systems (CAMS 2016)*. doi:10.1016/j.ifacol.2016.10.487

Perera, L. P., & Mo, B. (2016d). Data Compression of Ship Performance and Navigation Information under Deep Learning. *Proceedings of the 35th International Conference on Ocean, Offshore and Arctic Engineering (OMAE 2016)*. doi:10.1115/OMAE2016-54093

Perera, L. P., & Mo, B. (2017). Marine Engine Centered Data Analytics for Ship Performance Monitoring. *Journal of Offshore Mechanics and Arctic Engineering-Transactions of The ASME*, *2017*. doi:10.1115/1.4034923

Perera, L. P., Mo, B., Kristjansson, L. A., Jonvik, P. C., & Svardal, J. O. (2015). Evaluations on Ship Performance under Varying Operational Conditions. *Proceedings of the 34th International Conference on Ocean, Offshore and Arctic Engineering (OMAE 2015)*. doi:10.1115/OMAE2015-41793

Pettey, C., & Goasduff, L. (2011). *Gartner Says Solving "Big Data" Challenge Involves More Than Just Managing Volumes of Data.* Retrieved from http://www.gartner.com/newsroom/id/1731916

Pezeshkirad, G., Hajihashemi, Z., & Chizari, M. (2014). Use of Computer and Internet in Agricultural Extension as perceived by Extension Workers. *International Journal of Agricultural Management and Development*, *4*(4), 277–285. Retrieved from http://www.scopemed.org/?mno=177470

Phansalkar, S. P., & Dani, A. R. (2015b). Tunable consistency guarantees of selective data consistency model. *Journal of Cloud Computing*, *4*(1), 1.

Phansalkar, S., & Dani, A. (2015a). Predictive models for consistency index of a data object in a replicated distributed database System'. *WSEAS Transactions on Computers*, *14*, 395–401.

Post, F. H., Nielson, G. M., & Bonneau, G.-P. (2002). *Data Visualization: The State of the Art*. Research paper TU delft.

Postgre, S. Q. L. (2016). *The world's most advanced open source database*. Available online at https://www.postgresql.org/

Privacy Protection for Social Networking APIs. (2016). Retrieved April 10, 2016 from https://www.cs.virginia.edu/felt/privacy/

Qardaji, W., Yang, W., & Li, N. (2013). Differentially private grids for geospatial data.*Proceedings of 29th IEEE International Conference on Data Engineering (ICDE 2013)*,757-768. doi:10.1109/ICDE.2013.6544872

Rabbany, R., Takaffoli, M., & Zaıane, O. R. (2011). Social network analysis and mining tosupp ort the assessment of on-line student participation. *SIGKDD Explorations*, *13*(2), 20–29. doi:10.1145/2207243.2207247

Ranjan, N. (2015, January 03). *NoSQL database - Different types of NoSQL database*. Retrieved from http://www.devinline.com/2015/01/nosql-intorduction.html

Read, S. J., Monroe, B. M., Brownstein, A. L., Yang, Y., Chopra, G., & Miller, L. C. (2010). A neural network model of the structure and dynamics of human personality. *Psychological Review*, *117*(1), 61–92. doi:10.1037/a0018131 PMID:20063964

Redding, D., Florescu, D., & Kossmann, D. (2009, March). Rethinking Cost and Performance of Database Systems. *SIGMOD Record*, *38*(1), 43–48. doi:10.1145/1558334.1558339

RedHat. (2015). *Getting started with Hibernate OGM*. Retrieved February 1, 2016, from http://hibernate.org/ogm/documentation/getting-started/

RedHat. (2016a). *Hibernate OGM Documentation*. Retrieved October 1, 2016, from http://hibernate.org/ogm/documentation/

RedHat. (2016b). *ORM Hibernate Documentation*. Retrieved February 1, 2016, from http://hibernate.org/orm/documentation/5.0/

Redislab. (2016). *Redis Website*. Retrieved October 1, 2016, from http://redis.io/

RethinkDB. (n.d.). *The open-source database for the realtime web*. Available online at: https://www.rethinkdb.com/

Rhee, S. (2016, April). Catalyzing the Internet of Things and smart cities: Global City Teams Challenge. In *Science of Smart City Operations and Platforms Engineering (SCOPE) in partnership with Global City Teams Challenge (GCTC) (SCOPE-GCTC), 2016 1st International Workshop on* (pp. 1-4). IEEE.

Ricardo, C. M., & Susan, D. (2016). *Databases Illuminated* (3rd ed.). San Diego, CA: Jones & Bartlett Learning.

Ripon, S. H., Kamal, S., Hossain, S., & Dey, N. (2016). Theoretical analysis of different classifiers under reduction rough data set: A brief proposal. *International Journal of Rough Sets and Data Analysis*, *3*(3), 1–20. doi:10.4018/IJRSDA.2016070101

Rodesth, O. J. (2016). *Sustainable and Competitive Cyber-Shipping through Industry 4.0*. Singapore Maritime Sustainability Forum 2016: Smart Maritime Solutions and Overcoming Challenges, Suntec City, Singapore.

Rodesth, O. J. (2011). *A maritime ITS architecture for e-navigation and e-maritime: Supporting environment friendly ship transport*. IEEE ITS Conference.

Rodseth, O. J., Perera, L. P., & Mo, B. (2016). Big data in shipping - Challenges and opportunities. *Proceedings of the 15th International Conference on Computer Applications and Information Technology in the Maritime Industries (COMPIT 2016)*.

Romero, C., Ventura, S., Espejo, P. G., & Hervas, C. (2008). Data mining algorithms to classify students in Educational Data Mining. *Transactions on Educational Data Mining, 22*, 122–130.

Roy, D. (2013, May 22). The unvarnished truth about big data. *Computerworld*. Retrieved from http://www.computerworld.in/feature/unvarnished-truth-about-big-data-103412013

Saleh, E., & Meinel, C. (2013). HPISecure: Towards data confidentiality in cloud applications. In *Proceedings - 13th IEEE/ACM International Symposium on Cluster, Cloud, and Grid Computing, CCGrid 2013* (pp. 605–609). http://doi.org/ doi:10.1109/CCGrid.2013.109

Saleh, M. A., Awada, A., Belnap, N., Perloff, M., Bonnefon, J.-F., Longin, D., & Casacuberta, D. et al. (2016). A Logical Model for Narcissistic Personality Disorder. *International Journal of Synthetic Emotions, 7*(1), 69–87. doi:10.4018/IJSE.2016010106

Sang, T. (2013). A log-based approach to make digital forensics easier on cloud computing. In *Proceedings of the 2013 3rd International Conference on Intelligent System Design and Engineering Applications, ISDEA 2013* (pp. 91–94). http://doi.org/ doi:10.1109/ISDEA.2012.29

Sarathy, R., & Muralidhar, K. (2011). Evaluating Laplace noise addition to satisfy differential privacy for numeric data. *Transactions on Data Privacy., 4*(1), 1–17.

Sarna, G., & Bhatia, M. P. S. (2016). An Approach to Distinguish Between the Severity of Bullying in Messages in Social Media. *Violence and Society: Breakthroughs in Research and Practice: Breakthroughs in Research and Practice, 160*.

Sarna, G., & Bhatia, M. P. S. (2016). An approach to distinguish between the severity of bullying in messages in social media. *International Journal of Rough Sets and Data Analysis, 3*(4), 1–20. doi:10.4018/IJRSDA.2016100101

Saurabh, K. (2016). *Safe computing: University of Michigan sensitive data guide and Personally Identifiable Information (PII)*. Retrieved from http://safecomputing.umich.edu/dataguide/?q=node/89

Schalkoff, R. (1997). *Artificial Neural Networks* (1st ed.). New York: McGraw-Hill.

Schenker, A. (2003). *Graph-Theoretic Techniques for Web Content Mining* (PhD thesis). University of South Florida.

Shacklock, X. (2016). *From bricks to clicks: The potential of data and analytics in higher education*. Retrieved from http://www.policyconnect.org.uk/hec/sites/site_hec/files/report/419/fieldreportdownload/frombric kstoclicks-hecreportforweb.pdf

Sharma, U. C. A. (2013, October 22). *Karniti Part 7: Agricultural income and some misbeliefs under I.T*. Retrieved from http://www.caclubindia.com/articles/karniti-part-7-agricultural-income-some- misbeliefs-under-i-t-18678.asp

Shekar, M., & Otto, K. (2012). ICTs for health in Africa. In E. Yonazi, T. Kelly, N. Halewood, & C. Blackman (Eds.), *eTransform Africa: The transformational use of ICTs in Africa*. Retrieved from http://www.cmamforum.org/Pool/Resources/ICTs-health-Africa-2014.pdf

Shelby, Z., & Bormann, C. (2011). *6LoWPAN: The wireless embedded Internet* (Vol. 43). John Wiley & Sons.

Shen, E., & Yu, T. (2013). Mining frequent graph patterns with differential privacy.*Proceedings of 12th ACM SIGKDD International Conference on Knowledge Discovery and Data Mining (KDD 2013)*, 545-553. doi:10.1145/2487575.2487601

Shih, B., Koedinger, K. R., & Scheines, R. (2008). A Response-Time Model for Bottom-Out Hints as Worked Examples. *Proceedings of the First International Conference on Educational Data Mining*, 117-126.

Shyni, S., Joshitta, R. S. M., & Arockiam, L. (2016). Applications of Big Data Analytics for Diagnosing Diabetic Mellitus: Issues and Challenges. *International Journal of Recent Trends in Engineering & Research*, *02*(06), 454–461.

Silberschatz, A., Korth, H., & Sudarshan, S. (1997). *Database System Concepts* (Vol. 4). Singapore: McGraw Hill.

Simo, H. (2015). *Big Data: Opportunities and Privacy Challenges*. Cornell University Library. arXiv:1502.00823v1

Solove, D. J. (2010). *Understanding Privacy*. Harvard University Press.

Sood, S. K. (2012). A combined approach to ensure data security in cloud computing. *Journal of Network and Computer Applications*, *35*(6), 1831–1838. doi:10.1016/j.jnca.2012.07.007

Stansbury, M. (2016, May 9). *e-Campus News: 3 blossoming fields of study with massive potential*. Retrieved from http://www.ecampusnews.com/technologies/fields-of-study/

Statista. (2016). *The statistics portal*. Retrieved May 2, 2016 from http://www.statista.com/ statistics/273018/number-of-internet-users-worldwide/

Stinson, D. R. (2005). *Cryptography Theory and Practice* (3rd ed.). CRC Press.

Strasser, G., Takagi, K., Werner, S., Hollenbach, U., Tanaka, T., Yamamoto, K., & Hirota, K. (2015). A verification of the ITTC/ISO speed/power trials analysis. *Journal of Marine Science and Technology*, *20*(1), 2–13. doi:10.1007/s00773-015-0304-7

Subramanian, S. (2016, May 19). *A Primer on Open-Source NoSQL Databases - DZone Database*. Retrieved from https://dzone.com/articles/a-primer-on-open-source-nosql-databases

Subramanya, S. (2016). Evaluating and Deploying Sql-On-Hadoop Tool. *Bay Area Big Data Meetup*.

Sujansky, V., Faus, S. A., Stone, E., & Brennan, P. F. (2010). A method to implement fine-grained access control for personal health records through standard relational database queries. *Journal of Biomedical Informatics*, *43*(5Suppl), S46–S50. doi:10.1016/j.jbi.2010.08.001 PMID:20696276

Supplementary Account Opening Form by SBI. (2015). Retrieved May 5, 2016 from https://oaa.onlinesbi.com/sbijava/pdf/Supplimentary Form.pdf

Su, S., Xu, S., Ceng, X., Li, Z., & Wang, F. (2015, July). Differentially private frequent item set mining via transaction splitting. *IEEE Transactions on Knowledge and Data Engineering*, *27*(7), 1875–1891. doi:10.1109/TKDE.2015.2399310

Sweency, L. (2002). K-Anonymity: A Model for protecting privacy. *International Journal of Uncertainty, Fuzziness and Knowledge-based Systems*, *10*(5), 557–570. doi:10.1142/S0218488502001648

Sweeney. (2002). k-anonymity: A model for protecting privacy. *International Journal of Uncertainty, Fuzziness and Knowledge-Based Systems*, *10*(5), 557–570.

Talia, D. (2013). Clouds for scalable big data analytics. *Journal IEEE Computer Society*, *46*(5), 98–101. doi:10.1109/MC.2013.162

Tamane. (2015). Text Analytics for Big Data. *International Journal of Modern Trends in Engineering and Research, 2*(3).

Tamane. (2016). *Non-relational databases in big data.* 2nd International Conference on ICT for Competitive Strategies, Udaipur, India.

Tanenbaum, A., & Van, M. (2007). *Distributed System* (2nd ed.). Pearson Prentice Hall.

Tapia, D. I., & Corchado, J. M. (2010). *An ambient intelligence based multi-agent system for Alzheimer health care.* Retrieved from https://pdfs.semanticscholar.org/169e/2cc3edcdabe237c4b7b7bedb766734020c40.pdf

Tauro, C. J. M., Patil, B. R., & Prashanth, K. R. (2013). *A Comparative Analysis of Different NoSQL Databases on Data Model, Query Model and Replication Model.* Paper presented at International Conference on Emerging Research in Computing, Information, Communication and Applications, ERCICA 2013, Bangalore, India.

Tchepnda, C., Moustafa, H., Labiod, H., & Bourdon, G. (2009). Vehicular Networks Security. *International Journal of Ambient Computing and Intelligence, 1*(1), 39–52. doi:10.4018/jaci.2009010104

Tene, O., & Polonetsky, J. (2012). Response: Privacy in the Age of Big Data: A Time for Big Decisions. *Stanford Law Review.* Retrieved from http://www.stanfordlawreview.org/online/privacy-paradox/big-data

The Digital Enterprise A Framework for Transformation. (n.d.). Available at http://www.tcs.com/SiteCollectionDocuments/Perspectives/The-Digital-Enterprise-Vol-5-1013-1.pdf

The Top 20 Valuable Facebook Statistics . (2016). Retrieved March 2016 from https://zephoria.com /top-15-valuable-facebook-statistics/

To, H., Ghinita, G., & Shahabi, C. (2014). A framework for protecting worker location privacy in spatial crowd sourcing. *Proceedings of VLDB Endowment, 7*(10), 919–930. doi:10.14778/2732951.2732966

TPC. (2003). *TPC Benchmark W (Web Commerce) Specification Version 2.0r.* Retrieved February 1, 2016, from http://www.tpc.org/tpcw/default.asp

Transaction Processing Performance Council. (n.d.). *TPC benchmark C standard specification, revision 5.11.* Available online at: http://www.tpc.org/tpcc/

Truică, C. O., Boicea, A., & Trifan, I. (2013). *CRUD Operations in MongoDB.* Paper presented at International Conference on Advanced Computer Science and Electronics Information (ICACSEI 2013). doi:10.2991/icacsei.2013.88

Truica, C. O., Radulescu, F., & Boicea, A. (2015). *Performance Evaluation for CRUD Operations in Asynchronously Replicated Document Oriented Database.* Paper presented at International Conference on Controlled Systems and Computer Science(CSCS). doi:10.1109/CSCS.2015.32

Tutorial: Get started with Azure Data Lake Analytics U-SQL language. (2016). Retrieved 21 September 2016, from https://azure.microsoft.com/en-in/documentation/articles/data-lake-analytics-u-sql-get-started/

U.S. Department of Education. (2012). *Enhancing teaching and learning through educational data mining and learning analytics: An issue brief.* Retrieved October 13, 2016, from https://tech.ed.gov/wp-content/uploads/2014/03/edm-la-brief.pdf

UK Government, Department for Business, Innovation & Skills. (2015). *Combined triennial review of the industry training boards (Construction, Engineering Construction and Film) Final Report, December 2015.* Retrieved from https://www.gov.uk/government/uploads/system/uploads/attachment_data/file/485876/BIS-15-686-combined-triennial-review-of-the-industry-training-boards-December-2015.pdf

Union of Concerned Scientists. (n.d.). *Renewable Energy and Agriculture: A Natural Fit.* Retrieved from http://www.ucsusa.org/clean_energy/smart-energy-solutions/increase-renewables/renewable- energy-and.html#.V7_kQDUXVf4

Vaassen & Daelemans. (2010). Emotion classification in a serious game for training communication skills. *LOT Occasional Series, 16*, 155-168.

Vallverdú, J., Shah, H., & Casacuberta, D. (2010). Chatterbox challenges as a test-bed for synthetic emotions. *Creating Synthetic Emotions through Technological and Robotic Advancements*, 118-144.

Vallverdú, J., Shah, H., & Casacuberta, D. (2010). Chatterbox Challenge as a Test-Bed for Synthetic Emotions. *International Journal of Synthetic Emotions, 1*(2), 12–37. doi:10.4018/jse.2010070102

Vorhies, B. (2014, July 23). *Lesson 5: Key value stores (aka 'tuple' stores)*. Retrieved from http://data-magnum.com/lesson-5-key-value-stores-aka-tuple-stores/

Vu, D., & Slavkovi, A. (2009). Differential privacy for clinical trial data: Preliminary evaluations. *Data Mining Workshops, 2009. ICDMW'09. IEEE International Conference on*, 138–143.

Wang, B., Chow, S. S. M., Li, M., & Li, H. (2013). Storing shared data on the cloud via security-mediator. In *Proceedings - International Conference on Distributed Computing Systems* (pp. 124–133). http://doi.org/ doi:10.1109/ICDCS.2013.60

Wang, T., & Mitrovic, A. (2002). Using neural networks to predict student's performance. *Computers in Education, 2002. Proceedings. International Conference on*, 969–973. doi:10.1109/CIE.2002.1186127

Wang, C., Chow, S. S. M., Wang, Q., Ren, K., & Lou, W. (2013). Privacy-preserving public auditing for secure cloud storage. *IEEE Transactions on Computers, 62*(2), 362–375. doi:10.1109/TC.2011.245

Wang, J., Liu, S., & Li, Y. (2015). A review of differential privacy in individual data release. *International Journal of Distributed Sensor Networks, 2015*, 1. doi:10.1155/2015/743160

Wang, X., Gao, L., & Mao, S. (2016). Pandey, S., CSI-based Fingerprinting for Indoor Localization: A Deep Learning Approach. *IEEE Transactions on Vehicular Technology*.

Warwick, K., & Shah, H. (2014). Outwitted by the hidden: Unsure emotions. *International Journal of Synthetic Emotions, 5*(1), 46–59. doi:10.4018/ijse.2014010106

Wehrspann, W. (2016, April 12). Industry Insider: Robb Fraley. *Farm Industry News*. Retrieved from http://farmindustrynews.com/crop-protection/industry-insider-robb-fraley

Weinstein, R. (2005, August). RFID: A technical overview and its application to the enterprise. *IT Professional, 7*(3), 27–33. doi:10.1109/MITP.2005.69

Weiser, M. (1991, September). The computer for the 21st century. *Scientific American, 265*(3), 94–104. doi:10.1038/scientificamerican0991-94 PMID:1675486

Yadav, C., Wang, S., & Kumar, M. (2013). *Algorithm and approaches to handle large data-a survey*. arXiv preprint arXiv:1307.5437

Yang, L., Chen, Y., Zuo, W., Nguyen, T., Gurumani, S., Rupnow, K., & Chen, D. (2015, November). System-level design solutions: Enabling the IoT explosion. In *ASIC (ASICON), 2015 IEEE 11th International Conference on* (pp. 1-4). IEEE.

Yeh, Y. H. (2016). Dockerized Hadoop Platform and Recent Updates in Apache Bigtop: Apache Big Data. Vancouver: Academic Press.

Yildiz, M., Abawajy, J., Ercan, T., & Bernoth, A. (2009). A layered security approach for cloud computing infrastructure. In *I-SPAN 2009 - The 10th International Symposium on Pervasive Systems, Algorithms, and Networks* (pp. 763–767). http://doi.org/ doi:10.1109/I-SPAN.2009.157

Yonazi, E., Kelly, T., Halewood, N., & Blackman, C. (Eds.). (2012). *eTransform Africa: The Transformational Use of Information and Communication Technologies in Africa*. Retrieved from http://www.gsdrc.org/document-library/etransform-africa-the-transformational-use-of- information-and-communication-technologies-in-africa/

Zappi, P., Lombriser, C., Benini, L., & Tröster, G. (2012). Collecting datasets from ambient intelligence environments. *Innovative Applications of Ambient Intelligence: Advances in Smart Systems: Advances in Smart Systems*, 113.

Zappi, P., Benini, L., & Troster, G. (2012). Collecting datasets from ambient intelligence environments. In I. G. L. Global (Ed.), *Innovative applications of ambient intelligence: Advances in smart systems* (pp. 113–127). IGI Global. doi:10.4018/978-1-4666-0038-6.ch009

Zappi, P., Lombriser, C., Benini, L., Tröster, G., Baldauf, M., Dustdar, S., & Starner, T. E. et al. (2010). Collecting Datasets from Ambient Intelligence Environments. *International Journal of Ambient Computing and Intelligence*, 2(2), 42–56. doi:10.4018/jaci.2010040103

Zeng, C., Naughton, J. R., & Cai, J. V. (2012). On differentially private frequent item set mining. *Proceedings of VLDB*, 6(1), 26–36.

Zenodo. (2016, October 20). *Legal interoperability of research data: Principles and implementation guidelines*. Retrieved from https://zenodo.org/record/162241#.WHPHE_2FOic

Zhang, J., Wang, F. Y., Wang, K., Lin, W. H., Xu, X., & Chen, C. (2011). Data-Driven Intelligent Transportation Systems: ASurvey, . *IEEE Transactions on Intelligent Transportation Systems*, 12(4), 1624–1639.

Zhang, C., & Zhang, Z. (2003). Trading Replication Consistency for Performance and Availability: an Adaptive Approach. *Proceedings of the 23rd International Conference on Distributed Computing Systems*, 687-695.

Zhang, X., Meng, X., & Chen, R. (2013). Differentially Private Set-Valued Data Release against Incremental Updates. *Proceedings of 18th International Conference Database Systems for Advanced Applications*, 392-406.

About the Contributors

Sharvari Tamane, Ph.D, is an Associate Professor in the Department of Information Technology in MGMs Jawaharlal Nehru Engineering College, Aurangabad, Maharashtra, India. She has been appointed as a coordinator for BE and BTech in Computer Science & Engineering', 'Information Technology' and MCA branches for Dr. Babasaheb Ambedkar Marathwada University, Aurangabad. Her research interests include: Big Data Analytics, Watermarking, Neural Network, Fuzzy Logic, Wavelet analysis, etc. She is author of a book, Data Structures Using C and published more than 30 research papers in international conferences and journals. She has 20 years of teaching experience in Jawaharlal Nehru Engineering College, Aurangabad. She is a life member of ISTE, IETE, IEEE and CSI. She has also worked as an Editorial Board Member & Reviewer for many SCIE, Scopus indexed journals. She has also been invited for various institutes to deliver guest lecture talks on various research areas.

Vijender Kr Solanki is PhD research scholar in the department of CSE at Anna University, Chennai. Vijender has done B.Sc., M.C.A and M.E from Institution affiliated with Maharishi Dayanand University, Rohtak (MDU) Haryana, India in 2001, 2004 and 2007. Vijender has attended an orientation program at UGC-Academic Staff College, University of Kerala and a refresher course at IIIT-Allahabad. In addition, Vijender has participated in more than 15+ seminars, summits and conferences at various national & international levels, including IIT-Delhi, Bharathiar University, Coimbatore and Anna University, Chennai. Vijender has published 08 technical papers in the different journals & conference sponsored by IEEE, Springer, and Elsevier. Research interest includes Big Data, Smart city, Network security, and management. Vijender has 9 Years of rich academic experience with different institutions like Apeejay, KSRCE. Vijender has delivered many technical lectures in various institutions including AICTE Sponsored SDP-FDP Lectures at SETS, Pune, SNS College, Coimbatore and DAVIM, Faridabad. Vijender has also delivered lecture key note speaker in national and international conferences. Vijender is a reviewer of many SCIE, Scopus indexed Journals.

Nilanjan Dey, PhD., is an Asst. Professor in the Department of Information Technology in Techno India College of Technology, Rajarhat, Kolkata, India. He holds an honorary position of Visiting Scientist at Global Biomedical Technologies Inc., CA, USA and Research Scientist of Laboratory of Applied Mathematical Modeling in Human Physiology, Territorial Organization Of- Sgientifig And Engineering Unions, BULGARIA, Associate Researcher of Laboratoire RIADI, University of Manouba, TUNISIA. He is the Editor-in-Chief of International Journal of Ambient Computing and Intelligence (IGI Global), US, International Journal of Rough Sets and Data Analysis (IGI Global), US, Series Editor of Advances in Geospatial Technologies (AGT) Book Series, (IGI Global), US, Executive Editor of International

Journal of Image Mining (IJIM), Inderscience, Regional Editor-Asia of International Journal of Intelligent Engineering Informatics (IJIEI), Inderscience and Associated Editor of International Journal of Service Science, Management, Engineering, and Technology, IGI Global. He has 15 books and 200 international conferences and journal papers. https://www.researchgate.net/profile/Nilanjan_Dey3.

* * *

Rashmi Agrawal is working as an Associate Professor and Head of Department- Department of Computer Applications in Manav Rachna International University Faridabad. She is having a rich teaching experience of more than 14 years in the area of computer science and applications. She is UGC-NET(CS) qualified. She has completed M.Phil, MTech, MSc and MBA(IT). She has completed her PhD in the area of Machine Learning. Her area of expertise includes Artificial Intelligence, Machine Learning, Data Mining and Operating System. She has published more than 20 research papers in various National and International conferences and Journals. She has organized various Faculty Development Programmes and participated in workshops and Faculty development Programmes. She is actively involved in research activities. She is life time member of CSI (Computer Society of India). She has been member of Technical Programme Committee in various conferences of repute.

Abhijeet Dabre is Teaching Associate in Department of Computer Engineering at STESs Smt. Kashibai Navale College of Engineering, Pune. He has obtained his B.E in Computer Engineering from Pune University, Pune, India. Currently, he is pursuing his Masters in Computer Engineering at STESs Smt. Kashibai Navale College of Engineering, Pune.

Ajay Dani has obtained M.Tech in Computer Science from IIT, Kharagpur and Ph.D. from Hyderabad Central University. Working as Professor in Computer Engineering Department. Completed M.Tech. (Computer Science) from IIT, Kharagpur.

S. A. Demurjian is a Full Professor in Computer Science & Engineering at the University of Connecticut, and co-Director of Research Informatics for the Biomedical Informatics Division, with research interests of: secure-software engineering, security for biomedical applications, and security-web architectures. Dr. Demurjian has over 160 archival publications, in the following categories: 1 book, 2 edited collections, 65 journal articles and book chapters, and 99 refereed conference/workshop articles.

R. R. Deshmukh is currently working as Professor & Head in Dept. of CSIT, Dr. B.A.M. University, Aurangabad, (MS), India. He is Fellow & Chairman of IETE (Aurangabad Chapter). He is a Life Member of ISCA, CSI, ISTE, IAEng, CSTA, IDES, Senior Member ACEE & Member of IEEE. His areas of specialization are Human Computer Interaction, Digital Speech Signal processing, Computational Auditory Scene Analysis (CASA), Neural Networks etc.

Ritesh A. Gangwal is currently working as Software Engineer in an MNC. His work area includes Medical Image Processing, Machine Learning, Big Data.

Markus Gumbel is a professor for Medical Informatics at the Faculty for Informatics. His interests are the development of medical software systems, in particular bioinformatics applications and computer simulations of tissue and cells.

Neha Gupta is currently working as an Assistant professor, Faculty of Computer Applications at Manav Rachna International University, Faridabad campus. She has done her PhD from Manav Rachna International University, Faridabad . She has total of 11+ year of experience in teaching and research. She is a Life Member of ACM CSTA, Tech Republic and Professional Member of IEEE. She has authored and coauthored 18 research papers in SCI/SCOPUS/Peer Reviewed Journals and IEEE/IET Conference proceedings in areas of Web Content Mining, Mobile Computing, and Web Content Adaptation. Her research interests include ICT in Rural Development, Web Content Mining, Cloud Computing, Data Mining and NoSQL Databases. She is a technical programme committee (TPC) member in various conferences across globe. She is an active reviewer for International Journal of Computer and Information Technology and in various IEEE Conferences around the world. She is one of the Editorial and review board members in International Journal of Research in Engineering and Technology.

Trupti Kenekar has completed ME (Computer Engineering) from GHRIET, Wagholi, Pune under Savitribai Phule Pune University.

Jens Kohler is a researcher at the Faculty of Informatics at the Institute for Enterprise Computing in Mannheim. His research focus is Cloud Computing, Distributed Systems and Distributed Databases.

Sonali Kothari is pursuing PhD from Sant Gadge Baba Amravati University in Computer Engineering and Technology (Area of Research – Cyber Security). Completed Post Graduate Diploma in Information Technology (PGDIT), in 2012 from Symbiosis Center for Distance Learning, Pune, Maharashtra in First Class. Certified as Red Hat Certified Engineer (RHCE), Red Hat Inc. U.S.A., in November 2008. Completed MongoDB for Java Developer (M101J) and MongoDB for Python (M101P) certification from MongoDB Univdersity. Currently Working as Assistant Professor in Department of Computer Engineering in Engineering College Filed 3 IPRs in 2016. Worked as Project Coordinator for Department of Computer Engineering and guided 50+ students UG and 8+ PG students for project. Worked as HoD of Department and PG coordinator Published 2 books for Engineering and BSc students Worked as DCOE (Departmental Controller of Examination), DSB (Departmental Subject Board) Member. Worked as Student Association In-charge and organized various state and national level events under student association. Worked as Paper Setter and Checker for UG and PG Trained students for International Certifications Published 15+ papers in National/International Conference/Journals. Attended/organized various workshops/seminars/lectures for UG/PG students and engineering faculties.

Christian Richard Lorenz is a student of enterprise computing at the University of Applied Sciences in Mannheim. His research interest belongs especially to quality management and software testing of distributed systems most notably in the setting of Cloud Computing and Big Data.

Emmanuel M is currently working as Professor & Head in Dept of I.T, Pune Institute of Computer Technology, Pune, (M.S), India. His area of specialization are Database and Medical Image Processing.

Sandesh Mahamure is Teaching Associate in Department of Computer Engineering at STESs Smt. Kashibai Navale College of Engineering, Pune. He has obtained his B.E. in Information Technology from Shivaji University, Kolhapur, India. Currently, he is pursuing his Masters in Computer Engineering at STESs Smt.Kashibai Navale College of Engineering, Pune.

Brage Mo received the M.Sc. degree in Mechanical Engineering from the Norwegian University of Science and Technology in 1991. Currently, he is a Senior Research Scientist at Norwegian Marine Technology Research Institute (MARINTEK), Trondheim, Norway and his research interests include Maritime Systems, Energy Systems Efficiency, Emission Reduction Technologies, Instrumentation, Performance Monitoring and Maintenance.

Marmar Moussa is a Ph.D. student at the Computer Science & Engineering department at the University of Connecticut. Her research interests include machine learning, big data technologies, predictive analytics and differential privacy.

L. P. Perera received the B.Sc. and M.Sc. degrees in Mechanical Engineering and Systems & Controls from Oklahoma State University, Stillwater, Oklahoma, USA, in 1999 and 2001, and the Ph.D. degree in Naval Architecture and Marine Engineering from Technical University of Lisbon, Lisbon, Portugal, in 2012, respectively. He has won Doctoral and Postdoctoral Fellowships from the Portuguese Foundation for Science and Technology in 2008 and 2012. Currently, he is a Research Scientist at the Norwegian Marine Technology Research Institute (MARINTEK), Trondheim, Norway and his research interests include Maritime and Offshore Systems, Instrumentation, Intelligent Guidance & Control, Condition Monitoring and Condition based Maintenance, Energy Efficiency, Safety, Risk and Reliability.

Shraddha Phansalkar is Associate Professor in the Faculty of Computer Engineering at Symbiosis International University, Pune. Her research areas include Cloud Consistency model, Big data analytics and predictive modelling.

Kiril Simov is an Associate Professor at Linguistic Modelling Department, IICT, Bulgarian Academy of Sciences, Sofia, Bulgaria. His research interests are in the areas of Computational Linguistics, Knowledge Representation, Ontologies, Language Resources and related areas.

Thomas Specht is a professor at the Faculty for Informatics and leads the Institute for Enterprise Computing. His research focus is on Distributed Systems, Cloud Computing and Component-based Systems.

Krishnan Umachandran is a Corporate Consulting Academic (CCA) with over 28 years of business and consulting experience beginning as Shop Floor Engineer. He has done consulting for a spectrum of industries to include Beverages, Batteries, Chemicals, Tiles, Leather, Manufacturing, Facilities, IT, and

ITES. His personal quest is to expand boundaries using human potential. His major strengths include pedagogy; market promotions and customer retention; leadership and management; and organization building and development.

Snehal P. Wadibhasme is post graduate student in Department of Computer Engineering at STESs Smt. Kashibai Navale College of Engineering, Pune, India. She has obtained B.E. in Computer Engineering from Rashtrasant Tukadoji Maharaj Nagpur, India.

Index

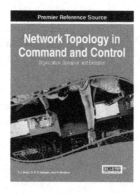

Stay Current on the Latest Emerging Research Developments

Become an IGI Global Reviewer for Authored Book Projects

The overall success of an authored book project is dependent on quality and timely reviews.

In this competitive age of scholarly publishing, constructive and timely feedback significantly decreases the turnaround time of manuscripts from submission to acceptance, allowing the publication and discovery of progressive research at a much more expeditious rate. Several IGI Global authored book projects are currently seeking highly qualified experts in the field to fill vacancies on their respective editorial review boards:

Applications may be sent to:
development@igi-global.com

Applicants must have a doctorate (or an equivalent degree) as well as publishing and reviewing experience. Reviewers are asked to write reviews in a timely, collegial, and constructive manner. All reviewers will begin their role on an ad-hoc basis for a period of one year, and upon successful completion of this term can be considered for full editorial review board status, with the potential for a subsequent promotion to Associate Editor.

If you have a colleague that may be interested in this opportunity, we encourage you to share this information with them.

Encyclopedia of Information Science and Technology, Third Edition (10 Vols.)

Mehdi Khosrow-Pour, D.B.A. (Information Resources Management Association, USA)
ISBN: 978-1-4666-5888-2; **EISBN:** 978-1-4666-5889-9; © 2015; 10,384 pages.

The **Encyclopedia of Information Science and Technology, Third Edition** is a 10-volume compilation of authoritative, previously unpublished research-based articles contributed by thousands of researchers and experts from all over the world. This discipline-defining encyclopedia will serve research needs in numerous fields that are affected by the rapid pace and substantial impact of technological change. With an emphasis on modern issues and the presentation of potential opportunities, prospective solutions, and future directions in the field, it is a relevant and essential addition to any academic library's reference collection.

Take An Extra

30% Off[1]

[1] 30% discount offer cannot be combined with any other discount and is only valid on purchases made directly through IGI Global's Online Bookstore (www.igi-global.com/books), not intended for use by distributors or wholesalers. Offer expires December 31, 2016.

Free Lifetime E-Access with Print Purchase

Take 30% Off Retail Price:

Hardcover with <u>Free E-Access</u>:[2] $2,765
List Price: $3,950

E-Access with <u>Free Hardcover</u>:[2] $2,765
List Price: $3,950

Recommend this Title to Your Institution's Library: www.igi-global.com/books

Printed in the United States
By Bookmasters